Johnny Olson

A VOICE IN TIME

Published in the USA by:
BearManor Media
P O Box 71426
Albany, Georgia 31708
www.bearmanormedia.com

ISBN 1-59393-471-8

Printed in the United States of America.

Book design by Brian Pearce.

Johnny Olson

A VOICE IN TIME

FROM THE BIRTH OF MODERN MEDIA
TO *THE PRICE IS RIGHT*

RANDY WEST

TABLE OF CONTENTS

With heartfelt thanks to Roz and Harold for the gifts, Debra for the patient love and quiet inspiration; the gifts of warmth, sensitivity, understanding, caring and beauty, and Cathy and David for their ongoing encouragement.

ABOUT THE AUTHOR

Randy West first met Johnny Olson at NBC in New York in 1969, and as a teenager, Randy followed his idol from studio to studio. Over time, the broadcaster included Randy in his audience warm-up act and arranged for his first appearance as a contestant on *What's My Line?* The relationship grew as Johnny mentored his protégé through an entry into radio.

Randy's disc-jockey career took him across the country from New York to Los Angeles. In 1979, he renewed his friendship with Olson. Following his mentor's advice, Randy continued to hone his broadcasting skills while making every opportunity to meet and work with game show producers. After a decade of appearing as a contestant on nine game shows and several pilots, Randy participated in development run-throughs reading the part of the announcer, and officiating as host for new game shows being presented to network programming executives.

Shortly after Johnny Olson's death, Randy realized his dreams, and began performing as the announcer and audience warm-up personality at game and talk shows hosted by Wink Martindale, Dick Clark, Chuck Woolery, Ryan Seacrest and Howie Mandel, among others. With poetic justice, Randy's career ultimately brought him the opportunity to stand in his mentor's footprints. During the 2003-2004 television season he worked with Bob Barker, behind Johnny's podium at CBS as the announcer on daytime and prime-time episodes of *The Price Is Right.*

Utilizing the skills he learned from Johnny Olson, Randy's good fortune continued with *Deal or No Deal, Weakest Link, Supermarket Sweep, Hollywood Showdown* and new episodes of Chuck Barris' classics *All New 3's a Crowd* and *Newlywed Game.* Although the jobs demanded very different styles, he also narrated the series *Hollywood and Crime* for CourtTV, and the annual Nickelodeon's *Kids' Choice Awards.*

In addition to his work on radio and television, Randy is continuing with his hero's signature show as the announcer on *The Price Is Right – Live.* The live version of America's beloved game show is presently in its sixth successful year and is staged in the 1,000-seat Jubilee Showroom at Bally's Hotel and Casino on the Las Vegas strip. Randy also serves on committees and is a convention delegate at AFTRA, the American Federation of Television and Radio Artists, is a member of the Pacific Pioneer Broadcasters, and is active in charitable causes.

Randy recounts, "Johnny was my mentor and friend, and he provided the inspiration and encouragement to pursue a career that I love. I can never repay that debt."

After Johnny Olson's death, Randy was entrusted with the personal notes, awards, clippings, scripts, and memorabilia that the performer collected during his more than fifty years of work. Penny Olson's retention of these materials was vital in making this history possible.

Randy's comprehensive work more than does justice to Johnny Olson's legacy of professionalism and passion for his work. He enthusiastically pursued research and conducted extensive interviews, as well as unearthed and reviewed kinescoped and videotaped interviews with Johnny Olson. During Johnny's lifetime, Randy spent hours in conversation with the popular broadcaster, extensively documenting his career and carefully observing his in-studio work. His mentor shared advice and counsel, as well as reminiscences that brought the history of American radio and television to life. Those first-hand accounts make "Johnny Olson: A Voice in Time" a unique read.

Randy's respect and appreciation for the career of one of American television's most familiar voice performers are apparent: "This is more than a tribute to a radio and TV pioneer. I'm thrilled to bring John's words, thoughts, and experiences to light for the first time, through his personal perspective on broadcasting's history."

Although the Olsons had no children, Johnny's grand-nephew, Barry Wick, volunteers to speak for the performer's descendents in endorsing and celebrating this work: "Your efforts to create a memory and a history of Johnny Olson is an act of love. You were very lucky to have known him as well as you did. On behalf of our family, those related to him, we thank you for his biography."

FOREWORD

While Johnny Olson is best known as the original announcer on CBS' *The Price Is Right,* he was a seminal figure in broadcasting whose prolific career is woven into the fabric of the development of radio and television.

This is the story of a journeyman entertainer who was born in the era of vaudeville, who as a youngster was fascinated by a new medium called radio, whose young adult years coincided with the big band era, who lived through the heyday of movies and Broadway musicals, and who was present for the birth and maturation of television. Johnny Olson's passion, versatility, and innate charm gave him the opportunity to enjoy a fifty-eight-year career participating in all of these forms

of entertainment, and allowed him to leave an impressive legacy in the history of American media.

Using Johnny Olson's own words and documentation of his career, as well as his remembrances of the birth and development of broadcasting as a guide, we trace radio and television from their experimental roots, through their growth to America's most influential sociological force, as experienced by a respected and celebrated participant.

This is the story of one of the most recognizable voices in television history, the voice of a man whose career parallels the birth and growth of broadcasting in America, and intersects with the stars, shows, and events that are part of our cultural tapestry.

CHAPTER 1
THE MAN, THE BOY

Bob Barker is American television's most celebrated personality, with nineteen Emmy awards as well as numerous lifetime achievement and hall of fame honors. With palpable admiration and sincere respect he reflected nostalgically from time to time on the years he worked with Johnny Olson. Barker first learned of Johnny's ability to make broadcasting magic from his mother. By coincidence, Matilda "Tillie" Barker Valandra remembered having been in the audience at an Olson personal appearance years earlier. When her son Bob first mentioned to her that Johnny had been cast as his announcer on the 1972 return of *The Price is Right,* she gave her immediate endorsement. Bob remembered being surprised that his mother was more familiar with Johnny Olson's work than he was.

Bob's mother was not unique. For more than half a century, audience members have always responded favorably to Johnny's enthusiasm and endearing personality. The same is true for the hosts, producers, and crew members who worked with him. Most echo similar sentiments of his likeability, engaging manner, upbeat demeanor, and personal humility, and all remember him as the consummate professional. At his final birthday party in 1999, game show host and former *Tonight Show* announcer Gene Rayburn commented on his twenty-year, 4,000-episode partnership with Johnny, recalling fondly and succinctly, "Johnny was simply the best." [1-1]

This is the story of a journeyman entertainer born in the era of vaudeville. As a youngster, he was fascinated by the new medium of radio. His young adult years coincided with the big band era. He lived through the heyday of movies and musicals, and he was present for the birth and maturation of television. Johnny's passion, versatility, and innate charm gave him the opportunity to enjoy a fifty-eight-year career participating in all of these forms of entertainment. A fortuitous decision made one cold night in Chicago in 1931 allowed John to leave an impressive legacy to American broadcasting.

Loved for his energetic studio audience warm-up, exciting vocal delivery, and his unfailing ability to read even the toughest tongue-twisting scripts, Johnny was a mentor to me. He nurtured a fascination with television when I was a teenager in New York, and he was always generous with his time when continuing to encourage my pursuit of a career in the field during visits years later in Los Angeles.

In 1999, our lives unexpectedly intersected again when John's family looked to find a respectful home for the souvenirs and memorabilia he had collected and saved during his decades in broadcasting. Stranger still, our fates crossed yet again in 2003 when I filled-in behind Johnny's old podium at CBS as the announcer on *The Price is Right* starring Bob Barker.

Johnny was thoroughly unassuming and actually a bit shy off-stage. He loved the business, took great pride in his work, and placed great value on the friendship and admiration of his co-workers. Always respectful of the industry that provided him a creative outlet and a gener-ous income, Johnny was present for the trials and tribulations, the hit programs and the flops, the successes and scandals, the good-heartedness and the greed, as well as the cooperative spirit and camaraderie of teamwork. He also bore silent witness to the inhu-manity of ruthless ambition and unbridled ego, as well as the aban-donment of people when their talents and labors no longer con-tributed to corporate profits.

A devoted husband, Johnny flew weekly from Los Angeles to West Virginia in his later years to spend days off with Penelope Olson, the love of his life and his wife of forty-six years. "Penny"

Johnny (right) at age 3.

had been his on-air co-host, vocalist, and occasionally, his producer on a number of radio programs, as well as some of television's earliest talk, variety, and game shows.

Johnny's story began decades earlier when he was born in the modest one-bedroom farmhouse of his Norwegian parents' eighty-five-acre dairy farm on the outskirts of picturesque Windom, Minnesota. It was a humble beginning for a broad-cast pioneer, who would later be celebrated by the Academy of Television Arts and Sciences, who would interview three sitting American Presidents, who would share stages with Frank Sinatra, Bob Hope, Bing Crosby, Jack Benny, and Jackie Gleason, and whose career milestones would parallel those of the very development of the broadcasting industry itself.

Both of Johnny's parents had been born in Norway. Papa Sivert was the son of a sea captain who sailed merchant ships through the icy arctic to Archangel and other Russian ports. In his youth, Sivert accompanied his father, Johnny's grandfa-ther, on many voyages.

Norwegians made the arduous voyage to the United States by the thousands — sometimes the entire population of a rural community or the membership of a church made the journey as a group. Johnny reported that his ancestors were motivated to immigrate to America simply to find a better, more affluent life, rather than by any political or religious oppression. They were spurred by advertisements of fertile land in Minnesota and Iowa, and they were encouraged by letters from relatives already in the great cultural melting pot and the jingle of coins in the pockets of some who returned to visit. Johnny wrote of his dad, "All his life, he dreamed and talked of returning to the sea. He never did."

It takes a village. The family in 1914. Sivert and Hannah Olson are second and tenth from the left in the back row; Johnny is third from the left in the front row. *(For a complete list of all the family members in this photo, see page 377.)*

Instead, in 1887, twenty-one-year old Sivert Olson emigrated directly to Windom. In addition to farming, he was a laborer, contributing as a bricklayer to the construction of the iconic Windom courthouse. Johnny recalled that his family's 85-acre farm was not sufficiently productive to support the family, so his father also had a job working for the highway department. The two horses that his father used in his road work were his dad's pride and joy, and he devoted hours to grooming them and cleaning their stables. Johnny remembered, "I recall mother once complained in a joking way that she wished she was a horse — father would have paid more attention to her and taken better care of her."

Mama Hannah Olson, nee Elness, was only one year old in 1871 when her parents made the fourteen-day journey with their three children from an area near Oslo to America. From their first homestead in northern Minnesota, the family of five traveled south by covered wagon to Windom. Johnny recounted that when they arrived, there was still some fear of Indians, so the expanding clan lived in a dugout cellar while building a log house. "As her younger brothers arrived, they slept on shelf bunks around the kitchen stove. She became an expert seamstress making their clothes."

Hannah was the only girl, and she had lots of practice with a needle and thread, as the family eventually grew to include ten children. Her nine brothers, Johnny's nine uncles, eventually owned sizeable grain and stock farms of their own in Minnesota and North Dakota.

Sivert and Hannah met as members of a Minnesota enclave of Scandinavians who were active in the Lutheran church. In 1889, less than two years after they met and when his mother was eighteen, they married and promptly began to build a family of their own — eleven children, including a boy who lived only twenty months. In order, they were Mabel, Ella, Sam, Laura, Alma, Pearl, Harold, Curtis, Richard, and Johnny.

On Sunday evening, May 22, 1910, upon learning that she had just delivered a 12-pound 8-ounce baby, Hannah Olson cried to Sivert, her husband, "Oh, Yonny!" That exclamation, combined with the fact that the blessed event caused Ella, his sister, to miss her date with Leonard Wick, her beau, was the inspiration for the newborn to be named Yonny, or Johnny Leonard Olson. Apparently, naming children became a less creative undertaking by the time of an eleventh birth.

Above: Johnny and his siblings' elementary school. Below: Johnny's father worked as a bricklayer in the construction of Windom's courthouse.

Johnny was the baby, and Mabel, his sister, was more than twenty years old when he was born. Johnny remembered, "Seeing all of us for the first time, a new neighbor of that faith once asked, 'Are you Catholic?' 'No, just passionate Lutherans,' answered one of my sisters."

Johnny saved home movies of the family that were taken in the 1930s in which the love is evident as John shares hugs and kisses with his then senior-citizen parents. In their forties when Johnny was born, and with the novelty of parenthood long expended, Barry Wick, Johnny's grand nephew, reported that Ella Olson Wick, his sister, watched after Johnny during much of his childhood. Wick recalled Ella, his grandmother, as "The salt of the earth and as tough as Minnesota winters." [1-2]

Johnny reflected on how being raised in such a large family taught him compassion and the art of compromise. It also imbued him with people skills that were essential to his becoming an adept entertainer, able to immediately develop a rapport with audiences, and relate to the contestants he selected to join in the fun on the audience participation programs he hosted.

Within a generation of their pilgrimages, the extended Elness and Olson clans grew to the size of a small village. While still in his teens, Johnny was an uncle to over a dozen nieces and nephews.

The Windom courthouse remains the centerpiece of downtown.

The Olson family mourned the loss of two daughters before Hanna took ill in the spring of 1938. She died several weeks later of unknown causes at the age of sixty-eight. Sivert Olson remarried in 1945, but died thirteen months later in 1947 on the day after Christmas. Johnny was touched by the outpouring from his audience following his on-air mention of his father's illness. He remembered that some 80,000 people, most of them entire strangers, were moved to send letters and cards, overwhelming the little local post office.

Despite Sivert Olson's extensive obituary listing that included the names of pallbearers, as well as the names of a soloist and a quartet that sang at the service, there was no mention of Johnny being present. At the time of his father's death, John was married, living in New York, and was a nationally known network radio personality in the third year of a hit show with a big national sponsor. John had already invested over twenty years building a career that had taken him from local radio in Minnesota and Wisconsin, to work as a big band vocalist in Chicago, to radio studios in Hollywood, and on to New York where he was among the early entertainers to have been seen on the infant new medium of television.

Although absent from his father's funeral, Johnny's love of family was evident in his writings. On several occasions in his life, Johnny invoked the words of Abraham Lincoln in honoring his parents: "All that I am or ever hope to be, I owe to my angel mother." At Windon High School, Johnny was the business manager of *The Cricket* yearbook, and Dorothy Clark, an early girlfriend, was its editor. They reprinted Lincoln's tribute and dedicated the annual "To our parents…realizing that only through their efforts, sacrifice, and love could all our opportunities have been made possible."

Johnny carried with him the imprint of his formative years in Windom, the county seat of Cottonwood County. It was a typical rural American town, a picturesque agricultural community along the Des Moines River in southwestern Minnesota. Johnny remembered that, like his brothers and sisters, he was born in the Windom house located on Sixth Street between Miller and Prospect Avenues, on the east hill with a view of Cottonwood Lake. Johnny recalled his childhood home as a modest frame structure with only one small bedroom on the second floor.

In Johnny's youth, train travel was still the primary means of transportation, and the tracks split through the town. The Windom High School that Johnny attended was only a block away from the ornate courthouse that his father helped to build in 1904. It is still standing today, with its impressive Corinthian-style marble columns and twelve-foot statue of the Greek goddess of justice atop its dome. The courthouse square remains the defining feature of the business district.

CHAPTER 2
THE BROADCASTING BUG BITES

When Johnny was fourteen years old, his broadcasting career had a humble beginning in downtown Windom, when electrician Oscar Estenson wired a crude radio transmitter in his electrical repair shop. During a break from his part-time job at a local jewelry store, young Johnny crooned "No, No, Nora" into a microphone that was fashioned from an old Victrola horn. Encouraged by his brother, Curt, who worked at the electrical shop, Johnny took to the air and reveled in the wonder of wireless during three more Sunday afternoon pirate broadcasts.

Those broadcasts generated phone calls, as well as letters and postcards from Mountain Lake, Fairmont, Worthington, and other neighboring communities. Dozens of people reported having heard the program. In fact, they were unable to hear anything else at the time because the home-made transmitter had no frequency control. Johnny recalled, "It was all exciting and exhilarating for me."

Johnny's father reviewed his performances with the comment, "I could take a rope and stretch it across a sick cow's belly and make better music than that." [2-1] Sivert Olson attempted to quash his son's excitement, preferring that his youngest choose a practical career as a mechanic or jeweler, as his siblings had. John recounted, "With only the encouragement of my sister Pearl, I began to sing. She alone of all the family was sympathetic to this ambition of mine. She was a good pianist herself, and she taught piano, and before dying young was on the Chautauqua circuit."

Johnny was not easily dissuaded by his father's lack of encouragement for a career in the entertainment field. He dreamed that his future would hold brighter promise. Years later, Johnny wrote of being inspired by others with Norwegian ancestry who immigrated to America and achieved greatness, including senators, governors, scientists, and educators. They included Knute Rockne, the great Notre Dame football coach, decorated Air Force Lieutenant General Lauris Norstad, son of a Chicago Lutheran minister, and Sonja Henie, the celebrated female ice skater, who had been a guest on many of his programs. Johnny noted, "In entertainment, there arose Ole Olsen, vaudeville partner of Chick Johnson, who was so famous as I grew up that Olsons found their names being spelled Olsen regardless of their wishes."

Johnny's name was misspelled in a great many radio and television program listings. Choosing to switch rather than fight, Johnny adopted the variant spelling of Olsen for a time in New York. He wrote, "To further confuse things, Ole Olsen had a son named Johnny, and when he died in a tragedy, my family received messages of condolence, and I had to spend part of my time for weeks reminding people that I was alive."

The thrill of Johnny's first amateur broadcasting experiences lingered despite his father's review and even after a man from the Federal Radio Commission, forerunner of the FCC, visited Estenson. There had been sufficient complaints about the home-made transmitter blotting out other stations in a sizeable area. After diagnosing the deficiencies of the electrician's crude equipment, the visitor made it clear that Estenson and the boys would need to obtain a radio station license. It was apparently an easy task in those days, as they were told a Catholic priest in Appleton, Wisconsin, had just gotten one by simply writing to Herbert Hoover, who was then the Secretary of Commerce.

Curt, Johnny's brother, was ready to work on adding frequency control to their makeshift radio apparatus, but Estenson wanted no more visits from the Federal Radio Commission. Johnny smiled in recounting that both he and Estenson quit broadcasting then and there, but that his own retirement was only temporary.

Radio was in its infancy. Wireless transmission was not originally intended to find a means for transmitting voice or music; it was to extend the capabilities of the telegraph to permit Morse code messages to reach beyond wires and allow for communication across great distances and with ships at sea. Any thought of families gathered around a device that brought voice and music into their living rooms was dismissed as nothing more than some futuristic fantasy. Rural families were still marveling at the availability of telephone service and contemplating the purchase of a "horseless carriage," as some of the first automobiles were called.

In 1895, Guglielmo Marconi sent and received his first wireless signals across his father's estate at Bologna, Italy. He became obsessed with the prospect of transmitting messages great distances through the air simultaneously to multiple receivers. When the Italian government failed to take an interest, the twenty-one-year-old inventor and his Irish mother set sail for England, where Marconi's work in the development of wireless transmission attracted financial backing.

In 1898, one of the earliest successful experiments in America was conducted at Notre Dame University in 1898, when telegraph tests were sent and received over a modest distance of about a mile. Two years later, Reginald Fessenden began experiments in the transmission of weather forecasts for the US Department of Agriculture. Fessenden's later work with voice transmission would feed Johnny Olson's fascination and help to lay the foundation for his life's work.

In 1901, a landmark test furthered the development of early broadcasting. That winter, Marconi checked into a room in the Cochrane Hotel in St. John's, Newfoundland. The decades-old, 32 room Victorian inn at the corner of Cochrane and Gower streets was located near the easternmost point of the North American continent. The hotel became famous during the next twenty years when pioneering aviators used it as a way station while waiting for favorable weather conditions for the first flights between the North America and Europe.

On December 12, Marconi sat bundled in his warmest winter clothing, in a cabin on Signal Hill, overlooking St. John's harbor. Buffeted by bitterly cold arctic winds, the inventor and two assistants flew a box kite 400 feet above the snow-covered Canadian tundra. From that kite dangled thin wires that served as an antenna, and another cable connected through makeshift electrical apparatus to a telephone receiver.

At a prearranged time, at the eastern reaches of North America, the inventor strained to hear a signal coming from 2,000 miles away in Poldhu, Cornwall, in southern England. As impossible as it must have seemed in that day, Marconi and his assistants reported that they heard three brief hissing clicks — the three-dot Morse code for the letter "S" — repeated over and over at regular intervals for half an hour through the crackling air. In the days to follow, more dots and dashes were hurled across the Atlantic in powerful flashes of electronic transmissions that beamed from equipment in a shack at the base of a circular array of twenty tall towers.

Within a decade of Marconi's experiments, telegraph operators were sending dots and dashes with clumsy, hand-held pump handles, facilitating communication across land and sea around the world, using exceptionally large, power generating equipment and towers that reached hundreds of feet into the sky. Wireless technology was a far cry from the simple fingertip-operated telegraph keys connected by wire, but soon hundreds of operators had mastered the technique and were working at remote land stations around the globe, as well as on ships at sea.

On June 24, 1910, one month after Johnny Olson's birth, the future of wireless was assured. The United States government approved an act requiring radio equipment on certain passenger vessels. On April 14, 1912, less than two years later, David Sarnoff, a junior operator working for Marconi, was stationed atop the Wanamaker Department Store in New York. The retailer used the wireless technology to communicate inventory and billing data with their other stores and to gain a competitive advantage by receiving timely information on fashion trends from Paris.

On that night in April, Sarnoff reportedly was among those who were monitoring the distress messages and passenger information from telegraphers Jack Phillips and Harold Bride aboard the doomed *RMS Titanic*. The young Sarnoff said he spent hours transcribing information about the disaster at sea and the names of survivors as relayed by the *Titanic's* sister ship, the *Olympic*. Few vessels received the distress calls because most shipboard radio operated only during daytime hours with a single radioman on board. Just a hundred days after the loss of 1,523 lives on that icy night in the North Atlantic, the United States passed the Federal Radio Act of 1912, which mandated 24-hour radio service for ships at sea.

Four years later, after hours spent in lonely silence monitoring the airwaves at various telegraph stations, Sarnoff had a vision for the future of wireless. His fertile mind, grasp of basic electronic theory, dogged perseverance, and talent for salesmanship would combine to eventually make Sarnoff the single most important person in broadcasting and a man who would create opportunities for Johnny Olson that exceeded both men's wildest expectations.

CHAPTER 3
SOS SARNOFF

In 1891, David Sarnoff was born in Uzlian, Russia, a small Jewish village near the city of Minsk. Nine years later, David traveled steerage to New York with his nine brothers and sisters. Knowing no English, he helped support his family as a messenger boy, by selling newspapers, and with other small jobs. At age fifteen, he bought a telegraph key, learned Samuel Morse's language of dots and dashes, and was hired as an office assistant at the Marconi Wireless Telegraph Company of America.

David Sarnoff, age seventeen, at the American Marconi Company wireless station on Nantucket Island, Massachusetts.

In 1916, Sarnoff wrote, "I have in mind a plan of development which would make radio a 'household utility' in the same way as a piano or phonograph. The idea is to bring music into the house by wireless…[it] need not be limited to music, [but could also be] a wireless classroom…Events of national importance can be simultaneously announced and received. Baseball scores transmitted…Farmers and others living at a distance could be greatly benefited…they could enjoy concerts lectures, recitals, etc." [3-1]

Sarnoff's grand scheme for broadcasting fell on deaf ears at the Marconi Wireless Telegraph Company of America. For several years, he pitched the idea in lengthy memos, as he worked his way through various stints at land stations and aboard ships at sea, before advancing to a managerial position that paid a respectable $5.50 per week.

The United States government ultimately helped to make Sarnoff's vision a reality, and World War I was the catalyst. The foreign-owned Marconi Wireless Telegraph Company of America controlled many important patents and had made an offer to General Electric for the purchase of the worldwide rights for their high-powered Alexanderson alternator that was proving vital for transatlantic communication. Led by outspoken misgivings from the Navy, the United States government came to believe that wireless technology was too vital to American security to be dependent on a foreign entity. The US Navy and several American corporations also held important patents, but none of them had all of the pieces necessary to move the technology forward.

In 1919, the US government paved the way for the formation of The Radio Corporation of America (RCA), a consortium consisting of General Electric (GE), Westinghouse, American Telephone and Telegraph (AT&T), and the United Fruit Company. Entities that would otherwise be competitors in radio pooled their patents. AT&T would manufacture transmitters, as well as keep its business of leasing distribution lines. GE and Westinghouse would manufacture radio receivers and supply them to RCA, which would act as their sales agent. The foreign-owned Marconi Wireless Telegraph Company of America's US holdings were folded into the new conglomerate in exchange for Marconi's right to use GE's Alexanderson alternator outside of the United States.

A July 1920 advertisement in *The Consolidated Radio Call Book* announced the new source for shipboard and land-based radio apparatus, informing, "Did you know that the Radio Corporation of America has taken over the assets and going business of the Marconi Wireless Telegraph Company of America and the radio interests of the General Electric Company?" With a nod to patriotism, the ad continued, "This reorganization has made the Radio Corporation of America an all-American concern, with practically all of its stock held in the United States."

By 1921, the RCA pie was sliced with GE controlling 30.1% of the new entity. AT&T was given 10.3% of RCA stock for the rights to its three-electron audion, a receiver component developed in 1912 by Lee De Forest for AT&T. In exchange for 20.6% of RCA stock, Westinghouse contributed the super heterodyne circuit. This invention by the young Edwin Armstrong radically amplified signals and suppressed interference. United Fruit had been using wireless to dispatch ships to profitable ports, and the company received 4.1% of RCA's stock for the rights to their work with crystal detectors and long-range antennae. The remaining interest in RCA was reserved for former American Marconi stockholders and for investors from the general public.

With numerous important patents now under the control of a single corporation, David Sarnoff set out to make radio the "household utility" he envisioned. Under his plan, programming would drive the demand for radio with RCA profiting from the sales of radio receivers. The affiliation of GE, Westinghouse, and AT&T also contributed to the formation of networks, multiple stations in different cities simultaneously broadcasting the same programming. While such hookups predated the formation of RCA, they were limited in scope and quality. Stations in New York, New Jersey, Boston, Providence, and Washington DC had been interconnected in various combinations, but the practice was limited and the sound quality was usually poor.

AT&T had refused its competitors access to high-quality telephone lines, relegating them to use telegraph lines leased from Western Union. These un-insulated wires were incapable of good audio transmission quality, and they were susceptible to both atmospheric and man-made interference. That stumbling block was removed with the 1919 marriage of RCA's underlying corporations. It allowed for President Calvin Coolidge's inaugural to be broadcast to the largest audience at that time for any single transmission. An unprecedented twenty-four stations were connected in a transcontinental network for the event.

By 1921, the RCA consortium held nearly 2,000 patents, and that young futurist, David Sarnoff, was finally being heard by Mr. Owen D. Young. Young had advanced from GE to Chairman of the Board of the new Radio Corporation of America. While working under Young, Sarnoff was given the ability to implement his idea of making radio the "household utility" he envisioned.

One detail of Young's plan did not include the most profitable aspect of radio — advertising. The philosophy behind forming RCA's radio broadcasting network was to create a demand for radio receivers. Because RCA controlled most of the important radio patents, the corporation received a 5 percent royalty payment on virtually every radio sold in America, no matter the manufacturer. With GE and Westinghouse part of RCA, radios built by those two companies were especially profitable, generating revenues from both sales and patent royalties.

Although AT&T's New York station, WEAF, which was subsequently purchased by NBC, had sold the first commercial time on August 28, 1922, advertising was not initially considered for RCA's new National Broadcasting Company. That intent was clear from the outset when Owen D. Young, RCA's Chairman of the Board, heralded the debut of NBC in newspaper ads in 1926:

> "The Radio Corporation of America is the largest distributor of radio receiving sets in the world. It handles the entire output in this field of the Westinghouse and General Electric factories. It does not say this boastfully. It does not say it with apology. It says it for the purpose of making clear the fact that it is more largely interested, more selfishly interested, if you please, in the best possible broadcasting in the United States than anyone else…The market for receiving sets in the future will be determined largely by the quantity and quality of the programs broadcast…If that

ideal were to be reached, no home in the United States could afford to be without a radio receiving set.

"Today, the best available statistics indicate that 5,000,000 homes are equipped, and 21,000,000 homes remain to be supplied. Radio receiving sets for the best reproductive quality should be made available for all, and we hope to make them cheap enough in that all may buy." [3-2]

Johnny Olson was only nine years old when RCA was formed, and it would have been beyond his and his parents' wildest dreams that the boy growing up on the Windom dairy farm would one day work at the National Broadcasting Company's magnificent headquarters in New York. It was far more likely that he would become a mechanic, or engineer, or work for a trucking company as his older brothers would, but radio was destined to become a reality faster than anyone could imagine, including David Sarnoff.

During the first half of 1921, there had been many experimental stations broadcasting on irregular schedules, but only Westinghouse's KDKA in Pittsburgh broadcast regularly scheduled programming. By the end of that year, there were twenty-eight stations, and by March 1922, there were sixty. On March 7, 1923, Herbert Hoover announced a conference to discuss the growth of the new medium. He reported that the number of stations had mushroomed to 576 in just twelve months.

CHAPTER 4
VOICES IN THE AIR

Despite the extensive growth in radio in the early 1920s, there were no local stations when Johnny Olson entered his teen years. The first broadcast in the state occurred in 1912, when the University of Minnesota attempted to describe the action of a football game using Morse code. A decade later, the university's campus in Minneapolis was home to WLB, the state's first licensed radio station, a low-power educational facility that went on the air for occasional spoken word broadcasts starting in 1922. In December of the following year, Minneapolis' KFMT (later WDGY), the state's first commercial radio station, began broadcasting part-time with a mere 231-watts of power. Both were inaudible 150 miles away in Windom.

To receive the signals from the higher powered, distant stations, Johnny and his brothers built a homemade crystal set. By wrapping wire around a household item such as a baseball bat or a cigar box and adding a few simple components, a crystal set grasped a radio signal from the air without a battery, using the power from the radio waves themselves when received by an adequately long outdoor wire antenna. Johnny remembered that when radio was first becoming popular in the middle twenties, his first set was fashioned with wire wound around a cylindrical Quaker Oats box that had been shellacked, a galena crystal (a pea-sized pebble of a naturally occurring mineral), a cat's whisker (a tiny wire adjusted to connect to a sensitive spot on the crystal), and a set of headphones.

In the early 1920s, most radios were assembled from scratch or from kits for hobbyists. Like the Olsons, those who wanted to tune-in to the world built their own receivers. In *How to Retail Radio*, a 1922 pamphlet written by F. W. Christian for shop owners thinking about stocking radio equipment, the author advised, "The dealer should be careful not to overload his shelves with many expensive cabinet sets for he will find that this sort of equipment does not move as fast as less expensive sets and parts will. The average amateur still derives a great pleasure out of building his own set in his spare time. This is all the better for the dealer, for the fellows who 'build their own' are forever changing and improving their sets. There is a larger margin on parts than on the assembled sets."

With his handmade radio, Johnny strained to hear the pioneering stations of that era. He recalled evenings monitoring KDKA, WGY, and WWJ, high-powered stations from Pittsburgh, Schenectady, and Detroit respectively. As radio always stirred the "theater of the mind," the big sounds from the big cities created an illusion greater than their reality. KDKA was actually a very humble affair born in the garage of Dr. Frank Conrad, an amateur wireless enthusiast and researcher for Westinghouse, who confounded his neighbors near the corner of Peebles and Penn Avenues in the Wilkinsburg suburb of Pittsburgh with the incessant noise from his experimentations.

Those amplified snaps, crackles and pops became music to the ears of the manager of the Joseph Horne Department Store. He was able to stock a few radio receivers, and he asked Dr. Conrad to provide the city's first public demonstration of wireless. The store's ad in the *Pittsburgh Sun* told readers that an "air concert played into the air by a wireless telephone" [4-1] was heard by listeners in the store at a receiving station installed by Dr. Conrad. The concert consisted of two orchestra selections played from records, a soprano solo that "rang particularly high and clear through the air," and a juvenile "talking piece." [4-1]

Pittsburgh Sun readers were encouraged to tune-in to another of Dr. Conrad's "air concerts" by purchasing one of the completely assembled and ready-to-use radio receivers, which just happened to be available in the store's "west basement" for "$10.00 and up." Westinghouse executive Harry P. Davis was among those intrigued by the ad and impressed by the broadcasts, and he provided space on the roof of the company's factory for Conrad to set up a higher-powered operation. Approximately 500 sets were sold in Pittsburgh during the intervening months before Davis and Conrad's application for a license was granted. Westinghouse's new KDKA was officially on the air in time to broadcast a summary of the 1920 election returns in which Warren Harding and his Vice President, Calvin Coolidge were swept into office, defeating Ohio Governor James M. Cox and running-mate, Assistant Secretary of the Navy, Franklin D. Roosevelt.

KDKA's success on election night inspired Westinghouse to build additional stations the following year. WBZ was born at the company's plant in Springfield, Massachusetts, where Westinghouse began to build fully-assembled tube radios. WJZ initially served the New York area from the Westinghouse meter-assembly plant at the corner of Plane and Orange Streets in Newark, New Jersey. A portion of the ladies' rest room in the factory was converted into a crude studio. Further west, KYW began broadcasting Chicago's Civic Opera Company, while a more permanent studio was built in the Commonwealth Edison Building.

Westinghouse had beaten Sarnoff in the plan to make radio a "household utility" and to "bring music into the house by wireless." AT&T also began staking an early claim in New York with WBAY, which became WEAF. Not to be left too far behind, on December 14, 1921, even before the formation of NBC, RCA took to the air from Roselle Park, New Jersey, with WDY, but just three months later, the station was shuttered. Sarnoff arranged to purchase the dominant WJZ from Westinghouse.

The new RCA consortium appeared to serve as a firm foundation for the developing medium, but with radio's incredible boom, it was not long before there was corporate in-fighting and unforeseen concerns over aspects of the agreements among RCA, GE, AT&T, and Westinghouse. In early 1926, AT&T sold WEAF to RCA for $1 million and left broadcasting. AT&T returned to its primary business of leasing telephone lines. AT&T was given all of RCA's business of connecting stations for network broadcasting.

Of his radio listening on the Olson farm, Johnny remembered his father first saying, "You're just imagining you are hearing something," but after he heard the voices from the air himself, Papa Sivert built a 60-foot antenna for his sons. With that upgrade, the headphones from the crude crystal receiver could be placed in a bowl to reflect the sound, enabling several family members to listen simultaneously. Johnny was further enthralled by the additional stations he could receive from other US cities, as well as from other countries. The first time he heard the Spanish language spoken, it was through the snap, crackle, and pop of radio broadcasts from Havana and Mexico City.

Johnny had been involved in various school activities, and he was active in the Boy Scouts, but no hobby could compete with radio. He told an interviewer, "We advanced from crystal to one-tube receivers with an immense improvement in reception. The tubes then cost $9 each, but my brother, Curtis, prophetically remarked that you would someday be able to buy a whole set for this amount."

The upgrade from the homemade crystal radio was funded by the tasks typical of a teenager. The first money Johnny earned came from mowing two lawns. One neighbor paid the going rate of 35¢, and for a much more thorough job, another gave the boy 50¢. When he took the coins home and showed them proudly to his mother, Johnny recalled that she found her purse and gave him 15¢ more. Mama Hannah said, "Now you have your first dollar." Johnny remembers changing the coins for a bill and later for a 1924 silver dollar that he kept for decades as a sentimental souvenir.

Johnny also worked afternoons and weekends at the local Olson Pharmacy. He delivered prescriptions, clerked, and presided at the soda fountain, as well as cleaned and stocked the store. The proprietor, Mr. Bordie "Doc" Olson, was no relation, but Johnny remembered him warmly. Doc treated Johnny like a son. He urged the teenager to become a pharmacist and offered to help him enroll at the University of Minnesota where he had studied, but the thought of studying to become a pharmacist was unappealing to Johnny. He later quipped, "I was not very studious. On a visit to the library, I was more likely to take out the young librarian than a book."

The magic of hearing those distant voices intrigued Johnny, and so he began reading about the brief history of wireless. Decades later, he spoke of the work of Canadian Professor Reginald Aubrey Fessenden, who built upon the earlier discoveries of James Maxwell and Heinrich Hertz. Each played a role in confirming that both electricity and magnetic energy travel in waves at the speed of light and could be manipulated. A former employee at both Thomas Edison's and Westinghouse's labs, Fessenden formed his own National Electric Signaling Company. Furthering Marconi's early experimentation with transmitting Morse code, Fessenden's voice was said to be the first ever to be carried by radio waves and heard by another person.

In December 1900, the Canadian inventor used a spark gap transmitter to speak to his assistant, who was one mile away. His first transmitted words were, "One, two, three, four, is it snowing where you are Mr. Thiessen? If it is, would you telegraph back to me?" [4-2] Mr. Thiessen had indeed heard the transmission.

Johnny's favorite historical moment in the development of wireless was what he referred to as "the first radio program." It occurred six years later in late December 1906, when Professor Fessenden staged a public demonstration of his work, transmitting from Brant Rock to Plymouth, Massachusetts. Beaming across the ten-mile mouth of the Bay State's Kingston Bay, the broadcast featured a female voice singing a Christmas carol, a violin solo, and a brief oration by Fessenden, all followed by recorded music.

Johnny wrote, "On that peaceful night, the human voice broke from the bondage of Earth and wires and leaped through the winter air for hundreds of miles. Huddled over their crude receivers, wireless operators listening for the usual dots and dashes were amazed by the strains of Handel's 'Largo' and Gounod's 'Holy Night' coming from their headsets. They summoned their ships' officers to hear what men had never heard before — voices and music coming through the air!"

CHAPTER 5
SPEAK UP!

The broadcasts he heard from KDKA, WGY, and WWJ during radio's infancy sparked young Johnny's imagination, but he certainly did not fathom that he would one day work at one of those stations, participating in an experimental broadcast that combined voice and picture. At that time, he channeled his fascination with radio in the auditions that led to him singing at local talent shows and between the silent pictures screened at Windom's Wonderland Theater. Once Johnny teamed with Glen Peterson, another precocious classmate, their fellow students were treated to free, impromptu performances at every opportunity.

Glen was a cheerleader at Windom High School, and Johnny helped him plan and perform in skits at their pep rallies, as well as at informal gatherings at friends' homes. After classes, the duo even climbed to the upper reaches of the school building and serenaded passers-by from the roof. Upon Johnny's death, Glen recounted for JoAnn Eaton's column in the October 23, 1985 issue of the *Windom Reporter,* "We'd just sing anything, 'My Blue Heaven,' 'Yes, We Have No Bananas,' all the songs of the day." Glen claimed that the teachers and principal enjoyed the performances, citing the fact that the faculty never discouraged the stage-struck teens nor removed them from their impromptu stage.

In his junior year at Windom High, Johnny was singing inside the school as well as on the roof, both as a member of the boys' glee club and in the school's theatrical productions. He was already playing character roles at age seventeen, when he portrayed Hop Sing Hi in the operetta, *Once in a Blue Moon.*

By his senior year, Johnny was writing, producing, and appearing in original presentations. One such offering entitled *The Magic Turban* was a short comic play in which Johnny co-starred with pal Glen Peterson and other classmates on stage at the Wonderland Theater. A couple of months later, Thelma Olson, his sister, joined Johnny in another senior class production at the Wonderland, a staging of the Drama League prize-winning comedy, *When's Your Birthday?*

Still another theatrical outing was a one-man show entitled *Seven Keys to Baldpate,* described as a "melodramatic comedy tragedy" with a program listing its sole performer, Johnny Olson, as The Hero, as The Heroine, and as The Crooks. So proud was this young theatrical impresario that he immortalized the event with graffiti on the theater wall, "Johnny Olson, lead in 'Seven Keys to Baldpate', Friday, Dec. 9, 1927 — senior class of 1928." The inscription remained for many years.

Johnny's outgoing personality, charm, and occasionally mischievous nature earned him fame among the school's most popular students. The 1928 Windom High School's *Cricket* yearbook bestowed on Johnny the honors of "most courteous" and "cutest boy," and referred to Johnny as "A good mixer, a royal kidder. Just the sort of fellow you like to have around." [5-1] The objectivity of those honors may be suspect considering the fact that, in addition to his pursuits in show business, Johnny served as the yearbook's business manager.

For his success on stage, in radio, and later on television, Johnny credits his mother. Because of her hearing impairment and her difficulty understanding English, Mama Hannah repeatedly demanded that her son "speak up" so she could hear him when he began to talk and read. Johnny spoke up when he acted in high school plays and began to sing and talk before audiences. Johnny said, "Because of her interest and demands, I amplified an average baritone voice into one that is loud and clear."

In that era before the Internet or television, when radio stations were few and far between, families typically spent evenings together at home, talking, reading, or playing parlor games. A weekly treat might be a family picnic, a weekend band concert, or a visit to the local theater to see a silent movie. "Talkies" were still years away, as the first feature length motion picture with synchronized sound

Above: Windom High School, where Johnny sang in the glee club, at theatrical productions, and occasionally from the rooftop tower. Below: The high school tower, Johnny's early stage.

that included dialogue was *The Jazz Singer* (1927) starring Al Jolson.

It would still be some time before talking pictures were in mass production, and years before rural theaters were equipped for sound. As such, local keyboardists and vocalists like Johnny were important and welcome performers. They were encouraged while honing their skills before audiences with limited expectations. Johnny spoke of one evening at The Wonderland before the era of talkies. "I have a poignant memory of singing 'I Don't Want to Play in Your Yard, If You Don't Want to Play in Mine,' while a film about the troubles of a little Negro boy was shown."

In the 1920s, vaudeville acts made for special nights at movie theaters, but Windom was not a regular stop on any of the major vaudeville circuits. It was only on rare occasions that a traveling performer or notable vaudevillian might find his way to Windom. One such act was billed as "Ed Mhyre 'The Norse Magician' and his wife Blanche."

Ed Mhyre was a trombone player, and Blanche was a trapeze artist in traveling circuses and wagon shows when their paths crossed in 1907. They made their home in Grand Meadow, Minnesota, but spent most of their time on the road playing hundreds of small towns from Washington State to Texas. In the classic style of journeyman vaudevillians, Ed and Blanche performed shows that featured trained dogs, trained bears, blackface comedy, singing, dancing, magic, Houdini-inspired escapes, and even contortionism. In the 1960s, Ed Mhyre reminisced about his career, reportedly saying, "Well, it might have been tough at times, but at least we always had enough to eat." Blanche, his wife, thought for a moment and was said to reply, "That may be true, but there were quite a few times I could have eaten a whole lot more!"

Although he became a show business jack-of-all-trades, music was Ed's forte, and he became accomplished at playing not only the trombone, but guitar, mandolin, and the accordion. Ed Mhyre's name is most often heard in an often repeated story about a night in a small North Dakota town, when he was approached by a local boy wanting to get into show business. Ed's suggestion was to take up the accordion, and that advice was taken to heart by the youngster whose name was Lawrence Welk.

Welk was only seven years older than Johnny Olson, and they performed in many of the same venues in the early years of their careers. The two would meet again in 1931, when Johnny was a vocalist and manager for a twelve-man musical group that auditioned for Lawrence Welk with the hopes of being added to the maestro's family of musicians, singing groups, and novelty acts. In the late 1940s, Welk and Johnny were together again when they shared the microphones at WJZ radio in New York.

Decades later, the two were fated to meet again in Hollywood, at least on one occasion when Johnny's work took him to the American Broadcasting Company's television studios on Prospect Avenue, where game shows, variety shows, and the occasional charity telethon shared the lot. The 20-acre property was originally developed as a film studio for Vitagraph Pictures, and it was subsequently owned by Warner Bros. During the 1960s and much of the 1970s, the facility was home to *The Lawrence Welk Show*. After ABC dropped the musical hour, the Welk program was distributed as a syndicated program and production moved to CBS Television City for the 1977 and 1978 seasons. There, the two Midwesterners exchanged greetings on numerous occasions as Johnny taped as many as two dozen episodes of *The Price is Right* and *Match Game* during some weeks at a studio adjacent to the maestro's.

Johnny especially enjoyed one of the stories Bob Barker regularly shared with *The Price is Right* audiences concerning an occasion when Barker and Welk were playing golf and Bob inquired as to how many strokes Welk had taken on the last hole. Welk's ambiguous answer matched his signature downbeat for his orchestra: "A-one-and-a-two."

CHAPTER 6

HOLY MACKEREL!

One year following NBC's debut in 1926, the seeds were planted for America's other great radio network, CBS. Its predecessor, United Independent Broadcasters, was started by talent agent Arthur Judson and promoter George Coats after David Sarnoff passed over Judson's clients in assembling a roster of performers for his new National Broadcasting Company.

For a cash infusion of $163,000, mostly intended to lease phone lines from AT&T, Judson and Coats merged the up-start enterprise with the Columbia Phonograph Company. On September 18, 1927, the network debuted as the Columbia Phonograph Broadcasting Company. Swimming upstream in a river of red ink, Columbia Records dropped out of the enterprise. Less than a year later, Judson sold the limited network to Philadelphia entrepreneur Jerome Louchheim and Ike and Leon Levy, the owners of affiliate WCAU.

Leon Levy was the fiancé of William Paley's sister. That connection inspired William, Levy's future brother-in-law, to take his first foray into broadcasting. He diverted a small portion of the advertising budget from his family's successful cigar business to purchase a weekly hour on WCAU. For $50, the Congress Cigar Company sponsored the music of a ten-piece orchestra fronted by the namesake of the company's best selling stogie, Miss La Palina.

After only a few weeks, Jake Paley, William's uncle, canceled the show. Sam Paley, William's father, observed that the company was spending $500,000 on print advertising without any direct measurement of its impact. Pulling Miss La Palina from local WCAU's air immediately resulted in numerous telephone calls. The Congress Cigar Company returned to radio, and sales promptly showed a dramatic increase.

William Paley learned that radio advertising offered greater sales potential than print advertising for certain products. With his family's backing, William offered his future brother-in-law and partners $400,000 for their holdings, and the Paleys began an association with a troubled chain of independent stations.

On January 18, less than a year before the 1929 stock market crash, twenty-seven-year old William took full control of fewer than two dozen stations. Simplifying the name of the enterprise to the Columbia Broadcasting System, Paley succeeded in growing the humble chain to prominence. It was the birth of the company that would grow to become the largest advertising medium in the world and bring Johnny Olson his greatest fame.

Radio became a true cultural force during the later half of the 1920s with the advent of national network broadcasting and the availability of affordable, pre-manufactured receiving sets. As Marc Fisher of the *Washington Post* observed, "Listeners bonded through their appreciation of characters, shows, phrases, songs, all the bits and pieces of sound that add up to a shared culture."[6-1] As the first real-time mass media, radio created a national unity and popularized the idea of being part of a generation.

Simultaneously with NBC and CBS providing the linking of local stations to carry programming, the consumer hardware necessary to be part of the radio generation reached the marketplace. The 1927 Sears catalogue featured a $34.95 table radio and counseled that "no family should be without its untold advantages."[6-1]

A catalogue from the Radio Specialty Corporation made the Sears pitch seem shy: "When the forces of the Almighty Creator of the Universe and the skill and genius of Man so combine to bring you untold blessings which may be yours to enjoy without even the asking, we ask you in all seriousness why you should not at once show your gratitude and appreciation and accept that which is so freely offered?"[6-1]

When the National Broadcasting Company was established in 1926, RCA announced it as the first commercial radio network in the world. It was celebrated with a live broadcast on November 15 from the stately grand ballroom of the old Waldorf Astoria Hotel, a majestic edifice that would be demolished a few years later to accommodate the new Empire State Building. Coincidentally, NBC's inauguration was celebrated at the future location of the company's experimental television transmitter and tower.

Twenty-five stations as far west as Kansas City carried the radio network's maiden broadcast. The grand affair lasted more than four hours. Stars from The Metropolitan Opera and the New York Symphony Orchestra, as well as dance bands, Will Rogers, vaudevillian George Olsen, and comedy team Weber and Fields all paraded past the microphones.

The following year, NBC signed-on a second radio network and distinguished the two as the Red Network and the Blue Network. Each provided programming to its affiliate stations across the country. For the most part, NBC Red distributed the more popular programs. NBC Blue was generally considered to be the less prestigious network, ultimately carrying the bulk of NBC's public affairs and cultural offerings, often without commercial sponsors. Despite that broad distinction, a number of noteworthy and popular programs such as *The Jack Benny Show*, *Little Orphan Annie*, *Jack Armstrong*, *Information, Please*, and the most popular radio show of the decade, *Amos 'n' Andy*, originally aired on the NBC Blue network.

In his adolescent years, Johnny's enthusiasm for the early network shows was infectious. Pearl and some of his other siblings derived only slightly more pleasure from the radio comedies than they did from sharing in Johnny's effusive joy listening to the programs' content and emulating the voices they heard on the radio. Among Johnny's favorites was the *Amos 'n' Andy* show.

Amos 'n' Andy enjoyed a popularity and longevity shared by few programs in broadcast history. At the show's peak, *Amos 'n' Andy* commanded an audience that exceeded 40 million listeners. In 1926, that landmark situation comedy first graced the airwaves in the Midwest as *Sam and Henry* on the Chicago Tribune's WGN. The performers were earning $250 a week and sought to supplement that sum by distributing recordings of the show to stations beyond WGN's broadcast range, but management refused. The rival *Chicago Daily News* owned WMAQ and was only too happy to welcome *Sam and Henry* to its studios, agreeing to the early syndication proposal. Since WGN owned the rights to the show's title, *Sam and Henry* was renamed and reincarnated as *Amos 'n' Andy*.

Freeman Gosden and Charles Correll, two white men, who had met in the vaudeville production *The Jollies or 1919*, brought to life the implausible exploits of Amos Jones and Andy Brown, the two African-American owners of the Fresh Air Taxi Company, an enterprise named for their one and only roofless wreck of a cab.

Born in 1899, Gosden was a native of Richmond, Virginia, and he was raised with an African-American nanny before staking a claim in show business. Nine years his junior, Correll was a singer, dancer, and performer in black-face minstrel shows that toured through the south. Although hailing from Peoria, Correll claimed to be a direct descendant of Confederacy President Jefferson Davis. With their Southern roots, the teammates said they were comfortable imitating the familiar African-American speech patterns they had heard in their younger years.

The basis for the show's comedy and its mass appeal lay in the struggle of the underdog to survive the Great Depression, a relatable theme rooted in a plight shared by nearly all Americans. Amos and Andy spoke in a dialect of African Americans from southern states, spiced with malapropos such as "Splain dat to me," "Ain't dat sumpthin'," and "I'se regusted." Gosden and Correll avoided humor based entirely on race; pointed racial slurs were never heard.

Among Amos' and Andy's family and friends in the cast of characters were the bombastic George "Kingfish" Stevens, also performed by Gosden, whose signature delivery of "Holy Mackerel, Andy!" always evoked laughs. Ruby Taylor was played by Elinor Harriet, and Sapphire Stevens was portrayed by Ernestine Wade.

The role of Madam Queen, the ever-infatuated girlfriend set on marrying Andy, was performed by Lillian Randolph, a black actress, who also performed the title role in the program "Beulah." Amanda, Lillian's older sister, played several roles on *Amos 'n' Andy* including Sapphire Stevens' overbearing mother. Amanda was a star in her own right, not recognized by the radio audience from her voice alone. Amanda enjoyed a twenty-four-year career portraying Aunt Jemima. Beginning in 1929, the fictitious African-American cook had her own radio show on CBS and served as narrator for many of the thirty-minute dramas. Aunt Jemima continued as a commercial spokesperson for the pancake mix that bore her name and image until changing times made her characterization socially inappropriate. Years later in 1944, Amanda Randolph had an opportunity to show off her singing talents when she appeared with Johnny on his first experimental television test. On that occasion, Johnny enthusiastically told the actress how much he had enjoyed her performances on *Amos 'n' Andy*.

In 1931, WMAQ was sold to NBC, and *Amos 'n' Andy* relocated to the network's headquarters in Chicago's Merchandise Mart. The comedy was broadcast from Studio F, a 26ft x 21ft studio on the 20th floor that was especially built for the hit show. There, one story above the rest of the network's facility, Studio F featured soft lighting, dark walls, and a desk draped with a tablecloth. Designed to resemble an English library, the room felt more like a den than a traditional, acoustical-tiled, brightly-illuminated studio.

During the course of *Amos 'n' Andy*'s long run, Gosden and Correll moved their production from Chicago to Hollywood, while the Amos and Andy characters moved

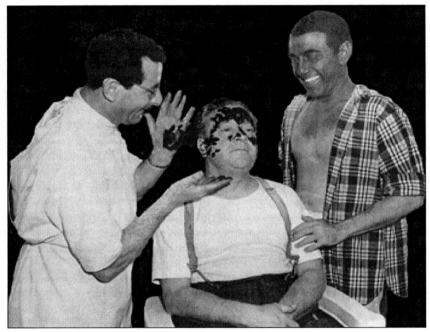

Young Johnny's favorite radio performers, Freeman Gosden (right) and Charles Correll (seated), are transformed into Amos and Andy for a personal appearance.

from Chicago to Harlem, New York. Later, the show moved from NBC Blue to NBC Red, and then moved to CBS, back to NBC, and finally returned to CBS. In the 1940s, the show changed from a fifteen-minute daily format to a weekly thirty-minute show with a live orchestra, a studio audience, and a cast of actors, many of whom were African American, taking over some of the roles that were originally performed by the show's two creators.

That change solved a problem that perplexed NBC for years. The network's archives contain internal correspondence outlining the policy instituted in the show's early years to withhold publicity photographs of Gosden and Correll without black make-up "because our client wishes to maintain in the minds of the public of Amos 'n' Andy as colored characters."[6-2] Another memo instructed "only blackface pictures are to be released [to maintain] the impression of Amos 'n' Andy as two living darkies."[6-2]

Amos 'n' Andy continued on network radio until 1960, ultimately as *The Amos 'n' Andy Music Hall,* while the show was reborn on CBS television in 1951 with an all-black cast. The television show was cancelled just two years later in a storm of protest led by the NAACP, which objected to the unflattering racial stereotypes. "Every character is either a clown or a crook." [6-3] CBS syndicated the television show's seventy-eight episodes until 1966, when the social outcry finally became louder than the show's laughs.

Clearly, the times had changed. During the first half of the 20th century, immigrants of all stripes poured into America through New York's Ellis Island. Numerous radio programs, without malice, often featured ethnic characters for comic relief and as a means with which to portray the human condition. Because it was not a visual medium, the radio characterizations were always played broadly in terms of both content and delivery.

For a five year run starting in 1948, CBS' *Life With Luigi* centered on a working-class Italian immigrant whose cultural conflicts and broken English were the source of much of the entertainment value. Likewise, Molly Goldberg's trials and tribulations as a European Jew adapting to American life propelled *The Goldbergs* through two decades of popularity on both NBC and CBS radio before being embraced on television. Certainly Desi Arnaz's Cuban ancestry was exploited for its comic potential. His character's abuse of the English language was an endearing ingredient in the success of *I Love Lucy.*

In the same decade, that did not hold true for *Amos 'n' Andy* despite exceptional writing and outstanding performances. The fact that the program employed a cast of talented African-American performers in an era when black faces were rarely seen on television in roles other than maids, the seventy-eight filmed episodes of *Amos 'n' Andy* have been officially withheld from the public nearly a half-century later.

During its unprecedented run spanning five decades, *Amos 'n' Andy* counted President Calvin Coolidge among its dedicated listeners. Huey P. Long took his nickname of "Kingfish" from the program. Even the famed Irish playwright George Bernard Shaw was among the show's fans, once commenting, "There are only three things I'll never forget about America: the Rocky Mountains, Niagara Falls, and Amos and Andy on the radio." [6-4]

Preceding and following *Amos 'n' Andy* and other network programs, when other radio listeners were turning the dial or leaving the room, Johnny found added entertainment in the commercials for an endless array of brand-name products, many of which he had never seen in rural Minnesota — heartburn remedies, laxatives, cereals, soaps, sodas, cigarettes, kitchen cleansers, and crackers. Brands included Cuticura, Eye-Gene, Astring-O-Sol, Double Danderine, Mem-Tone, Linit, Dolcin, Dryad, Drene, Dreft, Delrich, Rayve, Pebeco, Merita, Sal Hepatica, BiSoDol, Colox, Satina, Compana, Kolynos, Kriptin, Campana, and Teel. Johnny even heard commercials in which a Dr. John R. Brinkley advocated goat-gland rejuvenation transplants.

Johnny imitated the network announcers' stoic and formal voices, and he searched up and down the dial to hear local content from distant cities during station breaks, when local broadcasters filled the time between network programs.

CHAPTER 7
ON THE AIR!

As a teenager, Johnny was exhausting the show business opportunities available to him in and around his home town. Following his graduation from Windom High School, Johnny immediately set out to work in radio. The medium was coming of age as he was, and Johnny had his first opportunity to participate in commercial broadcasting at WIBU, "The Friendly Farmer Station," in Poynette, Wisconsin. Johnny worked as an unpaid vocalist in the makeshift farmhouse studio, billing himself as "The Buttermilk Kid."

Still in his teens, Johnny's ambition quickly brought him from tiny WIBU to WIBA in Madison, Wisconsin, for his first paid broadcasting employment. He adopted the persona "Don Parker" in order to give singer Johnny Olson a proper introduction. He also became "Uncle Johnny" for a WIBA kids' show.

With the enthusiasm one would expect from a young man starting to live his dream, Johnny wanted the world to know of his good fortune. Wearing a rented tuxedo, he posed behind a WIBA microphone just as the well known network broadcasters did for their publicity photos, and he sent the picture with a press release to about a dozen newspapers and maga-

Johnny Olson pursuing his dream with his first paying radio job at WIBA, Madison.

zines. The result was that Johnny's first national write-up appeared in the December 1931 issue of *Radio Digest*. John kept a copy among his most prized mementos that he toted from Wisconsin to Los Angeles, back to Wisconsin, to New York, back to Hollywood, and on to West Virginia over the course of the next fifty-four years.

At WIBA, Johnny's pay was meager, so in the spring of 1928, he contemplated an offer of a job repairing watches at his brother-in-law Leonard's jewelry store in Mitchell, South Dakota. Johnny recalled that his sister and her husband wanted to help him learn the trade, and offered to pay his way through the Elgin Company's school. On a visit to discuss that idea, Johnny learned that a new station had just signed on in the area. A letter to the owner netted a $25 a week offer to manage the new KGDA, 1280 AM.

Johnny commented that his relatives were none too happy, but resigned to his choice. He recalled that at the age of eighteen, he became the youngest station manager in the country. The responsibility further fueled Johnny's serious dedication to broadcasting. Simultaneously, the station's owner certainly got his money's worth. KGDA's broadcast day began at 5:30 a.m. with an hour of piano, song, and farm reports from Johnny. Then, a two-hour show of Johnny's patter and platters was followed at 8:30 a.m., when Johnny cracked the mike again as "Farmer Bill." Next on the schedule was a half-hour of religion during which Johnny preached the gospel. On Sundays, the religious program consisted of a live, remote broadcast of a church service, and it seemed impossible that one person could coordinate the seamless transition between studio and remote program origination.

In 1951, Johnny recounted for Minnesota's *Cottonwood County Citizen* newspaper how he overcame that logistical nightmare. KGDA regularly used music from *Gus Haenschen's Chevrolet Show* as fill-in programming. Johnny put a ten-minute transcription of that music on his home-made turntable at the studio, and then quickly packed a storage battery, microphone, amplifier, and portable radio into his car and drove to the church.

Johnny used the portable radio to monitor the transcription while setting up the microphone and wiring the amplifier to the phone line that connected the church with the station. At the end of the transcription, Johnny announced an introduction to the church service. During that remote broadcast he returned to the studio to prepare for the next program. Johnny then retrieved the equipment from the church later on Sunday afternoon.

The one-man operation demanded creativity in both engineering and in preparing content, sometimes simultaneously. Johnny wrote, sang, and acted in skits as a number of characters including his popular "Cousin Olaf" and "Bumpy, the Bus Boy." On a number of occasions, Johnny made repairs to studio equipment with screwdrivers, wire cutters, and soldering irons while singing, delivering farm and weather reports, or reading commercials.

Johnny did it all in small market radio: news, comedy, variety, audience participation shows, band remotes, and children's programs. He accompanied himself on piano, ukulele, and banjo, sold time, maintained the equipment, wrote scripts and commercials, composed and read poetry, preached religion, and covered every manner of sporting event.

For live coverage of a twenty-three-day bicycle race, enterprising Johnny hitched an amplifier to a telephone line, had the operator connect him to the station, and then connected a microphone with 150 feet of outstretched mike cable. Each time the cyclists peddled by, Johnny snatched an interview by jogging alongside the riders for 300 feet. Then, he continued the live coverage while recoiling the cable on his return to his starting point, preparing for another interview on the bikers' next lap.

Even a bout with measles did not keep Johnny from covering a state basketball tournament. A doctor accompanied Johnny to the broadcast booth to see that he did not contaminate anyone, and the physician watched with amazement while Johnny announced six games in one day. When the stock market crash of 1929 resulted in a salary cut to $18 a week, Johnny simply supplemented his income by working in plugs for local stores and restaurants that paid off in new clothes and free meals.

America's youngest station manager, Johnny at age eighteen, radio's jack-of-all-trades at KGDA.

Johnny began to develop a philosophy about announcing that he carried with him for many years and shared with his hometown newspaper, the *Cottonwood County Citizen*. "It takes a good voice to grab the audience's lethargic, wandering attention and hold it long enough to tell them what you and your sponsor want them to hear. A good voice involves more than a high decibel level; a voice without undue inflection may charm, soothe, calm, or arouse. A voice can also repel, infuriate, or actually make a listener ill."

As pay was low and the family did not want the teenager unsupervised, while working at KGDA Johnny lived with Ella, his older sister, and Leonard Wick, her husband.

John would laughingly cite a 1968 article in the *Medical World News* that a friend had brought to him from a doctor's office. The headline read "Sound of Announcer's Voice Jars Listener into Seizure." It was the story of a woman treated by Dr. Francis M. Forster at the University of Wisconsin's Epilepsy Center, who was literally thrown into fits by the sound of three specific radio announcers. In the article, Dr. Forster was quoted as saying that she believed it was not the broadcasters words, but their "prosody-variation in pitch, rhythm, and stress of pronunciation" that were responsible for the seizures.

Another such case came to light years later when Dr. Venkat Ramani, a Professor of Neurology at the Albany Medical College, reported in the *New England Journal of Medicine* that a woman named Dianne Neale was thrown into epileptic seizures simply by hearing the voice of Mary Hart, a host of the syndicated television program, *Entertainment Tonight*.

In the *New England Journal of Medicine's* July 11, 1991 issue, Dr. Ramani stated emphatically that his tests confirmed that Ms. Hart's voice set off the abnormal electrical discharges in his patient's brain that mark an epileptic seizure. The doctor said, "It was very dramatic" when he studied the seizures, reporting that Ms. Neale would rub her stomach, hold her head, "and then she would look confused and far away…(from) the expression in her eyes, she looked like she was far away and out of it." [7-1]

Dr. Marc Dichter of the University of Pennsylvania Medical School, an expert on epilepsy, said of those seizures, "It's the pitch and quality of the voice as a sound, rather than likely what she's actually saying." [7-1] The *New England Journal of Medicine* reported that Dianne Neale had not had any major seizures since she stopped watching the television show. *Entertainment Tonight* and Mary Hart continued successfully for more than twenty-five years despite losing the one viewer. Among the stories Ms. Hart delivered during her long tenure was that of Johnny's passing in which she reported that "Johnny Olson became more recognizable as an announcer than many stars who appear on camera."

Johnny Olson lived the vagabond life of a radio journeyman. Although he loved the work, he remained mindful of his father's admonition that a career in the entertainment world would not provide the security and pay that was necessary to support a family. So Johnny advanced from the KGDA experience through pharmacy classes at the University of Minnesota, as suggested by hometown druggist Bordie Olson.

In 1931, he went back to WIBA in Madison with part-time work as a soda jerk. Johnny recounted, "I managed to learn to type as fast as 97-words a minute, and enough shorthand to qualify as a court reporter and I was usually working part-time at some kind of job." Johnny even served as a short-order cook before trying his hand as a young adult in the world of music.

CHAPTER 8

CAREER CROSSROADS

John carried his mother's advice to "speak up" to new opportunities as vocalist with The Rainbow Revelers, typically earning $3 a night at fraternity dances. With that experience, John next founded The Rhythm Rascals, and he later fronted and sang for Heinie's Grenadiers. Jack Bundy, a fellow radio announcer on Milwaukee's WTMJ, adopted a German persona as leader of Heinie und his Grenadiers for performances of German folk music. Supported for a time by a Saturday morning radio show, the band enjoyed regional success for an amazing thirty-two years before disbanding in 1964.

The musical traditions fostered by German immigrants were woven into the cultural fabric of Wisconsin's Green County, the destination for thousands of nineteenth century Swiss immigrants. The cities of Monroe and New Glarus celebrated that rich Swiss heritage in their architecture, restaurants, and in their music. Embracing the Dutch, Swiss, and German stereotypes, the region has supported musical performers such as Yogi Yorgeson, Whoopee John Wilfahrt, The Six Fat Dutchmen, and The Happy Schnapps Combo. Even today, there are ethnic polka bands featuring Swiss-American yodelers performing in that area.

Jack Bundy was a shrewd promoter. With support from airplay on his Milwaukee radio show, Heinie's Grenadiers gained sufficient popularity to secure a recording contract with Decca Records. In the guise of Heinie, Bundy responded to fan mail with postcards that included a photograph of the band and a brief message employing his characteristic parody of the German-American accent and phrase structure. "Ve hopes you keep listenin' in, unt dot you writes again, so often vot you like."

After resigning his post as a Grenadier, Johnny served as vocalist and manager for Hip Haynes' The Hips Commanders. 78 rpm records of The Hips Commanders were pressed on which a young Johnny Olson made his recording debut crooning "Wabash Moon" and "Walking My Baby Back Home." Documentary filmmaker Leah Biel (*For The Record*, 2009) shared a copy of The Hips Commanders recording of *Wabash Moon* (Broadway 1439). It was a sentimental, almost dreamy composition co-authored in 1931 by radio personality Morton Downey, who used it as his theme song for several years.

"Wabash moon keep shining on the one who waits for me…" Johnny crooned the ballad's chorus as a tenor, in a style seemingly influenced by popular singer Nick Lucas. Lucas previously recorded the song for Brunswick Records. John's vocal was

accompanied by a primarily muted brass and woodwind orchestra that created a
sound common to the music that backed the Hal Roach Studio's two-reel comedy
shorts of the era.

Caleb Nelson, a musician and composer as well as a former member of *The Price
is Right* production staff, noted that the Hips Commanders' rendition meandered
through several keys, from B-flat major to A major. Of John's vocal he observed,

Vocalist Johnny Olson (left), wearing a white suit and fronting Heinie's Grenadiers. Jack
"Heinie" Bundy is standing at the right.

"The timidity in which he subdues his voice to the accompaniment provides a sharp
contrast to his later days of pushing his pipes to bellow above the raucousness of his
Price audiences."

In 1931, all twelve of Hip Haynes' Commanders crammed into a Buick that was
elongated and customized to serve as a bus, and they drove to Chicago to seek their
fame and fortune on the big band circuit. Johnny auditioned his band with Lawrence
Welk. Bandleaders Wayne King and Jan Garber also sampled the group, but it was
Jules Stein, the founder of MCA, who signed Johnny's troupe. The Music Corporation
of America began in Chicago in 1924 as a talent agency that specialized in booking
musical acts. Stein's and MCA's story are unique, and they laid the foundation for
what would become one of the world's largest entertainment conglomerates.

Dr. Jules Stein was a musician financing his medical education as a band leader.
After graduating from the University of Chicago, he received his MD degree from
Rush Medical College. Following postgraduate studies at the University of Vienna
and Chicago's Cook County Hospital, Stein began medical practice and was certi-
fied by the American Board of Ophthalmology. He continued to pursue his musical
career and began booking other musicians for professional engagements. With the
founding of the Music Corporation of America, Dr. Stein gave up the practice of

medicine to concentrate on his growing talent agency enterprise. In 1941, the business was boosted when CBS withdrew from the talent management field and sold its Columbia Artists Bureau to Jules Stein for $250,000.

By the mid 1940s, MCA represented most of the great name bands and began to expand to booking film stars, directors, and writers. Later, under the leadership of Lew Wasserman, one of the most respected moguls in Hollywood's history, Stein and MCA entered the promising new business of television soon after it became profitable. They became a major producer and distributor of programs.

MCA eventually acquired Universal Pictures and the bulk of Paramount Pictures' library of pre-1948 feature films. MCA purchased Decca Records and ultimately continued its growth into the music business with the acquisition of ABC Records, as well as the Chess, Motown, and Geffen Records labels. MCA further expanded into publishing and cable television.

Due to anti-trust regulations, MCA was forced to dissolve the original talent agency business in 1962. Finally, following a long series of mergers and acquisitions that included periods of both Japanese and French ownership, the company became known as NBC Universal and was 80% owned by General Electric, one of the original players in the nearly hundred year history of broadcasting.

During the intervening years, Dr. Jules Stein rededicated himself to medicine. In the late 1950s, urged by Doris, his wife, he directed his talents to blindness prevention. He was considered largely responsible for the passage of legislation that established the National Eye Institute as part of the National Institutes of Health. Dr. Stein died in 1981, but the Jules Stein Eye Institute at the University of California, Los Angeles, continues as a world-renowned research and treatment facility dealing with eye diseases.

Representation by MCA held the promise of future success for the Hips Commanders, but in 1931, Johnny suddenly left the group. He missed radio. At the age of twenty-one, Johnny was at a crossroads in his life, and he made the decision to follow his heart. He returned to South Dakota and KGDA, where he resumed his work as announcer, singer, and radio personality, as well as news and sports reporter.

Back behind the mike, Johnny hosted every manner of broadcast including audience participation shows, band remotes, amateur shows, dance shows, and courtroom coverage. He read comic strips, as well as obituaries, and announced sports play-by-play for football, basketball, wrestling, boxing, auto races, and track meets. Johnny's mastery of the medium led to his being hired as chief announcer for a dominant station in a larger market. Between 1933 and 1944, Johnny gained regional renown broadcasting on WTMJ, Milwaukee. The station was owned by and named for the *Milwaukee Journal*, and earned a footnote in the history of radio. In 1934, as reported by *Broadcasting Magazine,* a half-hour show was sold to six sponsors instead of only one as a way to stimulate sales during the Great Depression. It appeared to be the first documented instance of the business model for broadcast advertising that became the norm decades later.

Among the first to build radio stations were schools and churches. Businesses such as newspapers, stores, car dealerships, hotels, and other entities also sought greater recognition for their primary business, or saw the possibilities for the kind of cross-promotion that became known by the buzzword "synergy."

Like the *Milwaukee Journal's* WTMJ, some newspaper broadcast holdings incorporated names or slogans into their call letters, such as WGN for the World's Greatest Newspaper, the *Chicago Tribune*; the *Arizona Republic's* KTAR, Phoenix; North Carolina's WSJS, owned by the *Winston-Salem Journal-Sentinel*; WTAG, Worchester, Massachusetts, which was owned by the *Worcester Telegram and Gazette*.

Other newspapers to operate stations as early as 1922 included WSB, Atlanta, the *Atlanta Journal*; WFAA, Dallas, the *Dallas News and Journal*; WBAP, Fort Worth, the *Fort Worth Star-Telegram*; WWJ, Detroit, the *Detroit News*; KSD, St. Louis, the *St. Louis Dispatch*; WHAS, Louisville, the *Louisville Courier-Journal*; WHAM, Rochester, New York, the *Rochester Democrat & Chronicle*; WDAF, Kansas City, the *Kansas City Star*; WCX (now WJR), Detroit, the *Detroit Free Press*.

Retailers were also among the first to invest in radio, including WOR, Newark, New Jersey, which was owned by L. Bamberger & Co., and WNAC, Boston, which was established by Shepherd Stores. The Gimbel Brothers operated WGBS in New York and WIP in Philadelphia.

Like the *Milwaukee Journal's* WTMJ, other creative call letter requests were granted by the Federal Radio Commission in the 1920s. Chicago's WLS was owned by Sears and named to honor the World's Largest Store. That city's WCFL was operated by the Chicago Federation of Labor. Los Angeles auto dealer Earl C. Anthony built KECA (now KABC). Hartford, Connecticut was known for the many insurance companies headquartered there, and the Travelers Insurance Company owned WTIC.

The Edison Electric Illuminating Company in Boston operated WEEI. New York's Hotel McAlpin housed WMCA in a 24th floor glass enclosed studio. Likewise, Houston's KTRH broadcast from The Rice Hotel. A licensee in Atlantic City, New Jersey was granted WGP reportedly to honor the city as the World's Greatest Playground. Omaha's WOW was built by Woodmen of the World, a fraternal organization dating back to 1891 that offered life insurance and financial services to its members. WJJD honored James J. Davis, Director General of the Loyal Order of Moose in Mooseheart, Illinois.

Broadcasting legends Gary Owens and Joey Reynolds, with over a hundred years of radio history between them, reminisced about their time together at KMPC, Los Angeles, a station also on Johnny's resume. It was birthed carrying the monogram of its original owner, the MacMillan Petroleum Company. Joey's career benefited from divine intervention as he enumerated past posts and their presumed call letter derivations: Buffalo's WKBW, that stood for Well Known Bible Witness, and Philadelphia's WIBG, that stood for I Believe in God.

Owens added that Chicago's WIND was not named to commemorate the "Windy City," but for the location of its transmitter in Indiana. Always locked and loaded with a joke, Gary recalled the occasion when WIND's ratings bested those of WGN, and the station placed a questionably-worded ad in *Variety* heralding their success: "WGN no longer passes WIND in Chicago!"

Johnnny's hiring at WTMJ was a major vote of confidence for the young broad-caster, and he rose to the challenge. Johnny's audience in the Midwest grew, as he won regional popularity polls among listeners. For three consecutive years in the late 1930s, WTMJ's parent company, the *Milwaukee Journal*, proclaimed Johnny "Best Announcer." More objectively, in the June 29, 1935 issue of *Radio Guide*, the magazine reported that its readers had voted Johnny the nation's thirty-seventh most popular announcer in their "Star of Stars" election. His respectable placement between such notable, national names as Kenneth Niles and Ben Grauer was espe-cially encouraging because Johnny was not yet a network broadcaster, and he could only be heard on WTMJ.

His humorous introductions to the hit songs of the day earned Johnny a men-tion from Robert Ripley. "Ripley's Believe It or Not" called attention to John as the "veteran radio announcer who never announced a song correctly in his life." Typical of Johnny's creative introductions was "And now for a new song, 'I'm Sorry I Made You Cry, But it Made Your Face Cleaner.'"

Johnny extended his regional renown with a column, "Johnny Olson's Jottings," which was carried by several Wisconsin newspapers. His on-air popularity at WTMJ led to the first of several experiences with syndicated programming, a distribution model in which a station in another, often similar market purchased the rights to broadcast a specific program from a recorded transcription. Stations preferred to be on the receiving end of the transaction when a sponsor bought airtime to spread the popularity of a program closely identified with their product or service.

That was the case in a couple of Wisconsin farming communities. In 1939, Osh-Kosh B'Gosh, Inc., the state's well-known manufacturer of hickory-striped bib overalls, expanded Johnny's audience by syndicating *The Oshkosh B' Gosh Radio Pro-gram* from WTMJ to WSAU, Wausau, and WTAQ, Eau Claire. Likewise, Piggly Wiggly Markets sponsored an offering by the ambitious broadcaster the following year. WSAU also carried John's *The 1940 Laugh Parade*, while WTAQ aired his *Can You Beat It?*

CHAPTER 9
FINDING A LUCKY PENNY

Johnny interviewed three sitting Presidents during his career, Calvin Coolidge, Herbert Hoover, and Franklin Roosevelt. He recalled for the *Cottonwood County Citizen* that Roosevelt was seated on the back of a train that had stopped in downtown Milwaukee on a particularly hot and humid day. After pressing his way through the crowd, Johnny was perspiring profusely. While holding the microphone with one hand, he made a move with the other for a handkerchief in his hip pocket. He remembered being abruptly stopped by a Secret Service agent. "I wouldn't do that if I were you," the agent said. Johnny whispered off-mike that he was simply reaching for his handkerchief, but the President's guardian was unimpressed with that clarification. Fearful of being forced to stop the interview with the President, Johnny said, "I just kept talking…and sweating." [9-1]

The interview with Franklin Roosevelt was an important assignment for Johnny. Roosevelt's influence on the country during the difficult years of his presidency cannot be overstated. On the home front, the United States was in the throws of a deep economic depression. Overseas, the stage was being set for a worldwide conflict. With the memory of World War I still fresh in the American conscience, people looked to the eloquent statesman for his report on the current crises and for reassurance about the future.

In 1931, CBS staff announcer Robert Trout, one of America's most-celebrated news broadcasters, first took to the air, reporting on virtually every major news event during a career that spanned an amazing sixty-nine years. Trout was the newsman most closely associated with Roosevelt's broadcasts, and in later years, he reflected on the mood of the nation in 1933, when the newly elected President gave his first address:

> "After the March fourth inauguration…it was really a rather touchy time, and the President announced that he was going to make a talk from the White House to explain just what was going on and why the banks were closed and why nobody could cash a check and why, even if you had a job, you probably didn't have any money to eat on. The White House just said that there was

to be a talk by the President. So at the CBS Washington offices we prepared two introductions for me to use to put the President on the air." [9-2]

On March 12, Americans heard their President say, "My friends. I want to tell you what has been done in the last few days, why it has been done, and what the next

Franklin Roosevelt, a masterful radio communicator, and one of three sitting Presidents interviewed by Johnny.

steps are going to be." [9-3] It was the beginning of a thirteen-minute friendly talk in which complex economic theory and the steps being taken to preserve the nation's banking system were calmly explained in understandable terms.

Roosevelt was a masterful communicator. With a massive national audience delivered by the cooperation between both NBC and CBS, Roosevelt used the medium of radio as no President had before or has since with his thirty "fireside chat" broadcasts. That label helped to create a proper theater of the mind for the President's addresses, but contrary to many accounts, Robert Trout said he was not responsible for the name.

The newscaster explained, "The man who actually thought of the phrase 'fireside chat' was Harry Butcher, who at that time was the director and the general manager of CBS' Washington station. It was his idea that this would be just the kind of folksy touch that might do for the introduction for the President. And the whole little introduction was about the President is going to talk to you just as if he had come into your home and sat down beside the fireplace in your living room and gave a sort of fireside chat. It was that kind of introduction. So we sent both introductions over to the White House for the President to choose, and a little while later Marvin McIntyre, the President's secretary, telephoned Harry Butcher and said 'Oh, the President

Mrs. Eleanor Roosevelt, twentieth century America's most outspoken First Lady.

likes that folksy one,' and so I used it." [9-2]

In contrast to the notion of a fireside chat, Roosevelt usually broadcast in formal attire from a large White House ballroom that did not feature a fireplace, with members of the press and an assemblage of dignitaries in attendance. During the course of a dozen years, Roosevelt periodically utilized radio to address subjects of national concern with compelling familiarity and to apply pressure to legislators for support of his policies.

The President broke with the traditional formality associated with his high office to discuss family and personal matters, including making mention of his dog Fala. During one lengthy chat, he set aside the stodgy style typical of those heard on radio in the era and casually asked for a glass of water.

In the early 1930s, First Lady Eleanor Roosevelt took to the air as host of NBC's *The Pond's Program*. The cold cream company's weekly show featured classical and semi-classical music interspersed with Mrs. Roosevelt's commentaries on social issues, the war in Europe, and her husband's policies. In 1937, the First Lady was back on NBC on Wednesday nights with *Starring Mrs. Roosevelt*, interviewing literary and show business personalities, as well as commenting on the news of the day.

Although somewhat frail by the time of his final fireside chat in 1944, Franklin Roosevelt's words, as well as his tone, were always vital and powerful, and Americans tuned in to hear his every comment, as he guided the nation through an extremely difficult period in its history. It was with Arthur Godfrey's touching and tearful coverage of Roosevelt's funeral in 1945 that the rising broadcaster first endeared himself to radio listeners.

The following year, Godfrey began a twenty-eight-year reign on CBS radio and television as a favorite of both daytime and prime-time audiences, as well as advertisers. The effectiveness of Arthur Godfrey's ad-libbed, conversational, humorous, and sometimes critical pitches for everything from Lipton Soup to Scotch Tape to Wildroot Cream Oil hair lotion made him a darling of Madison Avenue.

Broadcasting Magazine reported that Godfrey was CBS' highest-paid employee in 1948 with a salary totaling $258,450, plus an additional $123,624 paid by the network to Arthur Godfrey Productions for "program services." At the peak of his popularity in the 1950s, the New York-born broadcaster's folksy, soft-spoken, Southern-styled delivery was earning him in excess of $1 million a year. According to Larry King, Arthur Godfrey, "The Old Redhead," understood broadcasting's ultimate business to such an extent that on his Florida driver's license he listed his occupation as "salesman."

Although Johnny worked with Godfrey years later after venturing forth from Milwaukee to New York, in the late 1930s and early 1940s, there was little motivation for him to move on. With WTMJ's regional Midwest reach, Johnny was enjoying salary increases commensurate with his expanding popularity and his willingness to work with management in all manner of sponsor-friendly promotions and tie-ins. The March 13, 1943 issue of *Boxoffice* magazine detailed Johnny's cooperation in supporting the Milwaukee opening of the movie *The Immortal Sergeant*. He invited women war workers to send letters detailing "How I am serving the Immortal Sergeants on the battle front." The ten best letters won dinner dates followed by a preview of the film with ten sergeants serving in the Milwaukee area.

On the air, Johnny was extremely versatile, hosting a wide variety of programs as diverse as *Romantic Balladier*, *Comic Caravan*, *Platter Puzzlers*, *The Falstaff Show*, and *Quiz Battle of the Century*. His knowledge of music helped Johnny in programming his popular *Masters of Rhythm* show, and he still sang on and off the air. For another program, Johnny borrowed a page from co-worker Jack Bundy's playbook.

As Bundy had with Heinie's Grenadiers, Johnny organized *The Rhythm Rascals* as a program for WTMJ, and as a five-piece jazz band for regional appearances. When the Eight Brothers Tobacco Company sponsored the quintet, Johnny happily obliged the benefactor's requests by altering the spelling of his first name and rechristening the group Johnnie Olson and His Eight Brothers Rhythm Rascals. In 1938 during a performance as a Rhythm Rascal at a Fourth of July dance in Iola, Wisconsin, Johnny first met Penelope Powers, his future wife.

Penny was working as a schoolteacher, but she had appeared in school and community productions, as well as talent shows, performing as a singer and dancer. She had even sung a few times on local radio. Penny attended a dance at the urging of her father and step-mother, both of whom were ardent fans of Johnny's. The Powers introduced the singer to their daughter, who gave him a cool reception at first. Johnny attempted to melt that chill by asking Penny what song she would like to hear, but the object of Johnny's interest again rebuffed him by saying she was not interested in hearing any particular song.

Penny's parents made up for her lack of enthusiasm and requested a couple of her favorites. Eventually, Penny warmed up a bit, and with her parents' encouragement, she accepted Johnny's offer to drive her home. They were certain that the fine young gentleman could be trusted to return their daughter safely to home because, after all, he was a broadcaster on the respected WTMJ. Unbeknownst to Johnny, it turned out that "home" for Penny was sixty miles away in Stevens Point. By the end of the long drive, a relationship had sparked.

Johnny's unique courting rituals included whispering sweet nothings to Penny via one of the Midwest's most popular radio stations. The Rhythm Rascals' theme song was a ditty entitled "Crazy Words," and Johnny sang the song when he introduced the band on their live broadcasts. He started writing new lyrics to the tune in which he broadcast secret messages to Penny. Johnny said that he wrote as many as 2,000 variations on the melody to keep Penny's interest over the months.

Penny shared much of Johnny's enthusiasm for radio, and she listened with great interest to his musings about the medium. On October 31, 1938, CBS broadcast Orson Welles' regular Sunday evening *Mercury Theater of the Air* program. That night's offering was especially appropriate for Halloween — an adaptation of H.G. Wells' *War of the Worlds* that resulted in many listeners panicking in response to the realistic accounts of New Jersey being attacked from Mars with poisonous gas spreading death across the Hudson River to New York. Johnny pointed out the irony to Penny that only a few years earlier, when radio was in its infancy, H.G. Wells predicted devastation, proclaiming in an interview, "The whole broadcasting industry will dry up." [9-4]

Following a proposal in Chicago's noted Blackhawk restaurant, a little over a year after their meeting at the Fourth of July dance, the couple tied the knot in October 1939 in Decorah, Iowa. During their forty-six-year marriage, Penny became an important partner in Johnny's success. She was co-host, sang, conducted interviews, selected contestants for Johnny's audience participation shows, and assisted him with the challenging logistics at thousands of remote broadcasts and personal appearances at state fairs, county fairs, agricultural expositions, bond drives, blood drives, polio fundraisers, and other charitable events.

In 1953, Penny wrote autobiographical liner notes for an album of hymns she sang:

> "She was born of a musical family...and fondly recalls the good
> times she had growing up in a home life that was packed with
> music and love. Her father, Fred Powers, employed in a paper mill,

her mother Agnes, two sisters, Helen and Irene, and a brother George were all musical and the family orchestra 'concerts' always included many of the family's favorite hymns."

"Penny started singing at the age of five and was one of the first to broadcast from her hometown. During her school and college years, she was always a favorite in the musical operettas and home town plays...Penny got the idea of this album of hymns while appearing in West Virginia when she attended a heavenly little church, St. Charles at White Sulphur Springs. Penny has always been a great believer in faith, having been tested many times by the Lord, and with the help of more than 50,000 loyal listeners from coast to coast who have written her of their favorite hymns, she has compiled and recorded ten of the tops, which she believes will bring hope and inspiration, to all races, color and creed."

CHAPTER 10

HOLLYWOOD, THE FIRST TIME

In 1940, Nescafé, the first mass-marketed instant coffee, as well as Fiberglass, Teflon, and antibiotics were all new, and Penicillin was soon to be on the market. Overseas, the Nazis were sweeping through Europe and Scandinavia. In America, a thirty-five-year-old Vermont widow received the first Social Security check in the amount of $22.54, and the first McDonald's hamburger was served in San Bernardino, California, by two brothers actually named McDonald. Although experimental television was being demonstrated at the World's Fair in New York, it was radio's golden age.

Johnny took a temporary leave of absence from WTMJ, and the newlyweds toured with The Rhythm Rascals. When the group arrived in Hollywood, in addition to playing dances, they were guests on several national radio shows. While standing behind those radio microphones, Johnny realized that broadcasting was still very much in his blood and his true passion. When the Rhythm Rascals returned to the road, Penny and Johnny remained in Hollywood.

In the summer of 1941, John found work at KMPC. With studios on Wilshire Boulevard in Beverly Hills, KMPC referred to itself as "The Station of the Stars" because its stockholders at the time included crooner Bing Crosby, orchestra leader Paul Whiteman, silent film comedian Harold Lloyd, and in a strange twist of fate, Freeman Gosden and Charles Corell, the originators of John's favorite show, *Amos 'n' Andy*.

At KMPC John performed on a program about adventures in aviation entitled *The Foreman of the Flyin' Y*, his own weekday afternoon *The Johnny Olson Show*, and was among the many Los Angeles radio personalities to deliver commercials for The Smilin' Irishman. Much as automobile dealers today flood television's fringe hours with hard-sell advertising, a disreputable used car dealer was saturating Los Angeles radio airwaves in the early 1940s.

Harry Bartell, another broadcaster of that day, conjectured about the dealer's choice of the appellation "Smilin' Irishman." He said, "I think that was supposed to imply warm, friendly, and generous attention...I couldn't very well apprise the public of the rumor that worn out brakes were being repaired with sawdust and molasses... I could never meet his demand that I describe his cars as gems in the Cadillac class when they were quite obviously clunkers even when washed."[10-1]

Johnny quickly advanced to host three local radio shows, *Missing Persons, Man on the Street*, and *Chef Milani*, all for Warner Bros.' KFWB. Johnny worked in radio studios adjacent to sound stages and a warehouse at the far rear of the ten-acre Warner movie lot that fronted Sunset Boulevard. He was less than a hundred yards from where the majority of the first "talkie," Al Jolson's *The Jazz Singer*, was filmed.

Unlike their war against television years later, the movie studios embraced radio.

Johnny made his Los Angeles radio debut on KMPC, Beverly Hills, the "Station of the Stars."

Most of the film companies were prominent radio advertisers, and in some cases, cross ownership made for partnerships in the movie and radio industries. The film studios saw radio as an allied business with abundant potential for the promotion of their product.

The call letters KFWB were publicized to celebrate the four Warner brothers who signed on the station in 1925. Soon after, both Paramount and MGM announced their intentions to form radio networks. MGM's parent company, Loew's, owned New York's WMGM (later WHN). In 1929, William Paley solicited an investment of approximately $4 million from Adolph Zukor's film company to help build the new radio network. Paramount Pictures became a substantial stockholder in CBS.

The "R" of RKO Pictures stood for "radio" as the studio was formed under the auspices of David Sarnoff's Radio Corporation of America and the Keith-Albee-Orpheum theater chain. At one time, RCA owned as much as 60 percent of RKO, entering the motion picture business in the new era of "talkies" with Photophone, a sound recording system designed to compete with the more popular Western Electric technology from AT&T.

In 1929, Sarnoff announced the deal negotiated with financier, politician and power broker, Joseph Kennedy. RCA's new interest in RKO was heralded in Sarnoff's customary bombastic style. Full page ads in the leading trade publications that featured flaring lightening bolts and flaming radio beacons proclaimed:

> "The Radio Titan Opens the Curtains of the Clouds and a New and Greater Year dawns for the Most Spectacular Show Machine of All Time! A New and Mightier Pageant of the Titans is forming... Titanic in Conception... Titanic in Development... Titanic in Reality... Sweeping on to a Mighty Destiny."[10-2]

The stars held under restrictive, exclusive studio contracts were made available to radio microphones for guest appearances on interview, variety, and dramatic programs. Among the earliest were *The Sunkist Musical Cocktail* and *Hollywood Hotel*. The movie moguls served up their prime talent for *The MGM Theater of the Air* on the Mutual Network, and CBS' *Silver Theater*. Louis B. Mayer, MGM's President, also opened his stable of stars and even guest hosted for the NBC variety series, *Maxwell House Coffee Time*. The film studios understood radio and utilized its promotional power, not considering the medium as competition for their visual offerings.

Some of the most celebrated film luminaries regularly appeared on *The Lux Radio Theater*. The program debuted in 1934, and for twenty-one years, presented adaptations of Broadway stage works and motion pictures in hour-long, live radio productions. For most of its extensive run, *The Lux Radio Theater* was introduced each Monday evening by no less a motion picture potentate than Cecil B. DeMille. The roster of film idols making guest appearances included Cary Grant, Bette Davis, Spencer Tracy, Joan Crawford, Clark Gable, Marlene Dietrich, Humphrey Bogart, Shirley Temple, Gary Cooper, Jean Harlow, Errol Flynn, Ethel Barrymore, James Cagney, Claudette Colbert, Wallace Beery, Loretta Young, Judy Garland, and Mickey Rooney.

In a similar vein, silver-screen celebrities of the caliber of Douglas Fairbanks, Jr., Ray Milland, Charles Boyer, and Rex Harrison were headliners in radio adaptations of motion pictures on NBC's *Hollywood Star Preview*. Likewise, filmdom royalty including Lionel Barrymore, Edward G. Robinson, Claude Raines, Charles Laughton, and Glen Ford performed on *Cavalcade of America*. During its eighteen-year run on CBS and NBC, the program dramatized true stories of lesser-known incidents and people in American history.

Frank Nelson, a well-respected actor and former national president of the broadcast performers' union, the American Federation of Radio Artists, AFRA, (later known as AFTRA when television came of age), was a familiar face from 1950s television. He is best remembered by situation-comedy aficionados from his countless appearances with Jack Benny and Lucille Ball, portraying a wide range of supporting comic characters, from a train conductor to a department store salesman, always with his animated wide-eyed smile, thin moustache, and supercilious "Yeeeeeeeeeeesss?"

Nelson devoted much of his life to the cause of improving wages and working conditions for broadcasters and actors. Once, in an impassioned discussion over the issue of residual payments, Screen Actors Guild President Ronald Reagan, in opposition to such compensation, angrily accused Frank Nelson of being a Communist. In truth, he was a conservative Republican, but the reckless charge foreshadowed the darkest days of the Communist witch hunt and the blacklist that split the union and destroyed careers not too many years later.

On the subject of film stars gracing the radio airwaves, Nelson recalled in 1980, "It was not until 1933 that any transcontinental shows emanated from Hollywood. The first of these was called *Hollywood on the Air*. I announced the show and also worked as an actor. Sometimes when a star scheduled to appear failed to show up, I did the star's part, too. The show ran 1933 and part of 1934." [10-3]

Nelson remembered that NBC's first outpost in the film capitol was only a single office on the RKO movie back lot, and that radio work was performed in the immense motion picture sound stages before broadcasting studios were built. The performer recalled, "The first sponsored transcontinental show out of here was an original Marx Brothers show." [10-4] That program was *Flywheel, Shyster and Flywheel*, a madcap comedy set in a disreputable law firm, starring only two of the brothers, Groucho and Chico, as a shady lawyer and his even shadier assistant.

Less than a decade later, the film community failed to understand the next wave of broadcasting. On the first day of commercial television in 1941, the great Jack Warner was in New York and had his first opportunity to see television. He allegedly told his dinner host, Tom Bragg, an investor in the new medium, "Can you imagine trying to produce a new movie for every night of the week? It's not possible." [10-5]

Johnny spent his first thirty years chasing the voices in the air, and he had finally joined their ranks, but he was only finding local success on KFWB radio in Hollywood. From the relatively humble studios at 5833 Fernwood Avenue at the rear of the Warner Bros. lot, Johnny occasionally walked a few short blocks north and west to the corner of Sunset Boulevard and Gower Street, the location of CBS' Columbia Square, to watch Jack Benny, Edgar Bergen, Fred Allen, and George Burns and Gracie Allen perform on their network radio shows in the magnificent Streamline Moderne palace of broadcasting. It was a facility so state-of-the-art that Al Jolson reportedly joked at its 1938 dedication, "It looks like Flash Gordon's bathroom."

The Red and Blue networks' star-studded west coast programs originated that same year at NBC's elegant $2 million art deco Radio City Studios located just two blocks further west along Sunset Boulevard at Vine Street. A few hundred feet north on Vine Street was the ornate Lux Radio Theater. Still another block further north at Hollywood and Vine were the offices of Benton and Bowles, Young and Rubicam, and other advertising agencies where performers were cast for many of the great network radio programs. All were within reach, but beyond Johnny's grasp.

With network success in Hollywood proving elusive, Johnny was hesitant to abandon the popularity he had nurtured in earning the *Milwaukee Journal's* crown as that city's preeminent broadcaster. Johnny continued *The Rhythm Rascals* radio shows by transcribing the daily, one-hour program on disc, complete with commercials, for his loyal WTMJ audience.

Variety lauded the long distance arrangement by reporting, "The return of Johnny Olson to Milwaukee, if only by way of a soundtrack, as is the case here, ranks as a shrewd bit of business action by a broadcaster... Several years ago Olson developed

CBS established its west coast presence in 1938 with the magnificent Columbia Square. It was a night and day improvement over Hollywood's earlier make-shift radio facilities.

into Milwaukee's top local mike personality with a reputation and popularity, competitor broadcasters here admit, which hasn't been matched since…The program is Olson at his smoothest as a personality, and adroitest (sic) as a showman. It didn't take long to get the hour pretty well sold to local merchants. Olson knows his Milwaukee audience and his Milwaukee merchandisers, and the three-way wedding looks like solid going for all concerned."

Above: In 1938, NBC opened its own state-of-the-art southern California studio complex. Below: NBC's art deco design and grand lobby mural in Hollywood were reminiscent of the network's New York's Radio City, which had opened five years earlier.

While Johnny and Penny were in Los Angeles, they dreamed up the concept for a program format that was to become their ticket to one of Johnny's greatest successes on radio, and later on television. Dennis Morgan was a Wisconsin-born radio singer, whose career had crossed with Johnny's in the Midwest. They became friends, destined to meet again years later as neighbors in Van Nuys, California.

Dennis had migrated west for film work. As a contract player at MGM, Para-

Left: Johnny's Hollywood smile disguised his initial discouragement in establishing himself as a Los Angeles-based national radio personality. Right: Dennis Morgan, film actor and fellow WTMJ performer, helped inspire *Johnny Olson's Rumpus Room.*

mount, and Warner Bros., he went on to a successful, thirty-five-year film acting career. In 1942, he had been announced to play Victor Laszlo in *Casablanca* before Paul Henreid was ultimately cast for the role. [10-6] While at a particularly lively Christmas party at Dennis Morgan's San Fernando Valley home, Johnny had the inspiration for his Rumpus Room program. That early "house party" idea debuted in Los Angeles on KMPC, and later originated back in Milwaukee on WTMJ.

In its initial incarnation, *Johnny Olson's Rumpus Room* was an energetic, 10:30 p.m. to midnight, informal music and variety show that had upwards of 300 teen-aged studio audience members dancing and crowding around the mike for live, ad-lib fun with Johnny. Involving the audience in a manner that *American Bandstand* did years later generated a six-week wait for tickets to visit the *Rumpus Room*. The show's popularity ultimately proved to be an important key to the Olsons' success when the program was picked-up by WJZ radio in New York, and then offered nationally by NBC's Blue Network. Originally airing on Monday nights, by 1946, the *Rumpus*

Room was open for fun, usually at midnight, as many as six nights during some weeks. The program continued on radio until 1948. The following year, an adaptation of the format brought Johnny fame, when *Johnny Olson's Rumpus Room* became the nation's first daytime network television entertainment series to originate from New York.

CHAPTER 11
BLUE IN NEW YORK

Johnny was establishing himself, developing his skills, and building a following as a broadcaster in local markets, but national exposure on network radio continued to elude him. The journey from WIBU's farmhouse studio to Milwaukee's top-rated WTMJ was a simple ascension compared to the challenging climb to the exclusive enclaves of NBC and CBS. Unnoticed by the networks in Hollywood and far from home and family, the Olsons returned to Wisconsin.

Milwaukee's top radio personality was warmly welcomed back to the WTMJ microphones, but John and Penny's retreat was short-lived. Trouble was brewing at NBC that would soon lead to a restructuring of America's #1 broadcasting company. Johnny was prepared to make the most of the moment with a bold move that would lead to his network radio debut.

Through the development of the Radio Corporation of America and the formation of NBC, David Sarnoff proved himself masterful in acquiring patents and collecting royalties. His protracted disputes with Philo Farnsworth, the inventor of electronic television, and former friend Edwin Armstrong, the inventor of FM radio, to control patent rights and steer the development of American broadcasting were beyond fierce. Sarnoff was also adept at currying favor with the government and developing relationships with FCC commissioners, as he leveraged clout and asserted political pressure towards achieving his goals for RCA's dominance. That included stalling the development of FM radio and having RCA's technical specifications for black and white television broadcasting (and later, color television broadcasting) adopted as the national standards. However, Sarnoff ultimately lost one important battle.

As the reach and popularity of radio grew, there began to be concern at the Federal Trade Commission that the government may have helped lay the foundation for what some regulators perceived as a monopoly. In 1926, the year that NBC debuted, the Federal Trade Commission held hearings on the charge that the field of radio manufacturing was unfairly controlled by RCA through its subsidiary partners, GE and Westinghouse.

The Justice Department was next to scrutinize RCA; they filed an antitrust suit against the company. In a 1932 consent decree, the organization's operations were separated. GE and Westinghouse were forced to sell their interests in RCA, which they had acquired in 1919, and divorce themselves from the conglomerate. The settlement worked to Sarnoff's advantage. He was now on his own and in complete charge, with RCA retaining licensing rights for the numerous patents, as well as full ownership of the National Broadcasting Company.

Within a few more years, the heat was on yet again. The FCC heard complaints from the rival Mutual Radio Network and from some of NBC's own affiliates. The FCC began to recognize the potential for anti-competitive practices at RCA's National Broadcasting Company. The single entity owned and operated some of the most influential major market outlets, and through onerous contracts with affiliates, lorded over a total of 154 stations tied to their two powerful coast-to-coast networks. Complaints also alleged that NBC was controlling the exclusivity of performers through an in-house talent department.

Indeed, NBC's Red and Blue networks shared common production and technical staffs, common studio facilities, and a common sales force. Further evidence that the Red and Blue were wielding weighty influence included the fact only a few stations were permanently assigned to either the Red or the Blue network full time. Other affiliates, such as Johnny's employer, WTMJ in Milwaukee, could be shifted by NBC management between the two chains to fit a sponsor's advertising strategy. There was also concern about the networks' one-sided contracts that gave NBC the right to dictate specific programming to local stations, thus skirting the FCC's highest mandate in the Communications Act of 1934 that stations serve the needs of their local communities.

In 1938, the FCC began a series of hearings investigating business practices of the radio networks. Under the leadership of James Fly, Franklin Roosevelt's appointee as Chairman of the FCC, the austere body published its report *On Chain Broadcasting* in 1941. It called for NBC to fully divest itself of one of its two networks. Between December 8, 1941 and January 9, 1942, RCA completed its reorganization of the Blue Network into a separate entity called The Blue Network, Incorporated. Blue was still owned by RCA, but with operations, staffs, and talent kept separate from the Red Network, government heat was off, as Sarnoff looked for a buyer.

Investment banking firms and insurance companies were among the interested parties, but true to character, Sarnoff ultimately closed the deal with the highest bidder. In July of 1943, on the heels of a Supreme Court decision upholding the FCC's right to compel compliance with its network anti-monopoly rules, NBC announced that the Blue Network was sold for $8 million to an unlikely buyer, Mr. Edward J. Noble. Although he had briefly served as an Undersecretary of Commerce during President Roosevelt's administration, and he had dabbled in the ownership of New York's WMCA, Noble, like Sarnoff, was best described as a shrewd, opportunistic businessman.

A resident of the luxurious Waldorf Astoria Towers, Noble also had an interest in United Drug, a conglomerate that owned several big pharmaceutical brands and the Rexall retail drug chain. In 1912, he made his sweetest deal by purchasing Life Savers candy from its inventor, Clarence Crane, for a mere $2,900 shortly after its invention. It was an investment that netted millions of dollars when the small, round candy in the shape of a ships' lifesaving floatation ring became a top seller.

After his broadcasting acquisition, Noble changed the name of the Blue Network. For $25,000, he bought the rights to the acronym ABC from the Associated Broadcasting Company, a smaller network based in Grand Rapids, Michigan, that subsequently referred to itself as ABS, the Associated Broadcasting System. The name American Broadcasting Company was reportedly purchased from the owners of WOL, Washington, DC for $10,000. [11-1] The moniker had also been used by George B. Storer, a radio pioneer and broadcasting legend active in wireless as early as 1928. Storer was the owner of major market stations, and during a long and storied career, he had signed-on his American Broadcasting Company network in 1934. Overnight, Noble had become a media magnate.

Johnny wrote Edward Noble a letter. The young host of Milwaukee's *Rumpus Room* show felt that the new owner of the Blue Network should certainly be made aware of the Midwest success of his program. There was no reply to Johnny's letter, a triviality that did not deter his determination.

In late 1943, Johnny made his first visit to New York. The morning after his arrival, he unpacked his best suit and promptly paid a visit to Edward Noble's palatial office in the RCA building in Rockefeller Center. He told Noble's two secretaries that he was John Olson, hoping that they might remember him as the broadcaster who wrote Mr. Noble from Milwaukee a year earlier.

As Johnny told it, "The girls looked at each other, and I realized suddenly that it might not be possible to walk in on a man who made $8 million deals. But one of the girls went inside and returned in less than a minute to say Mr. Noble would see me. His words were few, but were what I wanted to hear."

To the surprise of the two secretaries, Edward J. Noble was anxious to see the guy from WTMJ. It seemed that Johnny was mistaken for Jack Bundy, a.k.a. Heinie of Heinie's Grenadiers, the friend and former co-worker of Johnny's, who affected a German accent to host the WTMJ midday show, a show on which Johnny had often sung. Unbeknownst to Johnny, Bundy had apparently also sent a letter to Noble. In a case of mistaken identity, Johnny was hired to start immediately. Johnny reflected, "While I may have been given the job partly by mistake, I made good at it."

The meeting with Noble lasted no more than a moment before Johnny was dispatched with his first assignment. He was to return the next day to see George Hicks, a supervising announcer for the Blue Network. In their meeting, Hicks asked Johnny, "So you're Heine of Heine and the Grenadiers?" Johnny adeptly skirted the question, and luckily, Hicks moved on to explain that the host of a war plant show called *Swing Shift Follies* was going on vacation.

Johnny's initial New York job was to fill-in on that late night wartime morale-building program featuring amateur talent discovered among the ranks of second-shift workers. Johnny reported that he found radio-worthy talent in Connecticut among the war workers at Bridgeport Brass and The General Electric plant in Bridgeport, as well as on Long Island at the Sperry manufacturing plant.

Management must have been listening and favorably impressed because Johnny's second assignment came immediately. He was cast to host a weekly program that bowed on January 8 and had already been touted to the press without any mention of who would host. The *New York Times* reviewed the debut: "By design or happy coincidence, the first new program of 1944 was one which asks performers of some talent but little fame to step up to a microphone and try their respective specialties on the listening public, the show being known as *On Stage Everybody*, each Saturday at 11 a.m. on WJZ-Blue." [11-2]

Another simple talent contest, *On Stage Everybody* was not particularly note-worthy as a radio series and ran for only twenty-six weeks, but the program held the distinction of having inspired a major motion picture. In 1945, Universal Pictures released the movie named for the radio show that told the story of a veteran vaudevillian, Jack Oakie, and his daughter, played by Peggy Ryan, who were having difficulty facing the reality that the newfangled invention, radio, had eclipsed vaudeville. Ultimately, the old song and dance man embraced the future of entertainment by organizing a big radio variety extravaganza to showcase new talent.

With much of the movie set in a fictitious radio station, a couple of dozen performers paraded past the microphones. They ranged from the talented King Sisters and a young Julie London to a few acts that provided comic relief, including a dog impersonator and a skater. The *New York Times* stopped short of calling it a "B movie" by referring to *On Stage Everybody* as a "B plus musical."

Johnny did not appear in the film; his motion picture debut was still years away. The Olsons were fueled by encouragement from those early inroads, and they officially moved to New York. Arriving by train on a cold January day in 1944, the couple quickly settled into a $50 a month basement apartment in Forest Hills, Queens. It was a fiscally responsible commitment in a year when houses in that neighborhood were selling for $10,000, a loaf of bread cost 9¢, and the minimum wage was 30¢ an hour.

Johnny was proving himself a versatile performer and an able ad-libber. By March 8, 1944, he was given his own program, *The Johnny Olson Show*, which aired locally in New York on Wednesdays at 11:30 p.m., often sandwiched between Harpsichordist Sylvia Marlowe's fifteen-minute program at 11:15 p.m. and WJZ's midnight news. Starting on June 25, Johnny rotated with other staff announcers, occasionally lending his voice to the Blue Network's *Weekly War Journal*. On this Sunday half-hour news program, domestic and international reporters and commentators summarized the important events of the week from as many as a dozen outposts worldwide. Edward Tomlinson, Francis Drake, Frederick B. Opper, Clete Roberts, Major General Paul Malone, and the man who gave Johnny his first New York assignment, George Hicks, were among the regular contributors.

During the early morning hours of September 25, 1944, the original late night format of *Rumpus Room* was revived as a twenty-five-minute local offering on Monday nights following WJZ's midnight news. Johnny was also honored with his own daytime slot for *Johnny Olson's Pantry Party*. He described this, his first eponymous network outing, as "a fifteen-minute daytime music and humor show," a reincarnation of his venerable *Rumpus Room* program that he had adapted for the homemaker audience.

Johnny shared microphones with Milton Berle early in the comedian's career when he substituted for announcer Ken Roberts on a 1944 episode of *Let Yourself Go*. As Berle's popularity grew, *Let Yourself Go* moved from the Blue Network/ABC to CBS. Johnny was soon hosting other short-lived shows for his new employer, among them *Meet The Girls*. While his resume was quickly expanding in Radio City, none of the half-dozen shows Johnny hosted during his first months could be termed a commercial success. Several of his local programs continued into 1945, but Johnny's national series were all either short-lived or unsponsored programs. The infant ABC network was a weak competitor against NBC and CBS, and the Olsons saw the continuing cancellations as cause for concern. Milwaukee's favorite radio personality was a relative unknown in New York, just another one of hundreds of broadcasters seeking national notoriety.

In 1944, Johnny was developing his skills as a second banana, when he replaced announcer Clayton "Bud" Collyer in a pairing with a broadcaster of note on *The Mary Small Show*. Although Mary was only twenty-two years old at the time, she was a veteran behind the microphone. As a child, she had been featured as "Little Miss Bab-O," a precocious commercial icon and jingle singer for the household cleanser. Mary was soon making the rounds as a guest on numerous entertainment programs, including a stint as a featured singer alongside Dinah Shore, Jane Pickens, and Buddy Clark on *The Ben Bernie Show*, the orchestra leader's long-running popular music and variety series. During her teen years, the Baltimore native starred in her own programs, settling in with a Sunday evening berth on the Blue Network.

After Garry Moore (left) and Jimmy Durante ascended to stardom, Johnny became host of Garry's old morning show, the Blue Network's *Everything Goes*.

Johnny replaced Ted Malone as emcee of WJZ's *Yankee Doodle Quiz* in its second year, and was soon picked to replace Garry Moore, another up and coming broadcaster, who he would come to know well when their careers converged years later. By virtue of his boyish charm, quick wit, and versatility, Garry became one of the country's best-known and highest-paid radio and television hosts. Born Thomas Morfit, Garry began working in radio in 1935 as an announcer, actor-comedian-singer, and writer. With his crew cut and bowtie, the popular broadcaster went on to emcee his own very successful variety outing, *The Garry Moore Show* which quickly segued from radio to television. It then bounced from daytime to prime-time, ultimately enjoying a long, profitable run on CBS between 1950 and 1964.

Garry was responsible for bringing Carol Burnett, Don Knotts, Alan King, Jonathan Winters, and Lily Tomlin some of their earliest television exposure on his variety programs before adding to his on-air hours hosting panel shows. In that role, he shared the stage with Johnny on hundreds of episodes of Goodson-Todman's *To Tell The Truth* and *I've Got A Secret.* In 1944, twenty-nine-year-old Garry created the vacancy that gave Johnny his next break on network radio.

In a seemingly unlikely pairing, Garry was teamed with fifty-year-old veteran comedian and well-established star, Jimmy Durante. Nicknamed "The Shnazzola" for his prominent proboscis, Jimmy rose from a pianist in a Coney Island saloon, where he accompanied singing waiter Eddie Cantor through vaudeville to become one America's most enduring entertainers. Jimmy and Garry tickled America's funny bone for four years on *The Camel Comedy Caravan* with songs and skits that included a weekly feature showcasing Jimmy's signature comedic mangling of the English language. In one exchange, Garry described his previous occupation to Jimmy, and Jimmy repeated the story in his fragmented phrases.

Garry zipped effortlessly at top speed, "Jimmy, I used to work in Wauwatosa, Wisconsin at the Water Works as a reasonably reliable referee for the refrigerator repair wreckers, recluses, and renegade rum runners."[11-3] After a comedic pause and a long breath, Jimmy proceeded to plow through his version of the story, hitting only about every third word even vaguely correctly.

When the opportunity came to team with Jimmy, Garry left a weekday morning series called *Everything Goes,* and Johnny was ultimately tapped as the program's host. It was a high-profile opportunity, and Penny had the radio dialed in on 770 AM, listening excitedly from the couple's apartment in Queens to her husband's first Monday morning broadcast of the ABC network show over WJZ. Hopes were high that it would be Johnny's breakthrough opportunity, but only thirteen weeks later, *Everything Goes* was gone.

Johnny, in character in the 1940s, beginning to find national notoriety as NBC's Blue
Network became ABC Radio.

CHAPTER 12
A HIT WITH THE MISSES

Within twenty years of the formation of NBC in 1926, over 90% of American homes had radios. [12-1] The medium quickly evolved from a plaything of hobbyists and tinkerers to the source of the first truly national pop culture. With talent, discipline, humility, and his best business acumen, Johnny had worked through the ranks of local radio, moved to the epicenter of broadcasting, and was at the threshold of a career in network radio. While they exuded a quiet confidence at every turn, Johnny and Penny were in their thirties, living with limited savings in America's biggest city, and unsure of their future.

When the owner of a Milwaukee station offered Johnny a chance to return to the security of steady employment in a city where his success was assured, the Olsons seriously considered the opportunity. Determined to follow his dreams for a career as a national personality, Johnny remained in New York. He simply revived his *Rhythm Rascals* show for WMLO's 10 a.m. slot. Johnny and Penny rented studio facilities, producing and shipping five one-hour discs to Milwaukee each week, as they had years earlier from Los Angeles for WTMJ.

Perseverance paid off. The Olson's first truly big break in New York came quickly. In 1944, when former hosts Ed and Polly East departed their Blue Network/ABC daytime radio show *Ladies Be Seated*, Johnny and Penny inherited the popular audience participation program on June 27. Johnny adopted the variant spelling of his name, Olsen, and he worked in a glittering minstrel costume. He recalled that Penny not only served as his co-host, but was "masterful" as associate producer, preparing stunts and writing segments, helping him in pacing the show, and choosing interesting participants from the studio audience. Penny also worked to procure dozens of glamorous prizes on a budget that was limited to $6,000 per week.

At the height of its popularity, *Ladies Be Seated* was carried by 198 stations, airing weekday afternoons at 2:30 over the network's WJZ in New York. The competition was *Young Doctor Malone*, a CBS soap opera that aired locally on that network's flagship station, WABC (in 1946 WABC was renamed WCBS). *Women in White* was on NBC's WEAF (in 1946 WEAF was renamed WNBC); local news broadcasts aired on both WNEW and Mutual's WOR. Johnny and Penny's program often bested its competitiors. Jerry Collins of The Oldtime Radio Club reported, "*Ladies Be Seated* never recorded lofty ratings, its best being 4.9 (in 1947-48), the show sustained high interest among a segment of daytime fans who were drawn to lighthearted contests with a live audience."[12-2]

Ladies Be Seated ran for more than five years in several time periods, promoted as "audience participation at its best...where good sportsmanship and a sense of fun for the participants and spectators are the ingredients that pay off handsomely in attractive prizes."

Johnny found a successful niche hosting audience participation programs. *Ladies Be Seated* was a hit on ABC radio before it became one of television's earliest network programs.

Supporting players on *Ladies Be Seated* included "Million Dollar Penny," who joined Johnny for what the press releases referred to as the program's "hi-jinx." She authored the humorous "Penny Mystery" skits — sequences featuring detective clues that audience members puzzled over as they vied for prizes and tried to solve Penny's fun whodunits. The show's writer-director, Billy Redford, played "Professor Schnaaps," while Al Greiner was billed as Musical Director, accompanying the action and

Penny Olson (center) co-hosting the radio hi-jinx with Johnny (far right) in 1944. The beginning of the couple's five-year run on *Ladies Be Seated*.

providing transition music on the studio organ. The announcer was "good-looking and smooth talking" Bob Maurer, "the most eligible bachelor ever to leave Freeport, Illinois."

Ladies Be Seated segments also included "Johnny One-Note" games in which audience members won prizes by guessing the names of popular tunes on the basis of notes played. Audience members were also invited to try to stump Johnny and Penny, challenging the hosts to name songs the participants sang, hummed, or whistled. The "Kindly Heart" segment gave awards to people who had performed good deeds, and the "Johnny Crooner" spot featured Johnny selecting a young girl, usually under the age of six, to whom he sang a ballad. The interview that followed had a flavor similar to the conversations with youngsters heard on the *Art Linkletter's*

House Party program that debuted in January of the following year on CBS. Those chats with children became familiar over the decades in various incarnations of *Kids Say the Darndest Things*.

Johnny Crooners' youngsters publicly washed their family linen when they answered the host's questions such as "What does daddy do?" One girl responded with, "Daddy is a laundryman. It's good. We don't buy anything. He brings all our towels and clothes home free." Another answered, "he cuts piggies." It reportedly took Johnny ten fun-filled minutes to figure out that the girl's father was a podiatrist.

Press releases quoted Johnny recounting the stories of the four most loyal fans of *Ladies Be Seated*. They were two couples married as a result of meeting on his show. The first couple, an elderly pair, was waiting in a long line outside of Radio City in New York one wintry day to get in to see the broadcast. The gentleman invited the lady to have a cup of coffee, and four weeks later, they came up to Johnny and thanked him for making their marriage possible. The second couple consisted of a sailor and a young lady. While on leave, the young man was in the show's studio audience. The girl sitting next to him was munching on a box of chocolates and offered to share her sweets. The sailor said "her sweetness extended beyond the chocolates," and they were married on his next leave.

Audience members played games, sang, recited poetry, told stories, were tested with quizzes, and participated in stunts that included blindfolded challenges and spaghetti-eating competitions. For the audience participation segments, Johnny and Penny selected guests first by reviewing questionnaires that visitors filled out while in line to enter the studio. Once the audience was seated, the hosts wandered through the crowd chatting with the guests who had unique stories, interesting appearances, or unique voices. Johnny said that he was attentive to maintaining a balance among the participants in the audience participation segments — tall, short, stout, and slim — to create a sense of inclusion for all, which reflected his constant concern for never embarrassing his guests.

Ladies Be Seated was launched as an unsponsored, sustaining program. In 1945, the Quaker Oats Company picked up the tab for a two year period. Foote, Cone & Belding was the advertising agency producing the series during the period that Toni Home Permanents co-sponsored the program. Stefan Hatos, a junior producer in the agency's radio department, was assigned to work with Johnny and Penny, and introduced the "Toni Hot Seat Question" feature. It was the first audience participation program for a young producer who became legendary in the business. Johnny and Stefan were destined to meet again on the set of *Fun For The Money* in Chicago, and again decades later in Hollywood, when Hatos and his partner, Monty Hall, produced *Let's Make A Deal*.

During later years, *Ladies Be Seated* was sponsored by the Phillip Morris tobacco company. Johnny recalled that on one broadcast he purposely included the young daughter of a Phillip Morris advertising manager in his ad-lib interviews with audience members. The company was none too pleased when the girl unexpectedly said that her father smoked Lucky Strikes, a rival cigarette. The Phillip Morris folks took it in stride, later sending Johnny Roventini on the road with the show to provide a constant reminder of their brand.

Johnny Roventini had one of the most recognizable faces and voices in America in the mid-twentieth century as the living trademark and spokesman for Philip Morris cigarettes. He was only four feet tall as an adult and was always seen wearing a short-jacketed bellboy outfit. Roventini was the central figure in print and broadcast advertising for forty years as the bellboy who bellowed, "Call for Phil-lip Mor-rees."

Born in Brooklyn, Johnny Roventini was twenty-two years old and actually working as a bellman at the New Yorker Hotel when spotted by Milton Biow, president of the advertising agency handling what was then a lesser-known cigarette brand. Noticing the young man's similarity to the drawing of a bellboy that had previously been used in advertising for Philip Morris, Biow had an idea. He returned that evening with Alfred E. Lyons, an executive from the cigarette company.

Alfred E. Lyons ultimately became Executive Vice President, President, Chairman of the Board, and finally Honorary Chairman of the Philip Morris Company. From producing programs such as Mutual's *Name Three* in 1939, Milton Biow ascended to the highest ranks of Madison Avenue's pecking order. As an advertising executive, he created television programs for his clients, including *The Phillip Morris Musical Game* and a quiz for Eversharp pencils, *Take It Or Leave It*, the show known for posing "the $64 question."

Biow and Lyons sat in the lobby observing Roventini after giving him a dollar to locate a Mr. Phillip Morris. Roventini strode through the hotel shouting, "Call for Phillip Morris." Roventini recalled years later, "I went around the lobby yelling my head off, but Phillip Morris didn't answer my call." [12-3] Roventini was later quoted in *Variety* as saying, "I had no idea that Philip Morris was a cigarette." [12-4]

Starting in 1933, Johnny Roventini was featured on hundreds of radio and television shows wearing a bellboy's red-trimmed black cap, a black-trimmed, bright red tunic with gold buttons, red-striped black trousers, and white formal gloves. Paid $100 for his first radio commercial, Roventini's salary rose to an astronomical $50,000 a year during the depths of the depression. He was awarded a lifetime contract when Phillip Morris moved to the #4 position in national sales in five short years.

The trademarked cry, "Call for Phillip Morris," in B-flat that opened radio shows became so popular that the cigarette company insured Roventini's voice for $50,000. He closed those early radio shows saying, "This is Johnny again, returning now to the thousands of store windows and counters all over America. Look for me. I'll be waiting for you. Come in and call for Phil-lip Mor-rees."

In addition to being a spokesman in commercials, Roventini performed bit parts with many of the performers on the dozens of Phillip Morris sponsored programs in all manner of program introductions and promotional messages. Roventini shared radio microphones with an array of personalities from Johnny and Penny Olson to Milton Berle, and he shared the small screen with television stars including Lucille Ball and Desi Arnaz on *I Love Lucy*. Although only occasionally a program's host, in 1965 alone, Roventini was seen or heard on *The Red Skelton Show*, *The Jackie Gleason Show*, *Hazel*, *Hogan's Heroes*, *Thursday Night at the Movies*, *Slattery's People*, *Candid Camera*, *The Loner*, and even *The CBS Evening News with Walter Cronkite*.

The Phillip Morris Company, its advertising agency, and its publicist, George Weissman of the Benjamin Sonnenberg Company, as well as ABC radio's public-

Famed Hollywood gossip columnist Hedda Hopper stopped by the set of *Ladies Be Seated* to clown with Johnny.

ity agent John E. Gibbs and Company, all actively supported the Olsons' *Ladies Be Seated* with an extensive press kit designed for local media for when the show took to the road.

Such was the case when the program traveled to Chicago in mid-March 1946 for a simulcast from pioneering television outlet WBKB. That broadcast of *Ladies Be Seated* occurred hours before the station signed-off. *Billboard* reported that WBKB took a two-week hiatus and then changed frequencies. Johnny's seventy-five-minute "side-splitting" special was reviewed as "…plenty good video because it's based on visual humor supplemented by his comical line of chatter." [12-5] The magazine pointed out that Johnny performed magnificently despite the fact that the tight travel sched-ule did not allow time for him to do even a rudimentary walk-through rehearsal.

The network bought trade advertising to boast of the success of the remote broadcast: "The demand for tickets was so great the show moved from the studios to the Civic Theater. 33,000 letters in four weeks requesting more than 100,000 tickets to see Olsen put the ladies through their paces. Lines formed at the doors in the early morning…proving the Olsen motto, 'You can't beat fun.'"

Ladies Be Seated returned to Chicago to broadcast from the ABC network studios at WLS in mid-April 1947. More adventurous outings were arranged by promoters, who booked the show for live broadcasts from fairs and expositions. *Ladies Be Seated* traveled to all manner of events, from the Tobacco Bowl in Richmond, Virginia, to The New Jersey State Fair, and to the Fargo, North Dakota Diamond Jubilee Celebration.

Of those travels, Johnny spoke of an appearance in Orlando, Florida, saying, "We had 500 or 600 women in a tent, and as usual, a number of eight-month pregnant women were present. One was more so." Apparently the heat of the tent, the excitement of the show, and the thrill of winning a prize proved too much for the expectant mother. "She went into her pains, and we had to ask for a doctor on the air. One appeared promptly and found things so imminent that he got busy right there. Before the hour was over, the lady delivered a healthy, howling baby right in the middle of the audience while we were on the air. In fairness to me, as she explained, she named the boy Johnny."

CHAPTER 13
THIS IS ONLY A TEST

Ladies Be Seated proved to be an important addition to Johnny's resume. It was his first national hit program, and it remains his most enduring radio credit. After a five-year run, Johnny's substitute host, Tom Moore, borrowed upon the *Ladies Be Seated* format for his *Ladies Fair* show on the Mutual network that debuted the following year. Johnny stayed on in the same afternoon time period on ABC radio for the same sponsor, Phillip Morris, fronting *Johnny Olsen's Luncheon Club*. Having built a loyal radio following, Johnny was honing his ad-lib skills and further developing his energetic, fun, and friendly style during the birth of a new entertainment medium. *Ladies Be Seated* was a prime example of the value of being at the right place at the right time.

In its infancy, television was hungry for inexpensive programming. The economics of the new medium could not support star salaries, and Johnny was a perfect fit and an obvious choice for a notable television test. With his new success on network radio with *Ladies Be Seated*, he became a nationally-known personality with proven ability. He was also full of youthful ambition and passion. In network jargon, that meant he worked cheap.

On a Sunday morning in 1944, the entire cast of *Ladies Be Seated* headed to Schenectady, New York, the home of one of the few television stations in existence in the United States at the time. Johnny quoted Dr. Charles Alexander Richmond, a former President of the city's Union College, who classified the natives. "Schenectady," he said, "has three kinds of people: those who are connected with Union College, those who work for General Electric, and those who still live in terror of an attack by the Mohawk Indians." Johnny's business in Schenectady was with the people at General Electric's experimental W2XB.

In the government's earliest protocol for assigning identifiers to television stations, the "W" indicated North America, the "2" denoted the region of the country, the "X" specified an experimental and non-commercial status, and the simple "B" was all that was needed in a call sign for a station that began broadcasting so early in the medium's development. Three years before Johnny's visit, W2XB had moved to a new state-of-the-art facility, and in 1942, W2XB was re-christened WRGB. The new call letters were not derived from the red, green, and blue primary colors of television broadcasting, as some people have conjectured. As early as 1929, AT&T had written about a colorful future for television, but it was some time before GE would work in earnest on color television.

Johnny reported that WRGB had previously been the call letters of the Wellsville, Ohio police department. The Wellsville Police Chief had relinquished them to
Schenectady so that GE could honor Dr. Walter R. G. Baker, the first head of the
company's electronics division and the scientist who took a lead role in helping the
FCC set the technical standards for American television broadcasting. Although
Baker was then very much alive, the Police Chief told the press he was yielding his
call letters so that GE could honor a "deceased" scientist. Johnny said that Baker read
with amusement the newspaper clippings of the account.

Legend has it that GE's management had originally shown reluctance to authorize
experimentation with radio, only doing so when an enthusiast suggested that it might
save telephone charges in communications between the factories in Schenectady and
Pittsfield, Massachusetts. No matter the motivation, GE pioneered with many firsts
in both radio and television, many at the hand of Dr. Charles Steinmetz, who Johnny
and others referred to simply as "General Electric's famous hunchback scientist," and
his protégé, the stocky mustachioed Ernst Frederick Werner Alexanderson.

Alexanderson was the scientist who, years previously, developed the Alexanderson
alternator that Marconi wanted for his early development of transatlantic wireless
communication. The engineer was less enthusiastic about GE's work with television
than he was about wireless telegraphy, reportedly saying, "What I wonder is if the
public really wants television."

GE's experimental television station in Schenectady signed on as early as 1926
with occasional test broadcasts using the original mechanical system for broadcasting
visual images. Two years later, the FRC granted the facility its experimental license
as W2XB. Johnny noted that on September 11, 1928, GE was first to televise *The
Queen's Messenger,* a play by J. Hartley Manners, and on April 1, 1930, Dr. Peter Wold,
President of Schenectady's Fortnightly Club, became the first speaker to address an
organization via television. From a GE laboratory, he addressed a meeting of the club
in Dr. Alexanderson's home. The system used was a crude one involving whirling disks.
Johnny described the images as shadows and silhouettes rather than pictures.

GE and everybody else soon abandoned mechanical television in favor of an all-
electronic system, trading the spinning disks for vacuum tubes. In the late 1930s, the
company built its new electronic television broadcasting station, as well as a small, squat
white building and tower high in the Helderberg Mountains, west of Albany, New
York. GE used that receiving station to pick up signals from NBC in New York City,
relay them to the new WRGB transmitter in Schenectady, and from there, throughout
the capital district. Johnny said, "They had one of only six television broadcasting stations in the country." He characterized the owners of the other stations in New York,
Philadelphia, Chicago, and Los Angeles as guarding them like Ft. Knox because they
were either unable or unwilling to open their doors to outsiders and possible future
competitors. Johnny reported, "The attitude of the GE men was refreshingly different.
They were happy to share both their facilities and broadcasting experience."

Accompanying Johnny and Penny on that visit were Henry Cox, the producer of
Ladies Be Seated, and George Weist, the radio show's director, who came to broadcasting from a career in vaudeville. Tom Reddy, the program's announcer, was joined by

guest Jay Jostyn, who played the title role on *Mr. District Attorney.* The actress who portrayed Madame Queen on the popular *Amos 'n' Andy* program was another of the guests. Johnny wrote, "With us was Amanda Randolph, the great Negro actress. She was a very fine woman, and her commercial for the Quaker Oats Company's Aunt Jemima Pancake Mix was perhaps the first delivered by a Negro actress on television."

Since the broadcast was expected to garner press coverage, the newly crowned WJZ Radio's Miss New York City, a young, hazel-eyed Bess Myerson, was included in the entourage to add to the visual appeal of the event. Myerson was born in New York City's borough of The Bronx, on July 15, 1924, to Russian immigrants living in a subsidized housing development. She had intelligence, beauty, talent, and ambition that brought her from those humble roots to fame in both politics and show business. While studying piano and flute at the High School of Music and Art, Bess found opportunities to shine. She entered pageants and picked up part-time work as a model. She entered the New York transit system's Miss Subways contest before being crowned Miss New York City by WJZ. The station had narrowed 1,200 applicants to a field of 350 contestants aspiring to the throne. The selection was at the whim of two judges: orchestra leader Paul Whiteman and Danton Walker, a *New York Daily News* Broadway columnist.

The newly-crowned Bess Myerson, age 20, made her television debut on a test broadcast of Johnny's hit, *Ladies Be Seated.* Years later they would share the stage on several network game shows.

Bess Myerson's personal diary for the week of August 18th, 1944 even included this entry: "Morning train… with Johnny Olsen, the announcer. Olsen wants me on his radio show! Must get outfitted."[13-1] The year after her appearance with Johnny and Penny, Bess entered another beauty pageant. She showed off her charms in a bathing suit, played Greig's "Concerto in A Minor," and made the astounding leap from Miss New York City to Miss America of 1945. Despite several of the judges reporting that they had received threatening phone calls warning them not to choose "the Jew,"[13-2] Bess became the first Jewish woman up to that time to win the Miss America honors.

Bess was not looking for a launch to stardom; she said that she simply entered the pageant as a lark when she learned it offered a $5,000 top prize. She wanted to buy a new piano and was thinking about getting a master's degree in music. "I didn't do what other Miss Americas did," she said. "I didn't pose with Ford cars or in Catalina bathing suits. Those companies didn't want a Jew representing them." [13-2]

Bess was an attractive 5-foot, 10-inch, and 136-pound woman with a Bachelor of Arts degree from Hunter College, and she was in demand in early television. She sold Ajax soap powder, contributed to *The Today Show*, acted on *The Philco Television Playhouse*, and performed in comedy skits on *The Colgate Comedy Hour*. Bess handled every assignment with grace and intelligence. Over the years, she advanced from modeling furs on *The Big Payoff* game show to co-hosting *Candid Camera* with Alan Funt. Bess and Johnny were paired again when her game-playing skills and telegenic manner earned her dozens of appearances on Goodson-Todman game shows, including *To Tell the Truth*, *I've Got A Secret*, *The Name's the Same*, and *Beat the Clock*.

Bess Myerson was a lifelong Democrat. In 1969, New York Mayor John Lindsay, a Republican, asked her to head the city's Department of Consumer Affairs. Bess was lauded for her work as a consumer advocate, lobbying for New York City's Consumer Protection Act that made false advertising a prosecutable offense. Despite objections by the food industry, she introduced unit pricing and freshness dating, which became standard across the country. In fighting for consumers she said, "The accomplice to the crime of corruption is frequently our own indifference." [13-3] Bess continued her political presence in various capacities, including a stint as New York's Cultural Affairs Commissioner and a 1980 run for the US Senate.

In her later years, Bess fell from grace with an awkward, headline-making scandal surrounding her lover's divorce case. In an attempt to arrange favorable treatment from the judge handling the case, Bess allegedly hired the judge's daughter. She was charged with bribery and conspiracy, but after a fifteen-week trial, she was acquitted. In her personal journey, Bess Myerson survived ovarian cancer and a stroke. In her later life, she became a private person.

Johnny recalled the WRGB experimental broadcast with Bess. He said, "In 1944, I rode into the dawning world of television on a train. It was New York Central's old Empire State Express, once the world's fastest…[it] transported us swiftly along the lordly Hudson River to Albany and then a few miles west to Schenectady…At Schenectady, we walked under a cloudy sky from the New York Central station along State Street to the Van Curler Hotel, and then just across the street to the WRGB building." Johnny explained that the station overlooked the Mohawk River, and before it was reconstructed into a television facility, it had been a clubhouse containing a dance floor, a bowling alley, and similar recreational facilities.

Johnny reported that he was welcomed by G. Emerson Markham, a veteran of GE broadcasting, who toured the *Ladies Be Seated* entourage through the building. He had the staff help unpack their props and set their Quaker Oats and Chef Boy-Ar-Dee commercial art cards on easels. Johnny remembered being excited about the opportunity that was just hours away, and he was wide-eyed about the budding technology. He recalled being particularly interested in the large array of overhead and floor-level lighting equipment. He was also impressed by the futuristic-appearing control room where engineers had the choice of images from three live cameras and three film projectors.

Johnny had seen very little television and knew nothing about how the visual images were captured. Most experimental broadcasts and the first public television demonstration five years earlier had taken place in New York. Since Johnny and Penny had been in Milwaukee, they had only caught mere glimpses of television programs on the few receivers around New York.

New York was where NBC's Sarnoff, CBS' Paley, and Dr. Allan B. Du Mont, the innovative, pioneering underdog, had all been focused on developing television in anticipation of building powerful networks. DuMont Laboratories and RCA, NBC's parent corporation, focused on selling television sets to the public. Du Mont, a scientist new to the business of broadcasting, was embarking on a path that would lead to his becoming television's first self-made millionaire. Following work for Westinghouse, Dr. Du Mont's company was an early force in perfecting television receivers and contributing more durable picture tubes to the developing television science.

Musicians Fred Waring and Dick Haymes, ventriloquist Paul Winchell with his wooden pal Jerry Mahoney, and humorist Henry Morgan made early appearances on DuMont television. At the invitation of his brother, Lou Sposa, who was a DuMont engineer, Dennis James, an early television personality and jack-of-all-trades, enjoyed a ubiquitous presence announcing wrestling and serving as emcee for all manner of programs.

Starting in 1947, Johnny was a frequently seen face and a vital contributor to the fledgling network's programming, hosting sports, talent programs, game shows, and kids' shows until DuMont's demise in 1956. Dennis and Johnny were co-workers at Dr. Du Mont's facility, but neither had any inkling that they would share a stage in Hollywood thirty years later and preside together over a television program watched by millions of viewers from coast-to-coast simultaneously. In the 1940s, that technology was not yet possible.

Despite their generous funding of research and development, the networks' Manhattan facilities were limited in comparison to GE's WRGB in Schenectady, the first television studio Johnny ever saw. CBS had New York City's largest and most flexible laboratory above Grand Central Terminal, with a primary studio measuring 56-feet by 87-feet, and an available ceiling height of 34-feet. Although spacious, the loft lacked adequate air conditioning to counter the extreme heat generated by the high-intensity lighting that was needed to register a picture using the early cameras.

At NBC's magnificent headquarters in the gleaming Art Deco RCA building in Rockefeller Center, David Sarnoff converted radio Studio 3H to serve as the company's primary television workshop. While that modest 30-foot-by-50-foot room benefited from air conditioning, its 18-foot ceiling height had the lights so close to the performers that the heat was oppressive and the size of the sets was limited. Studio 3H was not made more television-friendly until 1955 when the skyscraper's structural beams on the third floor were moved and the space was remodeled to a 68-foot-by-61-foot room and re-christened Studio 3K.

DuMont's facilities on the forty-second floor of a Madison Avenue office building magnified the weaknesses found at NBC with a 15-foot-by-20-foot working space and a ceiling height of only 13-feet. A second DuMont studio was added that was larger but still limited by the building's 13-foot ceilings.

Johnny's first experience with television was in a superior environment at GE's upstate outpost, a facility that the company boasted was the first building in the United States specifically designed and constructed for television. Chicago television pioneer Captain Bill Eddy toured the facility several months after Johnny's inaugural broadcast and wrote that the studio was an immense 42 by 70 feet, topped by a 25-foot-high ceiling. That height enabled lighting to be placed far enough from the performers to keep the heat manageable. Combined with a water cooling system for the motor-controlled lights and the building's oversized air conditioning capacity, WRGB was comparatively comfortable among early television studios.

Johnny recalled that he did what little rehearsing he could without the audience participants, before the *Ladies Be Seated* cast and crew returned to the hotel for a couple of hours of rest and dinner. George Brengel, an executive whom Johnny and Penny knew from WJZ, introduced the couple to Mark Woods, the President of the Blue Network/ABC. The two had taken a later train and were ready to do what all broadcasting executives did to commemorate an event — drink. Johnny remembered, "Brengel…insisted on buying everybody a 'Brengel Buster,' a concoction of champagne and Canadian Club named for him. Despite this distraction we went on the air on time." Johnny's very first television appearance started with an introduction from announcer Tom Reddy. He then hopped out of a heart-shaped cardboard entrance wearing a glittering minstrel costume, and the cast sang the show's usual opening:

> *"Ladies be seated, the party has only begun.*
> *Ladies be seated, so let's all join in the fun.*
> *Ladies be seated, a laugh doesn't cost you a dime.*
> *Ladies be seated, and let's have a wonderful time!"*

Johnny reflected that the audience was lively and responsive. It was wartime, and many men and women were in uniform. Penny was decked-out in a striped dress with puffed-out sleeves. The audience members she selected enthusiastically competed in the planned stunts for prizes that included nylons, which were scarce at the time. He recalled that Bess Myerson and the participants in a beauty contest they staged were presented very sedately in full-length dresses. Besides delivering her Aunt Jemima commercial, Amanda Randolph sang a spiritual that drew tremendous applause.

Johnny reported, "There was only one incident. Lights became so hot they melted mascara on women's faces in early television. GE tried to lick the problem with a type cooled by water." In the course of the broadcast, one of those light assemblies exploded and sprinkled part of the studio audience with warm water. "'My God, my time has come,' shouted a pregnant woman caught in the downpour. When she found it hadn't, she laughed. Penny and some others wiped up the water. We finished the program with everybody convinced that television had great possibilities."

There was no time for Johnny and Penny to join the executives for another round of Brengel Busters. Because of Johnny's busy on-air schedule, the Olsons headed back to New York City to be ready for Monday's broadcasts. Johnny remembered the overnight train was so crowded with war travelers that one woman shared a double bedroom with three men, which annoyed and concerned the conductor, but not her. Johnny reported that for the only time in their lives, he and Penny slept together in an upper berth.

The view from GE's WRGB control room, overlooking one of early television's most sophisticated studios. A 1944 television test of *Ladies Be Seated* at the station was Johnny Olson's first experience with the new medium.

The debut of A. C. Nielsen ratings was eleven years in the future, so the infant medium used a crude ratings methodology for the *Ladies Be Seated* experimental television broadcast. A few days after the test, the GE staff sent a letter to the Olsons with an estimate of WRGB's audience. There was then only one station and only 300 television sets in the entire Albany-Schenectady-Troy area, but on that Sunday evening, 297 of them had been turned on. With 99 percent of the possible audience watching, John

Penny and Johnny adapted radio's *Ladies Be Seated* for early television simulcasts that debuted on February 25, 1945.

laughed that it must have been as high a rating as any program had ever earned.

In reflecting on his television test, Johnny said he felt apprehension about how the new medium, if it was to take hold, might impact his radio career. There was no shortage of conjecture in the trade press about the future of television, nor in the mainstream media of the day. Dr. Frank Stanton, the newly appointed Vice President of CBS, was broadcasting's most thoughtful and educated authority. With a PhD in psychology, Stanton's dissertation, "A Critique of Present Methods and a New Plan for Studying Radio Listening Behavior," had established his credibility and cemented his role as the era's most quoted media expert.

In his attempt to understand the future of his industry, Johnny researched Stanton's early writings. One article indicated that advertising directed to the ear was more effective than that directed to the eye. Johnny was skeptical because Stanton's essay promoted radio over print as an advertising medium; there was no mention of television. Johnny found the article further suspect as Stanton's employer, CBS, was in the business of radio, and not affiliated with any television receiver manufacturer, nor was the company as fulsome as RCA in advocating for the future of television.

RCA's David Sarnoff was more confident and proved more prophetic when he predicted at NBC's inauguration of television service in 1939, "The combined emotional results of both seeing and hearing an event or a performance at the instant of

Johnny toured the country in full minstrel regalia, taking time to share a smile at a charity appearance to benefit the fight against polio.

its occurrence become new forces to be reckoned with, and they will be much greater forces than those aroused by audition only." [13-4]

From personal experience, Johnny knew well that the success of any medium funded solely from advertising would ultimately be determined by its effectiveness in selling product. In assessing the future potential of television, he found logic in an often-quoted study of education that Thomas Edison had cited in a 1923 advertisement designed to help sell film projectors to school systems. That analysis concluded that learning was generally accepted to be a multi-sensory process. In his writings, Johnny repeated Edison's and the study's claim that "with all senses intact and functioning, knowledge is derived 83 percent from the eyes, 11 percent via the ears, 3½ percent through smell, 1½ percent from touch, and 1 percent from taste." The thesis concluded that when the sources of input are combined, the impression is naturally reinforced. It made sense to Johnny; he observed that when sight and sound were combined in motion pictures that the "talkies" had become more popular than silent films.

In 1949, the United States Department of Commerce confirmed what Johnny had already surmised when it reported, "Television's combination of moving pictures, sound, and immediacy produces an impact that extends television as an advertising medium into the realm of personal sales solicitation."

CHAPTER 14
THE TALK OF NEW YORK

Johnny came to believe that his greatest chance for success would ultimately lie in television, and that conclusion guided his future choice of opportunities. He and Penny looked to parlay their experience at WRGB into new ventures. Their first chance came within months; ABC offered to simultaneously broadcast *Ladies Be Seated* on radio and on television.

Only one script survives from *Ladies Be Seated*. It is from the debut radio and television simulcast of the program, which originated in New York City on the afternoon of February 25, 1945. No definitive record exists of which television stations carried the program because the American Broadcasting Company did not apply for television station licenses until 1947, and the company did not inaugurate its own television network until the following year.

In 1945, ABC originated television programs by purchasing time on other networks' affiliates and independent stations to clear programs on behalf of its sponsors. Author Michael Ritchie reported that the DuMont network aired nine-and-one-half hours of ABC-owned programming each week, charging ABC $625 per half-hour for the facilities, personnel, and airtime.

The *Ladies Be Seated* script is presented as an appendix in this book, and it is invaluable as a reference in gaining insight into the content of the most successful program Johnny hosted, as well as understanding the nature of the pre-production planning for a live daily broadcast in commercial television's earliest days. It can be considered a blueprint for the three-camera presentation of audience participation interviews and stunts.

Johnny's flair for showmanship was well-suited for the tube. Despite pitifully low pay, he jumped at the opportunity to appear as master of ceremonies on *Christmas Party*. It was television pioneer Dr. Allen B. Du Mont's holiday special, broadcast at 8 p.m. on Tuesday, December 24, 1946. Johnny's first appearance on DuMont's New York television outlet went so well that it laid a firm foundation for him to enjoy more camera time on WABD in years to come. Before he amassed a lengthy list of television credits, Johnny became one of New York's busiest radio performers. He ended the 1940s working at a hectic pace that continued for most of the next thirty-five years. In 1951, Johnny told his hometown newspaper, the *Cottonwood County Citizen*, that in 1948 and 1949 he was presiding over twenty half-hour radio programs from New York each week, as well as hosting a television program.

The *New York Times'* "Programs on the Air" local listings from a typical weekday of that period, Wednesday, June 8, 1949, bore out much of that claim. At 11 a.m., DuMont's WABD television aired the half-hour *Johnny Olsen's Rumpus Room*. Within an hour of that show's closing, Johnny was ready for his midday radio program, as WMGM carried *Johnny Olsen's Luncheon Club* at 12:30 p.m. from the ABC radio network, a highly rated staple that rose from the ashes of *Ladies Be Seated* in January, and had just been renewed following its initial six-month run. Then, at 4:30 p.m., Johnny was heard on WOR with *Johnny Olson's Prince Charming*.

The other radio programs of 1948 and 1949 of which Johnny spoke included four local outings that all debuted in 1948. One was a short-lived Monday through Friday quiz show that aired during the dinner hour. *Second Honeymoon* was a 3:30 p.m. interview show from WOR, targeted to women and promoted as "The program that brings back romance." *Get Rich Quick* was a question and answer cash competition that debuted at 9:30 p.m. over WJZ on Monday, July 19, 1948, only to be cancelled thirteen weeks later. Johnny also appeared as the quizmaster and queried contestants on *Whiz Quiz*. That program bounced around WJZ's schedule for nine months during 1948. The tally also included weekend broadcasts, such as his national Saturday morning *Johnny Olson's Get Together* on ABC.

Indeed, the busy entertainer's last name was being spelled differently for different series, apparently even on the same network. In addition, spellings in the program listings of various newspapers and magazines for the same show were often contradictory. When asked years later, Johnny shrugged off the inconsistency saying, "The checks all cleared!"

Geography played a role in Johnny's ubiquitous presence up and down television and radio dials. Although NBC utilized old Warner Bros. film studio space near Avenue M and 14th Street in Brooklyn for some of its programs, almost all of New York's broadcasting facilities were concentrated within one square mile of midtown, in and adjacent to what is known as the "theater district." Their proximity to production made Hurley's Bar and a drug store luncheonette, both on the ground floor of the Sixth Avenue side of the RCA building, the unofficial headquarters for the respective communities of technicians and talent. For a period during the 1950s, there was a telephone at the end of the bar at Hurley's that connected directly to the NBC operator.

The ability to finish a program for one network and arrive at another network's studio in time for a quick rehearsal and live broadcast was important to all of the city's performers. On fair weather days, most dodged the throngs on the sidewalks, while others fought the city traffic in cabs. Ray Collins would become best known for his role as the aging, stocky police lieutenant who arrested Perry Mason's clients each week on television, but in radio's heyday, he was one of the actors most in demand, sprinting between studios in the same building, or occasionally, even a block or two away during the closing credits of one show and the opening of another.

To make it all work, Collins employed a stand-in for rehearsals, who marked the actor's scripts with the directors' notes and handed it to the actor as the show began. Collins performed many roles cold, on-the-fly, having never seen the script before airtime. Orson Welles told of times when his schedule was so tight that he hired an ambulance to rush him between radio studios with lights and sirens clearing the way.

There was similar insanity in Hollywood. Beloved character actor Frank Nelson remembered, "I had a show at NBC, which was really one long block from CBS, and I had it at the last studio in the hall, that is, the closest studio to the CBS studio. I would conclude that CBS show, sign off that show, and then run out the side door, and have a page there — he'd have the door open — tear across the Palladium Ballroom parking lot, and slide through NBC Studio A...I'd slide to the middle of the stage and take one deep breath and say, 'Ladies and gentlemen, from Hollywood....' and open the next show...I was a lot younger then!" [14-1]

Between 1929 and 1964, CBS radio's New York facility was headquartered at 484 Madison Avenue at West 52nd Street, four blocks north and east of NBC's Radio City. CBS' television studios were located eight blocks south, above Grand Central Terminal's main waiting room, in a vast area that had previously been outfitted with tennis courts. In 1953, CBS added to its television facilities with the purchase of a Sheffield Farms dairy depot on West 57th Street which it later dubbed CBS Broadcast Center.

ABC still originates programming from a television studio on West 66th Street. For fifty years the space had served as a stable. Before automobiles choked New York City streets, and before the city's extensive subway system was built, horses provided transportation. In 1901, Durland's Riding Academy was home to over 600 horses. In the 1930s, the 100 ft by 200 ft facility operated as the private, elite New York Riding Club, which the magazine *Country Life* reported was home to several polo teams. The cavernous riding ring was even equipped for night polo. At David Sarnoff's urging, ABC vacated its previous Blue Network digs so abruptly in November, 1948 that technicians reported the former stables still had birds occasionally flying into camera range on early ABC television broadcasts.

The Mutual network's primary studios were at 1440 Broadway in Times Square, less than a half mile south of NBC's Radio City.

When Johnny first worked for the DuMont television network, the cramped studio at 515 Madison Avenue, two short blocks north of CBS radio, was little more than a couple of adjacent business offices with a wall removed. Maintaining tolerable temperatures was a problem at most of the early television facilities. When David Sarnoff participated in broadcasts from his NBC Studio 3H, he arrived with several identical dress shirts, periodically changing into fresh ones as perspiration deteriorated his appearance.

With the even lower ceilings at DuMont, heat generated from the intense lighting was unbearable for some performers. Men sweat through sport jackets and emitted tiny trails of steam. Harry Coyle, a DuMont studio assistant, remembered an on-camera appearance by a songstress from the Metropolitan Opera. Her costume was largely metallic and the metal conducted the intense heat. By the end of the fifteen minute show, her skin was blistered.

On April 15, 1946, relief came. DuMont moved most of its production to the same building where David Sarnoff had monitored distress calls from the *Titanic* three decades earlier. Larry White, the director of many of that network's early programs, recalled, "Our studios were in the Wanamaker Department store. In the old days, they had an auditorium where they would give piano concerts and turned it into a TV studio for us." [14-2]

The room was huge, with a small, high balcony from which guests and the occasional curious shopper could look down and see the sets for the various shows. There, at 770 Broadway, Johnny worked in relative comfort because the three studios were air conditioned, and there were even crude dressing rooms.

While the idea of a television studio located in a department store may have seemed strange, on many occasions it proved fortuitous; producers were able to quickly provide replacement wardrobe and last minute props. Most of the futuristic, science-fiction hardware used on *Captain Video and His Video Rangers* was fashioned from parts purchased at the store's automotive department.

As more people bought television sets, programming became more elaborate. DuMont expanded again and leased two theaters. The Ambassador on West 49th Street, west of Broadway, accommodated an audience of over 1,000 and had previously been utilized by NBC. The Adelphi at West 54th Street and Sixth Avenue had seating for 1,400, and was well-suited to *The Cavalcade of Stars*, the network's most extravagant presentation at the time. Later, Jackie Gleason, DuMont's biggest and brightest-shining star, returned to the theater even while under contract with CBS, when the DuMont Electronicam system was utilized to film the thirty-nine episodes of *The Honeymooners* that have entertained viewers for more than fifty years.

DuMont's use of the Ambassador and Adelphi Theaters was not unusual. In addition to their permanent studio facilities, NBC, ABC, Mutual, and especially CBS converted more than a dozen Broadway theaters for broadcasting. Radio's free entertainment had precipitated a sharp decline in box office business, and some traditionalists felt the networks added insult to that injury when they occupied those theaters.

After becoming a regular face on DuMont television, Johnny took to the stage of the Ambassador Theater on Saturday mornings for his *Kids and Company* program. Early in his network radio career, Johnny's *Rumpus Room* broadcasts originated from the Blue Network/ABC's Vanderbilt Theater at 148 West 48th Street, two blocks from the net's Radio City headquarters.

Studio historian and television production staffer Brian Conn traced the metamorphosis of one of the better-known of the Broadway houses where Johnny regularly worked. Oscar Hammerstein II opened the 1,200 seat neo-gothic Hammerstein Theater in 1927 to honor his father, the well-respected impresario and composer. In 1936, CBS leased the property, constructed a control room downstage right, and christened the theater CBS Radio Playhouse #3. In the conversion for television in 1950, seating in the stage left orchestra area was removed to accommodate the audio and video control rooms. Eventually, as CBS Studio 50 and The Ed Sullivan Theater, the old Hammerstein's stage, lighting, and sound facilities were expanded, and seating was reduced to accommodate no more than 400 audience members.

Ladies' Man, Johnny Olsen, a custom vehicle created for Johnny and piloted on WOR, became a network outing that utilized another one of those old so-called legitimate houses. Debuting on April Fools Day 1949, *Johnny Olson's Prince Charming* was another of the many audience participation and interview shows that became Johnny's specialty. For this 30-minute program women in the theater told Johnny why the men in their lives were "Prince Charmings." The local show was broadcast Monday through Friday at 4:30 p.m. from the 1,300-seat Mutual Guild Theater on West 52nd Street, west of Broadway (now known as the Virginia Theater). It was the former home of the Theatre Guild, a popular repertory company that included such distinguished members as Edward G. Robinson, Alfred Lunt, and Lynn Fontanne. The theatre opened in 1925 with George Bernard Shaw's *Caesar and Cleopatra*, before being leased to the Mutual radio network in 1943.

Johnny became a prodigious and popular radio personality. Starting in 1945 with *Break The Bank*, continuing with *Johnny Olson's Prince Charming*, and then hosting *The Mutual Movie Matinee, Movie Quiz, The Johnny Olsen Show*, and *National Wives Week* specials in the 1950s, he made merry behind the microphones of another national network, one now forgotten by all but broadcasters and historians.

With play-by-play coverage of the world's first nighttime baseball game, the Mutual Broadcasting System premiered on May 24, 1935. Eight months after being formed as the Quality Network, Mutual enjoyed a distinction that set it apart from CBS and NBC's Red and Blue chains. As the name implied, Mutual was a cooperative venture among independently owned radio stations, each contributing their own original programming, transmission, and promotion expenses, while sharing advertising revenues.

Time magazine reported that Mutual was born to serve the Gordon Baking Company's desire to advertise in only a few specific cities without the extensive reach of the well-established, large national networks. Anchored by WOR New York, WGN Chicago, WLW Cincinnati, and WXYZ Detroit, Mutual generated a little more than $1 million dollars in advertising income in its first year. Within three years, the cooperative boasted over a hundred affiliates and served as the launching pad for some of early radio's most popular shows.

In 1941, *Time* described Mutual's modus operandi as practical and profitable, explaining how its 173 affiliates "exchange programs and underwrite the network's wire costs…In the first eight months of 1940, its cumulative billings were $2,494,370; for the same period this year $4,024,680 (as compared with NBC's $30,960,519, CBS's $25,776,094)."[14-3]

The cooperative's WXYZ contributed *The Lone Ranger* and *The Green Hornet*, while WGN originated the *Lum and Abner* comedy series. WOR shared *The Adventures of Superman*, Orson Welles' performances as *The Shadow*, and commentary from Gabriel Heatter, a reporter who rose to prominence covering the "trial of the century," the 1935 prosecution of Bruno Hauptman, kidnapper of American aviation hero Charles Lindberg's baby. Johnny Olson was a perfect fit for Mutual, despite its roster of news and dramatic programming. For a time, Mutual was also home to kindred spirits Steve Allen and Henry Morgan, as well as a number of popular game shows.

On November 20, 1944, the door to the Mutual studios was opened for Johnny when the Blue Network's vice-president Ed Kobak became Mutual's new president. Blue's Phillips Carlin and Robert Swezey quickly joined Kobak at Mutual, and added audience participation shows to the program line-up, including *Juvenile Jury*, *Queen For a Day*, *It Pays to be Ignorant*, and *Twenty Questions*. Johnny was not bound by any exclusivity agreement at NBC Blue. He readily accepted an offer to fol-

lowing his former bosses, and to add to his on-air credits. Johnny's first time behind a Mutual microphone was as a fill-in on *Twenty Questions*, and he remained associated with Mutual's WOR until 1957.

In 1945, on Saturday nights, Johnny appeared on *Break the Bank*, bounding onstage to the strains of the theme song "We're In The Money." The top-rated series was initially a prime-time weekly game show, a tremendously popular series that moved from Mutual to ABC and to NBC, and then continued to bounce among those networks, enjoying a decade on radio. In 1948, *Break the Bank* transitioned to television for a nine-year run. Johnny was among several masters of ceremonies in the early seasons of *Break The Bank* during which listeners played by telephone from home and won prizes, including trips to New York to appear on the program.

The delightful Arlene Francis and Johnny first shared a microphone in 1949 on *What's My Name?* They regularly worked together during the next twenty-three years, as Ms. Francis ascended to the title of "The First Lady of Television."

Between 1948 and 1954, Johnny returned as a substitute host on *Break The Bank*, and then between 1954 and 1957, he served as announcer for the television version. In its final seasons, Johnny introduced host Bert Parks, who served as quizmaster as well as song stylist for musical questions. As it transitioned among the ABC, NBC, and CBS television networks, *Break The Bank* moved several times during its run, taking Johnny from the NBC Rockefeller Center studios 6B and 8H that were so familiar to him, to the huge Ziegfeld Theater located four blocks north on Sixth Avenue, and the 1,700-seat Century Theater on Seventh Avenue at West 58th Street.

Early in 1949, the same year that the Mutual Guild Theater was home to *Johnny Olson's Prince Charming*, the busy broadcaster could also be found two blocks west and three blocks south, back at NBC's facility in the RCA Building. There, where Johnny was first hired for the Blue Network, he was paired with Arlene Francis for *What's My Name?*

The popularity of the show's initial 1938 season on the Mutual network brought *What's My Name?* to NBC Red where access to big-name guests added to the program's success. This predecessor to *What's My Line?* changed networks between Mutual, NBC, and ABC over the years. The format also changed, often including live music. The basic game had players guessing the identity of a famous person, hearing only the mystery guest's voice and their responses to the contestants' questions. Early in 1949, *What's My Name?* was slotted Saturday mornings at 11:30 on ABC radio. Johnny received mention in a February 19, 1949 *Billboard* magazine review: "Johnny Olsen does another fine job as announcer and assistant emcee on the show." [14-4] With a switch in sponsorship from the Servel Gas Refrigeration Dealers to General Electric later that year, *What's My Name?* was moved to Saturday nights.

In 1949, on Saturday mornings, Johnny was behind ABC's radio microphones at 10 a.m. for *Johnny Olson's Get Together*, broadcast from the WJZ Playhouse. That 865-seat former legitimate theater was built in 1911 and converted for radio use the year of Johnny's weekly show. Before being demolished in 1969, the Playhouse stood at 137 West 48th Street, just one block south and one block west of NBC. *Johnny Olson's Get Together* featured community sings, "How I met my spouse" segments, children singing in "Why my kid has talent" features, as well as audience members crooning from their seats for prizes.

On the debut episode, Johnny got laughs interviewing an elderly woman. She met her second husband waiting on line at a radio quiz show and accepted his proposal of marriage on the subway going home. There was a "Public Eye" segment in which audience members acted out a humorous scene between a gangster and his moll, and a telephone interview with a 101-year-old woman. *Variety* favorably reviewed the premiere of *Johnny Olson's Get Together*, noting that he was "a tested emcee" and adding in their usual Variety-ese, "Olson himself sang well and should use more than the one vocal he did on the preem."

Ladies Be Seated was still on the ABC network weekdays at 3 p.m. when Johnny also presided over *Whiz Kids*. This was most likely the children's program that, years later, Johnny told interviewer Tom Snyder he hosted from CBS's Studio 52 on West 54th Street at Broadway. On Snyder's NBC *Tomorrow* show, Johnny mentioned it was coincidental that he worked there because it was the facility where he later teamed with Jackie Gleason for a legendary 1963 broadcast.

Whiz Kids was one of many radio quizzes for youngsters, not to be confused with the similar sounding *Whiz Quiz* which Johnny also hosted. The latter was an evening question and answer game that aired on ABC in 1948. The *Whiz Kids* format featuring intellectually precocious children had always been a broadcasting staple, enjoying success as *Juvenile Jury* and remaining popular sixty years later with Fox television's *Are You Smarter Than a Fifth Grader?*

The Mutual Movie Matinee was another radio question-and-answer challenge, while *The Johnny Olsen Show* was a Monday through Friday variety offering. Both were heard on the Mutual network. Using the alternate spelling of Johnny's last name, the 1954 namesake program presented more of Olson's popular mirth-making and featured a more hometown approach targeted for the Mutual network's majority of rural affiliates. Airing at 9 p.m. in the east, the show included children's prayers and closed with Penny singing a hymn.

The use of electrical transcriptions to record episodes in advance on large sixteen-inch discs helped Johnny add another daily program to his hosting schedule. NBC's *Second Chance* was a radio interview and game hybrid that originated from the network's Radio City studios, which by that time, likely felt as if it was Johnny's second home. Between 1953 and 1955, the show was promoted as "The program that brings you stories of real people who have won happiness by taking a second chance." With the opening "If at first you didn't succeed, there's always a *Second Chance*," Johnny presented people chosen from the audience in advance who felt they had taken a wrong turn in their lives.

Johnny's ability to pre-record *Second Chance* for NBC allowed him to add more hours of airtime. Before audiotape, the vibrations of sound were literally "cut" into large electrical transcription (ET) discs as an engineer brushed away the shavings of aluminum or cellulose nitrate lacquer. ETs were good for only a limited number of plays before the quality deteriorated.

On the premiere episode, announcer Fred Collins introduced Johnny, who entered to enthusiastic applause, explaining, "Few of us are able to succeed the very first time up at bat. But it's the person who has the nerve and courage to try again in the face of tough breaks and big odds who gets everybody's respect." On that debut, Johnny continued his long tradition of unobtrusively saying hello to or expressing his love for his "million dollar Penny," who faithfully listened to his shows' initial broadcasts.

On *Second Chance*, John interviewed his guests with great sensitivity and sympathy, dramatically building on the extraordinary moments in their life stories when they had been in trouble with the law, deserted their family, given up a baby for adoption, or simply wanted a second chance to marry a hometown sweetheart. On August 31, 1953, Johnny presented the especially compelling story of Mrs. Elka Johnson, whose husband was reported killed in Korea. After a year-and-a-half, she married her husband's best friend, only to discover that her first husband was alive, had been a prisoner of war, and was just released by the North Koreans. After telling their tales, contestants answered general information questions to earn money, presumably to help facilitate their second chance.

The program that "proves that opportunity can knock twice" was originally presented as "the quiz show that takes nerve," but in later years, the question and answer portion of *Second Chance* was dropped. Johnny then led more in-depth discussions about the guests and their predicaments, taking his microphone into the studio audi-

Johnny interviews contestant Joe Masaniello on NBC radio's *Second Chance*.

ence to include comments, suggestions, and occasionally high-spirited debate from audience members in a style that foreshadowed Phil Donahue's later approach to the issue-oriented talk show.

For a period later in the run, a mystery voice segment was added in which Johnny made a call to a listener with a chance to win a hodgepodge of prizes from a long litany of *Second Chance* sponsors. During the summer of 1955, participants who failed to correctly identify the mystery voice were awarded a memorable if not coveted consolation prize: a year's supply of Chicken of the Sea tuna.

Through all this work up and down the radio dial, Johnny had never lost his interest in singing. His original passion that was nurtured by early stage time vocalizing at the Wonderland Theater, and then successfully pursued with the Hips Commanders and The Rhythm Rascals, was in evidence again when he recorded a novelty song. In a Scandinavian dialect reminiscent of Heinie's Grenadiers, Johnny romped tongue-in-cheek through the up-tempo ditty "I Yi Yimminy Yi (The Smorgasbord Song)." With Henri Rene and his Musette Orchestra providing the polka rhythm behind Johnny's vocal, the tune's first line summed up the song: "*I yi yimminy yi* we just met a friend of I, all together, all aboard, we're goin' out for smorgasbord."

JOHNNY OLSON: A VOICE IN TIME

The "B-side" of the 78-rpm disc contained a similar satire, "The Rain Polka." With clout as a successful broadcast personality on RCA's radio subsidiary, Johnny's record was released by corporate sister RCA Victor in March of 1946. Johnny also lent his voice to at least one other RCA record, singing back-up on "More Beer." The performance credit on that disc's label read "Lawrence Duchow and his Red Raven Orchestra with Johnny Olsen and Chorus."

Johnny was also recording at home as a hobby. In the January, 1947 issue of *Mechanix Illustrated,* Johnny was pictured with his two-speed disc recorder and microphone. The accompanying article entitled "Candid Pickups" reported that the *Ladies Be Seated* host "rigged up an adapter and plugged it into his car battery through the cigarette lighter cord. Among the oddities he's captured in sound are the hiss and swish of Old Faithful geyser, the sniff of a Yellowstone bear (it refused to growl), and an interview with the engineer on a locomotive traveling 120 mph." Ever mindful of the value of publicity, Johnny granted interviews to a number of other magazines. They resulted in articles that brought the personal side of the broadcaster to life with features about his photography hobby and his home life with Penny.

Despite all the extra-curricular ventures, Johnny remained well-rooted in the world of radio and continually growing towards the bright lights of television. He remained a radio personality long after his income from television no longer made it a necessity. In addition to a few short-lived stints such as *Family Circle,* which was broadcast weekdays in 1951 on WJZ, in the later years of his radio work Johnny was heard primarily on the Mutual network and its local New York outlet, WOR. His *Johnny Olson Show,* which had been broadcast nationwide, Monday through Friday evenings at 9 p.m. during 1954, scaled down to a weekend feature heard Saturday and Sunday afternoons for the next three years, eventually becoming only a local program. After exactly thirty years, Johnny finally phased out of radio in July of 1957 when he relinquished his last Saturday afternoon time slot.

Focused on a future in television, Johnny took advantage of every opportunity to sample life before the lens. Within a few years of his 1944 television test in Schenectady, from experience with ABC's simulcast of *Ladies Be Seated* the following year, and work for the developing DuMont network, he became acclimated to the unique demands of being on camera. Perhaps from his years as a vocalist fronting bands and his countless personal appearances at fairs, remote broadcasts, and war bond drives, Johnny seemed to effortlessly expand upon the radio persona he developed as a young adult.

Pegged by one fan magazine as standing five-feet, eleven-inches in height, 165-pounds, and with blue eyes, *Television Forecast's* feature article on the emerging television personality described Johnny as five-foot nine-inches and 170-pounds. NBC's press department was likely most accurate in their write-up of him as five-foot nine-and-one-half-inches, with green-blue eyes. The details were inconsequential, as everybody on early television was less than ten inches tall with dark hair and grey eyes.

Although a handsome, fit man with an engaging smile, Johnny's appearance was not that of a traditional leading man, and his gestures and facial expressions would likely appear exaggerated by today's more contemporary, more intimate television standards. His energetic visual presentation was well-suited for the era's small-screen, fuzzy black and white picture, which was often received on set-top rabbit-ear antennae, on which subtlety was lost. His enthusiastic, likeable, and engaging manner was a timeless gift that was ideal for the visual medium, and most importantly, Johnny projected sincerity — a natural honesty. As television veteran Ed McMahon observed, "What you had to be was genuine. The screen, as small as it was, exposed phoniness. It was like a lie detector." [14-5]

CHAPTER 15
PICTURES IN THE AIR

Johnny Olson recalled, "Practical telecasting had begun with the visits of President Roosevelt and the King and Queen of England to the New York World's Fair in 1939." That broadcast of the British Royals was carried live on W2XB, GE's station in Schenectady. Johnny made his first television appearance there only five years later, but the work to fly pictures through the air started decades earlier.

Television was named long before it was born. "Tele" was taken from the Greek for "far off," and "vision" was adapted from the Latin "visio," the past participle of the verb "videre," which means "to see." The title was the combination of two languages, and the invention resulted from work in two technologies — mechanically rotating disks and electronic scanning.

Credit for the concept behind the mechanical system for transmitting pictures is generally given to Russian-German inventor Paul Gottlieb Nipkow, who proposed the idea as early as the 1880s. Scotland's long-haired, bespectacled John Logie Baird and Charles Jenkins, the American founder of the Society of Motion Picture Engineers, are the scientists primarily credited with developing the system, although both AT&T's Bell Labs and General Electric also experimented with mechanical television.

Watching television's earliest tests, Guglielmo Marconi observed in 1925, "It will soon be possible to transmit a picture or a whole page of print across the Atlantic by radio." [15-1] In an article for the 1929 *World Almanac*, AT&T wrote of its first experimental videocasts on April 7, 1927. Using the mechanical scanning system and telephone lines, Secretary of Commerce Herbert Hoover stood before a camera in Washington and was seen clearly on a two inch rectangular screen at the Bell Telephone Labs in the New York. Later that day, images were beamed through the air some twenty-two miles from Whippany, New Jersey, to the same small screen at the Bell Telephone Labs across the Hudson River.

In simple terms, a rotating disc with small holes placed in a spiral pattern around its outer edge was used to scan tiny light and dark parts of a scene. As the disc spun, variable levels of light were momentarily glimpsed through the holes and registered on a selenium photocell as electrical impulses. The complete picture was a collection of light and dark dots, similar to the way photographs were printed in newspapers. The scene could be crudely reproduced in a receiver using a second identical disk rotating in synch, at the same speed and direction as the first. *Time* magazine described Bell Telephone Labs' first small television screen as being comprised of "2,500 tiny squares of tin foil mounted in neon gas. As electrical current reaches each bit of tin foil, it leaps through the neon, which is instantly illuminated." [15-2]

The history of electronic television is a far more contentious affair, rife with patent battles, court cases, and human drama worthy of a network soap opera. If there had been a continuing daytime drama called *Television*, it would have been a spin-off of an earlier series called *Radio* because the story began with Guglielmo Marconi, the established star, and Germany's Ferdinand Braun, the man who shared the 1909 Nobel prize for physics with Marconi. While their shared Nobel award was for "contributions to the development of wireless telegraphy," the spin-off story featuring Braun began with his 1897 invention of the cathode ray oscilloscope — the basis for the television picture tube.

Over a dozen scientists from many countries played important roles in the drama. Philo Farnsworth and Vladimir Zworkin are generally recognized in America as the lead performers and the primary trailblazers in the development of electronic television. Like a good soap opera, their story featured greed, jealousy, trials, tribulations, heartbreak, alcoholism, disease, and even premature death. Much of it was motivated by David Sarnoff, a familiar protagonist.

There are many excellent books, papers, articles, and oral histories that document the development of electronic television. They tell the stories of Russia's Professor Boris Rosing enlisting Vladimir Zworkin, his student, to help further his work on the cathode ray tube. The stories also include Philo Farnsworth, a fourteen-year-old Mormon farm boy in rural Utah, who astounded his teachers with a theory for capturing light in a bottle and transmitting pictures line-by-line, back and forth, in the same manner that he tilled potato fields with a horse-drawn harrow.

Farnsworth found financing to further his work independently, while Zworkin immigrated to the US in 1919, where he worked for Westinghouse. In 1923, Zworkin applied for a patent for the design of his iconoscope, the basis for an electronic television camera. Farnsworth transmitted images on his working television system and applied for a patent for his image dissector in 1927. The relative status of those patents motivated the drama that, like the best soap opera conflicts, played out over many years.

David Sarnoff hired fellow Russian immigrant Zworykin from Westinghouse to further RCA's development of television, but the two soon realized that Philo Farnsworth had already patented vital elements integral to making quality electronic television a reality. Zworykin and Sarnoff visited Farnsworth's San Francisco laboratory in the spring of 1931 and offered the inventor $100,000 for the fruits of his labor and his patents. Farnsworth refused, asking instead for royalties from his invention. Sarnoff allegedly snapped in reply, "RCA doesn't pay royalties, we collect them." Sarnoff and Zworkin abruptly left and publicly downplayed the importance of Farnsworth's work.

Both inventions, Zworkin's iconoscope and Farnsworth's image dissector, can be described in simple terms as being similar. In both, the visual image is focused on a mosaic of hundreds of thousands of microscopic photosensitive specks that register the brightness of the tiny parts of the picture as an electrical current. An electromagnetic field is used to guide a steady stream of electrons that horizontally scan the mosaic, line by line, from top to bottom, to register the electric charge of each tiny photosensitive speck.

With both Farnsworth's and Zworkin's systems, those electronic impulses of brightness and darkness could be sent over wire or through the air to a receiver, along with synchronizing pulses, where a similar stream of electrons could re-create the light and dark portions of the picture when projected onto a phosphorescent coated surface in a vacuum tube — a picture tube based on Braun's cathode ray tube. While both inventors' prototypes required subjects to be bathed in immense quantities of light, Zworkin advanced the technology by increasing the camera tube's sensitivity. It was a vital step towards making television practical.

The drama grew intense during seemingly endless legal battles brought by RCA. Sarnoff attempted to prove that Zworkin had built a working system four years prior to the one exhibited by Farnsworth on September 7, 1927, the one that earned the former farm boy's patent #1,773,980 that was issued in August 1930. When it came time for RCA to produce material evidence that Zworykin had actually constructed and operated his television system in 1923, no conclusive documentation was submitted; only verbal testimony from two of Zworkin's colleagues was offered. In the realm of theoretical work on electronically transmitting pictures, Farnsworth's high school chemistry teacher stepped forward to present the young inventor's original drawings that demonstrated the basis for his later experiments — the earliest documentation related to the invention of electronic television.

In 1935, the government rendered its decision in RCA's claim of patent interference #64,027, stating "priority of invention awarded to Farnsworth … Zworykin has no right to make the count because it is not apparent that the device would operate to produce a scanned electrical image unless it has discrete globules capable of producing discrete space charges and the Zworykin application as filed does not disclose such a device."

Zworkin and Sarnoff appealed the decision. In 1939, the very year that RCA first presented television to the public at the New York Worlds Fair, the courts declared that the company was required to pay $1 million in royalties to Farnsworth for liberally borrowing from his patented work. Rather than write a check, Sarnoff's lawyers wrote more legal appeals. Finally, fifteen years after his initial application, Zworkin was granted patent #2,141,059 by a court of appeals reportedly over the objection of the patent office.

Ultimately, the lengthy ordeal took its toll on Philo Farnsworth. He had won the patent hearings, but lost the appeals, as well as in the marketplace. The young inventor suffered a nervous breakdown followed by depression and ulcers that were complicated by bouts of drinking. He was hospitalized and submitted to electric shock therapy, while his house burned to the ground in 1947. Farnsworth ultimately died of a perforated ulcer with little more to his name than a credit in his obituaries as "The father of television." On the occasion of Farnsworth's death, Johnny was diplomatic. He earned a significant income from RCA's NBC subsidiary, but he wrote that both Zworkin and Farnsworth deserved to share credit for flying pictures through the air.

It was not until April 30, 1939 that an appreciable number of Americans got to see a box with moving pictures. At the World's Fair in New York, David Sarnoff continued to build on his legacy of showmanship and promotion for NBC, introducing television to the world by broadcasting President Roosevelt's address at the opening of the event. Far more people viewed television at the RCA exhibit at the fair than saw it in their living rooms.

A small number of receivers began to be found in affluent homes and corner taverns, and inexpensive programming kept the tubes burning during evening hours. Television was still considered a novelty when commercial broadcasting began in 1941, just in time for World War II to temporarily slow further progress.

With manufacturing and manpower now dedicated to the war effort, suddenly NBC's and CBS' New York stations were on the air for only a limited number of hours per week with entertainment offerings replaced by public service programs. Dr. Du Mont's outlet gained early popularity by remaining on the air more hours than the others during the war years by virtue of dedicated employees. Many were factory workers by day, but they were persuaded to work evenings at Allen B Du Mont's W2XWV (later the eponymous WABD).

Television's development was halted by the war, but radio listening surged. Americans tuned their radios to hear vital news and for escapist entertainment. Television was broadcasting's poor stepchild throughout the decade.

As late as 1947, radio rights to broadcast the World Series cost $175,000, while television rights went for only $65,000. Just the same, an estimated four million viewers crowded around the fewer than one-half million television sets then in existence to see the New York Yankees beat the Brooklyn Dodgers. Overall, radio revenues were peaking at $415 million annually, twelve times that of television, but with forty-one television stations in twenty-three cities in 1949, the medium was on its way to reaching critical mass. No one knew what the future would bring for broadcasters and entertainers during and after the video revolution.

Johnny noted, "Some years ago, I stood before three cameras, a crew of eight, and in 22,000-watts of light — a veritable Turkish Bath — excitedly delivering my first TV commercial. What was it like? What was this new medium of TV to mean to me as an announcer-performer? What effect would it have on my career having just completed many years behind a radio microphone? No lights — no cameras — no crews surrounding you — no copy to learn?"

Radio and film superstar Bob Hope had yet to commit to the new form of entertainment. In a lighthearted letter dated July 13, 1949, and written to John Royal, his friend and Vice President of NBC, the comedian wrote about his thoughts on television and Milton Berle, television's first superstar. "Berle can have that medium all to himself for the next year." Hope went on to say, "Without a doubt, television will really be going in a couple of years and we will have to put on our very best manners and do a nice half-hour show every week. I don't think any less than that will do, as television will have to become a habit . . . maybe one of the nastier habits, but, nevertheless, an interesting one." [15-3]

In 1949, Bob Hope could afford to wait for television because radio ratings measured his share of audience at 23.8 percent. However, he was forced to quickly embrace the future of broadcasting. The following year, that number fell to 12.7 percent, and then plummeted to 5.4 percent the year after. [15-4] Radio's stars and top programs migrated to television along with audiences.

CHAPTER 16
DOINGS AT DUMONT

Johnny developed a reputation among producers and advertising agencies as one of the more reliable and versatile personalities. He worked for all four national radio chains, and his mike time was multiplying as he moved through the 1940s. Nevertheless, he maintained his focus on a future in television, believing more firmly than ever that it would ultimately eclipse radio.

While it may be hard today to appreciate the relative nature of the two media, work in network radio at the time carried prestige and was far more lucrative as it had become a respected, mature form of show business that was supported by generous advertising budgets. By comparison, television scarcely paid at all, was not yet covered by any of the performers' unions, and featured working conditions that were often abysmal. Hugh Downs recalled his earliest days under the bright lights, at age twenty-four, sweating through his sport jacket and dripping perspiration from the tip of his nose onto his script during a fifteen minute newscast on Chicago's WBKB in 1945, all to earn a total of $5.

Johnny was in his mid-thirties, and he relished his on-camera work at DuMont. He was among a number of radio performers who felt that their early experiences in television were investments in their future. Nevertheless, some of television's crew members referred to these radio personalities as "big shots" who acted like they were "slumming." DuMont's Harry Coyle told author Michael Ritchie, "They did anything they wanted to do, and if you were the director, you'd be subjugated to them. If you fought them, you were out of a job." [16-1] Johnny took opportunities to do that "slumming" to keep abreast of the latest technical and programming developments. He wanted to be prepared to stake a permanent claim in the new, emerging medium.

In the five year period that followed the 1941 inauguration of commercial television, during the war years, the number of television sets in the United States grew from a negligible few to a number quoted by a variety of sources to be between 6,000 and 15,000. Soon after, the market transformed; Americans had never bought any new device as quickly as they did television sets, and nothing had ever become such a major part of the culture in so short a time.

Early in 1946, RCA announced the commercial availability of the image orthicon camera tube that it had developed and manufactured for the military during World War II. Featuring an electron multiplier that acted as an amplifier, the improvement on Farnsworth's image dissector was so sensitive that it could capture a clear image using minimal illumination. David Sarnoff astounded the press when he demonstrated the new technology. He slowly dimmed the lights until a model's face was reproduced on a television monitor lit only by the glow of a single candle.

Gone forever was the heat that had resulted in some performers perspiring so profusely that microphones picked up the sound of their feet sloshing in sweat collected in their shoes. Upon the conversion of Studio 8G from radio to television, NBC publicized that the new camera technology allowed the lighting and the heat to be reduced by eighty percent. The impact of the image orthicon, nicknamed by engineers as the "immy," was so transforming that it was immortalized as Emmy, the winged muse of art holding an atom with orbiting electrons. Conceived by Louis McManus, a television designer and technician, and christened by Harry Lubcke, one of television's pioneering engineers, it remains the namesake of the award for excellence as recognized by the Academy of Television Arts and Sciences.

In February 1946, the same year that the new camera technology was made available, major radio manufacturers were at a meeting of the American Television Society in New York to announce that they had begun mass production and would have affordable television receivers on the market by that summer. The following year, an estimated 142,000 televisions were in homes, and by early 1948, the number mushroomed to over 500,000. With fifty-one television stations on the air, by all estimates there were over one million televisions in American homes by the end of 1948. Antennae were blossoming on rooftops and sets were being bought as quickly as they came off the assembly lines. *Time* magazine estimated that 1,000 new sets were being installed every twenty-four hours.

Budgetary considerations motivated programming decisions at local stations, as well as at DuMont and ABC, the networks without highly profitable radio divisions generating ongoing streams of revenue. Although Paramount Pictures ultimately invested as much as $200,000 of needed cash for a substantial share of Dr. Du Mont's company, the studio played no role in content. Visual offerings were produced on the cheap, as programming and viewership posed the classic dilemma of the chicken and the egg.

Without a significant number of viewers to attract advertising dollars, there was little budget with which to create quality programming. Without compelling programming, there was little reason for the masses to purchase television sets, and low viewership did not garner sufficient advertiser support. Television was considered a novelty reserved mostly for the affluent. The medium continued to operate at a loss after World War II and for the rest of the decade.

In 1949, the minimum wage was 40¢ cents an hour, the average annual salary was $3,600, and a new Ford sedan cost $1,230. Television sets were comparatively expensive. The January 1949 issue of *Science Illustrated* helped prepare consumers for the high price of going high-tech. A DuMont set with a twenty-inch screen, the largest direct-view television tube, sold for $2,500 — twice the price of a new car. DuMont's fifteen-inch model cost $700. The price of economy models were on their way down; an Admiral ten-inch set could be had for $250, and the Pilot Radio Corporation offered a portable model weighing fifteen pounds with a tiny three-inch screen at $100. Despite the required outlay, over two million television sets were purchased in 1949 alone, and *Variety* reported that the 1950s began with 3.5 million TV households.

Penetration increased as retail prices decreased; by the end of 1950, the tubes of 10 million television receivers were aglow. *Newsweek* reported that television broadcasting became a profitable enterprise the following year. By 1952, some 21 million homes had television sets, and CBS reported that its television business showed a profit of $8.9 million. In two more years, television's advertising revenue forever surpassed radio's advertising income. An FCC freeze on new station applications was lifted, and television's growth further exploded. By 1953, the new appliance was in more than half of America's households and was considered a necessity by the vast majority of families living within the range of a television station transmitter.

Television's boom coincided with the baby boom; the television generation was born as video came of age. In 1957, the all-time height of America's population boom, a record 4.3 million children were delivered, and 6.6 million new televisions were also brought home. In 1957, 50 million television sets were the focal points in American living rooms. That year, CBS accountants tallied their television net revenues at $22.2 million.

During the 1940s, Johnny looked to further hone his on-camera poise and presence, but there were far fewer opportunities available in television than in radio. There were dozens of radio outlets, but only NBC, CBS, and DuMont had television stations in the New York area until near the close of the decade. ABC did not sign-on WJZ-TV until August 1948, and the city's three independent stations were not up and running until the following year.

Radio was a 24-hour business, but most television outlets did not take to the air until late afternoons. Until the medium approached profitability, many stations broadcast test patterns for much of the day, allowing engineers, installers, and repair persons to make the sometimes confounding adjustments necessary for a viewable picture. A rare midday transmission would likely be a non-commercial, public affairs offering.

On Saturday, April 2, 1949, NBC's New York flagship station signed-on early for a noon broadcast to preview its future plans for the educational use of television. Some 2,000 school principals meeting at the Waldorf Astoria hotel watched the one-hour program in their conference room. Ever mindful of public perceptions that might impact the bottom line, David Sarnoff funded that kind of outing to help tip the scales in the ongoing social debate about whether television was "good" or "bad" for children. The issue was still far from resolved four years later, when the National Congress of Parents and Teachers conceded that television "even appeared to be an asset" in some homes. The PTA also acknowledged, "In the schools, too, where television was given proper recognition and guidance it seemed to foster both interest and learning." [16-2]

Regularly scheduled programming consisted of inexpensive fare, heavy on interview shows, cooking demonstrations, quiz shows, and especially sports. Coverage of the national pastime, baseball, was considered a must, even if with only one or two cameras. Roller derby, wrestling, and boxing were early favorites because of the tightly confined field of action in a controlled, indoor environment. Bars and saloons that invested in television sets for their patrons' viewing benefited, as thirsty sports fans spent hours gathered around their flickering little black and white tubes. Against this backdrop, Johnny stepped before the camera for his second television series.

Talent competitions had been a staple of entertainment on slow nights in vaudeville theaters, and the frugal format had segued easily to radio. *Major Bowes and the Original Amateur Hour* aired locally in New York in 1934 before being picked up by CBS months later. In 1935, its first year as a network radio show, *The Original Amateur Hour* auditioned more than thirty thousand acts, including "Frank Sinatra and the 3 Flashes." Their September 8 audition report showed that the group garnered an "A-1" rating for "singing, dancing, and comedy," and was renamed "The Hoboken Four," purportedly by Major Bowes himself. The quartet went on to win their on-air competition and joined one of Major Bowes's traveling vaudeville units. Sinatra soon left the tour to begin his solo career.

Edward Bowes was a rotund, balding, former realtor and theatrical producer, who earned his stripes as a Major during World War I. He continued to welcome hopeful performers to his popular program's microphones until

Major Bowes's created America's longest-running talent competition. In 1936, Walter Chrysler showed his appreciation for the broadcaster's salesmanship by presenting Bowes with a custom-made Chrysler Imperial Airflow limousine that featured a special console with exotic luxury features between the driver and passenger compartments.

his death in 1946. The following year, DuMont introduced an early video version of *American Idol* called *Doorway to Fame*, which was first hosted by Art Ford. On December 15, 1947, Johnny took over the show.

One press report stated that Johnny and his staff auditioned some 20,000 hopefuls during the series' two-year run. Each episode featured a guest star offering words of encouragement to the amateur participants. Originally airing on Friday and later on Monday nights, the program was noteworthy for its innovative approach to presenting the formulaic talent show. In his 1980 book, *Total Television*, Alex McNeil reported on ways that *Doorway to Fame* creatively used early multi-camera, scene-blending technology to project the performers into cleverly-constructed miniature sets and backdrops. While some of the talent may have been amateurish, the program was visually interesting.

In 1948, the show was reformatted and renamed to revive the popularity of *The Original Amateur Hour*. Ted Mack replaced Johnny as the new master of ceremonies. Ted was a protégé of Major Bowes, who knew the original program well, having been a talent scout and the show's director during its radio years. Primarily due to the on-going commercial support of Geritol, advertised as "America's number one tonic," the show held the distinction of having one of broadcasting's most extensive runs, ultimately airing on all four television networks before its demise in 1970. Other *Amateur Hour* alumni to achieve stardom after appearances on the show include Robert Merrill, Beverly Sills, Gladys Knight, Pat Boone, Jack Carter, Dorothy Collins, Ann-Margret, and Penny Marshall.

The picture rarely looked this good at home. On November 1, 1948 DuMont was the first network to drop the test pattern (used to assist technicians and installers in aligning and adjusting equipment) for regularly scheduled daytime programming. Johnny hosted America's first daytime network entertainment series.

At approximately the same time that Johnny was hosting *Doorway to Fame* in New York, Bob Barker, his future colleague, was hosting his own talent contest on the west coast. Barker recalled, "Westinghouse...hired me to host a local show called *Your Big Moment*. I would come out and say, 'Welcome to *Your Big Moment*, the show that gives you — if you have the talent — your big moment on television.' We gave a lot of people who had no talent their big moment on television, too. And it was my first appearance on television." [16-3] The host confided, "No one came out of the show and went on to play Broadway or anything like that, but we had some talented people on that show. Sometimes, though, we weren't completely booked, and I remember the producer going around to bars in Hollywood looking for someone to fill in." [16-4]

While Johnny had been jack-of-all-trades in Wisconsin radio, Barker was on-the-air in Springfield, Missouri, cutting his teeth on radio entertainment, news, sports, and interview programs. Both men migrated to the coasts to advance their careers, and both found themselves among the pioneers in early television. Although they had never met, nor even heard each others' work at the time, the similar experiences that Barker and Johnny shared in their parallel careers helped the two veteran performers to enjoy a unique bond that was evident during their time together on *The Price is Right* decades later.

For the period that Johnny fronted Doorway to Fame, Ned Harvey led the show's small orchestra, and Johnny's announcer was Joe Bolton. Johnny and Joe were both born the same year, and they were kindred spirits. Like Johnny, Joe had done it all in the world of entertainment. Starting in the 1920s, Joe performed as a musician, singer, local radio host, and network radio announcer. He later worked as a television sportscaster, weatherman, and game show host before a brood of pre-

"Officer" Joe Bolton, Johnny's announcer on DuMont's *Doorway to Fame,* enjoyed a long career hosting local children's programs as the favorite honorary member of New York's finest.

pubescent kids helped him find a more permanent niche.

Radio executive Charles King licensed Hal Roach Studios' *Our Gang* comedy series for television from Clinton Films, the company's bankruptcy trustee. The shorts were edited and sold as *The Little Rascals* on a station-by-station basis. Roger King recalled that New York's WPIX, the station of the city's self-proclaimed "Picture Newspaper," the *Daily News,* was his father's first customer in a deal that netted the family $50,000. Although virtually all of the proceeds from that initial sale went to Clinton Films, King World was in business.

WPIX management wanted Joe Bolton to present Spanky, Alfalfa, Buckwheat, Darla, Stymie, and the rest of the mischievous minors as a funny tramp character for *The Clubhouse Gang* afternoon show. Thinking it inappropriate for the school-aged audience, his 1955 decision to adopt the persona of Police Officer Joe Bolton brought the broadcaster his greatest fame. Presenting *The Little Rascals, The Three Stooges,* and an assortment of cartoon packages, Officer Joe Bolton reigned on afternoon television for the next twenty years as a hero of kids growing up in New York.

The venture that started with WPIX was successful enough for Charles King's tiny family-run company to next sell sixty-second news features from a one-room office above a barber shop. The small syndicator soon acquired other programs, including reruns of the 1953 series, *Topper.* That sitcom continued as a television mainstay for decades, often airing in the early morning hours on stations that carried King World's first-run hits.

Brothers Roger and Michael King learned the appeal of game shows in the late 1970s after being hired by distributor Dick Colbert to sell Jack Barry and Dan Enright's *The Joker's Wild* and *Tic Tac Dough.* That success led to a 1983 partnership with Merv Griffin, another of Johnny's former on-air partners. King World offered stations a new, nighttime version of Merv's *Wheel of Fortune.* Although it limped into the marketplace, the daytime, NBC word game was soon a smash in prime-time.

The following year, Merv's *Jeopardy!* was successfully revived as *Wheel of Fortune*'s companion in syndication. Ironically, *Wheel of Fortune* was the show that joined the NBC daytime lineup to replace *Jeopardy!,* when the answer and question game was cancelled in 1975. When teamed, the pair delivered a one-two ratings punch that knocked out the competition for more than twenty-five years. With subsequent hits from *Oprah* to *Dr. Phil,* a dynasty was born. King World and Charles' sons, Roger and Michael King, wrote new chapters in television distribution and salesmanship, both as an independent company, and later as part of the CBS-Viacom conglomerate.

During the medium's formative years, before behemoth multi-national corporations tamed television, Johnny's affiliation with the innovative DuMont network brought him a variety of assignments in addition to *Doorway to Fame.* Some, such as hosting the network's *Monday Night Fights,* were mundane, but one gave the versatile broadcaster a unique claim to fame in the history of television.

The first scheduled DuMont network series is believed to have been *Serving Through Science.* It premiered on the evening of August 15, 1946, on DuMont's two-station hook-up that linked New York and Washington, DC. Thomas T. Goldsmith, DuMont's engineering chief, reported that *Walter Compton and the News* aired evenings, simultaneously on DuMont's WABD and WTTG a year or two after the Washington station was named in his honor in 1946. Daytime television, an entirely unchartered territory, was about to be explored.

The November 1949 edition of *Telecast* magazine predicted, "In years to come, when historians are scribbling their chapters on television, The DuMont network will be saluted as a trail blazer." The article was entitled "Daytime Pioneer" and led with a picture of Johnny Olson. It reported, "Station WABD, the network's key outlet in New York, launched its first daytime schedule November 1, 1948. Operating without interruption from 7 a.m. until 11 p.m., this was the first television station in the country to offer a full day's entertainment."

Variety reported that "a nice, breezy informality" was the keynote of the entire day. WABD's mid-morning programs were low on production values and usually shared the same sets. They were presented in a manner that was enjoyed almost as much by listening as from watching. With no other station offering regular daytime programming, DuMont envisioned itself competing primarily with radio. As such, commercial spots were priced as low as $25, economical enough to draw even small business advertising from radio to television.

Johnny accurately and proudly boasted that he was host of the very first daytime network television entertainment show to originate from New York, *Johnny Olsen's Rumpus Room*. Initially a local offering inaugurating WABD's daytime debut, the historic program premiered on the five-station DuMont chain at 10 a.m. on January 17, 1949. It moved to 12:30 p.m. later that year, and then continued weekday afternoons until July 4, 1952.

During what was originally a fifteen-minute daily program, Johnny and Penny presented local singers, dancers, and people of interest, including an occasional celebrity enjoying their first appearance on television. Like the other shows that were inspired by the party at actor Dennis Morgan's home in Hollywood years earlier, this was another up-beat variety show that primarily relied upon Johnny's talent for light-hearted ad-libbing with guests.

Jim Young, then of Morristown, New Jersey, was five years old and wore an eye-catching dog and doghouse sweater knitted by his mother, when he and his sister were in the audience at a *Rumpus Room* broadcast in early 1952. Almost sixty years later, he remembered his impromptu interview with Johnny after being singled-out to be crowned "Prince of the Day." When Jim mentioned that his father worked for the A&P grocery chain, Johnny did not miss the opportunity to mention it was one of the fine supermarkets carrying Sauce Arturo — one of the show's sponsors. Jim recalled insisting that his mother carry his prize — a cumbersome metal "Mobo Pony Express" ride-on horse and buggy set — back to New Jersey on the train immediately after the show. [16-5]

In that era before satellites, DuMont pioneered among the television networks by making kinescopes available to its affiliates that were not yet connected by coaxial cable. With the crude technology of focusing a film camera on a television picture tube, a kinescope was the only way to preserve a video signal. Although delayed by several days or even several weeks, some of Johnny's work for DuMont made it as far west as the network's ever-changing Los Angeles affiliate over the years, KTSL, then KTTV and later, KHJ.

In its debut year, *Johnny Olsen's Rumpus Room* brought New York's first daytime network entertainment program's host recognition as "Favorite Man on Daytime Television," as awarded by *Radio and Television Mirror*. Although there was little competition for the honor, it served to embolden Johnny's dedication to staking a claim in the new but low-paying medium. As television matured, the publication again made mention of Johnny's work in 1950, 1951, 1952, 1954, and 1960.

Johnny Olsen's Rumpus Room was broadcast from a tiny studio at the original DuMont facility on Madison Avenue at West 53rd Street. Arthur Forrest rose through the ranks of television and enjoyed a reputation and the Emmys as one of the medium's most respected directors. He remembered the Olsons very well, saying, "I was a studio assistant at DuMont in the late 1940s and became a cameraman soon after. At that time, Johnny Olson had a morning show along with his wife Penny, two lovely people, and upon my promotion, Johnny very nicely mentioned it on the air and had everyone in the audience give me my first round of applause. He did it again when I got married. They were always very much in tune with the everyday people...I remember both of them with a great deal of fondness." [16-6]

CHAPTER 17
TODDLIN' TV

Johnny recalled that his early DuMont network series was seen live in New York, Philadelphia, Baltimore, Washington, and Pittsburgh. In late 1949, AT&T's coaxial cable and microwave relay system used to distribute live programming to affiliates in the pre-satellite world of broadcasting finally reached Chicago. That opened the opportunity for contemporaneous television to reach the Midwest, and for Chicago to become a vital city for program origination during television's pre-pubescence. That year, the *Chicago Tribune* celebrated the newly arrived New York programming by heralding "The end of dull sustaining filler on television screens appears to be in sight." 1949 was also the year that Chicago's Orchard Field Airport was renamed O'Hare Airport to honor Lieutenant Commander Edward "Butch" O'Hare, a World War II flying ace, who had been awarded the Medal of Honor.

Johnny Olson knew that well, as he flew to television's new frontier each week between June 17 and December 9, 1949 to further his on-camera aspirations as host of *Fun For The Money*. Again, Johnny was pioneering. *Fun For The Money* was one of the first prime-time game shows on the fledgling seventeen-station ABC-TV network. It originated Friday nights at 8:30 p.m. in Chicago, airing at 9:30 p.m. on New York's WJZ-TV, as well as the other east coast affiliates.

Fun For The Money featured contestants engaged in offbeat activities, as *Beat The Clock* and Nickelodeon's *Double Dare* would later. Two teams of four members each dressed in baseball uniforms and played nine "innings" of various stunts on a set that resembled a baseball stadium. Johnny's *Fun For The Money* was produced by the Foote, Cone & Belding agency for their client, Kleenex. The advertising agency's on-set producer was Stefan Hatos. Familiar to Johnny from their time together on *Ladies Be Seated*, Hatos would later breathe rarified air after he teamed with Monty Hall for the venerable *Let's Make A Deal*.

Johnny had developed a following in the Midwest from his years on WTMJ, and his Blue Network radio programs that aired in Chicago alternately on WCFL and WLS. His work hosting television's *Fun For The Money* caught the attention of local broadcasters and television critics alike. The July 9, 1949 Chicago edition of *Television Forecast* featured Johnny on the cover. The magazine carried a story on broadcasting and film star Eddie Cantor, and another article on *Fun For The Money*. It recounted Johnny's career from local radio vocalist through big band singer, through radio in New York and Hollywood, and to his new job as television host in Chicago.

"His main passion is for coffee, which he drinks in staggering quantities," the magazine reported. It also touched on Johnny's home life with Penny. Using the variant spelling of their name, the magazine observed, "If you want to find the Olsens during their off hours, you seldom have to look further than their own fireside. Strictly homebodys (sic), they do not care for night clubs and late hours, and when it comes to entertainment, they prefer the home variety — dinner, conversation, and quiet music. [17-1]

In building a presence in the Midwest, the networks utilized local talent, primarily from WMAQ and WBKB. In 1951, CBS plucked Massachusetts native Mike Wallace from the Chicago talk show he hosted with his wife to the network's New York studios for work as a staff announcer. Other Chicago television's talented jacks-of-all trades included Hugh Downs and prize-winning author Studs Terkel, who enjoyed a daily radio presence for forty-five years in addition to his early television exposure on *Studs' Place*.

Television Forecast identified Johnny (left) for its Chicago readers as the host of ABC's *Fun For The Money*, broadcast weekly from their city.

Studs' Place chronicled the activities at a mythical bar and grill. Producer Charlie Andrews wrote little more than an outline of the plot from which the actors improvised. The closing credits included an art card which read: "Dialogue by the Cast." "It was sort of like jazz in a way," Studs Terkel said in a 1997 interview with National Public Radio. "It was improvisational. People thought it was actually real."

Perhaps the most notable transplant was Dave Garroway, a gifted broadcaster, who would later become the first host of *The Today Show*. Gene Rayburn remembered Garroway, a Schenectady native, from the time the two young men served together as pages at NBC. While Rayburn stayed in New York pursuing his career on radio, Broadway, and television, Garroway traveled to Pittsburgh's KDKA, and then NBC's WMAQ in Chicago, where he developed the unique and quirky but friendly style that brought him back to NBC in New York, not as a page, but as talent.

The hallmark of what was called "The Chicago School of Television" was a sense of intimacy and informality that had not been fully exploited on radio. When Charles "Cappy" Cappleman, the senior statesman of CBS' west coast operations, was a youngster, he started his broadcast career in the Midwest, and he was present to watch some of Dave Garroway's earliest on-camera work. He explained that the New York television community was predisposed to treat the new medium as a way to bring Broadway into the home, and that Hollywood-based broadcasters saw television as an extension of film; both were played to theater-size audiences.

Chicago practitioners had no prejudice, and they approached television from a fresh perspective based on the medium's own unique characteristics. Marshall McLuhan was credited for saying, "The medium is the message," and Dave Garroway

exploited television's distinct attributes. His singular relationship with the viewer was subtly different from the way that New York broadcaster Arthur Godfrey's more "folksy" approach capitalized on the medium's intimacy.

On *Garroway at Large,* Dave roamed through his Chicago studio, gently leading viewers from one setting or situation to another in a calm, conversational style. He brought that technique to New York on January 14, 1952, for the inauguration of *The Today Show,* the program that has been on television more hours than any other single series. Long after her appearance as a "Today Girl" with Garroway, Barbara Walters observed, "I have never seen anyone in this business who could communicate the way he did. He could look at the camera and

Dave Garroway co-hosted America's first and favorite network television morning show with chimpanzee J. Fred Muggs from a 49th Street storefront window.

make you feel he was talking only with you." [17-2]

Garroway's casual, easy-going on-air manner was in direct contrast to his true demeanor in later life. Friends and co-workers, including Hugh Downs, reported that the broadcaster suffered from chronic depression, medicating himself with a concoction of liquid codeine, tranquilizers and amphetamines on the set to help maintain his energy for the daily grind of the early morning broadcast. Depressed, frustrated with the business realities of television and what he perceived to be a lack of gratitude for his contributions, Garroway told *Today* newscaster Frank Blair, "Nobody cares for old Dave anymore…I'm an old shoe, an old hat." [17-2] On July 21, 1982, Johnny was shocked by the news that was the talk of the entire New York broadcasting community. As his second wife had done twenty-one years earlier, the founding father of morning television, Dave Garroway, took his own life.

The March 17, 1951 issue of *Collier's* magazine observed the approach personified by Garroway: "In Chicago, they don't lavish money on costly trappings. They turn out quiet, casual little shows and the audiences love them."[17-3] Ten days later, in its March 27, 1951 edition, *Look* magazine wrote of the Second City style, "It's been called relaxed, intimate, friendly, natural, subtle — but the main thing about the 'Chicago School' of TV, more widely copied in higher-priced, higher-pressured areas, is this: The viewer doesn't always know what's going to happen next and next and next."[17-4]

Professor Joel Sternberg of the University of Illinois characterized the unique look and feel of early Chicago television as experimental, visual, intimate, and capable of presenting the unexpected. Radio producer Arch Oboler wrote in the July, 1951 issue of *Theater Arts* magazine, "For while Hollywood rushes to film, and New York frantically tries to force the theatre through the cathode tube, Chicago almost alone has recognized a new art form for the television medium." He discussed how the new relaxed intimacy reflected the fact that "...the television viewer is only a handful of feet from the performer."

Johnny enjoyed participating in the pioneering spirit among the Second City broadcasters. He was influenced by their style, and he admired their reputation for innovation on a shoestring. That skill was most evident in the many popular children's programs that originated from Chicago, programs on which creativity often compensated for a lack of budget. Dr. Frances Horwich created the Miss Frances character for her *Ding Dong School*; Burr Tillstrom fathered *Kukla, Fran, and Ollie*; Don Herbert amazed as *Mr. Wizard*; and Larry Harmon created a broadcasting empire overseeing *Bozo the Clown*, his alter-ego's image and the nationwide television franchise that enjoyed its greatest success in Chicago.

Johnny came to know another Chicago children's broadcasting icon, Ireene Wicker, *The Singing Lady*. Ireene added the third "e" to her first name at the suggestion of a numerologist, who said it would bring her good luck. The Illinois native was indeed fortunate, as she enjoyed a forty-five-year career hosting the nation's first network radio program for children. She told stories and sang simple songs to two generation of children, some 25 million at a time.

In 1930, she debuted on WGN, and within six months, Ireene's work was carried by NBC Blue, which provided a national audience for her program. The exposure helped to generate sales for the beloved broadcaster's books and records. Ireene moved to New York, just as Johnny and so many of the early Chicago broadcasters had done, and she continued her career on DuMont television along with Johnny.

The Singing Lady was on the air in syndication and on PBS until 1975. The show disappeared from radio and television stations when Ireene retired to a lifestyle more befitting her station in life. In 1941, she married Victor J. Hammer, owner of the prestigious Hammer Art Galleries and brother of Armand Hammer, the noted oil tycoon and art collector. She gave one of her last interviews a few years before her death at her magnificently furnished home in the famed Sherry-Netherland along Central Park. There, author Richard Lamparski reported that the Emmy winner spoke with great joy about her years in broadcasting:

"Miss Wicker had her hands stretched out before her and used them as she might before a studio audience of kiddies. The fingers spread when she spoke of the freedom of the imagination…They clutched at her heart when she told of the many letters she had had from fans…It was clear from the gestures that she was reliving the best years of her life as *The Singing Lady*"[17-5]

Johnny also came to know Chicago veteran Hugh Downs well, as the two broadcasters seemingly lived at 30 Rockefeller Plaza during much of the 1950s and 1960s. With a soft-spoken sincere style that was a hallmark of the Second City approach to television, Downs was one of the medium's most durable performers.

At various times, and often simultaneously, Hugh Downs hosted *The Today Show*, was Jack Paar's announcer on the network's late night show, joined Arlene Francis mid-days on *The Home Show*, and hosted the game *Concentration*, all on NBC. It was a schedule that earned Downs the honor of logging more time on television than anyone else in America, over 10,000 hours. Johnny Carson ran second in that race until the Guinness Book of World Records reported that Regis Philbin surpassed them both early in the twenty-first century.

Although the broadcasting industry largely migrated to the two coasts to be closer to advertising agencies in New York and studio and talent pools in Hollywood, much that was learned in the Chicago school assimilated into television's national presentation. The city continues to originate programming, primarily talk shows, most notably *Oprah*, the highest-rated program rooted in the Midwest.

Chicago has also been the setting for a great many fictional series, such as *The Untouchables, The Bob Newhart Show, Family Matters, Good Times, Webster, According to Jim, Life Goes On, Anything But Love, Punky Brewster, Coupling, The Hogan Family, Early Edition, Crime Story, Perfect Strangers, The Steve Harvey Show, Two of a Kind, Still Standing, My Boys, Samantha Who?, Special Unit 2, ER* (both the drama and the sitcom that shared that name), as well as *Chicago Hope, Chicago Sons, Chicago Story, and The Loop*.

CHAPTER 18
HIS MASTER'S VOICE

In 1950, President Truman announced the development of the hydrogen bomb, Shirley Temple retired from show business, Zenith sold the first television remote control called "Lazy Bones," the comic strip Peanuts debuted, and Diners Club, the first credit card, was first used. Television was so new that anyone with more than a couple of years in front of a camera was considered a seasoned veteran.

Those aspiring to careers in any business seek guidance from the professionals already established in the field. In 1950, Johnny was asked to provide advice for newcomers hoping to build a future in the burgeoning and exciting new sphere of show business. He continued to be generous with his knowledge and recommendations. Years later, I asked if he could provide any information that I could share with my fellow college students majoring in communications and broadcasting. Johnny gave me a copy of his previous essay with permission to copy and share it as I saw fit. His writings about the makings of a television commercial announcer in the early days of the new medium offer tremendous insight into his mindset and technique, as well as paint a vivid picture of the state of the art:

"Naturally, it's important that you first have some background of show business...before trying to crash the big-time centers of New York, Hollywood, or Chicago, however, spend at least a year in local TV stations in your area. The key cities mentioned are overcrowded with young men who have come to the big towns completely unprepared, and after months of no work at all, wind up doing restaurant work or one of a dozen different kinds of odd jobs and really never get the chance to make the big-time.

"I know from experience that it's rather disappointing to stay in a small city and work at the local TV station, when all the time your heart is clamoring for you to get to the top. But take it easy — don't rush into these things. You must have the experience and background before you'll get those opportunities and they come only after years of bitter disappointments and slow but steady building of contacts, plus keeping your voice and your acting ability in tip-top shape.

"Just look at the leading TV announcers of today. They may look young but, believe me, all are along in years. You have got to be, before you can command the respect and authority needed to sell successfully a sponsor's product. Every top announcer on TV today, gained his experience in selling in a small radio station and, when TV came along, those who were far-sighted enough, got into it at the early stages and developed along with the new medium. Many of the announcers from radio were unable to make the change-over to TV in spite of their elegant-sounding voices because of the illusion their voices created. Seeing them in person disturbed that illusion; appearance didn't fit the voice.

"So then, don't think of being a top TV announcer over night. By the same token, I don't mean that you must wait until you get to the 'Serutan age.' Start in right now, whatever your age, and you'll develop as all good things do, with age. That's why it's necessary to gain whatever experience you can in your local stations before hitting New York. The following paragraphs will be devoted to some suggestions I hope may steer you in the right direction.

"Start by learning the functions of the cameras, the difference between close-ups and medium shots, which are those most commonly used on the announcer. Learn the confinement of working area. This is very important, since in most cases, you must do all of your action within a space of four or five feet. Learn to walk gracefully in a rhythmic motion. Learn the best position in which to hold the sponsor's product when the director indicates a close-up view; move it gracefully so as not to cause a blur on the screen.

"The next thing I'd like to discuss is the copy. Now, if you've had radio experience you, of course, didn't have to learn the copy...maybe you learned copy points, if you delivered your commercials in an ad-lib manner. But regardless, since the timing is such an important factor in TV, it is absolutely necessary that you either know the copy thoroughly or are so familiar with it that you can breeze right through it, ad lib. If the copy indicates that you demonstrate a product, acquaint yourself with it before you go into the studio, so that you don't appear clumsy. Be sold on the product yourself, and you'll have no trouble selling it to the viewer.

"Remember, unlike radio, in TV, the viewer can both watch and listen to you, so it's necessary that you sell him in both mediums...sight and sound. He may like your mannerisms, but not your voice...or he may be entranced by the sound of your voice, but some little gesture done in a wrong manner will be enough to turn him away, and you couldn't sell him in a million years.

"Whatever you do, be familiar with the copy; try it out on yourself or your friends, do a 'walk-through' before you get into the studio, for studio rehearsal time is costly and in many cases, in the smaller stations, you get no rehearsal time on camera... your commercials are done cold...so you must be prepared. Remember, when you're doing the commercial, you're the star of the show. A philosophy I learned many years ago which still holds true is this. The only difference between a successful show and one not successful is a sponsor. On many of the top TV shows, the commercials get more rehearsal and better scenery sets and treatment than the content of the show, so be confident that your job is an important one.

"The next thing I'd like to discuss concerns your 'personality.' Now we all feel we have a certain something known as personality...something which gives us a bit more S.A. (sales appeal) than the next guy. And in many cases it's true. We have certain mannerisms that constitute our own personality. But right here, let me say, please don't try to copy any of the top TV announcers' mannerisms or voices. Learn by watching, yes, and study their movements but remember, each one has worked

The 1950s began strong for Johnny. Celebrating his silver anniversary in broadcasting, he was riding the crest of television's explosive popularity.

hard over many years to create and display his most attractive features. He has specialized in this 'creation'. It just can't be copied, and what he does well, you might do horribly. Let your own personal charms bubble forth…try to have an effervescent air about you…be enthusiastic…but be yourself above all else.

"Continuing with personality mannerisms, I know that each of you has a particular way of selling yourself…you do it every day when you shave. Talk to yourself occasionally…study your facial expressions. And just remember that, on camera you can exaggerate expressions a trifle more than what you would ordinarily do — then they'll come out just right on the screen. If you wink 'cutely', do it occasionally, but not to the point where it becomes negative. If it's an extra special charm-smile you have, use it but not to a point of over-doing, for it's just as easy, if not easier, for the audience to take a dislike to your personality because of some little thing which you have forgotten to underplay a bit.

"Be careful in your dress. Wear the proper clothes…and be careful of the accessories. Wear blue shirts, ties with some figure or design in them…neatly pressed suits. And look at your hands often…have your nails cleaned, for a camera close-up shows everything. Have your hair neatly combed, in a natural position, and don't look like a 'pretty boy.'

"There's also a matter of reading your commercial copy from a cue card held along side the camera. Now, in many cases on local stations, you'll be doing so many commercials you can't learn them all in a year…so the next best thing is a cue card. Many times the announcer prefers the copy written out completely. I, personally, just outline the basic points on it, so that my eyes don't focus continually on a card two feet from the lens of the camera. Also, I've learned from experience, that it's rather difficult to depend on someone to hold the card properly — first thing you know, you're at the end of the card, ready for the next one and the guy holding them engrossed in something else, and leaves you hangin' dry.

"I've seen more announcers lose their hair (and their options) by not being able to ad lib their way along when such a tragic incident occurs. But it does happen every day and one of the best ways to avoid it is to learn basic points, or to have an outline, so that you can get most of it on one card and don't have to depend on someone turning it for you. I'll never forget what went on in my mind the night a floor man picked up the wrong card for me, and while I was seeing an entirely different commercial in front of the camera. I had to ad lib through the one he was supposed to have held up. Talk about the power of concentration…radio was never like that.

"Another point in the concentration department: be not distracted by the many camera men, crew men, stage hands or the goings-on that are bound to occur in the average studio. The people on the outside can't see what's happening behind the camera, and don't let them know that you're aware of anything going on. I've done commercials with guys trying to break me up…I've had 'em sweep the floor, all around me…do all kinds of charades…funny faces, and a million and one other distractions. When they've taken medium close-ups of me doing a commercial, I've even had one crew man crawl on the floor, roll up my pants leg, light a match and move it against the hairy calf of my leg, just to try to throw me off equilibrium.

Success agreed with the Olsons. In New York with a new car, a new fur coat, and a new pet.

"It's necessary to have some equalizer in your sub-conscious mind to offset these distractions and keep you doing what you've set out to do. As an announcer many years ago in radio, I used to break-up at the slightest movement in the studio and eventually became known as the 'laughing boy' commercial announcer. It got so bad I could hardly get through an announcement without laughing. I was completely cured one day, when I happened into a hospital, ran into my doctor who was doing a post-mortem. He invited me to look for a moment. I did – result, a sobering experience which, when brought to mind, dampens my hilarity immediately. Now I can laugh at will, or stop at will. I don't recommend post-mortems to everyone getting into TV but I do suggest that it is necessary to have some sobering thought to offset distraction. As the Boy Scouts believe, in this business as well as theirs, it pays to 'be prepared.'

"If you do give your commercials from cue cards, learn to read without 'staring.' Take your eyes off the card even though it's right next to the lens, for you can't fool the audience…they can tell when you're looking them squarely in the eye. And what's more important in selling than looking the customer in the eye and telling him your product is the best?

"Speaking of reading from cards, they used to hold them above the camera so in reality you'd be looking above the lens. I was visiting a friend, a fellow announcer, and as we sat at dinner with his wife and three children, he became a bit annoyed and embarrassed by some of the things they said and did at dinner. Whenever I'd glance at him for a reaction, his eyes were always up in the air. After one of his children's remarks he looked up again, only to have his youngster blurt out, 'Daddy, you're reading from the cards again.' Thereafter, the cards were held on the side of the lens instead of above the camera, and written only on a 12 inch-wide card, so the home-viewer couldn't detect any typewriter carriage movement of the eyes.

"In summation, it's rather hard to say to you fellows who are bent on being TV announcers that you should be 'natural' or 'be yourself'…it's hard to say it to you because no one can actually tell you these things. We can only point out some of the short cuts…and through our mistakes, perhaps lessen yours…help you to get off to a good start. We pioneers spent hours doing many wrong things, but only through experience and hard work, were we able to continue building this great new medium. It's a fascinating career, and if you follow the rules of decency and good taste in your mannerisms, you'll be the best doggone commercial TV announcer there is. Good luck, and remember…don't get caught with your cue cards down."

CHAPTER 19
TURN ON, TUNE IN

One hundred years after the nation was first criss-crossed with copper and galvanized iron for telegraph communication, AT&T was burying the coaxial cable needed to extend video service beyond Chicago. In 1950, coast-to-coast live television was still not a reality, but the medium was approaching profitability and its future seemed assured. The Olsons felt confident that Johnny was establishing a bankable reputation within the new industry, while continuing to reap the rewards of his years in radio. With the couple enjoying a sense of security in the otherwise insecure business of broadcasting, Johnny and Penny soon moved from their small apartment in Forest Hills. Encouraged by the growing confidence that came with his achievements, the couple settled in for the long haul in New York and adopted three dogs, Lena, Sheba, and Gretel.

In May of 1951, ABC President Robert Kintner and ABC Vice President Joseph McDonald were among the dignitaries and performers gathered to celebrate Johnny's twenty-five years in show business. Actor Robert Alda, band leader Freddie Martin, and a dozen other entertainers were in attendance to hear recordings from Johnny's career and to roast the host. On that occasion, Johnny was inducted into the Radio Pioneers Club, and he received an award from The International Association of Fairs and Expositions. That organization's president, J. S. Dorton, cited Johnny for "doing more than any other single performer for America's great country fairs." [19-1] It was estimated that the celebrant had hosted 75,000 radio programs during his first twenty-five years.

During his 1951 transition from radio to television, Johnny and Penny were in the final months of their lengthy run of *Johnny Olsen's Rumpus Room*, which was seen weekday afternoons on DuMont. The Olsons always held a soft spot in their hearts for that show, as they had worked together on *Rumpus Room* through their years in Milwaukee, Los Angeles and New York radio, before it pioneered in daytime network television. Johnny's popularity on the program garnered a feature story in the New York edition of the May 5, 1951 *TV Guide*.

Simultaneously on ABC radio, *Johnny Olsen's Luncheon Club* continued its run sponsored by Phillip Morris, although its new 3:30 p.m. time period might be considered more appropriate for tea than for lunch. Broadcast from the old Blue Network's studios at NBC's headquarters at Rockefeller Center, the *Luncheon Club* was another Monday through Friday interview and audience participation radio show presented with Johnny's usual air of informality. Promoted with the phrase, "Where you meet America's most interesting people," *Johnny Olsen's Luncheon Club* was described in promotional materials as "friendly humor, music, audience participation, and a serious note when the occasion demands for worthwhile civic and charity projects."

Johnny was in good company during the week of November 16, 1951. Frank Sinatra, Milton Berle, and Johnny were the subjects of articles in that week's national pages of *TV Guide*. Johnny had just started another new show — a kids' program that he co-hosted for a time with Ham Fisher, the creator of the *Joe Palooka* comic strip. At other times, Johnny co-hosted the show with a large mechanical puppet goose.

Red Goose Shoes sponsored *Kids and Company*, a Saturday morning children's program that ran from September 1, 1951, through June 1, 1952, on DuMont television. Johnny was at his most sincere awarding "Kid of the Week" plaques to children who had exhibited citizenship in their communities. He was at his enthusiastic and effervescent best awarding watches, footwear, and defense bonds to precocious singing, dancing, and baton-twirling children, and occasionally, their stage-struck mothers.

Ladies Be Seated was Johnny's most successful network radio program. In studio, at remote broadcasts, and at stops along extensive promotional tours the host was always regaled in a memorable minstrel costume. For one magazine feature article he posed with a prototype Johnny Olson action figure.

Honors were given to kids who had overcome handicaps, were battling diseases, or exhibited courage in other ways. Among those recognized was a boy who grabbed the steering wheel when his school bus driver fainted. Among the talented prodigies to win a pair of Red Goose Shoes and a Bulova watch for singing prowess was a

young Leslie Uggams making her television debut with Johnny. In 1956, ABC-TV revived the *Kids and Company* format at the behest of Red Goose's advertising agency, D'Arcy MacManus Masius. Johnny was reunited with the big waterfowl for three, ninety-minute *Red Goose Kiddie Spectaculars.* Assuming that what was good for the caged ganders would be good for the red goose, the first of the specials was broadcast from the St. Louis Zoo.

Johnny became one of the era's most versatile television emcees, hosting *Kids and Company* for children, as well as variety, interview, quiz, and game shows for their parents.

In 1952, Johnny also fronted two television shows for the local New York audience on two competing stations, WJZ-TV's daily *Homemakers' Jamboree,* and the weekly *TV Auction Club* for WOR-TV. On *Homemakers' Jamboree,* Johnny included patriotic segments celebrating members of the armed forces, and he made appeals for charitable causes, as he had on most of his programs in the era of World War II and the Korean conflict. On *TV Auction Club*, viewers bid for merchandise that Johnny presented to the home audience. Items had to be paid for with "TV Auction Bucks" which were awarded free with purchases at participating retailers. The *Auction Club* debuted at 7:30 p.m. on Wednesday, April 9, and ran for thirteen weeks. The program is credited to Charles King Productions, and is believed to be an early creation from the Charles King who was patriarch of the family that later operated under the banner of King World Productions.

As a host, Johnny possessed the talent that made for success among the first generation of television personalities. Rather than excelling as a singer, dancer, comedian, actor, or juggler, the qualities most important for the new visual medium were proving to be warmth and likeability. Johnny recognized that while television was a mass medium, it was consumed singly, individually, and personally. His presentation was motivated by the realization, perhaps learned in the Chicago school, that television viewers were not part of any mass assemblage when watching at home. The ability to create a sincere rapport with the members of the audience proved to be the elusive ingredient for a long career as a guest in viewers' living rooms. Prolific game show producer Mark Goodson's adjectives: "comforting and trustworthy."[19-2]

In 1948, Milton Berle burst onto television, and within two months, amassed an audience of 86.7% of all television households. By 1951, he had ascended to the throne as "Mr. Television," when NBC signed him to a thirty-year exclusive contract. His explosive popularity was nothing less than a national phenomenon. Within a couple of seasons, Texaco pulled its advertising, and three years later, Buick's sponsorship hit the road. By 1956, Berle's broadcasting career had run out of gas. He had been television's greatest superstar, but by 1960, Uncle Miltie was hosting *Jackpot Bowling*. To add insult to injury, the show was pink-slipped after only six months.

It was becoming apparent that because of television's intimate nature, the audience would invite an affable, humble, friendly, likeable, familiar, non-polarizing personality into their home with open arms for a longer stay than a funny, loud comic or, in most cases, even the most soothing singer. Although his contributions to the new medium were immense, The Museum of Broadcast Communications credited Uncle Miltie as "the first TV personality to suffer from over-exposure and burnout."[19-3]

In 1948, CBS hired Ed Sullivan to stake a claim to Sunday evenings, traditionally an anchor night for broadcasting. If there was ever a television host with limited appeal as an entertainer in his own right, it was that newspaper columnist turned television icon. Columnist Harriet Van Horne said of Sullivan, "He is the commonest common denominator." Pat Weaver, NBC's visionary programming executive, observed, "He doesn't do anything on a stage. He's not a performer. Ed just knows the trick of putting together a variety show and it's a good staple. We were after him to switch to NBC, and twice I thought we had him."[19-4]

Indeed, as a streetwise New Yorker born in Harlem, Sullivan had a great sense of the public's taste and felt the early groundswell of trends. He was a shrewd, business-savvy producer, and leveraged positive press in his column to help book the television program. With a mere $475 talent budget for the June 20 debut of *Toast of the Town*, Sullivan managed to present eight acts, including headliners Dean Martin and Jerry Lewis in their television debut. In 1951, with three years of success behind him, America's favorite Sunday night host was quoted in the October 12 *TV Guide* crowing, "I was in on the ground floor of radio and dropped out of it like a big dope. Now I'm in on the ground floor of TV and I'm not giving up my lease until the landlord evicts me." The program's title was changed to *The Ed Sullivan Show* for the 1955 season, and it continued as a tentpole program for CBS. While Sullivan was often awkward in his presentations, he conveyed the friendly, honest sincerity that helped to cement his program as must-see television for twenty-three years.

Similarly, Arthur Godfrey, the popular broadcaster who likely logged the most on-air hours during the 1950s, reached stardom in the electronic media that would have been unattainable for him in any other branch of show business. Godfrey's voice was seemingly ubiquitous on the American airwaves, broadcasting sixteen hours a week with ratings for three of his shows among the weekly Top 10. In 1949, *Time* magazine aroused the ire of the ukulele-strummer with the observation, "The thing that makes Arthur Godfrey remarkable as a hit entertainer is his relative lack of a definable talent. He can neither sing, dance, act, nor perform with skill on a musical instrument. Yet today he is the top moneymaker and the outstanding personality on the air."[19-5]

Godfrey's seemingly natural, informal style was in evidence in 1948, when his long-running radio show, *We The People,* joined Johnny's *Ladies Be Seated* as one of the first programs to be simultaneously broadcast on both radio and television. In his book, *Arthur Godfrey: The Adventures of an American Broadcaster,* Arthur J. Singer quoted Godfrey starting his first simulcast saying, "This morning, we've got lights all around this place…and they're driving us crazy. They said, 'We'll come in, Arthur, and you won't even know we're there.' (He makes a face, thumbs his nose at the camera. The audience laughs. Then he addresses the radio audience.) For a penny postcard I'll explain that laugh to you folks."[19-6]

Still in his ascent as a star, *Variety* reported in 1950 that "The Old Redhead" was responsible for one-sixth of the Columbia Broadcasting System's total revenues. Bob Hope quipped that CBS was a subsidiary of Arthur Godfrey. With so many on-air hours each week, the broadcaster admitted that he almost missed one scheduled guest appearance. Stretched out on a Sunday night in front of the television, Godfrey heard the CBS staff announcer invite viewers to "stay tuned for *What's My Line?*" Having forgotten that he was that night's mystery guest, Godfrey jumped-up, dressed, and made it to the studio just in time to make his entrance.

Johnny was among the many broadcasters who studied Arthur Godfrey's off-hand, effortless presentation and its understated yet powerful attraction that drew viewers into his world. What Godfrey had was the newly-discovered nexus of attributes that made for an emotional connection with those who viewed the television tube. There was a new aura of intimacy that Godfrey fed with seeming sincerity, warmth, emotional vulnerability, and personal engagement. Arthur Godfrey's own observation of the phenomenon was summarized with a simple, "It's because people believe in me." Of his employers, Godfrey cynically surveyed, "They don't care what you say on the air as long as it sells." [19-5]

And sell, it did. Godfrey owned a vast estate in the Virginia horse country, maintained a huge duplex apartment in Manhattan, and piloted between the two in his own airplanes. With his chauffer-driven Rolls Royce that he preferred to drive himself with the chauffer relegated to the back seat, Godfrey lived a lifestyle that belied his folksy, common-man image.

In October 1953, Americans got a view of another side of the friend they had been welcoming into their living rooms. Godfrey's notorious behind-the-scenes arrogance was broadcast coast-to-coast, when he fired the increasingly popular singer,

Julius La Rosa, from his radio and television family. At the conclusion of a song, Godfrey stunned both the crooner and the audience by saying, "That was Julie's swan song with us."

Legend holds that La Rosa had angered his benefactor when he missed a Godfrey-mandated dance lesson due to a family emergency. Although the singer claimed he had advised Godfrey, when he arrived for work the following morning, he found a notice on a cast bulletin board indicating that he was barred from the show for a day as punishment. Feeing powerless, La Rosa signed with a talent agent to help buffer his relationship with Godfrey, as well as to expand his career opportunities. The move challenged Godfrey's autonomy, and the adored host told his audience that the singer was fired because he "lacked humility."

Tom Kennedy, the host of more than a dozen network television game shows whom Johnny worked with decades later, remembered, "When I started in broadcasting, one of the people I idolized was Arthur Godfrey…I loved everything he did." Thirty years later, Kennedy still cringed at the memory of LaRosa's legendary on-air firing and how it destroyed his reverence for Godfrey. "Oh my god, that was horrific. So unprofessional, and my opinion of him came tumbling down" [19-7]

Although Godfrey discovered La Rosa while the singer was serving in the Navy and been responsible for his initial popularity, America had already embraced La Rosa. In the wake of the incident, the public's adoration of Godfrey eroded. Within two years, his programs fell from television's Top 10 and the broadcaster's iconic status forever faded. Yet Godfrey's momentum carried him for years; the once honored and admired broadcaster lingered on the airwaves for another two decades in several futile attempts to recapture America's admiration. One 1963 outing featured Johnny.

While Godfrey was less emotionally intimate than some, many of the intangible attributes of his successful on-air persona turned out to be the secret ingredients in the success of other members of the first generation of television personalities, such as Art Linkletter, Hugh Downs, Ralph Edwards, and his discovery, Bob Barker. In Barker's words, "I don't sing, I don't dance, I don't act, I don't tell jokes, and I'm not about to start now…because I'm a star…My job is to make other people funny." [19-8] In his autobiography, *On Camera*, Downs confessed, "'I never quite fitted the stereotype of pitchman or announcer. Nor was I a comic, an emcee, or an entertainer or newscaster. Having no discernable talent in any performance category, I never fell comfortably into any particular niche."

Dick Clark's talent as a broadcaster and producer was immense, and his contributions as a midwife in the birth of a new form of popular music are legendary. Nevertheless, Dick Clark admitted that he was no singer or dancer, and he was only minimally impressive as an actor, as the 1966 final episode of CBS' *Perry Mason* series, "The Case of the Final Fadeout," proved.

Jack Paar, another extremely successful personality, could not dance, act, nor carry a tune if it were packed in a piece of Samsonite luggage, but he served up his great gift of wit with generous portions of heartfelt sincerity, emotional vulnerability, and a few tears. Paar said of his popularity, "It's almost impossible to dislike me because I do nothing." [19-9]

Those intelligent and gifted broadcasters developed an emotional rapport with audiences, despite the impersonal electronics that could have otherwise distanced them. Their legacies continue with media mainstays such as Regis Philbin and Ryan Seacrest. They all seem to have a stopwatch in their heads, and they possess an objective view of their on-camera presentation, as well as an innate sense of America's tastes. Their greatest talents as broadcasters are a familiar, friendly presence that simply makes their studio guests and home audiences feel comfortable.

Johnny's on-air persona was never as informal as Godfrey's, nor as emotionally intimate as Paar's, but he generously shared his gifts for warmth, compassion, and sincerity. After the initial challenge of minimizing the inhibiting effect that the omnipresent lights, cameras, cables, and stagehands imposed on his guests, Johnny perceived his role as television master of ceremonies to be similar to that of an adept host at a cocktail party. He contributed to the occasions by assuring a smooth intermingling, without intruding unnecessarily when the interplay was entertaining. The gracious, endearing host was capable of smoothing over any awkward moments, and he helped maintain the necessary and sometimes delicate equilibrium that kept events pleasant for all.

Then and now, skilled television hosts seem to effortlessly keep proceedings relaxed. They minimize the chances for any volatility due to a guest's lack of social graces. They enthusiastically greet guests upon arrival, and then briefly chat engagingly, sincerely, with lightness and humor. They help guests feel at ease in the potentially uncomfortable milieu, and they always offer a smile and a handshake when each guest departs.

Johnny had a natural affinity for people. His glib, friendly manner and his ability to soothe the jittery nerves of mike-frightened guests, young and old, continued to add to his reputation as a personable and reliable broadcast professional. His ad-lib skills were considered especially suited to working in the occasionally unpredictable audience participation genre.

It was a learned art. Johnny described the very first time he was required to ad-lib as "terrifying." The tale of terror involved Rudolph, Pratt, and Sherman, a trio of entertainers billed as "The Doctors." They joined Johnny in the tiny WIBA studio to perform their musical comedy act at the piano. Johnny vividly remembered that the mischievous mirth-makers called him over to the piano, and then one by one, they each walked out of the studio. Johnny said, "This was all live and I was alone with three minutes to fill. It scared the bejeezus out of me. Now what was I gonna do? So I started talking about the piano. 'The piano has three legs and eighty-eight keys....' I describe the piano, and then I start talking about the walls in the studio!"

Another war story of ad-libbing evoked more laughter than terror. Back in Milwaukee, Johnny was responsible for a WTMJ man-on-the-street broadcast outside of the Shraeder Hotel. One winter night, when the temperature dropped to 20 degrees below zero and few potential participants were anywhere in sight, Johnny said he simply filled the time doing different voices, repeatedly interviewing himself.

The lessons learned from all of the earlier escapades served to embolden the entertainer, and his speculative 1943 move to New York was a risk that had proved fortuitous. The Big Apple was broadcasting's hub, but the eyes of Hollywood soon focused vexingly on Manhattan, as television's growing popularity began to impact box office receipts. Filmed entertainment was one of the United States' top five money-making industries. In Hollywood's heyday, the major motion picture studios each churned out fifty-two features a year, and as many as 90 million Americans went to movie theaters each week. When it became apparent that television could change that habit and seriously erode ticket sales, the motion picture industry all but declared war on television.

Of the three fronts that were simultaneously attacking the movie studios' profitable status quo, television was the least able to defend itself and was the recipient of Paramount, Warner, Fox, Universal, Columbia, and the MGM lion's share of the return fire. Starting in October 1947, studio autocrats gave testimony before a Congressional committee concerning supposed un-American sentiment that was leaking into their product. One of the first waves of the Communist witch hunt broke on the motion picture industry, taking down stars, directors, and writers in a backwash of negative publicity.

The second insult also came from the nation's capitol. In May 1948, the Supreme Court decreed that studios must divest their nationwide chains of theaters. Block-booking contracts with independent exhibitors were outlawed. They were forced to submit to an open market model for product distribution, which brought an end to their anti-competitive exhibition monopolies.

The power to guarantee each film's access to theater screens and unilaterally schedule, advertise, and promote strategic release dates had allowed each of the major studios to generate a predictable cash flow and virtually guarantee a movie's success. In the words of Edward Dmytryk, an Academy award-nominated and controversial film director, it ended "the business that ensured a picture's profit, and incidentally, gave the filmmaker the means to make further works of art and enjoy a good living."[19-10]

The film studios continued to embrace radio, even while battling their perceived competitor, television. In 1948, Metro Goldwyn Mayer signed on an early FM station in Los Angeles, KMGM. Television was the enemy that had slowly snuck up in full view, but the studios had dismissed television as harmless until its numbers multiplied from several thousand to millions in only a few short years. Suddenly, with over three million television sets in use in 1949, television's impact was felt at the box office.

Hollywood studio moguls refused to produce content for the new entertainment medium and forbade their contract stars from appearing on the small screen. Additionally, they turned down healthy license fees for the use of their stockpiles of old product, withholding all but their least appealing films for exhibition on television. A few of the struggling, small studios swallowed their pride and sold second-rate programming to television, much of it re-edited versions of old films and theatrical serials. Republic, Monogram, and RKO under Howard Hughes'ownership were among the first, introducing viewers to the likes of Hopalong Cassidy, Hoot Gibson, and Charlie Chan.

Along came independent film producers, cranking low-budget action footage to provide content for independent stations, as well as to allow affiliates to keep the screens flickering outside of the few hours each evening when the networks fed their fare. Pat Buttram, Gene Autry's sidekick, remembered the singing cowboy shooting two films simultaneously to get more bang for the buck: "A heavy in one would be the sheriff in another...I was always Pat Buttram and he was always Gene Autry because we were doin' two at once, and he couldn't remember what name I had in what picture." [19-11]

Former radio syndicator Frederick Ziv had salesmen on the road across the country finding sponsors for his new television shows, *The Cisco Kid, Highway Patrol,* and *Sea Hunt.* They then brought the series pre-sold to local stations to ensure airtime. Ziv was successful by filming shows in as little as two days on production budgets as low as $20,000 an episode. By 1955, the television syndication business was grossing $150 million a year, and attendance at movie theaters was off by as much as 40 percent in the cities with multiple television stations. Despite the increasingly profitable business of providing programming, the major studios still remained reticent to team with television.

It took a mouse to prove that the lion could peacefully lie down with the lamb. Walt Disney believed in a cooperative future between TV and the film studios as early as 1936 when he affiliated his independent animation factory with RKO Radio Pictures. The deal with the studio partially owned by David Sarnoff's RCA was to distribute the cartoon producer's shorts and at least one feature a year. The March 3 issue of *Variety* heralded, "Radio Captures Disney." Mickey Mouse's creator told the press, "I'm looking to the future, and that includes television."

In 1953, Walt Disney was in need of capital to build Disneyland, his dream theme park. Following a merger with Paramount Pictures' former theater subsidiary, the third-rated ABC network was under the management of Leonard Goldenson, a man from the world of movies and theaters — a Hollywood insider — and the man who negotiated the first big television deal for first-run filmed entertainment. For $500,000 Disney would produce twenty one-hour episodes and relinquish a 35% ownership interest in the planned theme park. From its October 27, 1954 debut, ABC's *Disneyland* was a smash hit.

Emboldened by that success, ABC's Goldenson next broke the major Hollywood studios' embargo with Jack Warner. Cursed as a tyrant by some, Warner helped guide his family's empire in the early 1920s from also-ran status on the power of an unlikely actor, a German shepherd named Rin Tin Tin. Their gamble on the appeal of talking pictures took the studio the rest of the way from the dog house. *Fortune* magazine wrote of the Warner siblings' rise from a $16,000,000 operation in 1928: "Within two years, they were to be a $230,000,000 corporation. There has never been anything quite like that, even in the movie industry." [19-12]

In 1955, Warner Bros. followed Disney's foray into film for television with the debut of *Warner Bros. Presents,* an anthology series based on three of the studio's films, *Casablanca, King's Row,* and *Cheyenne.* At $3 million for thirty-nine one-hour episodes, the programming was fairly priced, but Jack Warner sweetened the deal for his studio by negotiating for each of the programs to include ten minutes of behind-the-scenes features that promoted the studio's new releases. In later deals for new programs, Warner's self-aggrandizing segments were reduced to five minutes, and were subsequently eliminated.

MGM followed, and by the mid-1950s, Columbia, Universal, and 20th Century Fox were producing television series. Initially, much of it was under the banner of subsidiaries, such as Screen Gems, Revue, and TCF that disguised the courtship between the once uneasy partners — partners who would later marry to form the multi-national entertainment conglomerates that today own both the studios and the networks.

With the influx of filmed dramatic programming, the look of television changed forever. Private eye yarns, police dramas, adventure shows, and especially westerns found berths on network prime-time schedules and shifted lower-budget fare to daytime and to the independent, local stations. According to *Broadcasting Yearbook*, in the nine years between 1952 and 1961, live programming was trimmed from 82 percent to 27 percent of network television time. The more economical audience participation shows that were Johnny's specialty were then largely out of fashion and programmed primarily in daytime and on lower-rated outlets. It was a sea change that limited his future opportunities.

That was just one of two major transformations that impacted Johnny's television career. Forced to adapt or retreat, he made both transitions with grace. Although serious about his work, Johnny never took himself too seriously. His sense of humor was in evidence in 1961, when he appeared as himself in an unusual motion picture, *The Sin of Mona Kent*. Johnny had top-billing in the low-budget feature, the final film from producer-director Charles J. Hundt, whose biggest credit was as a crew-member on *Singing In The Rain*.

TV Guide reviewed the motion picture as a "Citizen Kane-style film" tracing the career of a New York celebrity. It was a dizzying seventy-five-minute saga of young Elvira Kowalski arriving in the Big Apple after winning a phony beauty contest, and the story followed the trials and tribulations of her rise to stardom. Turner Classic Movies synopsized the plot: "New York City radio and television interviewer Johnny Olsen tracks down the true story of Mona Kent, a glamorous Broadway star, by contacting people who knew her before she achieved success."

In *The Sin of Mona Kent*, the protagonist takes a job as a hatcheck girl and meets an older gossip columnist, who changes her name from the ethnic Elvira Kowalski to Mona Kent. At a party, she takes a swim in his pool dressed only in her lingerie, which attracts attention that gets her parts in summer stock. A subsequent skinny-dip is captured by a photographer, who sells nude portraits of her. She turns down a marriage proposal from the photographer, dumps the pictures, and marries the older gossip columnist with the promise that he will make her a star.

The Mona Kent character was not a random fabrication. The real Mona Kent was a prolific radio and television scriptwriter, who contributed to the radio soap opera, *Portia Faces Life*, a show produced briefly by Mark Goodson. The real Mona Kent was also at DuMont during Johnny's tenure at the network. She was writing for the science fiction hit, *Captain Video & His Video Rangers,* which ran until 1955, only six years before the release of *The Sin of Mona Kent.*

Actor Victor Ramos Jr., who played the role of a friend helping the fictitious Mona Kent get the hatcheck girl job, went on to work in casting for several notable movies including *Apocalypse Now, My Bodyguard, Dressed To Kill,* and *The Blue Lagoon.* The year after working with Johnny as the Associate Producer of *The Sin of Mona Kent,* Paul Fanning served as Art Director on *The Brain That Would Not Die* — the story of a scientist, who keeps his wife's severed head alive until he can find a new body for her.

Johnny's tongue-in-cheek attitude about his only movie is obvious in a snapshot taken of him smiling under the New York theater marquee where the film was playing.

CHAPTER 20

THE HOST MEETS THE PRODUCERS

With a growing reputation for professionalism and versatility, Johnny was at the right place at the right time to form an important alliance. In late 1947, he was chosen to host a radio pilot called *Time's A-Wastin'*, a show that featured contestants answering questions in a race against the clock. *Time's A-Wastin'* was from the new producing team of Goodson and Todman, and was under consideration by ABC as a Thursday night replacement for the pink-slipped, Dr. Pepper-sponsored *Darts for Dough*.

That chance employment with New York advertising copywriter Bill Todman and former San Francisco radio announcer Mark Goodson would ultimately lead to Johnny's greatest fame, define the second half of his career, and provide his most lucrative employment.

By all essential measures of success, Mark Goodson and Bill Todman became the kings of the game show world, responsible for more hit program formats and more pioneering firsts than any producers in the industry. Among their programming innovations were having two contestants in direct competition, as opposed to one participant playing against a quizmaster. Goodson once called it "the basketball technique," in that two contestants tried to answer the same question at the same time. He said, "It was like throwing a basketball in the air and seeing who can get it first." Continuing the analogy, Goodson spoke of panel shows as "intellectual sporting events." [20-1]

The producing team's *Winner Take All* was the first program to hold a contestant over for subsequent episodes until he was defeated. That concept of the "returning champion" encouraged repeat viewership as audiences would tune in the following day or week to see how a known player would fare in subsequent battles. "Keep playing as long as you keep winning." Todman said, "I wrote that sentence. It's like king of the mountain." [20-2]

Among the technical innovations generally attributed to the producing team was the use of the "lockout", a mechanical and electrical device activated by a player to signal their intent to answer a question, simultaneously locking out his competitors' ability to signal. Quiz shows such as *Uncle Jim's Question Bee* and *Quick As A Flash* had used electric bells and buzzers as early as 1936, but none are believed to have had the added circuitry that prevented an opponent's participation. Among Goodson-Todman's business innovations was the extensive licensing of their games in foreign markets, a practice that generated countless millions of dollars for the partners long before other countries were viewed as parts of a global media marketplace. By 1956, after five years of success in the United States, *What's My Line?* was on the air in nine foreign countries.

Other than an appreciation for games, the two founding partners of that television empire seemingly shared little common ground. Mark Goodson was born in Sacramento, California, to a working-class, Jewish family. The son of a Russian-born masseur, who owned a chicken ranch, and later, a health food store, Goodson paid his way through college with a job at the Lincoln Fish Market near Berkeley.

Wilbur (Bill) Todman was three and one-half years older than Mark Goodson. He was born to a privileged New York family, the son of the owner of Frederick S. Todman and Company, a major Wall Street auditing firm. While Bill Todman mingled easily in society, Mark Goodson was described as "a very complex man," who was often ill-at-ease in social settings. [20-3]

Goodson first worked in broadcasting at his college radio station. Despite graduating Phi Beta Kappa from Berkeley, he chose to pursue a career behind the microphone. It began with a $30-a-week job as a staff announcer at San Francisco's KFRC, the same station where Merv Griffin enjoyed early success as a vocalist.

Three thousand miles away, Todman found his way into broadcasting as a copywriter with a small ad agency located in the CBS building. He reflected, "I was making very tiny money, so I ate in the cafeteria where the radio people hung out and got a job to freelance a couple of scripts." Behind the control room glass, Todman became a writer and producer at WABC, then the call letters of the CBS-owned station in New York. He was also a guiding force behind *The Connie Boswell Show*, a solo effort by one of the singing sisters cited as inspirations by Ella Fitzgerald and The Andrews Sisters.

In 1941, Goodson arrived in New York with encouragement from Ralph Edwards, a fellow Berkeley alumnus and KFRC mike-mate. Edwards had traveled east with aspirations for a career on Broadway, but found success as a CBS announcer and program creator. When Goodson arrived in New York, Edwards was the voice of *Major Bowes and the Original Amateur Hour*, and just one year earlier, at the age of twenty-six, he had created and sold *Truth or Consequences*.

Edwards lent a hand making introductions, and Mark Goodson soon found work briefly hosting the Mutual network's *Quiz of Two Cities*. It was a simple question and answer game that simultaneously challenged two contestants from different cities to answer general knowledge questions for their town's bragging rights and a prize. The experience was notable because it teamed Goodson with producer Dan Enright, who later rose to fame and infamy as Jack Barry's partner in game shows implicated in the quiz show scandals of the late 1950s.

Mark Goodson and Bill Todman crossed paths a number of times during those years when they were both freelancing in New York radio. They worked together as early as 1941 on a local show that Goodson announced, *The Battle of the Boroughs*. They later teamed on programs produced by the United States Treasury Department to help promote the sale of war bonds, but they were unsuccessful in selling their own concepts.

Mark Goodson had already tried his hand with game shows, having created and hosted a simple radio quiz at KFRC in 1939. *Pop the Question* was broadcast from the basement of a San Francisco newsreel theater. Of that early effort, the producer explained, "You threw darts at red, white, and blue balloons. The balloons were worth different amounts of money, and if you burst one, you got that much if you answered a question correctly."[20-4]

Goodson's hopes for a career as a performer were dashed by a serious and lingering case of "mike fright." In a moment of public introspection, Goodson said, "I'm a perfectionist who, above all, hates to be exposed in public. I am more terrified of failure than anxious for success."[20-4] The producer confessed that, as an introvert with extremely high standards for himself, he was not the easiest guy to live with. Observing that he retreated from social challenges, Goodson said his fears and self-consciousness kept him somewhat isolated and a spectator rather than a participant in activities such as skiing and golf. He shared, "What I do, I do aggressively. I'm a darn good dancer. I play the drums. What I can't do, I retreat from rapidly. I'm never satisfied. My lack of satisfaction is my greatest strength and my greatest weakness."[20-4]

With a constitution not well-suited to performing, Goodson transitioned to work primarily behind the scenes, and he was on staff at two successful shows. He served as one of several directors on the popular daytime drama *Portia Faces Life*, where Mona Kent was a scriptwriter, and he directed ABC radio's *Stop The Music* after acting as a middle-man in bringing the show's concept to producer Louis G. Cowan in 1947. Mark Goodson's wife, Bluma, played a role in garnering the grandiose gifts offered on *Stop The Music*, which included new homes, Hollywood screen tests, and even a two-week uranium prospecting tour.

When *Time's A-Wastin'* debuted on CBS in 1948, Johnny was passed over for the role of host in favor of Bud Collyer. Johnny and Goodson soon met again on the set of *Stop The Music*. Although Hal Simms and Doug Browning were the *Stop The Music* announcers, Johnny subbed on at least one occasion. The show was a breakout hit for the ABC radio network, and expanded to fill an hour of prime time Sunday night air. It proved so popular that comedian Fred Allen tried unsuccessfully to stem the tide of listeners by offering members of his audience a $5,000 bond to anyone who was called by the musical quizzer while listening to his show that aired simultaneously on NBC.

Stop The Music was based on bandleader Harry Salter's practice of challenging audience members to guess the names of songs he played at dances. They were instucted to shout "Stop the music" when they knew the answer. Both the radio and the later television formats of the show included a feature reminiscent of NBC's 1939 *Pot O' Gold* in which listeners at home were called by telephone and given a chance to win a prize by naming the song being played on the air. That contestant

JOHNNY OLSON: A VOICE IN TIME

could then try for cash and glamorous prizes by identifying additional mystery tunes.

On *Stop The Music*, Johnny also renewed his acquaintance with Harry Salter. The two had developed a friendship while working together on another Louis Cowan show, *What's My Name?*, as well as other earlier programs. Salter had pioneered the musical game concept as far back as 1937 with *Melody Puzzles* for NBC's Blue Network. During the years he led the *Stop The Music* radio orchestra, Salter created the similar but even more successful *Name That Tune* for television. Starting in September 1954, when Johnny's schedule permitted, Salter hired him to announce his new television musical game show in the latter seasons of its six-year run.

It was also on ABC's *Stop The Music* that Mark Goodson came to know hosts Bert Parks and Bill Cullen. When the Sunday night radio program sparked a sixty-minute weekly television version, Parks fronted both shows until Cullen ultimately took the radio reigns. Cullen's instincts and ability to instantaneously adapt to virtually any unforeseen circumstance during a live program motivated Goodson to refer to Cullen as an "on-stage producer" and to hire him to front many of his later creations. After Goodson moved on from *Stop The Music*, Johnny remained on producer Louis Cowan's radar; he was called in 1955 to fill-in as announcer on the television version that Bert Parks hosted.

After a difficult start, Bill Todman finally sold his and his partner's next original productions, *Hit the Jackpot*, *Spin to Win*, and *Rate Your Mate*, all to CBS over a two year period. Their first true hit was an innovative radio game show called *Winner Take All*, the idea for which Goodson had brought with him from San Francisco. It initially earned the partners $150 for three fifteen-minute programs per week.

In 1946, *Winner Take All* debuted on CBS radio and was hosted by Bud Collyer and Ward Wilson; Bern Bennett and Bill Cullen were among the announcers. After expanding to a daily afternoon radio feature, the program spun off a weekly half-hour television adaptation in the summer of 1948. There, Collyer, and later, Barry Gray, fronted on-camera while Cullen advanced to host the radio program.

Although Lever Brothers sponsored *Winner Take All* on radio, finding a sponsor for the television version proved challenging. As this was Goodson-Todman's first radio show to transition to television, the on-camera presentation was initially unwieldy. In retrospect, Mark Goodson reflected, "We tried too hard to dramatize, to make the game visual. We had questions about pictures; we paraded models and dogs around the stage. We had yet to learn that what's interesting on television is not appearance but content."[20-5]

After several format revisions, the television program was most successful anchored by Bill Cullen, the twenty-six-year-old Pittsburgh native, who had been the show's announcer and fill-in host on radio. *Winner Take All* was the first on-camera hosting job for the gifted broadcaster, who went on to enjoy a record-setting run as a preeminent television emcee and panelist.

February 25, 1952, was marked by a solar eclipse and the closing ceremonies of the winter Olympics in Norway. It was also the day NBC's staff announcer Don Pardo opened a revamped version of Goodson-Todman's first hit television show with an excited reading delivered over the sounds of the lockout devices. "Sound your buzzer! Sound your bell!" Pardo enthusiastically bellowed. "It's *Winner Take All* with your *Winner Take All* quizmaster, Bill Cullen!"

Goodson and Todman showed creativity in leveraging hit formats. They wasted no time exploiting the early success of their first hit by writing and selling a book to Crown Publishers. "The *Winner Take All* Home Quiz Book" by Bill Todman and Mark Goodson contained, as described on the dust jacket, "Two thousand NEW questions and answers, arranged in 'rounds' as the quiz is played on the air."

Johnny was yet to become Goodson and Todman's voice of choice, but the three would soon become inextricably linked working in game and quiz shows. It is a genre almost as old as broadcasting itself. By most accounts, the trailblazer was *The Pop Question*, a 1924 news quiz sponsored by *Time* magazine. On Saturday night, September 26, 1936, NBC invited America to listen to *Uncle Jim's Question Bee*, the first audience participation program, where participants' general knowledge was challenged for cash awards. The Blue Network's original press release promised that host Jim McWilliams "will call six members of the studio audience to join him before the microphone where he will ask each one, alternately, six questions on a wide variety of subjects. An answer, right or wrong, must be made within ten seconds."[20-6]

CBS' answer to Uncle Jim was Mr. Craig Earl, who billed himself as *Professor Quiz*. His show featured contestants from across the country as the program took to the road to broadcast from movie theaters in cities where the network had local affiliates. The professorial premise proliferated with *Dr. I.Q.*, *Doctor Dollar*, and *Dr. Peter Puzzlewit*. CBS' syllabus included *Crackpot College*, and bandleader Kay Kyser presided over his *Kollege of Musical Knowledge*.

Before long, radio waves cackled with a cacophony of quizzes. By the time Johnny arrived in New York, some eighty network radio games had come and mostly gone. Despite the FCC's attempt to ban the entire genus, arguing that it constituted a form of illegal gambling, the charm of game shows had forever seduced American audiences.

In 1939, the first televised competition outside of the world of sports was "The National Spelling Bee" broadcast on NBC's experimental New York station. There were fewer than a thousand television receivers in the entire country that year. As such, it was unlikely that many people saw *Visiquiz* or *Telewizzers*, the children's version of charades from radio's "Singing Lady" Ireene Wicker that appeared on David Sarnoff's experimental New York operation. Similarly, in Los Angeles during 1939, it was doubtful that many people were watching when Mike Stokey and his fellow students from City College and other local school drama departments played charades on W6XAO, a station that broadcast fewer than two hours most evenings.

From the earliest attempts at adapting games for the new visual medium, the first game shows produced for commercial television were *Uncle Jim's Question Bee* and Ralph Edwards' *Truth or Consequences*. Both were on WNBT (later WRCA and then WNBC), NBC's outlet in New York. They were one-time specials commemorating July 1, 1941, the government-decreed official first day of commercial television in the United States.

Truth or Consequences was not simply a game show; it was one of the longest running and most successful of the audience participation species, notable for a number of historic firsts in both content and production. Featuring stunts, practical jokes, hidden cameras, live remote segments, and surprise reunions, *Truth or Consequences* also brought Bob Barker his first national fame.

The following day, July 2, 1941, *The CBS Television Quiz* debuted on William Paley's network. It aired weekly for more than a year with a combination of stunts and questions-and-answers, and it was credited as being the first regularly scheduled game show. CBS's local New York station entered the fray a few weeks later with *Play the Game*, another early version of charades performed by in-studio guests with viewers calling in by telephone with guesses about what was being acted out. The host of *Play the Game* was Dr. Harvey Zorbaugh, a Professor of Education at New York University, who was awarded the honor of master of ceremonies by virtue of the fact that, with his wife's encouragement, he had brought the idea to the station just a few days earlier.

From *Information, Please* and *Pot O' Gold* to *Twenty Questions* and *Cash and Carry* in the early years, a great many broadcast quizzes and contests have been hits, and some extremely profitable for radio and television entrepreneurs. They were also the object of ridicule and even contempt by some executives in the industry, as well as by critics, who considered game shows less intellectual because they pandered to the tastes of an unsophisticated mass audience.

One humorous story that demonstrated the point was often repeated. Bill Todman was said to be carrying an armful of small prizes and appliances from his office to the studio for a broadcast of *Winner Take All* when he slipped, causing the prizes to crash to the sidewalk. Humorist turned broadcaster Goodman Ace, having witnessed the accident, shouted, "Hey Todman, you dropped your script!"[20-7]

In 1978, Mark Goodson lamented, "One of the prices I pay is that the game-show business is essentially without status. I regret it and resent it. The first thing people ask is, why is somebody as literate and articulate as you in games? It's like saying, why is an engineer taking out the garbage?"[20-8]

Despite a slow start, and the lack of respect for game and quiz shows, Goodson and Todman persevered and succeeded beyond anyone's expectations — including their own — and they took Johnny along for the ride. Goodson excelled at honing formats, and he had a discerning eye for staging. Todman trouble-shooted potential flaws in game play, and proved to be most gifted in managing the business and financial aspects of their partnership. As he explained, "I handle the contracts, sales, economy, budget; the minutiae."[20-4]

Todman's greatest gift was as a salesman. He was skilled at the art of the two-martini lunch that lubricated commerce among producers, network programmers, and especially advertising executives. Ira Skutch was a respected producer and director with the company for decades. He recalled that Todman sold at least one show based only on a title that Goodson had merely mentioned. Suddenly under the gun, Goodman had to quickly develop the game.

In 1979, Mark Goodson reflected on his specialty. "It's the greatest challenge in the world to invent a new game," he said, "when you finally get it down so that it looks very, very simple, that one has had the most complicated amount of work."[20-5] Bill Todman added, "Mark and me are very interesting chemistry. We argue constantly. If we both agree, one of us is not doing anything. I am very, very beholden to my partner."[20-4]

Contributing to Goodson and Todman's success was their cultivation of loyalty among a staff of creative contributors, such as Skutch. Many key employees stayed with the company for decades and were under salary as members of the company's creative team, even when not directly assigned to a particular program. Goodson-Todman Productions became home to a stable of gifted producers, directors, writers, set designers, graphic artists, and other creative contributors, in the style of the motion picture industry's structure during the so-called "studio era." They hired talented individuals who were willing to sublimate their desires for the fame and fortune they would have enjoyed from credit for authoring a hit. Instead they worked for job security, generous bonuses, and the benefit of the corporation.

While there are numerous anecdotes attesting to the fact that Johnny and Todman enjoyed each others' company on the occasions when they were together, there are a number of indications that Johnny and Goodson never shared a warm personal friendship. Perhaps it was simply Goodson's personality that led him to admit to author Gilbert Rogin that he was quite helpless at cocktail parties. One astute observer conjectured that Johnny's ease behind the microphone might have been a constant reminder of Goodson's early struggle with "mike fright," which was exacerbated by his self-proclaimed perfectionism. "I'm too critical. I hate failure. I loathe it."[20-4]

In the television industry, effusive praise generally flowed freely, nurturing egos and strengthening relationships. In 1985, that was not the case when Mark Goodson was asked about Johnny's contribution to the Goodson-Todman legacy of success. The producer coolly responded, "Oh, he was just a staff announcer."[20-9] His comment suggested that there might have been some animosity, past conflict, or professional envy. When asked about the snub, Roger Dobkowitz, who worked with Goodson for twenty years, observed that his employer "preferred to associate with higher society and the intellectual elite."[20-10] Bob Boden, a former Goodson-Todman staffer and programming executive, offered a simpler analysis of Goodson's dismissive response. He said, "I gather he didn't value the announcers as much as the hosts by light years. It was like if the host was number one, the announcer was number 57."[20-11]

CHAPTER 21
WHAT'S MY LINE?

With the innovative *Winner Take All* proving successful, Goodson-Todman next broke new ground in perfecting panel shows, programs that featured three or four public personalities usually celebrating the accomplishments of the common man, all within the context of a game. In that new paradigm, a person became the puzzle to be solved, as panelists probed to determine an occupation, accomplishment, or other unique attribute. The most important factor contributing to success with the new genre turned out not to be the contestants, their jobs, or secrets, but the chemistry among panel members.

In numerous interviews, Mark Goodson explained the importance of casting and taking care to balance contrasting personalities and styles in assembling a successful panel. The producer explained that it was a lesson learned from experience. "It takes a lot of trial and error, but . . . when a panel is finally working, each member possesses his or her own unique problem-solving talents that blend with and complement the personalities of the others."[21-1]

The producing team's first such panel show was fashioned from an idea presented by Bob Bach, formerly a disk jockey and producer at New York's radio station, WNEW. Bach was on the staff at Goodson-Todman's radio quiz, *Spin To Win*. As a personal pastime he often tried to deduce the occupations of total strangers while he rode the New York subways or was in bars. In late 1949, after overcoming the network's initial objections, Mark and Bill sold CBS on a concept they called *Occupation Unknown*.

As creator, Bach became the show's Associate Producer. John Charles Daly, one of Edward R. Murrow's team of respected CBS broadcast journalists, was chosen as moderator for the re-titled *What's My Line?* Daly had been CBS' White House correspondent during the Franklin Roosevelt presidency, and it was Daly's voice that broke into CBS's *Spirit of '41* at 2:25 p.m. Eastern Standard time on December 7, 1941, to announce that the Japanese had attacked Pearl Harbor.

Daly's new job on *What's My Line?* brought him a significant salary increase, but CBS was initially reticent to have their respectable newsman cross over into entertainment programming. Robert Trout had moderated the *Who Said That?* panel show for the network, but that offering was produced by the CBS News department. *What's My Line?* was controlled by outside producers and thus categorized as an entertainment program. A compromise was reached; to maintain his journalistic integrity, Daly was not called "host" or "emcee," and he was prohibited from participating in stunts, staged comedy, or commercial endorsements.

The February 1950 premiere broadcasts of *What's My Line?* were unsponsored, suffered from production problems, and featured a panel that failed to generate the necessary chemistry. Director Franklin Heller was brought on board to make a number of innovative changes. He designed an overall template for the production of the program that greatly improved the show, including the use of longer camera lenses as part of a schematic for camera placement that was less obtrusive and dis-

Moderator John Charles Daly (standing) with the recast panel that ultimately made *What's My Line?* a Sunday night television tradition. (Left to right) Dorothy Kilgallen, Steve Allen, Arlene Francis and Bennett Cerf.

tracting for the performers and audience. Still, there was no indication that *What's My Line?* would ultimately become an overwhelming success nor one of the two series that Johnny would be most proud to have on his resume.

By the third broadcast, *What's My Line?* found a sponsor in Stopette Deodorant, "The Original Spray Deodorant" from chemist Dr. Jules Montenier, who invented and patented a plastic squeeze bottle to dispense the liquid. Stopette stayed with the show so faithfully that at the beginning of the sixth year of *What's My Line?* broadcasts, the good Dr. Montenier even appeared as a mystery guest.

With an advertiser on board, the network renewed its commitment to the show until a re-cast panel gelled. The process required producers to assemble a quartet of public personalities that created the important, intangible quality that Goodson referred to as "chemistry." *New York Journal-American* columnist Dorothy Kilgallen was there from the start, but substitutes were soon found for the other three debut panelists.

Harold Hoffman, a former New Jersey Governor, and unrelated psychiatrist Richard Hoffman were replaced reportedly due to their lackluster television presence. Poet Louis Untermeyer abdicated his seat months later, after being implicated in the Communist witch hunt incited by political extremists and exacerbated in great part by US Senator Joseph McCarthy.

Over time, Dorothy Kilgallen was joined by actress and broadcaster Arlene Francis and publisher Bennett Cerf. The fourth seat regularly featured veteran radio comedian Fred Allen until his death. Then, unrelated Steve Allen took the fourth seat until that rising comedian was tapped by NBC to be the original host of *The Tonight Show* and appear on his own Sunday night program. Thereafter, that position on the panel rotated among other comedians, actors, and public personalities.

In 1927, Cerf had founded Random House, an enterprise he said was named for his motivation at the time. "We just said we were going to publish a few books on the side at random." [21-2] In 1934, he gained notoriety when he defied a ban by publishing James Joyce's *Ulysses*, and he gained recognition by bringing Dr. Seuss to America's children. Among the authors Random House published was Moss Hart, future husband of actress and game show panelist Kitty Carlisle. Cerf also authored a newspaper column and was well-known in New York society circles as a gifted punster and raconteur.

Bennett Cerf confessed that he had never heard of Mark Goodson or *What's My Line?* when the producer called him at Random House with an invitation to substitute for a panelist on that weekend's show. Goodson said, "Come down Sunday night an hour before the show. It's a very simple game. We'll explain it to you." [21-2]

Arlene Francis had been a radio actress and hostess with credit for presiding over *Blind Date,* America's first dating program. Between 1945 and 1949, she shared the microphone with Dorothy Kilgallen and Lucille Ball on Mutual's *Leave It To The Girls,* a feminine forum similar to today's *The View.* Before *What's My Line?,* Arlene was teamed with Johnny for radio's *What's My Name?* In total, the two worked together regularly, over a span of more than twenty-five years.

After becoming one of radio's favorite females, Arlene moved to television as Editor-in-Chief of *Home,* NBC's midday "service magazine of the air." With Kitty Carlisle's husband Moss Hart, she co-hosted NBC's *Answer Yes or No,* a program on which celebrity couples discussed the ins and outs of romance. With Robert Alda, she emceed *By Popular Demand,* a CBS summer talent showcase. Then she appeared on *That Reminds Me* and a litany of other television projects. Arlene adorned several covers of *TV Guide,* and she was celebrated on the cover of *Newsweek* as "The First Lady of television."

Dorothy Kilgallen was a popular newspaper columnist for William Randolph Hearst's New York *Journal-American.* She entered broadcasting as host of her own radio feature, *Voice of Broadway.* That show's success led to her celebrity news and gossip program, *The Dorothy Kilgallen Show,* which ran from 1947 to 1949. Later, Dorothy co-hosted a morning radio talk show, *Dorothy and Dick,* with her husband, actor Richard Kollmar. When *What's My Line?* debuted in 1950, her syndicated column was running in 146 newspapers with an estimated readership of 20 million. The untimely death of the reporter was the most shocking event in the history of *What's My Line?*

Although officially categorized as an accidental overdose of sleeping pills, the unusual circumstances surrounding Dorothy's passing in 1965 may forever remain mysteriously tied to her investigative journalistic efforts to expose the story behind President Kennedy's 1963 assassination. She had recently returned to New York from one of many trips to Dallas where she had interviewed Jack Ruby, the man who murdered the President's assassin, Lee Harvey Oswald, on live television.

Just hours before her own death on Monday morning, November 8, 1965, Dorothy told a number of staffers at the Sunday night broadcast of *What's My Line?* that she considered the Warren Commission Report on the assassination "laughable," and she vowed that she would "break the real story" and have "the biggest scoop of the century."[21-3] Bob Bach recalled for his colleague, Bill Egan, that Dorothy had been very excited that night about new developments in her investigation of the Kennedy-Oswald-Ruby affair. He also recounted that after the program wrapped that evening, the last member of the *What's My Line?* family to see Dorothy alive reported that he had escorted the columnist sometime after midnight to a midtown hotel, where she said she had a meeting with a man she described with a wink as "a new friend."[21-4]

Paul Alexander, author of *Good Night, Dorothy Kilgallen*, suggested that the columnist became obsessed with proving a conspiracy after landing the only interview with Jack Ruby for a book called *Murder One*. Reporter Sara Jordan noted that one of the biggest scoops of Dorothy's career came when she obtained the 102-page transcript of Ruby's testimony to the Warren Commission. "Readers were shocked at the hopelessly inept questioning of Ruby by Chief Justice Warren, and by Warren's failure to follow up on the leads Ruby was feeding him. Attorney Melvin Belli called Dorothy's scoop 'the ruin of the Warren Commission'"[21-5] One can only wonder what John Charles Daly, the moderator of *What's My Line?*, thought of all this, since he was married to the daughter of Chief Justice Earl Warren, namesake of the Warren Commission report on the Kennedy assassination.

Alexander's tome asserted that Dorothy died after turning in her book. The chapters about Kennedy are said to have mysteriously disappeared from the manuscript. The famed columnist was found under suspicious circumstances in her five-story townhouse, in bed in a room in which she reportedly never slept. The official cause of death: "Acute ethanol and barbiturate intoxication, circumstances undetermined." Jordan reported that as late as 1975, the FBI contacted Dickie, Dorothy's son, and they were still trying to locate his mother's papers. Her notes on the Kennedy assassination were never found.

On the episode following Dorothy's death, the show opened with a somber John Daly stating, "These are sad days for us." His one minute explanation concerning his friend's passing six days previously concluded with the statement, "The best tribute to Dorothy would be to do *What's My Line?* just as it was when she was here. That is what we will try to do." Then the show's usual opening animation was followed by Johnny's welcome that included an introduction of the panel which, uncharacteristically, was already seated.

Arlene Francis, Dorothy Kilgallen, and Bennett Cerf, always appeared on *What's My Line?* wrapped in tuxedos and evening gowns. The panel's collective, sophisticated wit imbued the simple parlor game with an air of elegance. Johnny joined the show in 1961, following original announcers Lee Vines and Hal Simms, and Johnny opened

his share of the 876 episodes with a rousing warm-up for the studio audience that he
ended just seconds before the 10:30 p.m. live broadcast was to begin. Johnny read the
show's scripted opening, and then he introduced the first panelist. Each subsequent
member of the panel was introduced by the preceding panelist. The final of the four-
some, almost always Bennett Cerf, introduced moderator John Charles Daly. Daly
shared a welcome and a witticism, and then he invited the first guest on stage.

Johnny just before airtime, thanking another audience for coming out late on a Sunday
night for a live broadcast of America's favorite panel show.

On Daly's cue to "Enter and sign in please," contestants wrote their name in chalk on a black art card, took their seat next to Daly, and whispered their occupation to the moderator, while the audience saw the occupation superimposed on the screen. Johnny rehearsed the audience before air-time, encouraging its members to register their recognition or amusement with the occupation vocally with a knowing "oooh" or laughter, followed by applause.

Then, Daly disclosed that the occupation involved a service or a product, or stated that the guest was salaried or self-employed. Then, to help them in divulging the occupation, the members of the panel began to ask questions that could be answered with simple "yes" or "no" responses. Each "no" response earned the contestant $5 and moved the questioning to the next panelist. After ten "no" answers, the panel was declared stumped, the audience applauded and cheered, and the guest won a grand total of $50.

On one occasion, Arlene Francis triggered laughter by asking a bed manufacturer, "Might Bennett and I use your product?" Steve Allen was first to ask whether a product was "bigger than a breadbox." Bennett Cerf confessed to playing for laughs, when a diaper salesman was a contestant. He recalled in 1967, "I asked, 'Does your work cover a large territory?' That brought a scream of laughter. Of course I knew exactly what I was doing."[21-2] Much of the entertainment value came from the erudite panelists and host indulging in cerebral discussions of comparative semantics, when questions and answers were open to interpretation.

Each episode included at least one segment during which the panel donned blindfolds for the entry of a mystery guest, whose identity was to be discerned by the panel, again by asking simple questions that each required only a "yes" or "no" answer. New York was considered the center of the universe for the cultured panel of Big Apple aristocrats, and they often asked, "Are you currently appearing on Broadway?"

In his 1978 book, *What's My Line?*, producer Gil Fates wrote about how seriously some of the panelists played the game. "Bennett prided himself on his ability to identify the Mystery Guest, and each Sunday night he used to come into the studio with a scribbled list of the suspects he knew to be in town. Just before the program took to the air, he would stand alone backstage with his glasses pushed up onto his forehead and a scrap of paper held close to his nose, squinting at their names in the dimmish (sic) light."[21-6]

Early in the show's run, some celebrities refused invitations to appear as mystery guests. Among their ranks were John F. Kennedy, and Greta Garbo, the actress noted for "wanting to be alone." Mystery guests were sports figures, politicians, major film and Broadway stars, and celebrities of every stripe, and their identities were always closely guarded secrets. The surprise guests ran the gamut from baseball's Phil Rizzuto and explorer Sir Edmund Hilary, to Bette Davis, Ronald Reagan, Salvador Dali, Elsa Maxwell, Frank Lloyd Wright, Sargent Shriver, Errol Flynn, Mayors John Lindsay, Sam Yorty and Richard Daley, Admiral William F. "Bull" Halsey, Jackie Robinson, Frank Sinatra, Eleanor Roosevelt, Yehudi Menuhin, Buster Keaton, Henry Cabot Lodge, Jr., Barbra Streisand, Groucho Marx, The Harlem Globetrotters, Senator Everett M. Dirksen, Earl Stanley Gardner, Muhammad Ali,

Walt Disney, Francis The Talking Mule, and moderator John Daly's father-in-law, Justice Earl Warren.

During its lengthy run, *What's My Line?* had its share of the kind of unpredictable moments that made live television especially compelling. During Milton Berle's 1959 appearance as a mystery guest, an audience member dressed in a suit unexpectedly stepped onstage and into camera range shortly after the panel guessed Uncle Miltie's

Backstage after a *What's My Line?* broadcast, Johnny (left) chats with mystery guest Frank Sinatra.

identity. The intruder shook hands with Berle, while blurting out what sounded like "I made it for Mothers Day." Then, as quickly as he entered the scene, the stranger exited stage left. Apparently he just wanted to meet his Uncle Miltie. No stranger to live television, Berle looked at John Daly and ad-libbed, "My agent."

Similar but more disturbing was a moment in 1962, when an unknown man suddenly stepped from behind the curtain and began to deliver an impromptu commercial for a dating or escort service just as that week's mystery guest, Melina Mercouri, was seated and asked the first question by Dorothy Kilgallen. Daly was heard saying, "We have a small problem. Gil, will you get the relieving unit in?" before the audio engineer turned down the input from the on-stage microphones. Johnny entered stage right from beyond the panelists' desk to join producer Gil Fates in escorting the intruder off the set.

Fates described the incident this way: "In the control room, Frank Heller yelled 'Who's that? What's he doing? Get him out of there!' Daly, spotting me bewildered in the wings, said 'Gil Fates, will you please remove this man from the stage?'" Fates remembered, "I signaled to our announcer, Johnny Olson, and together we moved in. Before 30 million people coast-to-coast, Johnny and I each grabbed an arm and eased the interloper — still into his plug — off the stage and into the custody of the stage doorman, who passed him on to the police."[21-6]

On another occasion, there was palpable animosity between panelists Bennett Cerf and Henry Morgan, when the latter's acerbic wit was in apparent overdrive. He interrupted Cerf's lengthy introduction of the moderator saying, "What time does this show go on?" Cerf was indignant, and cut short his remarks. When John Daly entered, he and Morgan had their own biting exchange. While extremely tame by today's standards, it was disturbingly out of character for the otherwise erudite and well-mannered socialites.

Panelist Shelley Berman once walked off the set in the middle of the program, explaining that he had a prior engagement. Another time, mystery guest Judy Garland suffered an attack of nerves and retreated to her dressing room just moments before she was to make her entrance. Mark Goodson hurried into the wings to serve as a last-minute replacement for the mystery guest segment. Less than thirty seconds before the celebrity spot, Garland rose to the occasion. She took the piece of chalk from Goodson's hand, entered on-cue, and was at her most charming.

Johnny did double duty on a few *What's My Line?* broadcasts. On April 4, 1965, he was both announcer and mystery guest. Two years later, on July 16, 1967, when Mark Goodson served as a panelist, John Daly called Johnny on camera to join a quartet of mystery guests, all hosts under Goodson's employ and all friends of Johnny's: Gene Rayburn, Allen Ludden, Ed McMahon, and Bud Collier.

The weekly broadcast moved from the studios above Grand Central Terminal to CBS' Studio 51, the Maxine Elliott Theatre on West 39th Street. A more permanent home for most of the 1950s was at Studio 59, the Mansfield Theatre (now the Brooks Atkinson) on West 47th Street. By that time, *What's My Line?* had found itself at home in American living rooms as a Sunday night staple and had further filled Goodson-Todman's coffers. In 1958, the team sold the format to CBS for a figure generally reported to be $1.5 million, but estimated by production executive Ira Skutch to be as high as $4 million.[21-7] The deal included a contract for Goodson-Todman to continue as the production company for as long as the network chose to run the show.

What's My Line? enjoyed seventeen years in prime-time. On September 3, 1967, Johnny took the stage of CBS' Studio 50, The Ed Sullivan Theatre, to perform his

In the closing moment of the final CBS broadcast of *What's My Line?*, moderator John Daly (right) called on Johnny (standing) to join producers Mark Goodson (far left) and Bill Todman (second from left) for a fond farewell.

final audience warm-up for the Sunday night stalwart, and then he opened the final network episode saying, "And now, live from New York, for the 876th and last time, let's meet our *What's My Line?* panel."

When Bennett Cerf introduced John Charles Daly for the last time, the moderator entered to a prolonged standing ovation from the studio audience. The first game featured a return of the original guests from the debut broadcast, followed by kinescope clips from each of the panelists' debut on the series. Next to attempt to stump the panel was a guest they would presumably be visiting the following morning, a representative from the New York unemployment office.

For the final segment, Daly left his moderator chair to make another entrance as the mystery guest. He alternated between the host and guest microphones, as he fielded the blindfolded panel's questions until Cerf ended the charade with a correct guess. At the close of that last episode, the panelists thanked the show's loyal audience, and Johnny was invited by Daly to join him, Mark Goodson, and Bill Todman for an on-camera farewell.

Within months, Todman engineered a creative deal with CBS for the production of a fresh run of the classic that the network's syndication arm would distribute. After a one year hiatus, *What's My Line?* returned as a Monday through Friday strip that was taped at NBC's Rockefeller Center facility. While CBS had felt the show's audience was too old for the network's new youth-minded mandate, the revival scored sufficient ratings to support a new seven-year run. Arlene Francis and Johnny were the only carryovers from the Sunday-night version, and it strengthened the bond between the two broadcasters that was forged in the early 1940s. Another newscaster, Wally Bruner, and later, actor Larry Blyden, hosted that syndicated version of the show. Both Johnny and Wally Bruner left the program in 1972. Johnny was on his way to Hollywood, and Bruner had put together a deal for his own home repair show.

Bruner had paid his dues as a correspondent with ABC News covering the easy White House and Congress beats, as well as trudging in the fields to report on wars in Santo Domingo and Vietnam. He settled into the anchor seat at Washington, DC's WTTG, where he delivered the nightly news with Maury Povich and weatherman Willard Scott.

Following his stint on *What's My Line?* in 1972, Bruner secured corporate funding to produce and host *Wally's Workshop,* one of the first do-it-yourself home improvement shows. Ever handy around the house, Bruner enlisted Natalie, his wife, on this syndicated outing to assist in demonstrating every manner of home repair project. To make it feel a bit more like home, Wally recruited Johnny, his one-time on-air partner, to announce the program via tape.

A few years after his relocation to Los Angeles, on an occasion when work took him east for a New York gig, Johnny returned to the syndicated *What's My Line?* Larry Blyden, the host at that time, was a respected stage actor and no stranger to television. His small-screen credits dated back to 1950, when he participated in live television dramas. Years later, Goodson-Todman had him signed to host *Showoffs,* a new game show, when Blyden met an untimely death following an auto accident while vacationing in Morocco. He was just shy of his fiftieth birthday.

That day's *What's My Line?* panel was almost stumped during the mystery guest segment until Arlene Francis guessed Johnny's identity just as the game was ending. The two old friends embraced warmly at the conclusion of the episode.

The landmark program enjoyed one last gasp in May 1975, when *What's My Line? at 25,* a ninety-minute special, was sold to ABC. Produced in New York on a limited budget without a studio audience, Johnny was not flown back from California for this retrospective finale. Sitting on a simple set, Mark Goodson, John Daly, and Arlene Francis reminisced and presented more than 150 clips featuring the best moments from some 2,000 episodes, including many of America's most memorable celebrities of the 20th century.

CHAPTER 22

GOODSON–TODMAN HAS A SECRET

The relationship between CBS, Mark Goodson, and Bill Todman, and the subsequent entities that acquired their company, continued for more than sixty years and occasionally expanded beyond game shows. The prolific producers' first foray into drama occurred in 1950, when the network needed to quickly find a replacement for their anthology series, *Suspense*.

The opportunity resulted in a four-year run for Goodson-Todman's *The Web*, which told the stories of people in peril, each caught in a web of confounding circumstances. During the subsequent decade, the production company enjoyed mixed results with several ventures into other dramatic television programs, including the westerns, *Jefferson Drum*, *The Rebel*, and *Branded*.

James Dean, before his breakthrough role as the *Rebel Without a Cause*, was among the up-and-coming performers from the famed Actors' Studio to appear in an episode of *The Web* anthology series. The young actor continued to earn extra money as a Goodson-Todman employee with a part-time job testing stunts for *Beat The Clock*. Ultimately, James was dropped from his job representing average contestants in performing the various physical feats reportedly because he proved to be far more agile and clever than the show's actual participants.

With the success of *What's My Line?*, Goodson and Todman focused on bringing more panel shows to market. Most were less successful than the original. *The Name's the Same* was the first reformulation. It debuted on ABC in 1951 and lasted four years, as amazing run considering that the show was based on the simple novelty of ordinary people with famous or unusual names, such as Paul Bunyon, Ima Hogg, Johnny Walker Black, or A. Mattress.

In 1954, another panel show failed so miserably that, according to its co-creator, Al Howard, it was cancelled after only five broadcasts. *What's Going On?* dared a panel of three celebrities to ascertain what was happening by questioning other challenging panelists about some specific activity taking place in another room or at some distant location. Ever the gentleman, Al Howard explained that the show's failure was most likely due to problems with the early technology's failure to deliver dependable, clear signals from remote locations, compounded by inadequate backup contingencies. That was indeed true for a segment originating from the Chicago stockyards, where a celebrity challenger was counting sheep.

Mark Goodson and his senior executives, as well as the program's producers, Frank Wayne and Allan Sherman, placed most of the responsibility for the failure of *What's Going On?* directly at the feet of host Lee Bowman. Faced with the challenge of ad-libbing on live television, the actor's true personality proved to be far from the bright, urbane, and sophisticated characters he portrayed on film. It became a reminder of how critical the specialized skills of proven performers were to the success of a program and a producer's reputation. The experience helped to cement the longevity of Goodson-Todman's roster of reliable regulars, including Johnny Olson.

In the mid-1940s, Allan Sherman, a young Chicago native with an ambition to be a songwriter, arrived in New York with Dee, his wife. The couple found themselves at the epicenter of the new television industry. Sherman did not find immediate success in the music industry, so he freelanced as a joke writer for Jackie Gleason and Joe E. Lewis, and he contributed comedy for several months at DuMont's *The Cavalcade of Stars*. Sherman then moved on to lend laughs to *Broadway Open House*, the forerunner of *The Tonight Show*, but that job lasted only three weeks.

In 1951, Sherman and Howard Merrill, another unemployed comedy writer, created a concept for a television show that the pair called *I Know a Secret*. Sherman and Merrill thought that its similarity to *What's My Line?* would assure a warm reception at Goodson-Todman. Mark Goodson saw the situation differently, and told the duo that their idea was clearly a derivative of his company's hit. Instead of retreating apologetically, Sherman's response was inspired, telling Goodson, "People are going to start imitating your show whether you like it or not. You might as well do it and make the money."[22-1] Goodson bought the pitch and the show, renaming the program, *I've Got A Secret* for CBS, and casting venerable Garry Moore to host.

Since 1944, Garry had grown from NBC radio's *Everything Goes,* creating the vacancy that Johnny filled, through his partnership with Jimmy Durante, and then on to establishing himself as a top television talent. Goodson-Todman's Gil Fates called Garry "the best emcee there ever was." [22-2] Responsible for one of television's most successful variety programs, Garry was minting money for CBS. The Museum of Broadcast Communications commemorated his status as a golden goose with the entry, "By 1951, *The Garry Moore Show* reportedly was the second largest revenue source for CBS, and for a time, the network could not accommodate potential sponsors awaiting the opportunity to advertise on the program." [22-4]

In a deal authored by Bill Todman, the game show empire offered Sherman and Merrill $1 for the rights to *I've Got A Secret* plus $125-a-week jobs as Associate Producers. They were also to earn another $62.50 in royalties per week. With little bargaining power, the unemployed partners agreed. Seven years later, Sherman was fired from the show he created, and Goodson-Todman went on to sell *I've Got A Secret.* CBS took a 75% interest with Garry acquiring the remaining 25% for a figure reported in 1960 by *TV Guide* as being $3 million, but estimated by Ira Skutch to be as high as $7 million. [22-3]

After its premiere broadcast on June 19, 1952 from CBS Studio 59, it was no secret that *I've Got A Secret* was in trouble. In an attempt to distinguish the new show from *What's My Line?* the more light-hearted *I've Got A Secret* was burdened with an imposing set resembling a courtroom. Garry presided as the judge, with members of the panel walking up to interrogate contestants seated in a witness stand.

Goodson promptly ordered the scenery scrapped, and a new set was built which

One of CBS' most popular and profitable personalities, Garry Moore was teamed with Johnny Olson on *To Tell The Truth*.

was simply a mirror-image of the *What's My Line?* arrangement. Despite the new presentation, CBS was prepared to cancel the program early in its run. The panel was repopulated and the show was saved. For the latter years of its lengthy and successful reign, *I've Got A Secret* was berthed at CBS's Studio 52 on West 54th Street. That historic theater had been The Gallo Opera House and The New Yorker Theater before being converted for broadcasting as CBS Radio Playhouse Number 4. In the 1970s, it was transformed into the Studio 54 disco, at one time the world's most famous and infamous dance club.

The twist that truly differentiated *I've Got A Secret* was the inclusion of an unpredictable and compelling added element that followed the questioning. On *What's My Line?*, the formally-attired panel remained removed from the person whose occupation they were to guess. After disclosure, the guest simply shook hands with the panelists and exited.

On *I've Got A Secret*, the revelation was followed by a demonstration that often involved the four members of the panel in activities such as milking a cow or tasting a chef's secret dish. Despite the danger of including unrehearsed and unpredictable elements in a live show, Allan Sherman was fearless, Garry Moore's ad-lib skills were seemingly up to any challenge, and the quartet of questioners was adept at making engaging television from almost any situation.

Elephants and Army regiments paraded across the stage; Garry wrestled an alligator, was a human archery target, and allowed a nine-year-old golfer to hit a ball from his nose. In the grand tradition of live television, the cow relieved itself while on camera, and the panel spit out the chef's secret specialty when it was disclosed that it was actually dog food.

While Johnny was not the show's announcer, he became an integral part of *I've Got A Secret* through the 1960s and into the 1970s. He regularly performed the studio audience warm-up, and on at least one occasion filled-in for the voice of the show, John Cannon. Over the decades, the panelists most identified with *I've Got A Secret* included stalwarts from the Goodson-Todman stable, Bill Cullen, Peggy Cass, Kitty Carlisle, Henry Morgan, Betsy Palmer, Orson Bean, and that former WJZ radio Miss New York City, Bess Myerson.

Among the hundreds of guests who exited from *I've Got A Secret* with a carton or two of Winston cigarettes under their arms, two were especially memorable. Samuel J. Seymour was ninety-six years old when he appeared with a compelling secret: in 1895 at the age of five, he saw John Wilkes Booth shoot Abraham Lincoln.

Philo Farnsworth, former farm boy and father of modern television, appeared in July 1957 as "Dr. X," inventor of "a machine." The first question from the panel was "Is this a machine that might be painful when used?" Farnsworth quipped, "Yes. Sometimes it is most painful." The panel was stumped.

I've Got A Secret emulated the success of the *What's My Line?* by adapting the mystery guest segment. In the program's original incarnation a celebrity was featured on each episode. Ernest Borgnine's secret was that he had posed as a cab driver earlier in the day and drove panelist Jayne Meadows to the show without her realizing it. Similarly, Paul Newman, while dressed as a hot dog vendor, had sold panelist Henry Morgan a frankfurter at a Brooklyn Dodgers game without Morgan recognizing him.

Likewise, Jack Lemmon appeared to reveal that back in 1948, when he was a struggling actor, he had been a contestant on a radio game show hosted by panelist Bill Cullen. Other celebrity secrets were of dubious interest and dubious veracity. Boris Karloff appeared on the very first episode with the revelation that, despite his professional reputation as a master of invoking fear in others, he was afraid of mice.

A later, similar celebrity segment hinted at the kind of creative license being taken by producers in that era when some quiz shows were rigged. Monty Woolley was a stage, screen, and radio actor with an outsized personality. His secret was that he slept with his prominent beard under the covers. When panelist Henry Morgan asked whether that was really true, Woolley reportedly responded, "Of course not, you bloody idiot! Some damn fool named Allan Sherman told me to say so."[22-4]

Indeed, co-creator Sherman had worked his way up to Producer on *I've Got A Secret* before being fired from the show in 1958. David Schwartz, a television historian and author, cited Gil Fates, the show's Executive Producer, as a source in explaining that Sherman and Mark Goodson butted heads on multiple occasions concerning the program's unrehearsed demonstrations. One legendary moment of Easter mayhem that aired on March 28, 1956, vividly demonstrated the point.

With 100 live rabbits placed on the stage floor, Garry Moore blew a whistle to cue 100 children from the National Boys Clubs to enter and each select a bunny. In the youngsters' exuberance, the scene resembled a wild stampede in which viewers could not help but be concerned about the fate of some of the live rabbits, especially two minutes later when some of the 100 boys still were not holding bunnies. Schwartz reported that the producers' working relationship further deteriorated beyond repair following a failed segment with Tony Curtis that aired on June 11, 1958. On that show, children's games were to be played with the panel. Although it was discovered

City slicker Gene Rayburn prepares to milk a cow. The kind of fun stunt that made *I've Got A Secret* unpredictable for viewers, and occasionally for its producers.

that Curtis was not familiar with the selected games, Sherman reportedly proceeded with the segment despite Goodson's suggestion that it be scrapped.

The firing precipitated a period of hard times for the gifted but troubled comedy writer. In 1961, Sherman moved to Los Angeles to produce the short-lived game show, *Your Surprise Package*. Then in 1962, Steve Allen hired Sherman to produce his new talk show, but Sherman was fired before the program even hit the air.

In Los Angeles, Allan and Dee Sherman were renting a home near Marilyn Monroe and other celebrities in the tony Westside community of Brentwood. Their next-door neighbor, comedy legend Harpo Marx, invited Sherman to several of his star-studded parties. Sherman entertained Harpo's famous friends, performing the song parodies that he had been writing for years. Bullets Durgom, Jackie Gleason's manager and a guest at one of those parties, made a series of introductions that led to interest at Warner Bros. Records.

Paul Lieberman wrote in the August 16, 2003 edition of the *Los Angeles Times* that August 6, 1962 was a pivotal day in Sherman's life. He reportedly picked up a $55 unemployment check in the morning and went before the microphone to record a comedy album in the afternoon. The unexpected success of that disc resulted in more parodies from the prolific comedian and his two collaborators, Lou Busch and the un-credited Stanley Ralph Ross. One song from his third LP, "Hello Mudda, Hello Faddah (A Letter from Camp Grenada)," about a child's unhappiness at summer camp, won a Grammy. Lyrics by Sherman, Busch, and Ross were perfectly married to the bouncy melody of a movement from "The Dance of the Hours," the ballet from Act Three of *La Gioconda* by Ponchielli. The success of the hit song began a whirl-wind of success that suddenly catapulted Sherman to fame and a reported income of over $1 million.

In 1962, appearances on *The Ed Sullivan Show*, *The Tonight Show*, and even in the Macy's Thanksgiving Day Parade thrust Sherman into fame. He recalled the dizzy-ing life of hotel suites and late nights winding down with double shots of J&B. In his autobiography, *A Gift of Laughter*, Sherman recalled, "I was drinking two bottles of Scotch every day. I couldn't sleep. Or eat…I got those terrible depressions. And muscle spasms. I was in a whirling madness."[22-1]

In his book, Sherman lambasted both Goodson and Todman as pompous elitists. He ridiculed Goodson's penchant for writing copious memos from his ostentatious office that was complete with original Picasso artwork and a desk once owned by Napoleon Bonaparte. He recounted that he had been in Todman's office the day he was on the telephone ordering a custom-made Lincoln directly from industrialist Henry Ford. Just the same, Goodson and Todman were happy to exploit Sherman's star power. Between 1963 and 1967, the former producer appeared as a mystery guest on *What's My Line?*, and participated as a guest panelist on his original cre-ation, *I've Got A Secret*.

Just ten years after catapulting to stardom, Sherman was living at the Motion Picture Country Home. "I suppose this meant that he had run out of money," Steve Allen is said to have written. On November 20, 1973, ten days short of his forty-ninth birthday, Sherman died of emphysema. Coincidentally, his ashes rest at Hillside Memorial Park, not far from where Mark Goodson was interred two decades later. As he had years earlier with his father, Goodson hired Sherman's son, Robert, as a writer. Over the next twenty years, Bobby Sherman rose to become a producer, helm-ing *Super Password*, *Password Plus*, and *Blockbusters* among other series.

With host Garry Moore, Sherman and Merrill's *I've Got A Secret* was among the A.C. Nielsen Top 20 television programs for seven years of its twelve-year run, and was still going strong in 1964, when CBS cancelled Garry's long-running prime-time variety show. Recorded history reflected that Garry took that opportunity to retire from his daily grind, but those present at the time clearly remembered the contentious confrontation between Garry and CBS executive Jim Aubrey over that cancellation. It led to Garry walking off of *I've Got A Secret* that September.

Garry was not alone in his altercation with Aubrey. The controversial program-ming executive's legacy of success was undeniable in bringing ratings hits to the air, but Jim Aubrey's abrasive arrogance was also well-documented. Press reports indicated that the network president unceremoniously cancelled Jack Benny's weekly series despite its Top 20 rating, when the star expressed displeasure with Aubrey's choice for a lead-in show. It was reported that the executive called up Benny and terminated his show with the line, "You're finished, old man!"

Likewise, CBS superstar Lucille Ball refused to deal with Aubrey, referring to him as "that S.O.B." The executive also failed to endear himself to Allen Ludden, when he forced the host to choose between two CBS shows he was hosting, *The GE College Bowl* and *Password*. Aubrey created similar sentiments in what were described as his Machiavellian dealings with Red Skelton, Danny Thomas, and Arthur Godfrey. Respected actor and director John Houseman, after dealing with Aubrey, was credited with imbuing the programmer with the enduring if not endearing nickname, "The Smiling Cobra."

Steve Allen took over the hosting duties for three more seasons of *I've Got A Secret*. In that era, Madison Avenue began to covet youthful viewers, and *I've Got A Secret* drew aging audiences. When ratings lagged after fifteen years, CBS pink-slipped the hit and pulled the plug on Goodson-Todman's other primetime stalwarts, *What's My Line?*, *To Tell The Truth*, and *Password*. They also fired Aubrey, all in a period of only six months. *I've Got A Secret* proclaimed the end of its network run on April 3, 1967, by simply returning from the final commercial break with Steve Allen sharing the words, "That's the end of another show, and in fact, that's the end of *I've Got A Secret*."

In 1972, Steve Allen returned to host a syndicated revival of the program. He was assisted by Johnny, who regularly appeared on camera in demonstrations and in audience participation segments. In one, he shared the stage with Bob Barker, who was a guest on an *I've Got A Secret* episode, demonstrating the kind of game play planned for the return of *The Price is Right*.

CBS took one more shot with Allan Sherman's old evergreen. In the summer of 1976, *I've Got A Secret* was brought back for only four episodes with Bill Cullen in the host's chair. The first two shows of that brief summer run were recorded as pilot episodes on September 28, 1975, close to nine months before they aired. According to David Schwartz, they were taped at CBS' Broadcast Center on West 57th Street, with Richard Hayes announcing. The other two episodes were taped on June 11, 1976, at the Ed Sullivan Theater. Johnny flew in from Los Angeles to announce and excite the audience for one more fling. The revival struggled for an audience opposite ABC's blockbuster *Happy Days*, and the show did not see air again for many years. Like many of the classic Goodson-Todman games, *I've Got A Secret* passed into the hands of new owners and producers, and was retooled in subsequent decades for new audiences.

CHAPTER 23
GETTING IN THE GAME

Johnny became a consistent ingredient in the Goodson-Todman recipe for success, but not before his work as the voice of *Masquerade Party*. That prime-time hit bounced among all three major networks over its eight-year reign as one of the era's most successful panel shows. During the long run, Johnny was one of the show's consistent elements, working with no fewer than six different hosts.

Masquerade Party premiered in 1952, just one month after *I've Got A Secret*, emulating the Goodson-Todman formula in challenging a panel of four regulars to ascertain the identity of a celebrity by asking questions that could be answered "yes" or "no." The celebrity not only disguised his voice as the *What's My Line?* mystery guest did, but was disguised behind extensive make-up and elaborate costumes, and often appeared with an object that was an additional clue. After peeling off the latex facial appliances and wig, the celebrity's charity was awarded $1 for each second the panelists used in their sleuthing.

Besides being seen on three networks at different times over the course of its eight years, *Masquerade Party* also held the unusual distinction of once being broadcast on NBC, CBS, and ABC simultaneously. On a special Sunday afternoon episode a few weeks before Election Day in 1954, an unusually light-hearted Vice President Richard Nixon played via a remote coaxial cable link from Washington, DC. More memorable for our hero was the time that comedian Bert Lahr, who had portrayed The Cowardly Lion in *The Wizard of Oz*, walked right past a surprised Johnny as he made his on-stage entrance, in disguise, with a live lion in tow.

Allan Sherman found work as a producer on *Masquerade Party* after his dismissal from *I've Got A Secret*, which was indicative of the small world that was the early New York television community. The show was produced by Wolf Productions, and Herb Wolf was among the producers to perpetuate the intimate and sometimes pleasantly incestuous nature of the business. He utilized Bud Collyer as host on several of his shows, and he hired Johnny for his other productions that ran concurrently with *Masquerade Party:* the quiz show, *Break The Bank*, the 1957 musical game, *Hold That Note*, and *Keep Talking*.

Keep Talking featured six celebrity panelists attempting to casually work secret phrases into ad-libbed stories without the opposing celebrities identifying the phrases. As with *Masquerade Party*, *Keep Talking* was presented by several hosts during its run, including Monty Hall, Carl Reiner, and future icon in the game show business, Merv

Griffin. Johnny's hosting opportunities were on the wane as the 1950s came to a close, and he enjoyed occasionally being featured on-camera, as the celebrity-laden, prime-time *Keep Talking* transitioned from CBS to ABC between 1958 and 1960.

Johnny found greater joy during the early years of *Masquerade Party*'s run by utilizing his early experience as a vocalist when he danced and sang on *The Strawhatters*. That talent competition was one of several shows that DuMont televised from across the Hudson River at New Jersey's Palisades Amusement Park. On May 17, 1953, the network announced its plans for the one-hour, local summer variety show to be staged during the warm weather months. Debuting ten days later, amateur acts competed to impress a team of three celebrities and one park customer who judged the performers.

On June 3, 1953, *Variety* reviewed the show, citing, "Despite enthusiastic encouragement from emcee Johnny Olson, the amateurs' efforts were lulling and generally embarrassing." Notwithstanding the trade paper's appraisal, DuMont returned to Palisades Park for another run of *The Strawhatters* the following summer. The 2003 edition of *The Complete Directory to Primetime Network and Cable TV Shows* called the show "essentially an hour-long advertisement for Palisades Amusement Park." It was certainly no more shameless a promotional vehicle for an amusement park than the *Disneyland* series that debuted on ABC in 1954.

DuMont was once considered by many to be the most innovative network and the place where television viewers first tuned for some of the earliest televised wrestling and boxing matches, but like a defeated pugilist, DuMont ultimately fell on the ropes. In the late 1930s, Allen Du Mont sold all of the class B shares of his company's stock to Paramount Pictures to raise operating capital. The deal brought in desperately needed cash, but the plan backfired. Paramount acquired half of the seats on DuMont's Board of Directors, and the company's future was hampered by the lack of a cohesive overall business plan. The network's Thomas T. Goldsmith recalled, "Paramount wouldn't let Dr. Du Mont go to Wall Street for more investment capital. They were afraid of what the television business would do to their movie business... [they] never invested more and vetoed Du Mont's many attempts to attract additional investors." [23-1]

The FCC's interpretation of DuMont's relationship with Paramount further handicapped the network's chances for survival. While CBS, NBC, and ABC were each allowed to own and operate a full complement of five stations, DuMont's count included Paramount's other properties — KTLA, Los Angeles, and WBKB, Chicago — even though they were not DuMont owned or even DuMont affiliates. The network struggled competitively with only three stations under its direct control. Even a proposed merger between DuMont and ABC failed to materialize, reportedly because of a veto from Paramount soon after its spun-off United Paramount Theaters purchased ABC.

On April 1, 1955, under assault from CBS, NBC, and a newly capitalized ABC, DuMont drastically cut back its prime-time programming, but it was no April Fools Day stunt; it was the beginning of the end. Goldsmith remembered, "By September 1955, DuMont programming had been reduced to NFL football on Sunday afternoons, boxing on Monday nights, and college football on Saturday afternoons. On

August 8, 1956, the DuMont network's final broadcast was a boxing card. CBS inherited the rest of the DuMont/NFL football deal." [23-1]

DuMont was Johnny's early employer in television, and although they were fading from view, his career was on the rise.

Starting on Monday, February 22, 1954, Johnny announced the short-lived *Manhattan Honeymoon*, weekday mornings at 10:00 a.m. on WJZ-TV. The local program featured married and engaged couples, recommended by friends who sent letters to the show. Honeymoon vacations were awarded after interviews with Neva Patterson, and musical performances from vocalists Martha Lou Harp and Jerry Leighton.

That year, Johnny also appeared as a panelist. On September 19, *I Made the News* debuted as a weekly, half-hour feature, produced and sponsored by The New York *Daily News*. It aired in a prime slot, Sunday evenings at 7:00 p.m., on the newspaper's WPIX television. Johnny anchored a panel that attempted to identify famous news personalities from clues given by the program's host, Daily News feature reporter Bob Sullivan.

Future *Password* host Allen Ludden and television personality Eloise McElhone served as regulars on the panel with Johnny. Ludden had recently won a Peabody award for his radio show aimed at teenagers, *Mind Your Manners*. McElhone was recognized in *Time* magazine for her "indefatigable smile, a capacity for continual astonishment ('Is that so?' 'You don't say!'), and the ability to talk endlessly about nothing." They were joined each week by a different Broadway performer, each anxious for the added exposure on local televison, and anxious to curry favor with the newspaper's columnists and reviewers. *I Made the News* ran for thirteen Sundays, before being replaced during Christmas week.

In addition to an ever-evolving roster of daily and weekly programs, Johnny was always happy to step in to substitute for other performers. His reputation for reliability, professionalism, versatility, and adaptability made him a logical choice when a last-minute call for help was required by a live show in need of a sudden substitute. With his apartment near Central Park South, just blocks away from most of the studios, his availability on short notice made him a producers' ace in the hole.

Such was the case for at least one spring 1955 prime-time telecast of *A Penny to a Million* from the Ritz Theater on West 48th Street. Hosted by Bill Goodwin, George Burns' and Gracie Allen's former announcer, Johnny was called to substitute for broadcaster George Ansbro, another legendary radio voice, who was the series' announcer. That ABC game show was produced by the familiar Herb Wolf and quizzed participants for the chance to continually double a jackpot until it reached a grand prize of one million pennies.

Johnny was also called by Wolf to substitute as television emcee on *Break The Bank*, a show he had hosted for a time on radio. He returned to the series as announcer between 1953 and 1957, working in prime-time with the eternally enthusiastic host, Bert Parks. In 1948, three years into its radio run, *Radio Mirror* dubbed the show "the highest paying quiz program in the world," with winnings that occasionally exceeded $9,000. In its later years on television, during the era of the big money quiz shows, *Break The Bank* kept its king's crown by tempting players with a potential top prize of $250,000.

Bert Parks' leading-man appearance helped him transition with *Break The Bank* from radio to television in 1948, and he was on his way to becoming one of early television's more popular hosts. In one incarnation of *Break The Bank,* the program featured contestants from the studio audience attempting to answer a series of nine questions in a row. Answers to the final question earned award money banked along the way by previous players failing to successfully complete the challenge. When not cautioning the audience with the admonition, "No coaching, please," or clarifying for the contestants that he would accept their "First answer before the bell," Parks found opportunities to pose musical questions by singing with Peter Van Steeden's orchestra.

His ultra-enthusiastic presence, mile-wide smile, and super-energized delivery were assets that powered Parks' prominence among the era's emcees. However, his style occasionally approached mania and proved to be too effervescent for a program that was already cast with nine celebrities. Although Bert Parks hosted the original pilot for *Hollywood Squares*, Peter Marshall, an actor and singer with previous experience as a comedy straight man, was ultimately awarded the job. Parks' high-octane energy was perfect for officiating over the annual Miss America pageant, where he crowned twenty-four consecutive beauties, including future broadcast personalities Lee Meriwether, Mary Ann Mobley, and Phyllis George.

After *Break The $250,000 Bank* ran its course, it was suddenly replaced on January 22, 1957, in its Tuesday night time period by the short-lived *Hold That Note.* After a brassy six tone fanfare and tympani drum roll, Johnny opened each episode from the Ziegfeld Theater with a strident welcome to "The biggest money-paying musical show on the air," and then introduced the familiar Bert Parks. On that NBC-TV offering, players tried to beat their opponent to the lockout button and identify tunes played by the familiar Peter Van Steeden orchestra, winning cash for each un-played note. Johnny participated throughout each episode, regularly tallying and announcing the scores. To add to the entertainment, Parks was occasionally joined by Johnny and the audience to sing one or two bonus songs each week.

Work on *Hold That Note* came during the five-year period when Johnny was already announcing the similar and more popular musical game, Harry Salter's *Name That Tune.* Johnny joined that weekly tune-title tester when the program moved from NBC to CBS on September 2, 1954. Johnny reported to Studio 52 for most of the episodes broadcast during the next five years, until *Name That Tune* ended its six-year prime-time run from Studio 59 on October 19, 1959.

Johnny's role was off-camera while paired with host and song stylist, George DeWitt. He watched contestants race across the stage to be first to ring a bell for the right to name the popular hits played by Ted Raph's musicians. He was far more involved during Bill Cullen's reign, visible while introducing the contestants, walking them on and off the set, and during his good-natured kidding with the host. Johnny led the audience applause on Tuesday night, September 24, 1957, when future astronaut Major John Glenn, Jr. competed in the show's Golden Medley for $15,000.

It was unusual for a program host to front two similar shows, and only a limited number of emcees in television history worked simultaneously for competing networks, but Johnny regularly hop-scotched across schedules and channels. He served as an announcer on both *Hold That Note* and *Name That Tune*. The peculiarity was also illustrated by the fact that while announcing CBS' *Name That Tune*, he was seen and heard on NBC's *Tic Tac Dough* and ABC-TV's *Keep It in the Family*. The latter show enjoyed only a brief run on Saturday nights between October 12, 1957, and February 15, 1958, with a setup that foreshadowed an element of Goodson-Todman's *Family Feud* — two clans of five members each competing against each other. Unlike *Family Feud*, the questions on *Keep It in the Family* were not based on surveys; they were simply rooted in general knowledge, similar to those used on so many of the era's quiz shows. The series was hosted by Bill Nimmo. At that time, Nimmo was Johnny Carson's announcer on *Who Do You Trust?* before Ed McMahon and Carson were teamed.

Although game show icon Wink Martindale is best remembered as the emcee of *Tic Tac Dough* from his successful run with the series in the 1970s and 1980s, Johnny was among the program's early hosts in its original incarnation. Producer Jack Barry, the ever-popular Gene Rayburn, and on occasion, Johnny, the ever-ready pinch-hitter, posed the questions that players answered to capture the nine squares of a tic-tac-toe board. He later briefly inherited the announcer and warm-up work on *Tic Tac Dough*, moving from in front of the camera to behind the microphone, when Bill Wendell, the previous announcer, took on the role of host. There was quick re-casting of the prime-time version of the show, as NBC bounced it around their schedule from Thursdays to Fridays to Mondays.

In part, the parade of personalities presenting *Tic Tac Dough* was prompted by the investigation of alleged game show rigging that ultimately resulted in Jack Barry and Dan Enright, his producing partner, being banished from American television. While the heat of the quiz show scandal was primarily focused on the big money competitions, *Tic Tac Dough* was implicated when a teenaged contestant named Kirsten Falke testified that one of the show's producers had given her questions and answers in advance.

In 1958, Nikita Khrushchev became Premier of the Soviet Union, the Brooklyn Dodgers and the New York Giants were moving to California, Bud Collyer was president of AFTRA, the performers' union, and *My Fair Lady* was on Broadway. CBS invested $500,000 in the stage musical in exchange for all rights beyond its live performance — the bet netted over $32 million after the Broadway cast recording became the biggest selling album to date. [23-2] In 1958, Johnny joined forces with Merv Griffin, another former band singer, who was on his way to leaving an impressive legacy in American television.

While continuing on *Name That Tune* and the other programs he juggled, in June 1958, Johnny was happy to be hired by Goodson-Todman for *Play Your Hunch*, an additional Monday through Friday daytime game and variety show. It was his first series for the producers with whom he partnered for twenty-seven years. It was also an assignment that gave him the chance to put some of his ad-lib and singing skills to good use again, performing in skits designed to showcase Griffin's musical talents.

The show previously had brief runs on both CBS and ABC, but the sudden cancellation of an NBC program in the wake of the quiz show scandals resulted in a call to Goodson-Todman for a quick replacement. That call precipitated another to Merv Griffin, Goodson's first choice to host, who was vacationing in the Caribbean. With less than two weeks between the show's sale and its debut, the new *Play Your Hunch* clicked, enjoying a successful four-year run on NBC's daytime schedule and benefiting from a few forays into prime time.

On-air, Griffin described *Play Your Hunch* as "a game of observation and deduction." It involved simple challenges in which two teams, usually married couples, earned points by guessing from X, Y, or Z choices in a wide range of questions or puzzles that involved one person or object from among three. The pilot episode set the tone for the game with contestants guessing which of three children could play the violin, which of three women married a serviceman, and which of three dogs was the father of the other two. Ira Skutch, *Play Your Hunch* Producer, described the program as a spin-off of *To Tell The Truth*, featuring a demonstration instead of a series of questions.

Other *Play Your Hunch* segments were simple challenges to determine which contestant couple could come closer to guessing the actual number in a quick question that tested their powers of estimation. While far from his most flattering moments on camera, Johnny happily participated in several memorable segments. For one, he lay on a table with his head on a scale, while everyone in the studio stared at him. The challenge was to guess how much his head weighed. In recounting the incident, Skutch remembered it was somewhere around ten pounds.

On another occasion, thirteen-year-old Stephen Press appeared on the show as the actual child magician from among three. Each started a trick before contestants were asked to choose the actual illusionist from the two imposters. When it came time to perform, Stephen took Johnny's necktie and cut it up with a pair of scissors. He then loosened Johnny's shirt and unbuttoned his cuffs. The young magician then borrowed a dollar bill from Johnny's wallet and burned it to cinders. The act stopped for the contestants' responses with the thirteen-year-old promising that he would restore the tie and the bill, as well as pull off Johnny's shirt without removing his jacket. Forty years after the incident, Stephen Press reported that the couples guessed that he was the actual magician, but he failed to recount how well he did in completing the magic routine. At the end of that day's *Play Your Hunch,* Johnny may well have been without the dollar or the tie. [23-3]

A small orchestra accompanied the *Play Your Hunch* action. At times, show segments seemed little more than a means to present music, songs, and skits with guests that included Burt Bacharach, Troy Donahue, Mary Tyler Moore, Sam Cooke, and Kaye Ballard. Johnny's musical background was an asset on the two occasions when he filled-in for Merv as host.

Although *Play Your Hunch* was far from an athletic competition, in 1963, *Sports Illustrated* dispatched a writer to a live broadcast to report on television games. Johnny's enthusiastic entrance instantly earned him the focus of the lead paragraph, albeit with the alternate spelling of his name:

"Every weekday morning at 10:15 a cheerful middle-aged man named Johnny Olsen bounds up the aisle of NBC's Studio 6B in New York to warm up the audience attending the telecast of a program called *Play Your Hunch*. One of the first principles of warming up an audience is to make sure everyone applauds, and Olsen relentlessly ferrets out delinquents during commercials. Not long ago he upbraided a man who hadn't been clapping. The man showed Olsen his empty right sleeve. 'Well,

About his boundless energy, Johnny said, "Every night is opening night." On *Play Your Hunch*, opening night was every weekday morning at 10:15.

snap your fingers,' Olsen told him. 'Everybody works on this show. It's a wing-a-ding-a-ding-a-ding-ding.'" [23-4]

Indeed, *Play Your Hunch* was broadcast each day from NBC's second most-famous studio, Studio 6B, which was two floors below and 40 feet east of the celebrated Studio 8H. Studio 6B was the same stage where Milton Berle enjoyed his greatest success, and Studio 6B was home at various times to *The Ernie Kovacs Show*, *Ted Mack and the Original Amateur Hour*, *The Paul Winchell Show*, *Tic Tac Dough*, *Juvenile Jury*, and *Broadway Open House*. Each day following Merv's *Play Your Hunch*, the show's sets were struck and the studio was reset for *The Tonight Show*, American television's favorite, long-running, late-night nightlight.

One day during Jack Paar's reign in late night, he came to work much earlier than usual and walked into the studio that was regularly vacant in the early afternoon. He found himself in the middle of a morning broadcast of *Play Your Hunch*. Realizing that he was unexpectedly on live television, Paar quickly headed for an exit, but it was too late. The audience's wild reaction, led by Johnny, drew Merv's attention to the unintended guest and he dragged Paar on-stage for some spontaneous interplay. Together, they made the most of the unplanned encounter, creating some truly inspired unrehearsed comedy. Feigning complete surprise that his studio was being used every morning by another program, Paar joked, "So this is what you do in the daytime?" [23-5]

Paar, also a former game show host, was impressed with Merv's instincts and ad-lib skills. The prince of late night was well aware that Merv had made magic of the unexpected moment. Chris Carroll, Paar's army buddy and staffer, acted as a matchmaker when he subsequently arranged for Merv to appear on Paar's show. Before long, Merv was offered fill-in opportunities as guest host. Those nights went so well for Merv that he was given future shots in the late-night time slot after Paar left, and he was ultimately under serious consideration to take over *The Tonight Show*, while NBC waited for Johnny Carson to serve out the remaining six months on his contract with the ABC series, *Who Do You Trust?*

Play Your Hunch was a springboard that launched Merv into decades of success as a talk show host, and even led to Johnny Olson making late-night appearances on NBC with both Jack Paar and Johnny Carson. That exposure helped lead to occasional opportunities to work with legends such as Frank Sinatra and Bob Hope, when Johnny announced series and specials hosted by Sammy Davis Jr., Kate Smith, Victor Borge, Dom DeLuise, and Peggy Fleming.

Gene Rayburn stepped in to host *Play Your Hunch* after Merv. Rayburn was another familiar NBC face and a radio and television veteran. He had been Steve Allen's sidekick on *The Tonight Show* in earlier years. Just a few weeks after fronting *Play Your Hunch*, Rayburn relinquished the reigns to actor-broadcaster Robert Q. Lewis, when he was teamed with Johnny on Goodson-Todman's *The Match Game*.

CHAPTER 24
A PERFECT MATCH

The Match Game, like most of the Goodson-Todman hits, was a collaborate effort in refining the format and game play, as well as perfecting the on-air presentation. At the core of the company's creative team was about a dozen senior producers, directors, and other specialists. They spent hours and sometimes days working in committee, contributing ideas, making suggestions, and experimenting with variations on the basic formats and the staging of the games in development.

Most members of that team agreed that Mark Goodson's greatest gift was as a judge, an evaluator, an editor, and an arbitrator, as he firmly steered the development process. Among the members of that brain trust in the early years were Frank Wayne, Bob Stewart, Ira Skutch, Chester Feldman, Frank Heller, Paul Alter, Gil Fates, Bob Bach, Jerry Schnur, Willie Stein, and Lloyd Gross.

Bob Stewart, creator of some of the genre's most enduring concepts, reported that Goodson's "greatest ability is to recognize good ideas and then edit them."[24-1] Stewart also looked askance at the team approach to invention saying, "Nobody ever created an idea with twenty people in a room."[24-2] Skutch concurred: "They never came out with an original concept at the meetings, but we did push other concepts along."[24-2]

Frank Wayne was credited for the premise that became *The Match Game*. A former song-and-dance vaudevillian who studied and taught at the New England Conservatory of Music in Boston, Wayne was among the pioneers in Boston television. He enjoyed one of the longest associations with Goodson and Todman as a vital contributor to their think tank and as Executive Producer of some of their biggest hits. Ira Skutch recalled that a new game was born on the day that Wayne gathered a few staffers and asked them to "Write down something about an elephant." Among the answers were "Big," "Gray," and "Trunk."

With the added motivation of trying to match the answers that would be given by the others, the basis for a game was quickly apparent. As pairing civilian contestants with celebrity players had been a successful innovation for *Password* the previous year, it was added to the recipe. As simple as it all may sound, Mark Goodson summarized the complex development process to get *The Match Game* air-worthy. He described the essential concept of coming up with the most likely answer as being similar to "the old Italian game of matching fingers or matchsticks."[24-3]

From there, an idea in which contestants bid and risked points was tested and discarded. Goodson reported that the inclusion of a celebrity player then came under scrutiny and was rejected at first. He asked, "What was he there for, anyway?"[24-3] He then concluded that a betting game had little interest for an audience because it was difficult for a viewer to keep track of the action. The producer remembered next experimenting with a system of elimination. "We put six contestants in a room," he said. "'Name an American President not living.' Say three named Franklin Roosevelt. We eliminated the other three like in a spelling bee ... The trouble with that, once

Straight-laced and buttoned-down, the early years of *The Match Game* gave viewers no clue to the linguistic mayhem to come in its later seasons. Master of ceremonies Gene Rayburn was always masterful in balancing the fun with the game play.

you're down to three, two must match. It might take forever."[24-3] That approach was abandoned because of the complex staging needed to get people on and off the set without unnecessary, distracting movement and awkward breaks in the game rhythm.

Next, the team idea was explored. As team captains, celebrities would have a function. Goodson said, "We still felt a lack, however, so we developed the idea of the audience match."[24-3] Before the show, studio audiences would be polled with a simple question such as "Name a famous American landmark," and the teams would try to guess the most frequent answer. The producer observed, "It allowed the viewing audience to say, 'You're all crazy.' It gave them a feeling of triumph if the contestants didn't get it. It was more definitive." [24-3]

The fruits of all that labor joined the NBC lineup on the last day of 1962. Over the theme song "A Swinging Safari" by Bert Kaempfert, Johnny opened each of the

1,760 episodes during the seven-year initial run of *The Match Game* with the words, "From New York City, it's time to play *The Match Game*." The teams attempted to match answers to pedestrian questions that included "Name a President whose picture is on money," "Name a way to prepare eggs," and fill-in-the-blank challenges such as "*(blank)* muffin."

Cancellation of *The Match Game* was precipitated by both lackluster ratings and a change in programming philosophy by the network's executives. The program was marked for extinction after a single year, but then the show's fate was reversed by the whimsical inventiveness of Dick DeBartolo. DeBartolo had a background in television that began with work as an office boy and writer for producers Jack Barry and Dan Enright. By the 1960s, he was utilizing his off-beat sense of humor as a contributor to *MAD* magazine. The confluence of those creative streams gave birth to an idea that proved to be pivotal for the survival of *The Match Game*, and ultimately cleared the way for the show to enjoy runs on all three networks. It was adapted and piloted for new generations of viewers almost fifty years later.

Producer Bob Noah brought Dick DeBartolo to the attention of Goodson-Todman three months before the show's debut, and he was hired as a free-lancer to begin writing the sedate questions for *The Match Game*. DeBartolo recalled, "After about ten months on the air, Mark Goodson called me into his office and told me that the preceding Friday was the pick-up date from the network, and that they didn't call. He told me there were six weeks of shows left to do and then production would stop."

The writer continued, "After thinking about the show's demise over the weekend, I came back to Goodson-Todman Productions Monday morning and set up a meeting with Mark Goodson. I said, 'You know Mark, I also work for *MAD* Magazine and I've being thinking about bringing a *MAD* approach to the questions.' I suggested we try some silly questions. Mark asked to hear an example of one, and I said, 'Mary liked to pour gravy on John's *(blank)*.'

"That was the first silly *Match Game* question I ever wrote. Goodson laughed and said, 'what the hell are people gonna say?' I told him they would most likely laugh like he did and then give acceptable answers like meatloaf or mashed potatoes. They'll give serious answers, but it just sounds funny. Goodson said, 'Do what you want. The show's cancelled, so write what you like. Do all the silly questions you want. NBC can't cancel it twice.' So I started writing those questions and we started alternating the new off-beat questions with the regular ones. After five weeks of that, Goodson called me in and said, 'Dick, the ratings are up enough that it's going for another year.'" [24-4]

DeBartolo earned a substantial raise and assured an eighteen-year future for himself at the game show factory, contributing to several long-running hits. With the kind of loyalty often seen at Goodson-Todman, DeBartolo continued into the 1970s as a member of the team. He cast contestants for the syndicated years of *What's My Line?*, as well as created comedic moments for *I've Got A Secret* and *To Tell The Truth*. Although he turned down company-paid moves to Hollywood for a revival of *The Match Game* and for its spin-off, *Family Feud*, DeBartolo contributed to both from his home in New York.

Johnny played a role in all five of those shows on DeBartolo's resume, but because of his already full schedule, he announced only on the 1976 pilot for *Family Feud*. Johnny forged working relationships with all of those shows' hosts, but he developed a permanent bond based on mutual respect with Gene Rayburn on *The Match Game*.

In his on-air presence, Johnny had developed a knack for complementing but never over-shadowing a program's star. Always ready with a laugh in response to a host's quip, Johnny's extensive experience honed his instincts to where he was perpetually prepared to contribute a line when the host looked to him for support, or when he sensed an awkward moment. More challenging a skill was John's sensitivity to know when to withhold a comment that could add to the program's comedy if it might upstage the star. Rayburn had an appreciation for the delicate art.

Johnny had the lead role in his interplay with the studio audience, and he was skillful at respectfully deflecting an audience member's desire to speak to a host during commercial breaks when the emcee's attention was necessarily focused on the program's next segment. Yet Johnny knew how to instantly eclipse his leading role with the audience when he sensed that a program's host wanted to address those in-studio guests. It was a balance that required skill and grace, and as a former second banana to Steve Allen, Gene Rayburn fully understood and valued Johnny's ability to handle the challenges with aplomb. Their chemistry made Johnny a valued on-air partner and Rayburn's first choice as announcer for all of his future work.

The Match Game was produced in NBC's Studio 8H, a historic facility that encompassed a specially constructed section of the eighth and ninth floors of the RCA building. The magnificent edifice was the third tallest New York skyscraper when it opened in 1933, and its roof was later equipped with the world's largest gasoline-powered air raid siren that was often manned on a 24-hour basis during World War II, ever ready to warn America's most populous city in the event of an enemy attack.

The centerpiece of the Rockefeller Center development, the RCA building (now rechristened to honor GE) is a full block wide between 49th and 50th Streets. It fronts along Sixth Avenue, the Avenue of the Americas to the west, and tiny Rockefeller

Facing page: Created with the theme "New Frontiers," the magnificent Rockefeller Center development was crowned by the RCA building. The complex was constructed during the darkest days of the Great Depression. Above: NBC Studio 8H in the RCA building, in the days before television. Johnny worked regularly in the world's largest broadcasting facility, the origination point for many of radio and television's most memorable moments.

Plaza to the east. The building was planned with broadcasting in mind; the lower nine floors constructed for NBC's studios incorporated a number of unique architectural features.

Studio 8H's design was most elaborate, with a studio floor that floated above the building's floor on felt-covered steel springs in order to trap any noise and absorb any vibration from the subway line that ran below the building. The load-bearing walls around the massive studio's perimeter were reinforced to allow the 132-foot long, 76-foot wide, and 30-foot high room to be unencumbered by support columns. When NBC moved to 30 Rockefeller Plaza on October 1, 1933, Studio 8H was the largest broadcasting studio in the world, and just one feature of David Sarnoff's dream for America's magnificent headquarters for broadcasting that he unashamedly christened Radio City.

Indeed, Sarnoff much preferred that NBC's new headquarters in Rockefeller Center always be referred to as Radio City, and he preferred that his employees refer to him as "The General." His work organizing the extensive communications required for the D-Day invasion earned him the title of Brigadier General, which he relished. Radio City, the General's new citadel, was outfitted with deep plush carpeting, magnificent murals, and gleaming black marble and gold Art Deco appointments that were nothing less than lavish. The facility undoubtedly felt like home to Johnny. He had regularly worked there, often on a daily basis, since eighteen years before the debut of *The Match Game.* Johnny was hired amidst all that grandeur soon after the Life Savers candy mogul purchased NBC's Blue Network.

Gene Rayburn reminisced about his own days surrounded by that opulence, when he worked as an NBC page in the 1930s. He remembered the hours he spent standing at the doorway of Studio 8H, watching in awe, as the renowned Arturo Toscanini rehearsed the NBC Symphony Orchestra. Sarnoff had coaxed the celebrated maestro from his home in Italy to command an honored assemblage of 130 musicians, in defiance of Thomas Edison's claim that "radio, so far as music is concerned, is a failure." [24-5]

Without a sponsor, David Sarnoff committed the first investment of what eventually totaled over $400,000 to the NBC Symphony Orchestra. Author John J. Floherty reported during Toscanini's heyday, "Before the final notes of the initial broadcast had melted into the ether, telephone calls created a traffic jam on the NBC switchboard. Next day, an avalanche of mail poured in and continued to arrive from all parts of the country . . . all of it reflected gratefulness for the opportunity of listening to the world's greatest music interpreted by an acknowledged master and rendered by an orchestra composed of many of the country's finest musicians." [24-6]

Sarnoff's investment paid off financially, when General Motors stepped up to sponsor the orchestra's broadcasts "to the tune of a million dollars a season." [24-6] The NBC Symphony Orchestra generated additional black ink for the corporate balance sheets with the sale of its popular recordings on RCA Victor Records. The tradition of the NBC Symphony continued on television before the orchestra was disbanded in 1954.

In addition to the origination of countless live hours of classic symphonic and operatic entertainment programming, news coverage of presidential elections and NASA space missions were broadcast from Studio 8H. After being remodeled for television during the summer of 1950, the remaining 115 by 58 feet comprised one of the largest video facilities in Manhattan. Producer Al Howard remembered staging his *Sale of the Century* game show in that huge studio on one of the few, two-story game show sets ever constructed. Witnesses confirmed his recollection that large prizes, including numerous cars, had to be cut in half to fit into the freight elevator, and then re-welded on the eighth floor.

In 1963, Studio 8H was transformed for color broadcasting. Since 1975, Studio 8H has been the home of *Saturday Night Live.* Instead of the NBC Symphony

Orchestra's performances of the classics, The Rolling Stones, George Harrison, Billy Joel, The Grateful Dead, and Elton John have been among the classic rockers to play the room. One can only conjecture what maestro Toscanini would have thought of the music more recently performed there by Kid Rock, Amy Winehouse, Foo Fighters, Five For Fighting, The Red Hot Chili Peppers, and Korn.

CHAPTER 25
WHO DO YOU TRUST?

Johnny was born at a politically tumultuous time, when the world was entering the conflict that was to be "The war to end all wars." World War I ushered in an era that was marked by a distrust of foreigners. At times, our nation seemed to be overwhelmed with suspicions about many of its own citizens. Thousands of Americans were in prison for violating the newly enacted Espionage Act of 1917 or its amended 1918 version known as the Sedition Act. Both usurped freedom of speech, as dissenting voices were judged to be a threat to national security. Likewise, the 1918 Alien Act was passed to protect Americans from spies and disloyal subversives, who were feared to be lurking among us.

Poet Carl Sandburg was arrested for violating the 1917 wartime law known as the Trading with the Enemy Act when he returned from Stockholm and set foot on American soil because of writings he had mailed back to the states. The November 21, 1918 edition of *The Nation* reported that distributors of political leaflets were snared in the web, as was a man who simply told a Liberty Bond salesman that he wished the "government would go to hell."

Staffs of The US Postal Service, The Secret Service, The Office of Naval Intelligence, the army's Military Intelligence Division, and the forerunner of the FBI — The Justice Department's Bureau of Investigation — were all soliciting information from thousands of private citizens who were self-appointed sleuths. They were members of dozens of organizations including The American Protective League, The Liberty League, The American Defense Society, The Home Defense League, The National Security League, The Knights of Liberty, and The American Anti-Anarchy Association. These extremists were fierce and fearless in ferreting out suspected spies, subversives, anarchists, and Russian Bolsheviks.

That radical chapter in our history seemed as if it could never be repeated, but only thirty years later, America was embroiled in another internal witch hunt. Johnny was spared, but he bore silent witness as many of his co-workers were destroyed by rumor and innuendo. The late 1940s and early 1950s was a period of patriotic paranoia. Americans feared that Communists were infiltrating our culture and attempting to indoctrinate our citizenry with the ultimate goal of taking over the country.

A 1945 report issued by the US Chamber of Commerce, "Communist Infiltration in the US," warned of the inroads made by subversives, particularly in the entertainment industry. A budding hysteria was intensified by the rhetoric dispensed by

Wisconsin Senator Joseph McCarthy. New Jersey Congressman J. Parnell Thomas rode the wave of distrust to become Chairman of the House Committee on Un-American Activities, before he was indicted on charges of conspiracy to defraud the government, and subsequently convicted of fraud.

The loyalty of neighbors, friends, government officials, and especially film and television writers and personalities, became suspect. Blacklisting became the darkest chapter in broadcasting's history, and the careers and lives of many talented directors, performers, and scribes drowned in a wave of fear.

A decade earlier, newspaper columnist Walther Winchell had created controversy on his popular Sunday night network radio program when he accused politicians and private citizens of being spies and communists. Winchell's conjecture even included a 1937 claim that "the Duke of Windsor was to be employed by the motion picture industry to censor pictures for world distribution." [25-1] Most of the columnist's musings were dismissed as sensationalist rhetoric; there was little to suggest that such innuendo concerning political ideology and patriotism packed the potential for a pandemic panic of paranoia.

The United States and Russia had been allies during World War II, but the relationship became increasingly strained. Josef Stalin was *Time* magazine's 1942 Man of the Year, but in the years that followed, there was growing distrust between the two former allied nations. Soon after America developed, tested, and used the atomic bomb against Japan at the end of the war, Russia developed its own atomic weapons during peacetime. In February 1950, as the Cold War heated up, Wisconsin Senator Joseph McCarthy warned America about a communist threat from within the US government and how communism had the potential to destroy America's security, as well as the American way of life.

At a speech in Salt Lake City, McCarthy announced, "The State Department, which is one of the most important government departments, is thoroughly infested with Communists." Waving documents that he never presented to any investigative body, McCarthy warned, "I have in my hand fifty-seven cases of individuals who would appear to be either card-carrying members or certainly loyal to the Communist Party, but who nevertheless are still helping to shape our foreign policy." [25-2]

During a speech the previous day in West Virginia, the Senator had proclaimed, "I have here in my hand a list of 205, a list of names made known to the Secretary of State as being members of the Communist Party." Eleven days later on the Senate floor, McCarthy cited eighty-one "cases," including "three big Communists." [25-2] It all turned out to be political posturing, but fanning the flames of mistrust brought on a firestorm. One of the few breaths of levity came from Bob Hope, who chided, "Senator McCarthy is ready to name two million Communists — he just got a copy of the Moscow phone book."

Red Channels, a 213-page paperback publication edited by former FBI investigator Vincent Hartnett, was issued on June 22, 1950. It singled out 151 actors, writers, producers, and literary figures by name as being Communists or affiliated with causes sympathetic with Communism. Although the report was loaded with innuendo and many of the allegations were untrue, being tainted by suspicion was enough to end a career. During the post-World War II "Red Scare" and the chilling days of the Cold War, obsessive mistrust and fear all too often resulted in advertiser and network pressure to fire anyone even suspected of disloyalty.

Henry Morgan and Orson Bean, Goodson-Todman's ubiquitous panelists, fell under suspicion. Bennett Cerf watched, as one of his fellow *What's My Line?* panel

members was dragged through the mud. "Louis Untermeyer is no more a Communist than J. Edgar Hoover, but he had joined several suspect societies — that made him rather conspicuous." Cerf noted that the era of the blacklist "was an unfortunate time…a lot of people in television lost their jobs outrageously." [25-3]

The political controversy became a financial brouhaha when a fanatical grocer in Syracuse, who owned a small chain of stores, threatened to start a boycott of products from sponsors hiring people of whom he disapproved. He alerted manufacturers that he was prepared to enlist other retailers in placing signs on store shelves indicating which products were from companies sponsoring television and radio programs that employed Communists.

Naming names. Johnny was spared in the Communist witch hunt that destroyed the careers of many of his co-workers and friends.

With their bottom lines in jeopardy, networks and ad agencies looked to appease advertisers; they succumbed to the demands of all manner of activist groups. Bennett Cerf remembered, "The Catholic War Veterans were also raising hell about Louis Untermeyer. Goodson-Todman held out against this as long as they could, but finally the veterans started picketing the theater where *What's My Line?* was done." [25-3] Under pressure, Mark Goodson reluctantly released Untermeyer from the program.

In 1950, General Foods dropped actress Jean Muir from NBC-TV's *The Aldrich Family* after her name appeared in Red Channels. An organization calling itself The Joint Committee Against Communism took credit for the firing as part of its drive to "cleanse" the media of pro-Communist forces. To no avail, *Broadcasting* magazine, a widely-read trade publication, reported Miss Muir's denials before Congress of any Communist affiliations or sympathies. That same year, CBS asked all employees to sign loyalty oaths, while NBC inquired as to its employees' possible Communist Party membership going back to 1944.

Actor and game show regular Tony Randall recalled, "People made money out of the blacklist...Everybody was cleared through that man Hartnett. He made a living from clearing people."[25-4] Vincent Hartnett's *Red Channels* was affiliated with a weekly newsletter called *Counterattack,* which was circulated by three other former FBI agents. In addition to listing more names of alleged subversives, those agents' American Business Consultants acted as a clearinghouse of information. For a fee, they investigated and evaluated directors, performers, and writers, and provided the networks and advertising agencies with the confidential information they supposedly needed to determine who was fit or unfit to be employed. Ed Sullivan was said to have been one of Counterattack's most loyal customers, using its staff to check on the loyalty of blacklisted and tainted talent.

Johnny knew several victims of the witch hunt, including Jackie Gleason's original Alice Kramden, actress Pert Kelton, who disappeared from public view in 1952 after being tainted by the red scare. While audiences were told that she was suffering from heart problems, the cover story might not have been too far from the truth. Pert was born into a family of vaudevillians and had performed since the age of three. There was little doubt that her heart was broken when she was unable to find work for a full decade. Kelton ultimately was welcomed back to Gleason's troupe in the 1960s to play Alice Kramden's mother.

Johnny's friend, Ireene Wicker, the children's television hostess, was off the air after it was erroneously reported that she had signed a petition on behalf of a Communist Party candidate. Only after her lawyer obtained a court order to identify all 30,000 names on the petition did the editors of *Counterattack* admit that a mistake had been made. Leonard Bernstein, Aaron Copland, Lena Horne, Burl Ives, Gypsy Rose Lee, Burgess Meredith, Arthur Miller, Zero Mostel, Dorothy Parker, Edward G. Robinson, Pete Seeger, Artie Shaw, and Orson Welles were all named and shamed. Even Jane Wyatt, the wholesome mother on *Father Knows Best,* came under suspicion. After being cast for that great, all-American sitcom, Columbia Pictures arranged for the actress to read scripts that were broadcast on Radio Free Europe in order to purge her anti-American stigma.

No less a comedic icon than Lucille Ball, television's most beloved redhead, was feared to be too red to trust. There was an audible gasp at CBS' New York offices that could be heard as far away as Desilu Studios in Hollywood, when columnist Walter Winchell implicated their top star in the scandal. Lucy was among the many brought before the House Un-American Committee in Washington. Years before, she and her brother registered as Communists at the urging of their grandfather. Unlike other accused people who never worked again, once Lucy denounced her controversial affiliation and President Eisenhower excused her transgression, Americans were told it was once again safe to love Lucy.

The impact of the blacklist continued far beyond the life of its instigator. Senator McCarthy died in May 1957, but his legacy of accusations and insinuations lingered for more than a decade. Joan Boniface Winnifrith was a British-born motion picture and television actress known simply as Anna Lee as early as 1939, when she was one of the pioneering film actresses to appear on W6XAO Los Angeles, the first television station in the west.

In 1991, on the occasion of Mark Goodson's seventy-sixth birthday, the seventy-eight-year-old actress recounted her experience as a regular panelist on Goodson's game shows when her name unexpectedly appeared in *Red Channels*. Anna Lee referred to the blacklist as "diabolical," and she thanked the producer for personally vouching for her to the network and sponsors that had asked for her removal.

As a corporate entity, CBS was among the media and advertising firms that bowed to political pressure in its programming and casting. Edward R. Murrow, CBS' most-respected newsman, took advantage of the network's long-standing policy of empowering its news department with journalistic freedom. Once the word was out that a show dealing with McCarthy was being prepared, the Senator mounted a preemptive attack, telling people that he had documents proving that Murrow was a Communist.

After much pre-production and extensive gathering of footage of McCarthy's impassioned oratories, Murrow's March 9, 1954 *See It Now* program took on the Senator. Murrow exposed McCarthy's rhetoric as being based on half-truths, innuendo, and outright fabrication designed to further his own political agenda. CBS President Frank Stanton recalled, "The broadcast obviously was a bombshell; it wasn't that we didn't expose anything that hadn't been known because *Look* magazine had done a very rough piece on McCarthy and others had done individual stories. But Murrow, with [Fred] Friendly's help, put together a *See It Now* broadcast that shook the whole journalism field." [25-5]

On the *See It Now* broadcast, Murrow quoted from newspapers that had been critical of the Senator. From the *Chicago Tribune,* he read, "McCarthy will better serve his cause if he learns to distinguish the role of investigator from the role of avenging angel." From the *New York Times,* he quoted, "The unwarranted interference of a demagogue — a domestic Munich..." From the *New York Herald Tribune,* he read, "McCarthyism involves assaults on basic Republican concepts..." From the *Milwaukee Journal,* he quoted, "The line must be drawn and defended or McCarthy will become the government..." From the *New York World Telegram,* he read, "Bamboozling, bludgeoning, distorting way..." The *St. Louis Post Dispatch* had written, "Unscrupulous, McCarthy bullying. What a tragic irony it is that the President's political advisors keep him from doing what every decent instinct must be commanding him to do..."

On April 6, 1954, CBS presented McCarthy's rebuttal. The Senator called Murrow "a leader and the cleverest of the jackal pack, which is always found at the throat of anyone who dares to expose individual Communists and traitors." McCarthy also reviewed the work of his Senate committee, claiming, "84 witnesses refused to testify as to Communist activities on the ground that, if they told the truth, they might go to jail; twenty-four witnesses with Communist backgrounds have been discharged from jobs [in] which they were handling secret, top-secret, confidential material, individuals who were exposed before our committee."

Of the Communists that had infiltrated our government, McCarthy explained, "If there were no Communists in our government, why did we delay for eighteen months, delay our research on the hydrogen bomb, even though our intelligence agencies were reporting day after day that the Russians were feverishly pushing their development of the H-Bomb? And may I say to America tonight that our nation may well die — out nation may well die — because of that eighteen-months deliberate delay. And I ask you, who caused it? Was it loyal Americans? Or was it traitors in our government?" [25-6]

In his review of the *See It Now* program on McCarthy, Jack Gould, the *New York Times* television critic, wrote that "last week may be remembered as the week that broadcasting recaptured its soul." [25-7] It was also the beginning of a rift between network founder, William Paley, and his star newsman. Facing pressure from advertisers and from friends in his lofty social circles to reign-in Murrow's controversial and liberal-minded reports, Paley's relationship with America's most-respected broadcast journalist cooled.

The disagreement over the network's role in reacting to the blacklist ultimately led to the 1958 cancellation of the newsman's pet project, *See It Now*. That contributed to Murrow's departure from CBS two years later to head the United States Information Agency, the parent of the Voice of America, for President Kennedy. Paley's public explanation for the cancellation of *See It Now* concerned itself with finances. With each episode reportedly budgeted at $90,000, the program was expensive for news fare.

John Crosby, the *New York Herald-Tribune* television critic, slammed CBS and Goodson-Todman simultaneously with his commentary. "*See It Now*," he wrote, "is by every criterion television's most brilliant, most decorated, most imaginative, most courageous and most important program. The fact that CBS cannot afford it but can afford *Beat The Clock* is shocking." [25-8] Harsh criticism, but game shows were already well on their way to their own ultimate indignity.

CHAPTER 26
TO TELL THE TRUTH

Mark Goodson and Bill Todman focused on panel shows and celebrations of ordinary people instead of big money quizzes. They managed to avoid being sullied in the greatest scandal in television history, an ignominy that the medium brought upon itself by rigging game show competitions in search of higher ratings.

In much the same way as celebrities on *Hollywood Squares* would be provided with joke responses to questions in later years, Goodson-Todman's celebrity panelists were occasionally given questions to ask that would elicit laughter when juxtaposed with the identities and secrets of contestants. Panelists were never given those identities or secrets, contestants were never scripted, and the Goodson-Todman games were played for real.

There was little financial incentive to rig the company's shows. Stumping the entire panel on *To Tell The Truth* resulted in each participant winning $333. *What's My Line?* was on the air for twenty-four years on network and in syndication, and no contestant was ever awarded more than $50. The one time the idea was floated to raise the maximum prize on *What's My Line?* to $1,000, the thought was quickly rejected. According to Goodson-Todman veteran director and producer Ira Skutch, John Daly said he would not be interested in continuing as moderator as any significant increase in the $50 maximum honorarium would change the nature of the program. In the January 30, 1960 issue of *TV Guide*, Garry Moore said he felt slighted that *I've Got A Secret* was not investigated by the grand jury exploring the extent of the rigging. He joked, "Apparently, they figured that as only $80 was given away on our show, we were too cheap to be crooked. They were right."

By contrast, big money quiz shows were awarding life-altering sums of money to average Americans — the more average and in possession of vast knowledge, the better. A dock worker earned $10,500 for his scholarly prowess, and a police officer who knew Shakespeare captured $16,000. A grandmother who worked as a typist tapped $32,000 answering questions on the Bible. A shoemaker who knew opera sewed-up $64,000, as did Billy Pearson, a jockey who rode to riches as an expert on art.

Charles Van Doren, who earned $4,400 a year as a Columbia University instructor, climbed to $129,000. Elfrida Von Nardoff, a student at that respected university, amassed $220,500, while Teddy Nadler, a minimum-wage warehouse clerk and occasional cab driver, pocketed $252,000. As Steve Carlin, executive producer of *The*

$64,000 Question, described the casting dichotomy, "Good honest three-dimensional people [with] a depth you wouldn't suspect." [26-1]

The money was big and so were the ratings. Within six weeks of its debut, *The $64,000 Question* with quizmaster Hal March became America's top-rated television program. The night when a marine captain, who was an expert on French cuisine, cooked-up the first grand prize on *The $64,000 Question,* the show served-up the largest audience for a weekly entertainment program in the entire, albeit brief, history of television — a national Trendex rating of 68.2 with an 85 percent share of the television audience — ratings that far surpassed the legendary popularity enjoyed by *I Love Lucy.*

As icing on the cake, Louis Cowan, the show's producer and a Chicago native with a degree in philosophy and a well-developed social conscience, was soon crowned as the new president of CBS. Cowan's career subsequently deflated faster than a soured soufflé. Despite asserting his innocence, he later realized that the show's competition was merely a charade. Cowan's next pursuits were in academia. He accepted a position at Columbia University, the same institution from which Charles Van Doren resigned in disgrace after his role on the rigged quiz shows was revealed.

Teddy Nadler was the biggest winner of the era with a bounty of just over $250,000 from *The $64,000 Question.* The equivalent of that sum would be over $2 million dollars today after accounting for inflation. He immediately wrote a sixty-four-page paperback book with the inflated title, *Secrets of My Million Dollar Memory,* in which he taught his method of memorization. Other high-profile participants wrote books on their areas of expertise, from Shakespeare to cooking.

After winning $64,000, spelling whiz Gloria Lockerman became a guest speaker at the Democratic National Convention. Catherine Kreitzer, the grandmother with seemingly total recall of the Bible, returned to television to read from the scriptures on *The Ed Sullivan Show.* Baseball expert Myrtle Power was made a sports commentator on CBS. Gino Prato, the shoemaker with a specialty in Italian opera, was given a $10,000-a-year job with the manufacturer of replacement heels and soles to serve as goodwill ambassador to cobblers everywhere. [26-2] Prato was also brought to Italy for a special performance at la Scala, and he was honored by an audience with the Pope. [26-3]

In the late 1950s, the excitement, the fabricated human drama, and the huge ratings garnered by *The $64,000 Question, Twenty One, The Big Surprise, Tic Tac Dough,* and *The $64,000 Challenge* built to a frenzy before imploding. On Friday, April 15, 1958, the Colgate Palmolive Company suddenly cancelled *Dotto,* their top-rated show, from CBS' daytime and NBC's prime time schedules.

Dotto contestants' correct answers to questions allowed them to connect dots to reveal a drawing of a celebrity. There were no isolation booths or heavy drama, and the questions were not particularly difficult. Just the same, players were being given information that would manipulate the outcome of the games. Marie Winn was the eighteen-year-old contestant who created what became the smoking gun in the quiz show scandals; in a school notebook, she wrote down answers to questions that she suspected would be used on the program.

As Winn wrote in a rare reflection on the matter, "They'd throw sample questions at me, and I'd give them the answer as if I were playing *Dotto*. If I didn't know an answer, they would casually throw it in...in fact, the warm-up session included real questions." [26-4] Once it surfaced in the media that suspected rigging was the reason behind *Dotto*'s abrupt cancellation, a domino effect began that led to a New York grand jury investigation and an eventual Congressional probe. *The $64,000 Challenge* was gone after September 7, and on November 2, the end came for *The $64,000 Question*, the show that started the big-money rage three and one-half years earlier.

When the decision was made to abruptly yank *Dotto* from airwaves, host Jack Narz recalled that he was invited to the producer's home, offered a couple of martinis, and told the news. He said he was at a loss for words, unaware that the outcome of his simple game had been manipulated for maximum drama. The host recalled forty years later, "That night when I was told what was going on, I saw my whole career flash before me. I knew this was going to be in every newspaper and magazine in the country as a big black mark for television. I wasn't sure I'd ever work again." [26-5] Narz said he had never even met the standby player who brought the charges, and a lie detector test cleared the affable host of any wrongdoing. Narz continued his long and successful career, working often with Johnny Olson in the years to come.

Despite his on-camera longevity, Narz wondered in retrospect if the association with *Dotto* had cooled his career. He told Steve Beverly, Professor of Broadcasting at Union University in Tennessee, "I always felt that I was a 'day late and dollar short' kind of guy. From that point on, that maybe there were some shows I didn't get because they said, 'He was on that show, maybe we shouldn't take a shot on him.'" [26-6]

While the manipulated competition on big money quiz shows was considered by some in the television and advertising communities to be an open secret among their ranks, it seemed unbelievable to the general public that contestants, who appeared to struggle with the questions, actually knew the answers all along. *Twenty One* producer Albert Freedman, who was later indicted for perjury for his role in the hypocrisy, more recently reflected, "Everybody knew what was going on — the agencies, the sponsors, the networks." [26-4]

Advertising agencies, sponsors, and the networks denied any wrongdoing. CBS stated that a week-long internal investigation failed to uncover any impropriety. In addition, the big money winning players were outspoken in denying any collusion. The public refused to accept the reality of having been duped even after accusations by other former contestants fed months of headlines in the country's most respected newspapers and magazines. Those were indeed innocent times.

Despite an article in the April 22, 1957 issue of *Time* that explained how questions were being tailored to winning participants' specific areas of expertise, and a story in an August 1957 *Look* magazine specifically alleging that the outcome of the intellectual battles on *Tic Tac Dough* and *Twenty One* were controlled, the producers' and winning contestants' denials rang true. Most believed that the accusations from players such as Herb Stemple, the socially awkward former GI and student who lost to the handsome, engaging, and erudite Charles Van Doren on *Twenty One*, were undoubtedly sour grapes.

Elfrida Von Nardoff responded to the most difficult question asked of the winning quiz show players, "It was inconceivable they could have been fixed." Teddy Nadler said, "They never told me a damn thing." George Wright III, a $100,000 winner on *The Big Surprise*, stated, "They never gave me answers to any questions." Robert Strom, a twelve-year-old science prodigy, earned $224,000 from his correct responses, but his mother answered by sidestepping the most relevant question, saying, "I think meeting the boy speaks for itself about the authenticity of the show." Jockey Billy Pearson could not have been more wrong when he conjectured about the sponsor, "Revlon is too close to the shows...it would never allow its product to be jeopardized" [26-7]

Johnny almost certainly knew the way that some shows were being subtly manipulated. Producers he knew well were among those plotting the competitions. Panelists on *What's My Line?* were provided with questions calculated to produce humorous double entendres. Johnny's friends at *Stop the Music* seemed to telephone listeners at random with a chance to name the mystery tune, but in reality, the calls were auditioned and put on the air in the most dramatic order.

At NBC's Rockefeller Center headquarters, where Johnny reported to work almost daily, *Twenty One* administered a four-hour, 363-question test to ascertain information about contestants' areas of knowledge that was being exploited to influence the outcome of competition. *The $64,000 Question*, its spin-off, *The $64,000 Challenge*, *The Big Surprise,* and *Dotto* all engaged their players in warm-up sessions that included questions and answers that were later included in the games.

Johnny was among those watching in horror, as his industry came under attack for violating the blind trust that Americans had for game shows and for television in general. During his work at DuMont, Johnny had come to know Jack Barry, one of the people deeply embroiled in the controversy. Barry was hosting *Wisdom of the Ages* for DuMont during the years when Johnny was a regular face on the network and the two became friendly. Barry and his producing partner, Dan Enright, had met a decade earlier when Barry was a local radio announcer and Enright an audio engineer. Suddenly, the two were at the center of television's biggest scandal.

Enright recalled that the debut episode of *Twenty One* on September 12, 1956, was less than compelling viewing. Indeed, NBC's short-lived revival of the show in 2000 proved that the game's format, when played purely, lacked much of the desired tension and drama. In a 1989 interview on NBC's *The Today Show*, Dan Enright said that he received a call from Pharmaceuticals, Inc., the sponsor, on the morning after the lackluster 1956 premiere. They admonished that they never again wanted to see anything like what they had seen the night before. That somewhat cryptic message began a sequence of events that forever changed the lives of that show's host, producers, and participants, and contributed to the most damning chapter of American television history.

Columbia University instructor, Charles Van Doren, was the thirty-year-old, fair-haired offspring of a respected family of literary honorees. On the evening of

November 28, 1956, he made his first appearance on *Twenty One* and quickly garnered attention that boosted NBC's Wednesday night ratings. By the time of his final appearance the following March, he had outwitted a string of challengers and had become an American celebrity. During his reign, he competed in a series of nail-biting tie matches against the less erudite Herbert Stempel, a student at the City College of New York, who went on to work for the city's transit system. By appearance, pedigree, and even in the sound of their names — Van Doren and Stempel — the two were polar opposites, and their battles captured the public's fascination.

By December 5, 1956, the drama of their academic sparring matches had played out, and as directed to do, Stempel reluctantly gave an incorrect answer to a question about *Marty,* his favorite movie, that he said would never have stumped him. Van Doren remained on the show to meet new competitors, was a guest on *The Steve Allen Show,* and was even featured on the cover of the February 11, 1957 issue of *Time* magazine, while Stempel quickly grew bitter after having been deprived of his newfound popularity. Fame was indeed a drug, and Stempel's public withdrawal was graceless.

An iconic moment from game shows' great disgrace. Producer and host of NBC's *Twenty One,* Jack Barry (center) officiates over the staged intellectual struggle between Charles Van Doren (left) and Herb Stempel (right).

He watched his former competitor's continuing victories with increasing agitation. He repeatedly called *Twenty One* producers Dan Enright and Albert Freedman and asked for more television exposure. In one of his meetings with the producers, he inadvertently learned that Van Doren was scheduled to, in Stempel's words, "take a dive" on March 11. Stempel said he quickly gathered $5,000 in cash that he successfully bet against Van Doren at 2-to-1 odds.

Van Doren's retirement from NBC's *Twenty One* was far more celebrated than that of any other defeated contestant. He became a contributor to the network's morning show, which awarded him a Mercedes Benz on April 22, 1957. The following year, Van Doren became host of his own NBC series entitled *Kaleidoscope.* It all served to fuel Stempel's anger, which led to his telling his story to newspapers and magazines. With no hard evidence and denials from every corner failing to corroborate his claims of wrongdoing, Stempel received little ink at first.

Joseph Stone of the New York City District Attorney's office believed the dominoes started to fall after the producers of *Dotto* failed to appease the standby player who discovered Marie Winn's writings. Edward Hilgemeier, a part-time nightclub comedian, had ripped a page of correct answers from the teenager's notebook. While Hilgemeier was reading the scribbled names from Winn's notebook — Barry Fitzgerald, Donald Duck, and Dagwood — the young lady was on-stage giving those correct answers.

When confronted by the contestant's attorney, the producers offered Hilgemeier $2,500. He soon seethed when he learned it was a figure far less than they offered Winn's on-air opponent as a quiet settlement for any potential disadvantage he might have been given in the show's controlled competition. In retrospect, Stone says that it was Hilgemeier's subsequent visit to the *New York Post* with his story and the first piece of tangible evidence — the torn page containing answers — that triggered the official inquiry.

With quiz shows under a cloud of suspicion, the state of New York mounted the initial investigation into the integrity of the programs, questioning approximately 150 witnesses during the course of a nine-month inquiry. Soon, despite attracting over 50 million loyal viewers each week, *Twenty One* was among the shows to be cancelled, pulled from NBC on October 16, 1958. Ironically, it was shortly after the network purchased Barry and Enright's programs for a reported $2.2 million.

The New York investigation was fruitless; it failed to conclusively prove any wholesale wrongdoing. No charges were brought because there were no laws that made rigging television games illegal. Attorneys consulted by *Life* magazine conjectured that if answers were being sold, it would constitute commercial bribery, but with no testimony to suggest such a scenario, that angle was never pursued.

Herb Stempel was then being taken more seriously, when he told his fantastic tales of manipulated competition and contestants' orchestrated performances that had previously been dismissed. He was back in the limelight, enjoying another fifteen minutes of fame by granting interviews. *Life* reported that Stempel spent more than twelve hours telling his story to the district attorney, but it still was in conflict with the testimony of other participants. Charles Van Doren continued to deny collusion. As late as November 1959, Van Doren told the *New York Times*, "I lost honestly...at no time was I coached or tutored." [26-8]

The prospect of perjury before a body no less impressive than a subcommittee of the United States Congress resulted in humble recantations of earlier grand jury testimony by producers and the less forthcoming contestants. The Congressional hearings during October and November 1959 played to a standing room only crowd, and they were almost as dramatic as the quiz shows. In reviewing the scene in Washington, Walter Karp of *American Heritage* magazine invoked *Time*'s description of the witnesses as "a tawdry succession of fixers and schlockmeisters, corrupters, and corrupted."

The most damning evidence of manipulation came from Hilgemeier and from Greenwich Village artist James Snodgrass. Snodgrass had mailed registered letters to himself with the questions and answers to be featured on *Twenty One* on the date of his appearance. The letters were postmarked May 11, two days before the contest.

In hindsight, it was obvious that the original New York grand jury hearings featured a parade of perjurers. State District Attorney Frank Hogan reflected that of the 150 who testified, "Maybe 50 told the truth." [26-9] As *Life* reported, "The public was learning that what it had assumed to be bright, clean fun was perhaps not so bright or clean as it looked." [26-10] Harold Craig, an upstate New York farmer, who won $106,000 on *Twenty One* explained, "They can keep you as long as they want, get rid of you when they are ready." [26-10] Ethel Richardson of Los Angeles had taken home $100,000 on *The Big Surprise*. She explained, "Before the show, we'd talk about everything I knew…Whatever I told them most about, the question would be about." [26-10]

Tic Tac Dough contestant Kirsten Falke testified that she had been shown question cards in advance: "I was told to just memorize them as best I could because the questions that would be asked of me were included in these card files. I wrote as many down as I could remember, which were quite a few, and took them home and studied them, faithfully." [26-11] Falke further told the Congressional subcommittee what happened when she defeated a challenger she had been instructed to tie: "Immediately after that there was a station break and Mr. [Howard] Felsher came rushing across the stage, pulling his hair out, and he said, do you realize what you have done? I said 'Yes.' I didn't, really, but there was not much else I could say." [26-11]

Ever since Robert Kintner was among those on hand to celebrate Johnny's 25th anniversary in broadcasting, Johnny considered Kintner a friend. Both men had been hired by Life Saver's candy tycoon Ed Noble, and the two had shared light-hearted greetings at various studios and at numerous industry events. Robert Kintner had recently been named President at NBC and his tone was now serious as he gave testimony before the Senate subcommittee.

Johnny had seen enough to strongly suspect that Bob Kintner was being less than candid when the executive claimed that the networks were duped along with the public by the producers who rigged the quizzes. Asked if NBC executives such as Kintner knew about the wholesale manipulation of the televised contests, Dan Enright responded, "You would have to be very unsophisticated or very naive not to understand that certain controls have to be exercised." [26-12] In retrospect, it was obvious why Barry and Enright felt it necessary to exercise control. *Time* reported in 1957 that "Geritol's contract with Barry & Enright limits its annual outlay for prizes to $520,000; anything over that comes out of the producers' pocket." [26-13]

Despite Dan Enright's assertion that the network could not have been unknowing, Robert Kintner vouched for NBC's legitimacy and honesty, promising that controls were in place to "investigate and safeguard the integrity of the shows." [26-10] His counterpart at CBS, William Paley, was more conciliatory: "The quiz show scandal had led us to re-examine the whole area of our responsibility." [26-10]

Although working in New York during the hearings, Johnny followed the action in Washington with great interest, especially the testimony offered by Mark Goodson and Goodson-Todman employees. Howard Felsher, Johnny's co-worker and producer of *Tic Tac Dough*, testified that 75 percent of contests on the evening version of the series were fixed. Felsher explained, "I was trying to put together an exciting show, and I never did feel there was anything wrong with it."[26-14] He further admitted lying to the grand jury and encouraging about thirty contestants to do likewise. Like Felsher, most of the production personnel who testified took the position that they were merely presenting entertainment.

Eric Lieber, who supervised the drawing of the caricatures on *Dotto*, explained that the dramatic turns in each episode, including which players would win and lose, were carefully plotted at regular meetings. Edward Jurist, the show's producer, explained that the world of information was so vast that "you cannot ask random questions of people and have a show. You simply have failure, failure, failure, and that does not make for entertainment."[26-15]

Jurist testified about *Dotto*, "We took some people who were bright and amusing people and we put them on a television show that millions of people watched. We gave them the biggest experience of their lives. If they were lucky they won a lot of money; if they were not so lucky they won a little money. They were not injured or maimed. All they had was a lot of fun and additional reward. I don't consider that immoral, particularly if you have grown up in the entertainment business as I have."[26-16]

Shirley Bernstein, composer Leonard Bernstein's sister, was an Associate Producer on *The $64,000 Challenge*. She testified that the show was frequently rigged on instructions from the sponsor, and that she personally briefed participants at the direction of Executive Producer Steve Carlin: "There were many meetings with the sponsor, where Mr. Carlin would come back with anger…Often I would say, 'Why do it this way?' Mr. Carlin would say that it was not his wish, but the sponsors wanted it that way."[26-17]

Mert Koplin, producer of *The $64,000 Question* and *The $64,000 Challenge*, admitted that practically every winner on his shows who had amassed more than $16,000 had received help. Koplin explained that the collusion was designed to fulfill the sponsors' wishes for super sized ratings, and that Revlon, his show's sponsor, insisted on controlling the comings and goings of the contestants. Attention soon focused on those advertisers.

Twenty One champion Charles Van Doren became the primary object of scorn and ridicule among all of the contestants who could not resist the temptation of easy money. Despite his ongoing denials, in October 1959, the Columbia instructor was suspended by NBC and subpoenaed by Congress. The following month, he finally recanted. Van Doren's testimony began with his reading from a prepared statement, "I was involved in a deception,"[26-12] and ended with his firing from his $50,000 a year job as a contributor to *The Today Show*. On the morning of November 10th, *The Today Show* host, Dave Garroway, cried on the air, as he expressed heartbreak over his friend's ordeal.

Van Doren told America, "I would give almost anything I have to reverse the course of my life in the last three years…I have deceived my friends, and I had millions of them."[26-18] He explained the deception that began with a private discussion with Barry and Enright staffer Albert Freedman in which the producer asked for his cooperation in staging a game with Stempel.

In his ninety-five minutes of testimony, Charles Van Doren's included every detail of his being briefed and coached in how to respond to the questions and how to act. "[Freedman] would tell me how to answer them: pause here; add this or that remark or aside; always seem to be worried, anxious; never answer too quickly, let the suspense build up." [26-19] The college instructor said he almost persuaded himself into believing that the charade was enhancing the national attitude towards teachers and promoting the value of education and "the intellectual life."

In the July 23, 2008 issue of *The New Yorker*, Van Doren broke decades of silence to again illuminate the dark secrets of competition on *Twenty One*. Van Doren said Freedman "appeared nervous" when he explained, "You remember I told you about this fellow Stempel? Well, the sponsors want him to be beaten. He'll walk away with a bundle but they want someone more sympathetic." Van Doren recalls that when he asked if they have a right to do that, he was told by Freedman, "Hey, come off it, Charlie. Don't be naive." [26-19]

Van Doren recalled the young producer suggesting that he would be the perfect player to beat Herb Stempel, saying it would be a secret only between the two of them: "'Jack Barry — the show's host — won't know and Dan Enright won't, either. Stempel won't know — I've got a way to handle that. The sponsors won't know — anyway, they'll be so happy they won't give a damn. And the audience will never know, because I won't tell them, and you won't, either.'" [26-19] At that point, Van Doren said Freedman began to portray a scenario of staged matches that would culminate with a victory for the telegenic literary protégé. So began the deception of which Van Doren spoke back in 1959.

Van Doren's four-month, on-air sham culminated with his stunning defeat by attorney Vivienne Nearing. Games between the two intellectual titans ended in ties for several weeks. Then, when it appeared that Van Doreen could have won more than $150,000, the contestant said, "I couldn't, because Al had informed me that I would lose to her." [26-19]

On the evening of March 11, Jack Barry asked both Nearing and Van Doren to name the kings of Norway, Denmark, Sweden, Jordan, Iraq, and Belgium. Both were isolated in their sound-proofed booths, and both contenders performed their scripted parts flawlessly. In the orchestrated intellectual Olympics, Nearing won the gold; Van Doren finally stumbled after he seemed to prod and probe every fiber of his grey matter for the name of the king of Belgium.

In offering his story's dénouement, Van Doren recalled that 1959 was a year of agony, as he and Vivienne Nearing were among a total of seventeen who were indicted, arrested, and arraigned. Albert Freedman, a man who started in television getting hit with pies, sprayed with seltzer, and taking pratfalls with slapstick comedian Pinky Lee, five short years later was taken into police custody in handcuffs. Van Doren wrote, "We were marched through the streets of downtown New York (accompanied by photographers), forced to hand over our valuables, take off our belts and shoelaces, and get fingerprinted." [26-19] He pleaded guilty to second-degree perjury, a misdemeanor, for lying to the grand jury about being provided with answers. Ultimately, none of the seventeen was sentenced to jail.

Van Doren lost a great deal more than simply his dignity with his firing from Columbia University. Once the truth was revealed, his participation in the fraud disgraced his family's good name that had been held in such high esteem in literary circles. He moved to Chicago and worked editing the Encyclopedia Britannica, where he reported that he earned about 20 percent of what he'd been getting with NBC. Jack Barry and Dan Enright found work in Canadian television producing what would later be referred to as "reality television" programs. Despite escaping prosecution, it was a difficult time for both. Barry recalled, "For five years, I was virtually unable to conduct my life. I could not focus. I was drinking a lot. I almost lost my life." [26-20]

Jack Barry found an opportunity to return to American television, albeit in a behind the scenes capacity. In 1967, Barry was the uncredited creator and producer of *Everybody's Talking*, a short-lived ABC daytime game. In 1969, he produced a pilot for *The Joker's Wild* starring Allen Ludden. In an industry that coveted ratings, both Barry and Enright were eventually welcomed back to the fold for as long as viewers followed.

While popularity was fickle and America's love returned for all things television, game shows included, a great deal of trust was lost forever. The scandal added to the growing cynicism for American institutions that became an identifying attribute of the 1960s and would be manifested in slogans such as, "Don't trust anybody over 30," and "Question authority."

Although rigging game shows was not illegal at the time, the mass deception had great cultural impact. At least two members of Congress' House Telecommunications Subcommittee proposed banning quiz and game shows completely from television. President Dwight Eisenhower was motivated to register his personal disapproval, saying that orchestrating the outcome of quiz shows was "a terrible thing to do to the American public." [26-21]

It was a different era, long before 24-hour news channels disseminated daily doses of deception, disinformation, and distortion from the worlds of big business, politics, and sports. Americans had yet to become calloused by endless disingenuous claims denying Wall Street insider trading, steroid use in sports, and Presidential transgressions. "I am not a crook" and "I did not have sexual relations with that woman" became little more than comic punch lines.

Johnny surveyed the wreckage of the quiz show scandal, as Congress looked to ensure that history would not repeat itself. In 1960, it became illegal for the outcome of any on-air contest of skill or knowledge to be pre-arranged or unduly influenced in any manner. It was now a federal crime for any individual to participate in rigging a broadcast quiz or game show. On a corporate level, while networks were not licensed, the greatest assets of CBS, NBC, and ABC were the portfolios of stations each owned and operated in major markets. To protect those valuable licenses, each of the networks instituted internal oversight of contests with new Standards and Practices or Program Compliance departments.

In-house attorneys forevermore supervised a small army of staffers, who evaluated the rules of game shows in advance of production and approved the manner in which game material was handled and protected. Hosts and announcers, including Johnny, were subject to scrutiny along with each member of the production company's staff and each member of the crew. Prior to production, game show police executed signed affidavits of compliance from all persons on the set.

Studios and contestant green rooms became more crowded, as Standards and Practices personnel were on-hand to review the rules with each player and to officiate as each participant completed a probing questionnaire. NBC's Compliance and Practices Department required all potential participants to respond with a "yes" or "no" to queries such as, "Were you induced to refrain from winning by anyone or to engage in any conduct contrary to the object of the rules of the game? If so, please explain." During production, members of the team were present in and around the studio to monitor all of the game play, as well as the safety measures in place to protect the programs' honesty, even accompanying contestants on bathroom breaks.

Hugh Downs, a veteran broadcast personality and host of *The Today Show* and *Concentration*, recalled that for a period immediately following the institution of the new regulations, the network security squad protecting the integrity of *Concentration* became suspicious of certain persons on the set who seemed to be especially interested in aspects of the game play. In a case of "Spy vs. Spy" those mysterious observers turned out to be another covert team of investigators hired by the producer to assure the purity of the program's competition.

The final chapter of the game show scandal was written when Dan Enright marked the thirtieth anniversary of his appearance before Congress. He returned to 30 Rockefeller Plaza, not as a game show producer, but as a guest on *The Today Show*. On November 2, 1989, Enright humbly reflected, "We, at the time, deluded ourselves into believing that what we were doing was not that wrong." He apologized publicly to Herb Stempel, saying, "I should have been more mindful and far more sensitive," and he apologized to America, saying, "We were driven by ambition and greed." Enright's demeanor was slightly less repentant when he added, "The Congressional hearings into the rigging — the hearings were rigged, too. We rehearsed the questions and answers."

CHAPTER 27

A WORD FROM OUR SPONSOR

Network executives took the position that they were unknowing victims of the game show scandal and deception. Attention next turned to the advertisers who had obviously benefited from the rigged shows' massive viewership. Revlon took to sponsoring *The $64,000 Question* to recover a diminishing market share eclipsed by Hazel Bishop. Once actress Wendy Barrie started pitching Revlon's new Living Lipstick, the product literally sold out. While host Hal March urged the public to be patient for the factory to catch up with demand, Living Lipstick commercials had to be temporarily replaced by ads for Touch and Glow make-up foundation. Retailers from coast-to-coast clamored for stock. Charles Revson, Revlon's principal, could not ignore the power of *The $64,000 Question* to move merchandise.

On November 4, 1959, Revson was called before the Subcommittee on Interstate and Foreign Commerce of the House of Representatives. He denied any knowledge of rigging. The cosmetics king testified, "Sure, I was the sponsor, but I was just like the rest of the millions of Americans, who had been caught up in the drama of the program. And yet, I heard for the first time last week, and you heard the testimony yesterday, that they were rigging the show right from the start with some of the earliest contestants. I was absolutely flabbergasted." [27-1] Revson ultimately acknowledged making suggestions to the producers, but added that he "never imagined that the producers would tamper with the [show's] honesty." [27-2] Testimony from others clearly suggested that he took an active and direct hand in guiding the program's intellectual clashes.

In the case of *Twenty One*, Pharmaceuticals Inc. had reportedly been in constant contact with Barry and Enright, commenting on the appeal of players and outspoken in its desire for the largest possible audience for the program's live commercials that extolled the benefits of its products, including Geritol, the iron and B-vitamin tonic. Ultimately, the hearings failed to produce any hard evidence to conclude that the sponsors were aware of the means utilized to maximize the programs' drama.

The networks sensed it was time to change the nature of their relationship with Madison Avenue and wrest control of program content back from advertisers and their agencies. A business structure had been in place since the earliest days of radio, and change meant an upheaval in the comfortable status quo between broadcasters and the hands that fed them. As Johnny explained, "Most important shows were then owned and produced by advertising agencies. Firms like Young and Rubicam, J. Walter Thompson, and Foote, Cone & Belding had huge radio departments." Johnny knew well that the sponsors called the shots, and for reasons unknown, had even changed the spelling of his first name from Johnny to Johnnie for one advertiser.

Ad agencies controlled programs and shaped performers' careers. It was a practice that dated back to the 1920s with *The Eveready Hour* and *The A&P Gypsies,* and continued with radio's most popular programs. For a modest talent fee of $150, ventriloquist Edgar Bergen and dummy Charlie McCarthy made their radio debut on December 16, 1936, as guests on crooner Rudy Vallee's NBC program, *The Royal Gelatin Hour.* Soon after, it was the advertising agency for Chase & Sanborn coffee that tapped Bergen for his own series, launching his ascent to stardom.

Sponsor control was evident in 1946, when Bing Crosby, already an American favorite from his hit recordings and his work on *The Kraft Music Hall,* was off the program following a dispute with the underwriter. Kraft forbade the singer from using the new technology of tape recording that Bing had helped to develop for commercial use to record his show in advance. Within weeks, the crooner signed a $30,000-a-week contract with a new sponsor, Philco, for an ABC show that he could transcribe prior to broadcast.

Radio's superstars brought listeners to the networks' hit programs, and the shows were firmly controlled by and often named for the sponsors. Some of Bob Hope's early radio appearances were on *The Fleischmann Hour,* a program owned by the yeast manufacturer. In 1938, the Lord and Thomas advertising agency signed Hope to an exclusive contract to host their pharmaceutical client's radio program. Hope then became irrevocably linked with Pepsodent, the sole sponsor of his NBC show, *The Pepsodent Hour.*

Al Jolson was a top singing star, but his radio show was controlled by the Lever Brothers soap manufacturer and called *The Lifebuoy Program.* Milton Berle was the headliner of *The Texaco Star Theater,* and later, *The Berle Buick Hour.* Even when product names were dropped from the titles of shows and the sponsors' logos were no longer emblazoned on the set, advertising agencies continued to lord over the content of the vast majority of entertainment programs.

Talent agencies such as Jules Steins' Music Corporation of America expanded their realm into packaging and brokering deals. MCA agent Jerry Zeitman recalled that the agency sold shows to advertisers, not to the networks. "We sold *The George Burns and Gracie Allen Show* to Carnation Milk, who then bought time on CBS. We did a show called *The Bob Cummings Show* that we sold to R. J. Reynolds, and they used it to introduce Winston cigarettes." [27-3]

Networks took control of the programs in the aftermath of the quiz show scandals. As the costs of production rose beyond sponsors' budgets, advertising agencies were sold "participations" for their clients. Ironically, the idea of shifting control away from advertisers was championed by Sylvester "Pat" Weaver, a former Vice President from the powerful Young & Rubicam agency. Weaver crossed Madison Avenue, traveling two blocks west, to head the emerging television business at NBC. In 1953, Weaver was installed as President of the network under David Sarnoff, and he left his mark with many programming innovations, including *The Today Show* and *The Tonight Show*. Despite his many successful contributions, Weaver was soon pushed out of NBC's presidency by David Sarnoff so that the General could install his son, Robert, in that position. In response to that insult to Weaver and his many loyal supporters at 30 Rock, Gene Rayburn and Johnny invoked a play on words based the title of an Ernest Hemingway novel and joked, "The Son Also Rises."

A crude recreation of the composition of television's first commercial. New Yorkers with televisions watched the second hand of a Bulova clock make a full revolution to the tune of Valse in D-flat major, "The Minute Waltz" – Opus 64, Number 1 by Frédéric Chopin.

Before he resigned in his dispute with the Sarnoffs, Weaver had advocated for what he called the "magazine concept," in which broadcasters maintained editorial control and advertisers were sold insertions. *The Today Show* was born in that magazine model. CBS President Jim Aubrey, Garry Moore's antagonist, espoused the same philosophy. He allegedly once ranted, "I program the network. If you want to buy Monday night at eight o'clock, you'll buy what I put there." [27-3]

In the decade between 1955 and 1965, the number of network programs sponsored by a single advertiser dropped from seventy-five to twelve. [27-4] NBC, ABC, and CBS assumed government of program content, and members of the network sales force began to act more like their counterparts at local stations. Instead of selling blocks of time, they pitched the attributes of a television show, its anticipated success, its intended audience, as well as the environment for the advertiser's message and the unique, exploitable opportunities that a program would present for a client to reach potential consumers.

The old business model was retired; the new model was more of a flashback to the broadcast of the very first legal television commercial. The spot aired in New York at 2:29 p.m. on July 1, 1941, the medium's first day of commercial broadcasting. For a full sixty seconds, NBC's WNBT played "The Minute Waltz," while a camera focused on the face of a ticking clock with the name of the sponsor, Bulova, superimposed over a map of the United States. The minute of time reportedly sold for $9, and another identical spot that same evening set back the clock manufacturer a few more bucks. Bulova contracted for thirteen weeks of similar commercial breaks without a thought of controlling the adjacent program content.

Advertising agencies were buying minutes, and later, half-minutes of time. Also for sale were all manners of sponsorship identifications described by terms such as "intro," "outro," "billboard," "cow catcher" (a commercial announcement at the beginning of a program that advertised a different product from the one advertised on the program itself), and "hitch-hike" (a commercial announcement at the end of a program in which a different product was advertised from that mentioned during the program).

The new archetype resulted in new scripts for Johnny and other announcers. Fresh phrases entered television's lexicon, such as, "This program is brought to you in part by..." as well as, "And now here's a word from our alternate sponsor." Even though programs had multiple benefactors, many advertisers continued to utilize their own commercial pitchman when serving up their valuable thirty and sixty-second spots.

The ability to communicate persuasively through the lens and into the living room was a prized art. Advertising agencies paid handsomely for the talents of the commercial announcer, who might only work two or three minutes during a half hour program. Television personalities including Ed McMahon, Dennis James, Jack Narz, and Don Morrow worked during their careers in this sub-specialty, extolling the virtues of dog food, cigarettes, cereal, hair care products, flour, laundry detergent, and a vast variety of consumables. Early in their careers, Dick Clark touted Tootsie Rolls on bandleader Paul Whiteman's *TV Teen Time,* and Mike Wallace pitched peanut butter on the kids' show, *Super Circus.* Respected female news personalities, Barbara Walters and Betty Furness, logged early camera time peddling a potpourri of products.

Johnny wrote about commercial spokespersons in his 1950 essay on the makings of a television pitchman:

> "There are actually three types of announcers on TV: (1) the personality-type (most commonly seen), (2) the hard-hitting radio-salesman type who is usually heard but not seen and, (3) the direct-selling demonstration-type announcer who has become so very popular, not to the viewer, I'm afraid, as much as to the station for which his direct selling 'pitches' bring in the lucre in large amounts. All three types pay well but, of course, the personality-type is the one most admired and most in demand."

Johnny continued as the omnipresent announcer of programs, but many of his contemporaries began to lose work. They had been performing as commercial pitchmen, but the relationship between sponsors and networks changed. Under the new structure, more and more commercials were filmed insertions that replaced live endorsements and demonstrations. Don Pardo continued as the program announcer on the original *The Price is Right,* but the sponsor's announcer, Don Morrow, moved on to a career in filmed plugs, including years appearing as The Shell Answer Man, and ultimately to the specialized world of voicing movie trailers.

Dennis James' family told the *New York Times* that the television pioneer delivered the very first television commercial in the early 1940s, an unpaid sample pitch for Wedgwood china, to demonstrate television's commercial possibilities. Later that decade, Nick Keesely of the advertising agency Lennen & Mitchell was said to have steered Old Gold cigarettes to sponsor *The Original Amateur Hour.* "For $150 a week, I hired Dennis James to do the commercials." [27-5] As sales shot up, so did James' salary.

James recalled that by the mid 1950s, he was earning $850,000 a year hawking products as diverse as cigarettes and cereal on thirteen live shows a week. "I worked for P. Lorillard for a tremendous amount of money — $350,000. With Kelloggs, it was $250,000 a year." [27-6] With changes in the sponsors' role, lucrative contracts were not renewed, but James' future was assured. He resumed a hosting career that started at DuMont in the 1940s and continued in the 1970s working with Johnny on Goodson-Todman's syndicated *The New Price is Right*. His extensive broadcasting career ended in 1981 after a seven-year run fronting a syndicated revival of *Name That Tune*.

Dennis James may have delivered the first sample television commercial, but the very first advertising message carried on television was for the fur industry, and it has been extensively documented. In 1930, Boston's experimental W1XAV rebroadcast the audio from CBS's radio program, *The Fox Trappers*, which included a commercial message for America's furriers. Stations licensed as experimental were forbidden from carrying advertising (commercial licenses were not issued until 1941), and the indiscretion was sufficient for the Federal Radio Commission to take action. The regulating agency did not have the television monitoring capabilities necessary to witness the offense first hand, but they still fined the broadcaster.

Advertisers no longer controlled program content, and their biggest concern was being assured that their commercial spots were placed in the programs with the greatest viewership. With ratings becoming more important in the competition for advertising dollars, television also began to emphasize youth, visual appeal, and style along with substance.

Johnny was then in his fifties, with a well-receded hairline. He soon found himself making a necessary transition to a new niche. His ubiquitous, on-camera presence peaked in 1956, when he was seen weekly on CBS, ABC, and NBC, but slowly and surely, he was heard far more often than seen. As late as 1964, he continued to occasionally host and appear on programs such as *On Broadway Tonight* for CBS. He also enjoyed other on-camera moments as a sidekick for the remainder of his career, but for the most part, the television pioneer became almost invisible to home viewers, and it was the biggest disappointment and adjustment in his professional career. As Johnny and television both matured, the veteran performer invented a new niche for his next thirty years in the business by redefining, elevating, and setting new standards for the role of game show announcer.

The greatest testament to his character was the poise, grace, and dignity with which Johnny made that transition; he looked ahead and made the most of the opportunities still before him. For the rest of his career, he remained most proud of his work as the anchor of the many shows he had emceed on radio and television. He took at least one opportunity to inform a producer too young to remember his background that he had been a well-respected host before adapting to his new role.

Ultimately, Johnny's greatest recognition and financial rewards came as the most prolific announcer and audience warm-up performer in the world of television game shows. In a 1968 interview with a *Time* magazine reporter, he gave the world a rare peek behind his seamless veneer: "He concedes that it is a comedown to be warming up someone else's audience. But he is consoled by the fact that he makes more money now." [27-7]

Starting with *Masquerade Party* and *Break The Bank*, Johnny's was the signature voice for over thirty audience participation programs, including some of television's most successful and memorable game shows of the black and white era. In the 1950s and 1960s, he announced Goodson-Todman's biggest hits, *What's My Line?*, *To Tell*

In 1963, Johnny was teamed with a television icon and various vertebrates on CBS' *Arthur Godfrey Loves Animals.*

the Truth, and *The Match Game*. In the 1970s, Johnny was most closely identified with *The Price is Right*, the *Match Game*, and *Concentration*.

In addition to his reign as the undisputed king of game show announcers, Johnny was associated with the television outings of a number of musical variety artists. Between January and July of 1960, he introduced Kate Smith on her weekly half-hour CBS-TV program. It was a re-partnering between the popular singer, William

Paley, and the network where she had spent decades. Their collaboration began in 1931 with *Kate Smith and Her Swanee Music*, sponsored by the Paley family's La Palina cigar brand.

Before the use of videotape became ubiquitous, network television shows often produced thirty-nine weeks of episodes per year and relied on summer replacement shows instead of reruns to fill the time period when viewership was low. In 1961, Johnny announced *Glenn Miller Time* on CBS during the warm weather weeks. Four years later, he was the announcer on CBS's *The Steve Lawrence Show*. The affable singer and alumnus of Steve Allen's television coterie fronted his own variety offering between September and December 1965. In an October 17, 2003 interview with Larry King on his CNN show, Lawrence recalled that his program was "the last variety show on CBS in black and white."

In 1963, Johnny worked with Arthur Godfrey, the once-brightest star in the television firmament. Godfrey was formerly broadcasting's most powerful and prodigious personality, and he had an ego befitting his popularity. By 1963, he was a bitter, fallen icon. CBS continued to manufacture vehicles for his potential return to prominence.

Johnny was there for *Arthur Godfrey Loves Animals*. It was not an educational program for kids about the world of zoology, nor a showcase for animals performing tricks; in fact, there was nary an animal in sight. It was a big-budget, prime-time musical variety show with original songs and comedy sketches all loosely related to animals and his real-life horse ranch in Virginia.

The March 18, 1963 episode featured footage from Marineworld. Godfrey joked and sang with guests Mel Blanc, Shari Lewis, and Paul Lynde. Blanc did the voices of Bugs Bunny, Porky Pig, and the entire Warner Bros. cartoon menagerie. Shari Lewis, a former winner on *Arthur Godfrey's Talent Scouts*, was well-known for her animal puppets, Lamb Chop, Hush Puppy, and Charlie Horse. Paul Lynde played a racetrack regular, who bet on the ponies, and whose wife was also a nag. Johnny called an imaginary horse race, as well as performed his usual announcer and warm-up roles.

Godfrey sang with all of his guests, and was at his most sincere pitching Clairol hair color in his usual casual, conversational style. He closed by thanking the dogs, cats, and canaries that watched, despite the fact that their viewership was not measured by Nielsen. A CBS press release stated, "Arthur Godfrey believes that animals are the most misunderstood people. Tonight, in comedy and song, he tries to enhance our appreciation of our finned, feathered, and four-footed friends"

Of all of his work with celebrities, Johnny was most proud of his long association with Jackie Gleason. He rarely failed to mention his work with "The Great One" when introducing himself to studio audiences during pre-show warm-ups throughout the remainder of his career.

CHAPTER 28
WITH "THE GREAT ONE"

Herbert Walton "Jackie" Gleason first appeared on the home screen in 1949 as Chester Riley on NBC's sitcom, *The Life of Riley*. On July 8, 1950. Gleason rocketed to fame on DuMont's *The Cavalcade of Stars*, where he created characters that America enjoyed for decades. The show was a hodgepodge of entertainment that featured music, dance, vaudeville specialty acts, and guest stars, along with both dramatic and comedy skits, all produced on a shoestring budget.

Comedians Jack Carter and Jerry Lester preceded Jackie Gleason as hosts of *The Cavalcade of Stars*. After Carter was hired away by NBC and Lester was fired for on-air insubordination, Gleason accepted the challenge of transitioning from nightclub work to television. He was initially paid $750 a week with a mere four-week commitment. By the final week of *Cavalcade*, he was reportedly making $1,500 per episode. Johnny first met Gleason at DuMont's Madison Avenue facilities, and he contributed to *The Cavalcade of Stars* at the Adelphi Theater on at least one occasion.

After CBS featured Gleason in a guest shot with Frank Sinatra, founder and President William Paley personally courted Gleason, offering him five times his DuMont salary. In September 1952, Hubbell Robinson, Paley's lieutenant, Bullets Durgom, Gleason's manager, and the finest dealmakers at MCA forged television's biggest talent bonanza up to that time — a two-year, $11 million contract that included a $150,000 circular, custom-built home in Peekskill, New York, for the thirty-six-year-old comedian. In exchange, Gleason appeared in a weekly television show.

The deal gave CBS a high-profile weapon to take to battle against NBC in signing the more powerful affiliate stations in the major cities. The pact promised Gleason a $120,000 budget each week to fully exploit the seeds of his creativity that were evident on his DuMont program. Supporting player Art Carney made the move to CBS with Gleason, and Audrey Meadows and Joyce Randolph were later added to the cast. After three years as a regular feature in the CBS variety hour, one of the recurring comedy skits first created as a six-minute sketch for the DuMont show become one of CBS's most-viewed programs. The Brooklyn-born comedian's co-star, Audrey Meadows, reported that it was no one less great than Orson Welles who was then responsible for honoring her *Honeymooners* hubby with the nickname, "The Great One."

In 1955, *The Honeymooners* was spun off for CBS as a half-hour, weekly situation comedy sponsored by Milton Berle's old benefactor, Buick. The contract that totaled

$14 million called for a two-year run of seventy-eight episodes, but after a single season, Gleason halted production, telling CBS "the excellence of the material could not be maintained, and I had too much fondness for the show to cheapen it." [28-1]

Later, Gleason told biographer James Bacon, "Everybody thought I was nuts turning down $7 million bucks to film that second year of my contract. I know CBS and Buick thought I had gotten a better offer someplace else. They offered me more money and I turned it down. They wouldn't believe me when I said we couldn't come up with the same high quality of scripts that second year. It was that simple." [28-1]

While friends derided the Brooklyn-born comedian's business acumen, Gleason's creative instincts were often impeccable. His foresight as a producer resulted in those CBS shows being filmed using a technology developed by DuMont called "Electronicam." Piggy-backing a 16mm or 35mm film camera with each television camera created permanent images far superior in quality to the kinescope recordings of the era.

With Electronicam, a kinescope of a broadcast was later used as a reference to edit the film from each of the cameras into a re-creation of the original electronic switching between views during the live program. In later experiments, a director's live switching between the video cameras imbedded editing in and out points onto the film with each switch of the cameras to assist in re-creating the director's live version of the program.

The pristine look of Electronicam allowed for the thirty-nine filmed episodes of *The Honeymooners* to survive through decades of syndicated reruns, much in the way that the use of film has enabled *I Love Lucy* to continue to entertain the world. Although the thirty-nine immortal half-hour shows were produced for CBS, Gleason owned the program. He shocked his business associates in 1957, when he sold his rights to the shows to MCA for only $2 million. Bullets Durgom told James Bacon he estimated Jackie lost $100 million in the deal, which meant that Durgom was out $15 million in commissions. Bacon quoted Gleason: "I knew what I was doing. Hell, if I still owned those thirty-nine shows, I would need a small army of people to keep track of them. I'm not cut out to be a tycoon." [28-1] Later, those episodes were augmented for syndication by a cache of kinescopes of the Kramdens from the earlier sketches that Gleason had stored decades before.

Following the success of Gleason's variety hour and *The Honeymooners*, William Paley considered the performer such an asset that CBS paid the star a guaranteed retainer of $100,000 a year for his exclusivity, whether or not he was seen on-air. The appeal of an early, paid retirement did not appeal to Gleason and the entertainer did not remain idle.

Johnny reprised his work with Gleason on Friday night, January 20, 1961, the evening of President Kennedy's inaugural gala. Gleason's new CBS game show, *You're in the Picture*, is tied for the record as the shortest-running program in television history. It was the first of a grand total of only a dozen shows in sixty years of network television to be canceled after just one broadcast. (*Secret Talents of the Stars* was the most recent to suffer that fate, in April of 2008). [28-2]

The format of *You're in the Picture* was a benign premise designed to bring four celebrity players together to create comic opportunities to showcase Gleason's ad-lib skills. The game was to be secondary to the comedy, much in the way that NBC's *You Bet Your Life* was less about any competition than it was a vehicle for Groucho Marx's hi-jinks. It was a worthy inspiration because the 1950 to 1961 success of *You Bet Your Life* made it the longest-running prime time game show in NBC's history, often placing among the Top 10 most-viewed shows and occasionally challenging *I Love Lucy* for popularity.

The big difference between *You're in the Picture* and *You Bet Your Life* was that Groucho's show was filmed with the intent to subsequently edit together the best of his interplay with the contestants. This was the original idea of producer John Guedel, a former scriptwriter for Laurel and Hardy and advertising executive, and it was the technique he used with Groucho's earlier radio version of the show. The concept for *You Bet Your Life* was born on April 27, 1947, when Guedel was producing a radio comedy program sponsored by the Walgreen drugstore chain. While Bob Hope and Groucho Marx were reading a prepared comedy sketch, Marx suddenly started ad-libbing. Hope then threw his script on the floor and joined in for a volley of quick quips.

Guedel later asked Marx if he could be so spontaneously witty all the time. Marx responded that it would be almost impossible not to be. Typical of Marx's style of illogical non sequitur: When a guest said she was from South Wales, Groucho shot back: "Did you ever meet Jonah? He lived in whales for a while." [28-3]

A staff of twelve worked full-time for Guedel on television's *You Bet Your Life* to find four contestants a week with attributes unique enough to provide comic fodder for Groucho. Not all were civilians. Some players, including Phyllis Diller and Pedro Gonzales-Gonzales, were up-and-coming performers or lesser-known vaudevillians, and others, such as General Omar Bradley and boxer Rocky Marciano's mother, had their own claims to fame.

Albert Freedman, who later became embroiled in the quiz show scandals, was one of the writers on the show. He remembered the filmed interviews ran as long as an hour to insure that there were adequate funny moments to string together for twenty-four minutes of program content. In fact, eight 35mm film cameras each cranked for as long as ninety minutes some weeks before Guedel called "cut," certain that he had the makings for a half-hour of hilarity.

In addition, the staff of writers scripted questions for Groucho that played into the contestants' humorous stories previously explored in interviews. They then bolstered the host's comic skills with hastily penned one-liners written with grease pencil on an overhead projector visible only to Groucho. Even after the show's extensive editing, Groucho can occasionally be seen looking over the heads of the guests at suggested comic lines.

Guedel took audience participation programming to a new level with his use of extensive pre-production interviews with participants to prepare questions. Variations on his innovation did not surprise the producer. To Fred Allen's perverted proverb about "imitation being the sincerest form of television," Guedel told *TV Guide* in a 1960 interview, "There can be no such thing as a giant step in TV. Steps forward must be taken in inches." [28-3]

When it came to light that the practice of extensively pre-interviewing and pre-testing contestants was secretly being mutated to manipulate big money quizzes instead of simply to elicit laughs with Groucho, Guedel shamelessly observed for *TV Guide,* "So far as TV is concerned, the public is getting exactly what it deserves." [28-3]

In contrast to the care taken to maximize Groucho's comedic mayhem, Jackie Gleason's show was broadcast live and unrehearsed. After Johnny's opening and

"The Great One," Jackie Gleason.

introduction of Gleason and "The Great One's" live pitches for Kellogg's and L&M cigarettes, very little was written or prepared.

Four celebrity players poked their heads through four holes in a painted scene that they were unable to see, in the way that visitors to Coney Island had their pictures taken as they provided the faces for cartoon drawings of muscle-bound men and seemingly emaciated women. While positioned in a scene such as "Goldilocks and the Three Bears," the celebrities asked questions of Gleason with the goal of guessing who they were and the nature of the tableau, thus the title, *You're In The Picture.*

The show was produced by Steve Carlin, who enjoyed tremendous success with *The $64,000 Question* before being taken down in the quiz show scandals. While the premise may have sounded hilarious when pitched in the network's and sponsors' offices, there was clearly very little that was funny about the broadcast unless the audience enjoyed watching a performer die with dignity and a smile. By virtue of his engaging presence and quick ad-lib ability, Gleason narrowly escaped that death.

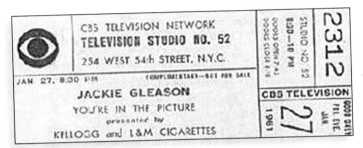

A ticket to an unforgettable television broadcast. Johnny performed the warm-up and introduced Jackie Gleason for a live, thirty-minute unscripted and unrehearsed monologue apologizing for the premiere episode of *You're In The Picture*.

It was a poorly conceived concept, and the performer apparently realized that as the show progressed. He thanked the studio audience at the end of the half-hour for their good nature, saying, "You have braved a blizzard." The best thing to come out of the entire affair was the thirty minutes of riveting television that appeared in the show's time period the following week.

At 9:30 p.m. on January 27, Johnny welcomed viewers at the show's opening to "...what will probably prove to be a very unusual program." Then, Gleason appeared live from CBS' Studio 52 on West 54th Street at Broadway, standing on a naked stage adorned only with a comfortable chair, two small tables, an ashtray, a cigarette lighter, and a coffee cup containing an undisclosed liquid. In a half-hour, hysterical, off-the-cuff monologue about good ideas gone wrong, he apologized to the audience for what he called "the biggest bomb ever put on television."

Gleason said, "Honesty is the best policy...Last week, we did a show called *You're In The Picture* that laid, without a doubt, the biggest bomb in the history of television! I'm telling you friends, that I've seen bombs in my day. This would make the H-bomb look like a two-inch salute." He continued, "You don't have to be Alexander Graham Bell to pick up the telephone and find out it's dead." Gleason discussed the inexact science of television programming, explaining show business an "intangible endeavor." He reviewed the behind-the-scenes process of creating television shows, discussed the genesis of *You're In The Picture*, disclosed the details of his staff's post-mortem analysis of the failed episode, and generally conjectured about the anatomical location of network executives' brains.

The comedian's brilliance was undeniable, as he self-mockingly shared humorous stories of his show biz escapades, including other flops in his career. Critics had panned the previous week's game, but they raved about the half-hour public apology. Audiences seemed to love the vulnerability of a big star admitting with great candor and humor that he had blundered. Of *You're In The Picture*, Jackie Gleason said, "The only good show was the second one, in which I apologized for the first one." [28-1]

Cope Robinson, an advertising executive at Liggett & Myers Tobacco, recalled years later that Gleason and the people at the William Morris Agency had packaged the production. "Together with CBS, they pitched the program to me and a few others at Liggett & Myers. I remember thinking that the show could be risky for it was quite removed from anything that Gleason had done, and the premise of celebrities sticking their heads through a painted plywood board and guessing what historical character they were supposed to be was pretty shaky."

Robinson reflected on the show's failure. "Everybody knew it. Gleason, William Morris, CBS, and, for sure, Liggett & Myers. The real question after the first show was 'What do we do now?'" [28-4]

For the next eight weeks, *The Jackie Gleason Show* was in the time slot. Known for his disdain for extensive preparation and rehearsal, Jackie returned with a simple, one-on-one, ad-lib interview show in which he played host to stars including Bobby Darin, Mickey Rooney, Jane Mansfield, and Gleason's comic partner, Art Carney.

The *You're In The Picture* experience that would have ended any other performer's television career only inspired CBS to give Jackie Gleason an hour of prime time on Saturday nights. For the new show that premiered the following year, Gleason changed a great many staff members, cast, and crew, with the exception of the announcer, whom Gleason recalled did a masterful job with the audience in the minutes leading up to airtime. In an interview for *Time* magazine, Gleason lauded Johnny's warm-up performance. He said, "Johnny is electric. He gets the people in a frame of mind for what's going to come out, just like a burlesque show when the girl starts peeling delicately and gets the audience anticipating." [28-5]

Johnny remained for the new and hugely successful, big-budget, one-hour variety format that rose from those ashes. On September 29, 1962, Gleason's *American Scene Magazine* debuted; Johnny's voice rang loud and clear, "From New York City, the entertainment capitol of the world…" He closed his opening billboard and cued the orchestra with a rousing "And away we go!"

Gleason also hired Johnny for all of his subsequent television shows and specials that utilized a live audience, including his *Honeymooners* retrospectives. He flew Johnny between New York, Atlantic City, and Florida, as needed. In addition to his announcing and warm-up roles, Johnny performed occasional bit parts in Gleason's sketches, and he was credited as the "Town Crier" in a *Honeymooners* episode that included Ralph Kramden staging a skewed performance of Charles Dickens' *A Christmas Carol* in an effort to curry favor with his boss at the Gotham Bus Company. For nine years, Johnny's was the voice that opened the Saturday night show. In later seasons, he spoke over the music of Sammy Spear's Orchestra, "From the sun and fun capital of the world, Miami Beach, we bring you *The Jackie Gleason Show*."

Goodson-Todman's creative guru, Dick DeBartolo, remembered: "Since Jackie Gleason insisted on Johnny doing his warm-ups, we would sometimes move tape dates around so that Johnny could do both *Match Game* and Jackie's show. Friday *Match Game* schedules were built around how soon Johnny had to leave for the airport" [28-6]

Mark Evanier, a veteran television writer, saw Johnny's warm-up and understood why Gleason had come to rely on Johnny as the maestro of mirth-making. Evanier wrote:

> "The late Johnny Olson was the undisputed heavyweight champ of thawing-out an audience. By the time Johnny was through with you, you'd give a standing ovation to a potato race.
> "Jackie Gleason, a man of ego unbounded, would not go before the TV cameras without a Johnny Olson warm-up preceding him. When Gleason moved his CBS show from New York to Miami, he arranged (at great expense) for Johnny to be flown to Florida each week, just for the day, just to do the warm-up.
> "A Johnny Olson warm-up had to be seen to be believed. He would boogey out to an Aretha Franklin record played full-blast, and he would quickly have the house on its feet and clapping along. For about ten minutes, he would race through the audience, sit on fat ladies' laps, kiss everyone who wanted to be kissed (and a few who didn't), pass out prizes...once, I saw him turn a cartwheel in the aisles...He did the best warm-ups I've ever seen." [28-7]

Gleason decided that he preferred to do his weekly program from Miami to accommodate his penchant for golf. With no network production facilities in town, CBS made a major investment to upgrade and equip the old Miami Convention Center for color television. Now known as The Jackie Gleason Theater of the Performing Arts, the huge facility was remodeled. Gleason brought in key personnel, including Johnny, for tapings. Penny Olson usually joined him for the working weekends. In later seasons, she was added to the payroll and received an on-screen credit as a member of *The Jackie Gleason Show* program staff.

With an audience of 2,500 to cajole, Johnny worked one aisle while his "million-dollar Penny" worked the other. The warm-up routine was much the same, but far more energetic as Johnny ran up and down the aisles to make a personal connection with as many audience members as possible. The building seemed to shake when Johnny cued the throng of Gleason's fans, "Now give me a real belly-buster laugh!"

CBS also contracted with Gleason's Peekskill Productions for a 1968 summer replacement program, *The Dom DeLuise Show*. It starred the versatile performer, who had honed his acting skills with early appearances on television series including *The Munsters, Please Don't Eat the Daisies,* and *The Girl From U.N.C.L.E.* DeLuise was just gaining fame as a comedian in appearances with Mike Douglas, Merv Griffin, The

Smothers Brothers, and Dean Martin, as well as from two guest shots on *The Jackie Gleason Show*. Like Gleason's own program that year, *The Dom DeLuise Show* was produced in Miami and featured the June Taylor Dancers. To assure a responsive audience, Jackie utilized ever dependable Johnny on each tape date.

Johnny joked, "From 300 or so New York to Miami flights for Jackie Gleason, I know a lot of Eastern and National Airlines stewardesses." Discussing his fifteen-year

On the stage of the Miami Convention Center for Jackie Gleason's Saturday night CBS show. Johnny (left) emulated Gleason's style by wearing his own red boutonnière.

relationship with Gleason and his longevity working with other high-profile hosts, Johnny advised keeping a respectful distance from their personal lives.

Johnny shared stages with a great many stars. They appeared as celebrity panelists on game shows and as guests on interview and variety shows he hosted. They also participated in the superstar specials he announced, as well as in the personal appearances he made over the course of his career. The list included Frank Sinatra, Bing Crosby, Jack Benny, Groucho Marx, Gene Kelly, George Burns, Milton Berle, Tony Bennett, Phil Silvers, Wayne Newton, Maureen O'Hara, Mickey Rooney, George Carlin, Rodney Dangerfield, Donald O'Connor, Johnny Carson, Bob Crosby, Lena Horne, Lionel Hampton, Ozzie and Harriet Nelson, Roy Rogers, The Andrews Sisters, Gene Autry, Count Basie, Woody Herman, Roddy McDowall, and Kate Smith.

Johnny advised, "They'll invite you to all the parties, but that doesn't mean you have to go all the time."

CHAPTER 29
THE TALE OF THE TAPE

Early television was live. Because electrons and broadcasting transmissions fly at 186,282 miles a second, the speed of light, what the camera saw, America saw. With the exception of theatrical movies shown on the tube, and the few situation comedies and dramas that were previously filmed, all news programming, variety shows, soap operas, game shows, and interview and talk shows were broadcast live.

In the 1980s, Sid Caesar found great humor in a question asked by students at his college lectures when discussions turned to *Your Show of Shows*, his live, break-through comedy series of an earlier decade. "How long did it take you to perform the weekly ninety-minute program?" they invariably asked.

The mechanics of recording audio began as sound vibrations cut into a continuous groove on rotating wax cylinders. Flat discs made from shellac, lacquer, or acetate followed. The next development was tape, which came into use in the wake of World War II. Recorded sound came from magnetically arranging metallic particles on a spool of oxide-coated tape. Bing Crosby championed the use of tape after Jack Mullin, an audio engineer serving as a GI, shipped vital parts from two German-made tape recorders back to the United States.

Capturing a complex visual signal proved baffling, but once mastered, it was a dangerous, engineering nightmare. At first, to move the tape at a speed necessary to record the vast amount of information, the large metal reels holding the tape were required to spin at life-threatening speed, and the length of a recording was limited to just a few minutes. Bing's "Crosby Video" captured a quality signal, but its one-inch tape unwound at 100-inches-per-second from an 8,000-foot reel. RCA's 1953 proto-type was even more unwieldy, using huge, 36-inch-diameter reels that unwound seven miles of tape at 60 miles per hour — a mile a minute — for a maximum recording time of seven minutes. After three more years of research and development, Sarnoff's engineers came a far way towards harnessing the horror, pulling tape from whirling 20-inch reels at only 20-feet per second — approximately 14 miles per hour.

NBC visionary Pat Weaver spoke of his visit to a lab, where an early model of an Ampex videotape machine was being developed, "The spools had to be so big and the speed so fast that if the tape would break…the guy who was running it had to run for his life." [29-1] Ampex was the first company to make a practical video recording machine, introducing its VR-1000 at the National Association of Broadcasters Conference in Chicago on April 14, 1956. Ampex tallied over $4 million in orders in just a few days, selling ninety machines at a cost of $50,000 each. The new 2-inch tape format remained the industry standard for nearly three decades.

In October 1956, NBC reported that it first used videotape to present a recorded musical number with guest singer Dorothy Collins in a live broadcast of *The Jonathan Winters Show*. CBS first utilized the new technology on November 30, 1956, to replay *The CBS Evening News with Douglas Edwards* to the western states. In 1958, Paley's network boasted that it aired the first entertainment program produced entirely on videotape, an episode of *Playhouse 90*.

Even with tape taking hold, there was a lack of confidence in its reliability, and the networks were still using film kinescopes as back-up for many broadcasts. The day soon was at hand when the technology proved trustworthy and the production of television programming experienced a revolution.

In network contracts with program providers, the producer typically paid for the performing talent and creative expenses, referred to as "above the line" costs. The networks provided the "below the line" services associated with production, including the facilities and crew. Game shows' transition to tape was instigated by the networks and motivated by the economics of scale. The ability to produce two episodes in one taping session resulted in immense, below the line savings over the course of the run of a series. Labor costs were greatly reduced, and facilities were utilized more efficiently. With careful scheduling, each studio could accommodate multiple programs.

Experiences at *The Price is Right* and *Play Your Hunch* were typical of the transition to tape. NBC came to Goodson-Todman producers, Bob Stewart and Ira Skutch, with requests to change production schedules from the live broadcast of one show each day, to producing two episodes each day in the studio. Skutch reported that he reluctantly started the transition with Merv Griffin and Johnny performing two shows on Thursdays, the second taped to air on Friday. Stewart recalled that his host, Bill Cullen, was resistant at first, as were many staffers, who were required to prepare two entire shows' prizes, scripts, and contestants for each day in the studio; it seemed like double work. Stewart delayed NBC for as long as possible, but within a few weeks, he reluctantly retooled for the new scheduling. Soon after, the production company from Bill Cullen and Bob Stewart on down enjoyed working half as many days.

Cullen reportedly loved the use of videotape so much that he was among those soon advocating for the production of an entire week's worth of programs in two days. Completing two episodes on one day, and then three on the next became the norm for the Goodson-Todman shows on which Johnny worked in the mid 1960s. By the end of the decade, producers and networks were confident enough to begin taping five episodes during a single day in the studio. For the first time ever, production costs were slashed by stockpiling episodes. Furthermore, people associated with an on-going hit program enjoyed the luxury of vacations.

It was a transition that changed television forever. Soon, little more than news programming was broadcast live, and the producers of videotaped entertainment shows began editing their errors. While a boon to the business of broadcasting, it marked a moment when television forever lost much of its immediacy, spontaneity, and urgency, as well as the sense of danger in the knowledge that anything unexpected

could happen at any time. Many media historians and pundits point to the introduction of videotape as sounding the death knell for the dramatic anthology series cited
as the hallmark of the so-called "Golden Age" of television.

It was only with the use of tape to record multiple episodes of a program on a
single day that Johnny truly became the ubiquitous voice of American game shows.
AFTRA, his union, helped support the transition to tape by including in their con-

Johnny, Penny, and their three pet poodles recreated a bit of the Midwest at the first of
their two homes in Greenwich, Connecticut.

tracts with producers an incentive to utilize the new technology. Since a performer
would be free to accept more work if multiple episodes, even an entire week's worth
of a daily show, were produced in one session, the union instituted what it called a
"multiple program discount." The formula reduced talent fees to three-fifths of the
usual union scale for a week's worth of shows that taped on the same day and aired
in the same calendar week.

Videotape changed the game show industry forever and allowed Johnny to do the
seemingly impossible — announce programs that were broadcast on different networks and in syndication on over 150 local stations simultaneously. Johnny happily
accepted more work than ever, including a revival of *Concentration*, which taped its
entire 1973 season of 195 shows in only nine weeks, recording seven episodes each
day in the studio. The following year, Johnny told *Tomorrow* host Tom Snyder that
his record was his being featured on forty-one shows in one broadcast week.

As Johnny considered the financial rewards of his work secondary, there is little
motivation to multiply the union scale minimum salary by the number of episodes

on which he performed. Johnny loved the work and the friendships too much for the money to have ever become an issue. Suffice it to say he was earning more than ever before in his career, and his six-figure income far exceeded any expectation he had for his future back when he toiled in local radio in Minnesota and Wisconsin, or in the early days of television at DuMont.

Most important to Johnny was that Penny and he were enjoying a gracious lifestyle. He lavished his loyal lover with furs, fine dining, and the kind of furniture, china, crystal, and household appointments that brought them joy. Although they employed Joyce Lyle, a housekeeper for a time, and each of their residences was large and well-decorated with elegant furnishings and artwork, one guest to their homes observed that the couple entertained exclusively in their kitchen. Ira Skutch remembered evenings with the Olsons in Connecticut during which the party never left the supper table. It was almost certainly a reflection of Johnny and Penny's Midwest upbringings as members of large families where the kitchen was the nexus of household activity, and there was always something cooking on the stove.

Success agreed with Johnny. In 1951, he told southern Minnesota's Cottonwood County Citizen, "I do have an apartment which doesn't face the park on Central Park South in New York, a house in Greenwich, Connecticut, and a Cadillac with 'JOTV' license plates." Johnny continued with typical modestly, "I also have at least a nodding acquaintance with a great many executives, producers, cameramen, elevator operators, pages, and receptionists at all the networks."

By 1960, Johnny truly had been employed by all four television networks, and he had contributed to some of their most popular daytime and prime-time programs. At a time when the minimum wage was $1.00 an hour and the average annual salary for Americans was $5,500, Johnny was earning well over $100,000 a year.

As for the "nodding acquaintances," Johnny was one of the more respected and beloved workers in the New York broadcasting community. He told his hometown newspaper, "I have come up the hard way. It took 35 years, but the time was well spent and I think I have established a good stake in the future. From where I sit now, I like the looks of tomorrow." [29-2] Johnny had far exceeded what he set out to do when he first starting in radio, yet he maintained every ounce of his original passion and humility, as well as his highly contagious, electrifying enthusiasm.

Words could never fully capture the magic, but in their November 1st, 1968 edition, *Time* tried with a description of John's energetic pre-show performance. The magazine reported Johnny's warm-up preceded seventeen different television broadcasts each week. "Ten minutes or so before air time, Olson crouches backstage like a half-miler, waits until he feels the 'right psychological moment,' and then bolts out before the audience, shouting 'Hey! Helloooo everybodeeee!' As the applause sign flashes on and off, he bounds about like a cheerleader and cries: 'Good morning, everybodeeee! Good morning! Say good morning, everybodeeee! [Audience shyly replies.] Oooh, that was bee-yoo-tee-ful!" [29-3]

Time's reporter wrote of some of the clowning that entertained over two million audience members through the years. Even before saying a word, Johnny's soft-shoe shuffle could warm any room. His bird ballet in honor of NBC's peacock never failed to evoke laughter, as he flapped his arms and pirouetted around the stage. The dance culminated with Johnny turning his back to the audience, bending over, and flipping-up his coattails to reveal a picture of the NBC peacock pasted on the seat of his pants. Invariably, the audience roared. Network programmers and sales representatives, sponsors, and ad agency account executives smiled at each other, confident that the infectious, in-studio excitement would pour into viewers' living rooms.

CHAPTER 30
WORKING MORE AND MOORE

The inspiration for the failed original courtroom set for Goodson and Todman's *I've Got A Secret* foretold the presentation of the producing partners' third iconic panel show, *To Tell the Truth*. In keeping with the judicial theme, participants were introduced with the reading of an affidavit, and their questioning was often referred to as a cross-examination. The program debuted on December 18, 1956, with CBS staff announcer Bern Bennett asking contestants and imposters, "Number one, what is your name, please?" Four months after Bennett was reassigned, Johnny became permanently associated with this evergreen hit when he manned the mike for a twelve year run that started on Halloween, 1960.

To Tell the Truth sprang from an idea from Bob Stewart, the possessor of the most fertile mind in the creation of game shows. While Mark Goodson and Bill Todman led a think tank that expertly refined the formats and sold and produced the programs, *To Tell the Truth*, *Password*, and *The Price is Right* were all based upon inspirations from Stewart, and each has its own claim to fame for innovation.

The Price is Right took the simple auction concept to new heights with elaborate prizes, fun bonuses, and home-viewer showcases. Although tried on *Take a Guess*, a 1953 summer replacement show on CBS, *Password* was the first hit series to team civilian contestants with celebrities, bouncing control of the game back and forth between the teams. *To Tell The Truth* was the first game in which ordinary citizens were entrusted to carry much of the program, with the difficult challenge of bluffing in response to tough, unrehearsed questioning.

Stewart remembered being met with skepticism in 1956, when he suggested that he could present three persons all claiming to be the same individual, and that the imposters could stand up through a no-holds-barred inquiry, leaving the identity of the real person a mystery. He recounted, "I presented Mark [Goodson] an idea called *Three of a Kind*...I brought in three people. One of them had been in the infantry in World War II and was then managing a grocery store. Mark brought some of his producers and they questioned these people for fifteen minutes. Then they had to vote separately. I said, 'Before you vote, if anybody is positive about who the real person is, raise your hand.' Nobody did. The show went on that December." [30-1]

In a series of office run-throughs, the Goodson-Todman staffers were unable to consistently identify the true individuals from the pairs of imposters after rigorously questioning all three. Mark Goodson recalled one format test in which he and his collection of creative collaborators walked into the office to find three people seated side-by-side. "They all said their name was Jerry Something, that they used to sing with Frank Sinatra, and that they were expert gardeners and painters. 'Boy,' I said, 'this is going to be a cinch.' We cross-examined them for twenty minutes. Then, all of us picked the wrong one." Thinking it was a freak occurrence, the guru of games had Stewart deliver another trio the following day. Goodson remembered, "One of them had won a photography contest, received his award from Ike and worked for the fire department. We all picked wrong once again. Within a matter of five months the show was on the air."[30-2]

CBS agreed that it was an intriguing and innovative new twist for a panel show. The name was changed to *Nothing But The Truth*, and the details for the show's presentation were the next concern. When thoughts turned to casting the role of host, the success of *What's My Line?* with moderator John Charles Daly was a motivating force. Mark Goodson again looked to the ranks of CBS' newscasters and staff announcers.

Mike Wallace filled the bill. He had proven himself a versatile broadcaster before becoming America's preeminent investigative reporter, fronting innovative talk and interview shows, as well as performing as an announcer and actor on radio. He had even worked as a costumed character on Claude Kirchner's circus-themed kids' show. Born Myron Woleck, Wallace was a commercial pitchman for products as diverse as Parliament cigarettes and Fluffo shortening. He was adept at comedy having worked opposite Spike Jones, and he had even appeared briefly on Broadway. He had already hosted game shows, including *I'll Buy That*, *Who's the Boss*, and *The Big Surprise*, and he had been hired by Goodson-Todman in February 1954, just two years previously, for a dramatic role in the company's anthology series, *The Web*.

Although Mike Wallace hosted the new panel program's pilot, *Nothing But the Truth* was scheduled to premiere at 9:00 p.m. on December 18, 1956, from CBS Studio 59 with another newsman moderating. NBC had only recently dropped John Cameron Swayze as the anchor of *The Camel News Caravan* in favor of a revamped newscast with Chet Huntley and David Brinkley. Among Swayze's strengths were an almost photographic memory, a gift for ad-libbing, and a sponsor-friendly reputation from his years as a commercial spokesman for Timex watches.

John Cameron Swayze briefly became Goodson's choice to front the series, but the program's fate took two more twists just days before its debut. Paramount Pictures objected to the title because it had used *Nothing But the Truth* for two different films, one starring Bob Hope. In addition, the role of host was again recast. The warm, friendly, and familiar Bud Collyer ultimately took the helm for the twelve-year network run of *To Tell the Truth*. The catchy "Peter Pan" composed by Metropole Orchestra leader Dolf van der Linden was initially used as the theme. When it was first played, Swayze was relegated to a seat on the panel with Polly Bergen, Hildy Parks, and Dick Van Dyke for the debut episode. Mike Wallace appeared as a panelist the following week.

It was reported that Wallace turned down the original opportunity to host *To Tell The Truth* in order to focus on more journalistic endeavors, but that account has been brought into question. Wallace later expressed his disappointment at being passed over twice for the emcee job in the 1950s, having performed well enough on the pilot to have helped sell the show. While taping an interview for a 1960s episode of CBS' *60 Minutes,* Mark Goodson was face-to-face with Wallace discussing game shows.

The tone of the interview changed after the newsman mentioned *To Tell The Truth*, and Goodson registered a complaint on camera: "I must say, that I'm not terribly happy to be talking with you knowing that you are going back to New York and edit this any way you choose." Goodson was well aware that Mike Wallace's career included several stints as a game show host going back to 1951, including helming one program that came under suspicion during the scandals. Goodson then asked, "Suppose I said something about you being the host of *The Big Surprise.* Would you have left that in, or taken it out?" Wallace responded, "I would have taken it out."[30-3]

Johnny Olson was occasionally caught on camera during his years with *To Tell The Truth,* the program that Mark Goodson called "the most golden game show idea of all."

Decades later, Wallace chided Goodson about being passed over for the job. In a 1991 taped greeting in which he wished the producer a happy birthday, Wallace recalled the incident, stating that Goodson had promised him the position if the pilot show sold. Thirty-five years later, Wallace said he was still waiting for the call.

With a daytime version added on June 18, 1962, *To Tell The Truth* bounced among several facilities, including Studio 52, the same CBS theater where Johnny worked with Jackie Gleason on *You're In The Picture,* and the network's Broadcast Center on West 57th Street, the former Sheffield Farms dairy. Johnny finished the series' primetime network run on May 22, 1967, and the daytime run on September 6, 1968. After a fifty-two-week rest, the format returned, and Johnny was teamed with Garry Moore in 1969 for a syndicated version of the show that debuted on September 8 from CBS'

Ed Sullivan Theater on Broadway, and later from Studio 6A at the familiar NBC Rockefeller Center facility.

In retrospect, Goodson referred to *To Tell The Truth* as "the most golden game show idea of all." Its legacy of lengthy runs bears out that claim, as versions of *To Tell The Truth* have been broadcast in all six decades from the 1950s to the 2000s. Only one person has been involved with all of those incarnations, popular panelist Kitty Carlisle Hart. She celebrated the experience saying, "I spent quite a long time in my life in television…It's turned every town into a small town for me, because people come toward me smiling and they remember me from *To Tell The Truth* and other shows long before that."[30-4]

There was a bump early on along the show's long road of success. During the first year of *To Tell The Truth*, Chicago television columnist Harriet Van Horne noticed the similarity between the Goodson-Todman program and a segment called "Detecto" on Art Linkletter's audience participation series *People Are Funny*. She erroneously reported that Linkletter had stolen the idea from *To Tell The Truth*, when in reality, "Detecto" predated the new game show by years. Van Horne apologized, but drawing public attention to the similarity resulted in Linkletter and his producer John Guedel filing a plagiarism suit. The affair was settled out of court with the payment of the biggest prize in the history of *To Tell The Truth*, a reported $3 million.

When *To Tell The Truth* premiered a week before Christmas 1956, *What's My Line?* was about to start its seventh year, and *I've Got A Secret* was halfway through it's fifth season. The three panel shows became consistent ratings performers, regularly among the A.C. Nielsen Top 20 television programs, and Johnny was proud to ultimately be associated with all three. He witnessed far more drama behind the scenes at *I've Got A Secret*. After a disagreement with CBS programmer Jim Aubrey in 1964, Garry Moore walked off the show vowing to never return to CBS.

Aubrey, not Moore, never returned to the Tiffany network. The executive was fired soon after his altercation with the host. Still in his forties, Garry was not ready for retirement. After an extended vacation travelling the world with his wife, Moore wanted more. In 1966, the network premiered *The New Garry Moore Show* on Sunday nights opposite NBC's stalwart *Bonanza*, but the series quickly fizzled. Garry was gone again in January 1967.

With Steve Allen having taken his seat at *I've Got A Secret*, Garry was sidelined until 1969, when Mark Goodson returned him to the spotlight as host of the new syndicated run of *To Tell the Truth*. Garry was a good match for the show, orchestrating a perfect balance between the game play and light-hearted fun with the panel. Despite the slow erosion of viewership for the aging Goodson-Todman shows on the networks, *To Tell The Truth* enjoyed a relatively smooth sail in syndication. It was most memorable for its multi-colored, Carnaby Street-inspired "mod" motif, just one of many creative sets designed by Ted Cooper, and for its catchy theme song co-written by director Paul Alter.

Then in 1977, Garry suddenly left *To Tell The Truth*. As he had developed a rapport with audiences during his forty years in broadcasting, gracing more than a dozen covers of *TV Guide* over the decades, television viewers and reviewers immediately sensed something was amiss. No explanation was offered.

Bill Cullen assumed the hosting responsibilities for *To Tell The Truth*, but Mark Goodson's keen eye for casting sensed that Cullen's change of seats had affected the chemistry with female panelists Peggy Cass and Kitty Carlisle. Bill Cullen returned to the panel and Joe Garagiola, a sports legend turned television personality, was then hired to host. Through all of the musical chairs, Garry's fate remained unexplained to the audience.

Johnny knew the truth; Garry had developed throat cancer and had taken time off from *To Tell The Truth* for surgery and recovery. He decided it was time to retire, but to address the audience's questions about his fate and to take a well-deserved final bow, he came back to the show literally to tell the truth. Garry hosted *To Tell The Truth* for one last time at the beginning of the 1977-1978 season.

Garry's surprise entrance at the top of the program stunned the studio audience, and the respected emcee received one of the more enthusiastic welcomes in television history. Garry bantered with the panel displaying his usual good nature, and then in a more somber moment, he explained in the most general terms that he had experienced some health problems and had chosen retirement. To more applause, Garry then figuratively passed the hosting baton to Joe Garagiola before making his final exit from the show and from America's living rooms.

It was well known in the industry that Garry was a recovering alcoholic, as well as a heavy smoker, both on and off the air. Before smoking became controversial, he entered at the top of the show in a swirl of smoke with a cigarette between his lips, as did other hosts, newscasters, and pitchmen. In live commercials, he praised Winstons as the best-tasting filter cigarette and the one that is "more fun to smoke." Garry exalted the brand's two-year rise from its introduction to the best-selling filter cigarette in the country as a "success story that has never been equaled in the history of the American tobacco industry." In later years, after tobacco advertising was banned from the airwaves and on-camera smoking was on the wane, rare backstage documentary footage shows Garry taking one final deep drag from a cigarette and tossing the butt at the last second while making his entrance.

Garry Moore came out of retirement for two final television appearances in 1984. One, to honor Carol Burnett, and the other for a Goodson-Todman prime-time retrospective of game shows, on which he reminisced and showed memorable clips from his long run on *I've Got A Secret*. Garry later lost his clear diction as a result of multiple surgeries, and he died on Hilton Head Island in South Carolina on November 28, 1993. Out of respect for the tobacco sponsors, who had contributed to his decades of success, Garry never publicly used the word "cancer" in describing his illness. The cause of his death was listed as emphysema.

Much has been written over the years about the period of time during which the tobacco industry aggressively marketed cigarettes while desperately trying to keep the lid on research that linked smoking to cancer. Celebrities from Lucy and Desi to Fred Flintstone and Barney Rubble pitched tobacco products, and many television personalities, including Garry Moore, were encouraged to smoke their sponsors' brands on-air. In another of many sad ironies like Garry's, Old Gold cigarette's perennial commercial spokesman, Dennis James, was ultimately felled by lung cancer, although he had given up smoking many years previously.

In his book, *Here's Morgan!* venerable *I've Got A Secret* panelist Henry Morgan wrote of one incident in which Garry came to his aid during the era when the tobacco sponsors wielded great clout over programs and personalities. "One night, I was doing my own local TV show, and in lighting a cigarette, I remarked that I was creating my *own* cancer. It didn't occur to me, of course, that *Secret* was sponsored by Winston...they fired me at dawn. Garry flew down to North Carolina and talked them out of it. What can you do with a guy like that? More to the point, what can you do *without* him?" [30-5]

During the 1950s and 1960s, an especially prolific period for television game shows, Johnny performed his enthusiastic studio warm-ups while announcing NBC's *Split Personality* in 1959 and 1960. Taped at the network's historic Studio 8H, *Split Personality* teamed Johnny with Emmy award-winning Tom Poston. That versatile performer first became popular to television audiences as a supporting player on *The Steve Allen Show*, and he remained a familiar face in their living rooms through the 1990s with his extensive work on sitcoms, including three series with Bob Newhart. *Split Personality* featured players feeding clues to each other about a famous person to help their partners in attempts to name the celebrity. The bonus round challenged the champion to name two famous people, whose pictures were combined into one image.

For thirteen weeks at the end of 1961, Johnny was back working with children as he had when hosting *Whiz Kids* for CBS radio and *Kids and Company* for DuMont television. *On Your Mark* was an early ABC-TV prototype for the decades of Saturday morning children's shows and the Nickelodeon cable network fare that followed. Produced and hosted by Sonny Fox, kids aged nine to thirteen answered questions and faced challenges relating to different professions.

Irwin "Sonny" Fox was one of the original staff writers on Alan Funt's *Candid Microphone* and a CBS news correspondent before chosen as the original host of *The $64,000 Challenge*. He was miscast in the role and awkward in his performance, and he was replaced a few weeks into the series. As "Officer" Joe Bolton had done after he was the second banana on Johnny's *Doorway to Fame*, Sonny Fox found years of steady employment and unlimited goodwill as one of the heroes of local television. He became a favorite kids' television personality in New York hosting *Wonderama* on WNEW-TV, the new identity for the city's Channel 5 after the demise of the DuMont network and its flagship, WABD.

In addition to spending those two notorious Saturday nights on CBS with Jackie Gleason for *You're in the Picture*, Johnny Olson returned in front of the cameras in 1963 to emcee the Mrs. America pageant. It was one of the last hosting roles of his career. The beauty competition was a 1930s invention of publicist Bert Nevins for his client, New Jersey's Palisades Amusement Park. Nevins knew Johnny and his work from the 1950s, when Johnny anchored DuMont programs that originated from the park. As he had with many of the shows he most enjoyed working, Johnny saved mementos from his performance with the fifty-one Mrs. America hopefuls, including the program's script, contestant information, and his interview questions.

The following year, Johnny was back on the CBS network's prime-time schedule with *On Broadway Tonight*. That summer replacement series was a one-hour variety outing hosted by one of old time radio's superstars, Rudy Vallee. The show was produced by Irving Mansfield, an entertainment manager and the husband of novelist Jacqueline Susanne. *On Broadway Tonight* boasted a contemporary, youthful feel that included a theme song sung by Frankie Valli and The Four Seasons. Each episode presented six acts, including some of the best of new talent. Some of the performers, such as Richard Pryor, George Carlin, and Rodney Dangerfield, were making their earliest network appearances.

Despite his occasional forays into variety and children's programming, the bulk of Johnny's work in the 1960s and 1970s was on game shows. In 1963 and 1964, he joined hosts Ed McMahon and Dick Clark on *Missing Links*, initially for NBC, and then through its subsequent pick-up by ABC. In 1964, Johnny announced ABC's short-lived *Get The Message* from the network's 885-seat Elysee Theater on West 58th Street at 7th Avenue. The following year, Johnny teamed with Goodson-Todman's long-time producer, Bob Noah, for a six-month run on *Call My Bluff!*

Between 1967 and 1969, Johnny again shared the stage with Ed McMahon for approximately 500 episodes of NBC's *Snap Judgment*. He assisted Joe Garagiola on the syndicated *He Said, She Said*, which also taped at NBC in 1969 and 1970. He stayed with the former baseball star and *Today Show* co-host for *Joe Garagiola's Memory Game*, which debuted on February 15, 1971, for a six-month run on the peacock network.

On *Missing Links*, contestants received cash based on the ability of three celebrity panelists to fill in the blanks in a story of a real life incident that was read to them. Despite the best efforts of two popular hosts, time slots on two networks, and a guest appearance by Johnny Carson, *Missing Links* was missing an audience. It has been said that every member of a generation of Americans remembers where he was when President John Kennedy was assassinated. Johnny Olson was in a midtown New York theater that Friday, working with Dick Clark and producer Ira Skutch, his long-time colleague and neighbor in Greenwich, on the ABC incarnation of *Missing Links*. While the show's cancellation soon sent staff and crew members scurrying for their next jobs, it created an opportunity for Johnny to step behind the mike for yet another Goodson-Todman outing.

As *Password* had pioneered in pairing civilian players with celebrities, *Get the Message* teamed a contestant with two celebrities in their combined effort to outscore a similarly cast opposing team. Again, one-word clues were in play, one from each celebrity, as their teammate attempted to discern a message about a person, place, or thing. With the clues "explorer" and "America" from the team's celebrities, a contestant was likely to get the message "Christopher Columbus." Neither host Frank Buxton nor Robert Q. Lewis could keep the show compelling enough to survive longer than nine months. The combination word-panel game ended its run on Christmas Day, 1964.

Bob Stewart's innovation of pairing celebrities with contestants was again mutated for *Call My Bluff!* A grouping of one celebrity with two civilian players challenged another similar team to identify the one accurate definition of an obscure word from among three, two of which were bluffs. Graphic artist Eric Lieber, who had drawn the caricatures for *Dotto*, survived the quiz show scandals and was credited as Word Editor for *Call My Bluff!* It was a six-month stop on a career that later included Pro-

Johnny (left) with multi-talented, actor-author-director-host Frank Buxton on the set of ABC's *Get The Message*.

ducer credits with talk shows starring Dick Cavett, Sammy Davis Jr., Mike Douglas, and Chuck Woolery. Lieber reached his greatest success as the creator and producer of the 1983 dating show, *Love Connection*.

Instead of a glamorous visual of the set or a close-up of an enthusiastic player, early episodes of *Snap Judgment* opened with a view from the wings. Johnny explained, "This is backstage at NBC Studio 8H in New York City just about to go on the air. Our contestants for today are hurrying to complete their associations to the key words we have given them. Out on stage waiting to meet them for the first time are their partners...and the game they're on their mark to play is *Snap* (audience members snap fingers) *Judgment*."

As Gene Rayburn and Hugh Down had done previously, Ed McMahon, the *Tonight Show* sidekick at that time, could be found moonlighting in daytime games. McMahon presided over a contest that abandoned its original word association guessing game format after eight months to adopt a closer derivative of the familiar *Password*.

A condensation of the opening did not help to adequately explain the game nor create sufficient excitement to hook the audience into viewing. "This is backstage and our contestants for today are completing their word associations. Out on stage are their partners...and the game they're on their mark to play is *Snap* (audience members snap fingers) *Judgment*." It was becoming a tough time for television games, and despite the behind-the-scenes teamwork of both Bob Noah and Ira Skutch, no amount of retooling could keep the struggling *Snap Judgment* alive beyond the spring of 1969.

Joe Garagiola's Memory Game, like *Jeopardy!*, was hatched from a skewed twist on the game show world's preoccupation with the earlier quiz show scandals in which players were given answers. As *Jeopardy!* provided answers to its contestants and challenged them to come up with questions, the five players on *Joe Garagiola's Memory Game* were each overtly given some of the questions and answers to be used on the program. Either by their own knowledge or by virtue of having seen the material in advance, the players earned points for each correct answer. Both formats found their way to NBC from the fertile imagination of Merv Griffin, although he chose to remain unaccredited on the memory game.[30-6]

Between 1960 and 1968, Johnny was behind the microphone and audience merriment for the network run of *To Tell The Truth*, making the series' move in 1969 to syndication. Throughout those years, Johnny was still the voice on the stalwart *What's My Line?* In 1968, when CBS' weekly *What's My Line?* transitioned to a syndicated daily show, Johnny continued as its voice for the five weekly episodes that were taped at NBC. Concurrently, between 1962 and 1969, he was on the set with Gene Rayburn for 1,760 episodes of NBC's *The Match Game*.

Johnny was always glad to accept as much work as he could, and Goodson-Todman accommodated his workload when scheduling tapings. It added to the illusion that Johnny defied the laws of physics, when he seemed to be present in multiple studios for different networks simultaneously. The fall of 1969 was Johnny's busiest television season during his twenty-eight years based in New York. With *The Match Game*, *To Tell The Truth*, *What's My Line?*, and *He Said, She Said*, counting only game shows, the fruits of Johnny's labor were heard on twenty different half-hour nationally broadcast programs each week. During most weekends between 1962 and 1970, he also joined Jackie Gleason for the superstar's Saturday night CBS show.

In 1970, Johnny told his hometown newspaper, the *Cottonwood County Citizen*, that his current schedule included *The Peggy Fleming Show*, as well as his continuing work on *To Tell The Truth*, *I've Got A Secret*, *The Jackie Gleason Show*, *The USIA Worldwide Show*, *What's My Line?*, and *He Said, She Said*. Either Johnny or the newspaper reporter erroneously included *I've Got A Secret* in that list, as the program had concluded its New York run, and was still two years away from its syndicated revival from Hollywood.

Goodson-Todman's *He Said, She Said* was rooted in the earlier NBC pilot, *It Had to be You*. *He Said, She Said* was hosted by Ed McMahon, and featured civilian contestants instead of celebrities. Joe Garagiola was recruited to host a second pilot, as well as the series, when McMahon was tapped for *Snap Judgment*. *He Said, She Said* presented four celebrity couples, each recalling funny moments from their marriage, triggered by clues from their spouses. It was advertised as a "fun-filled new game of marital quotes and misquotes."

He Said, She Said ran for only one year, but served as the prototype for Goodson-Todman's 1972 pilot, *Celebrity Matchmates*, starring Gene Rayburn. That adaptation of the evolving format was later streamlined to include only three couples, and ultimately became the 1974 hit, *Tattletales*. With Rayburn already leading the successful *Match Game*, Goodson and Executive Producer Ira Skutch cast another multitalented performer, Bert Convy, as host. From minor league baseball player, to rock and roll singer, to theatrical actor, Convy appeared in the original Broadway casts of *Fiddler on the Roof* and *Cabaret* before joining Johnny and announcers Jack Clark, Gene Wood, and John Harlan at Television City for *Tattletales'* four-year run.

The USIA Worldwide Show of which John spoke was far more meaty fare. The program was a product of the United States Information Agency, the Eisenhower administration's program that used the media to influence overseas listeners. Its purpose, and the purpose of Johnny's show, was to create a positive image for America and to make foreign audiences receptive to US foreign policies. The best known of the USIA's operations was the Voice of America, which included programs in more than fifty languages that were beamed from dozens of transmitters to every hot spot on the globe during the Cold War.

The balance between entertainment and propaganda on *The USIA Worldwide Show* cannot be judged, and the program is not available to be studied as an artifact of the times. Outside of governmental auspices, it has never been heard in this country. By congressional order, the United States Information Agency's services cannot be distributed within the United States.

In 1972, an election year, Johnny had another indirect connection with the United States government, when he appeared as himself in *The Selling of the President*, a Broadway musical about politics, media, and the American presidency. With much of the production set in a television studio, Johnny shared the stage with singers, dancers, and actors portraying US Senators, advertising executives, and members of the press.

The show was an adaptation of a 1969 book of the same name by Joe McGinniss, a young columnist for the *Philadelphia Inquirer*, who followed Richard Nixon's 1968 campaign. The non-fiction work reported on the candidate being packaged and sold to the American public through television, as McGinniss said, "...like so much toothpaste or detergent."[30-7] Turning the political satire into a bona fide Broadway musical proved to be almost as hellish as the Nixon presidency.

Tony Award-winner Jack O'Brien, the author of the book and lyrics, recalled in 2009 that the story was depressing. He reported that it ended with, "[the] assassination of the newly elected President, wherein the participants simply closed ranks and went on as if they would easily find another image to sell. Not exactly an 'up' ending, considering the history of [John] Kennedy, Bobby Kennedy, and Martin Luther King, but there you are!"[30-8]

After try-outs in San Francisco, O'Brien said, "It was decided to make the show more 'real' and less fantastic, and that was when it seemed logical to hire Johnny Olson, then practically a household hero." Of Johnny's role, author O'Brien explained, "The point was that he was a 'commercial' rather than a political figure, which added to the satiric aspect of 'selling,' as it were." Of Johnny, O'Brien echoed the universal sentiments, "He was bright, eager, happy to be there…polite, and a complete pro."[30-8]

Johnny's commitment to the Broadway show impinged upon the broadcasting career that had brought him fame and a very comfortable lifestyle. Work on the Great White Way not only demanded his presence for regular evening performances, but for matinees as well, typically on Wednesdays and Sundays. The added weekly salary he stood to earn was less than a single appearance on one of his regular television series. It was prestigious work, but compensation for theatrical performers other than headlining stars generally fell below that of even union scale minimums for television.

The beginning years of the 1970s had been a down time for game shows, and Johnny saw *The Selling of the President* as an opportunity to re-establish himself in a new milieu with another transition like those he had taken from radio to band singer to television. Jack O'Brien specifically confirmed Johnny's presence for all rehearsals and performances, "I don't remember 'conflicts' being a problem, and, of course, he was very much 'live,' and not on tape."[30-8]

Following rehearsals, *The Selling of the President* enjoyed six preview performances that began on March 16. Hopes were high that the show would be a hit. Had it been, Johnny might not have made the move to Hollywood for *The Price is Right*, *Match Game*, and the other programs that defined his career during the final thirteen years of his life.

The Selling of the President officially premiered on March 22 at the famed Shubert Theater on New York's Great White Way. The musical was ill-timed; it not only opened during Nixon's presidency, but it was just months after the White House "plumbers" unit, so named because of their orders to plug leaks in the administration, burglarized a psychiatrist's office. Their goal was to find files that would discredit patient Daniel Ellsberg, the man who leaked the government's secret "Pentagon Papers" to the *New York Times*. The subsequent break-in at the Democratic National Committee headquarters at the Watergate Hotel complex soon filled America's psyche with a view of presidential politics that was not the least bit conducive to the success of a musical on the subject.

In the midst of that turmoil, neither a light-hearted romp nor a darkly sarcastic satire could have held much promise for mass appeal. In the wake of less than complementary reviews, the under-financed production folded on March 25. Johnny's entire experience on Broadway consisted of fewer than three months and only five official performances. It was perhaps the most poorly timed musical entertainment offering since a string quartet performed during the sinking of the Titanic.

CHAPTER 31
JUDGMENT CALL

In 1960, the FDA approved "the pill" for birth control, America's secret U2 spy plane was shot down over Russia, Xerox introduced its first automatic plain-paper copier, and gasoline was 25¢ cents a gallon. In little more than a decade, television had taken a place of honor in the majority of American homes for its ability to deliver entertainment, and it had grown to become the single most powerful force in shaping public opinion. Its newfound power to impact politics was never so well in evidence than during the 1960 presidential campaign, when debates between candidates John Kennedy and Vice President Richard Nixon were simulcast on radio and television.

Johnny spoke of that milestone in television's maturation, quoting Theodore Sorensen, Kennedy's principal aide, who wrote, "The four debates, and the first in particular, played a decisive role in the election results. Some 70 million adults, nearly two-thirds of the nation's adult population, watched or listened to the first debate, clearly the largest campaign audience in history."

Television's impact on politics was graphically demonstrated by the fact that a far greater number of radio listeners thought that Nixon had won the debate, as compared to the overwhelming majority of television viewers, who were adamant that Kennedy was more presidential. Kennedy's telegenic qualities and controlled demeanor were in stark contrast to Nixon's. Almost fifty years later, NBC's Sander Vanocur, one of the last surviving network newsmen present at the debates, still recalled how television's unblinking eye colored people's perceptions. "We saw only with our natural eyes. And looking with the naked eye at [Nixon's] gray suit with a gray background didn't seem so terrible in person."[31-1]

The first debate was broadcast from CBS' Chicago outlet, WBBM, and was directed by Don Hewitt, later known as the guiding force behind the network's *60 Minutes*. Hewitt recalled asking Kennedy if he wanted makeup, but he declined because he had a natural tan from his recent campaigning in California. Author Beverly Merrill Kelley also acknowledged the candidate's tanned appearance. She reported that he had prepared for the debates while aboard his sailboat.[31-2] According to another account, Kennedy's healthful glow was the result of having recently begun cortisone treatments for his chronic Addison's disease.

Having heard that Kennedy refused make-up, Nixon did likewise. The Vice President's advisors were worried about his appearance, and they applied a product called Lazy-Shave to cover the visible stubble of his beard. The result was that Nixon looked pale with beads of sweat clearly visible on his upper lip. He looked gaunt and ashen compared to Kennedy, which caused some supporters to report that their candidate suffered from a low-grade fever. Others said that he had just returned to campaigning after two weeks of recuperation from a knee infection.[31-2] To make matters worse, Nixon periodically mopped his face with his handkerchief, as the Lazy-Shave began to streak with perspiration.

Although radio and television audiences heard the same dialogue, Nixon's appearance overshadowed what he said. After watching a videotape of the event, Kennedy fully grasped the role that television had played. He said, "We wouldn't have had a prayer without that gadget."[31-3]

While Johnny Olson was best-known to television viewers for announcing, "Come on down!," and "Now, let's all play *What's My Line?*," and for describing Proctor Silex toasters and Sarah Coventry jewelry, he was a thinking man, aware of the sociological impact of his industry. Johnny wrote, "Even Newton N. Minnow, the former Federal Communications Commission Chairman, who in 1961 termed television 'a vast wasteland,' three years later paid eloquent tribute to its vast power."

Johnny referred to Minnow's book, *Equal Time*, in which the medium was celebrated: "Television is the most powerful instrument ever created to reach the minds and hearts of men; an instrument that any President or dictator, any Congress or army must reckon with forevermore…nothing in the history of man approaches the potential of television for information and misinformation, for enlightenment or obfuscation, for sheer reach and sheer impact."[31-4]

Johnny cited the case of Nelson A Rockefeller, whose chance for a third term as Governor of New York was very poor in 1966. He had twice raised taxes, and he had been divorced and re-married. His media-savvy campaign started as early as the July 4th weekend, and it included heavy use of television. Rockefeller won by a margin of 392,263 votes.

Johnny also pointed to Michigan Governor George Romney's fate as evidence of television's power to negatively impact public opinion. In an off-the-cuff remark during a 1967 Labor Day interview with commentator Lou Gordon on Detroit's WKBD-TV, Romney mused that US officials in Vietnam had "brain-washed" him. The incident was credited with dashing Romney's hopes for the Republican Presidential nomination in 1968.

Maturity brings with it an inevitable loss of innocence, and an awareness of the evil as well as the good that surrounds us. By 1968, it seemed that television's maturation was complete. The medium no longer turned a blind eye to civil unrest, war, assassinations, and race riots. Television brought into our living rooms, in full living color, battlefield deaths in Southeast Asia, race riots in America's inner cities, the murder of a President and his assassin, as well as the bloody confrontation between anti-war protesters and the Chicago police outside the 1968 Democratic National Convention.

In that year, Johnny reflected that he had seen television broadcasting stations in the United States grow from six to 1,200. He noted that there were 1.2 sets per American household in 1968, an increase from 7,000 in 1944 to more than 78 million.

Johnny observed that in one year, fifty-five motion picture theaters closed in New York City, and that the proliferation of television was credited with the demise of five, once-great New York newspapers. Of its economics, Johnny observed, "Television broadcasting revenue was only $1,900,000 in 1947. It passed $1 billion in 1958, $2 billion in 1966, and $3 billion in 1968."

Television's maturation included a heightened focus on ratings and demographics. The once-sacred network news departments fell under direct pressure to produce programming that delivered audiences considered attractive to potential sponsors. Even successful entertainment programs were under increased scrutiny to ensure that youthful viewers were delivered to advertisers. Madison Avenue wanted buyers at the peak of their acquiring years and not yet permanently loyal to favorite brands. They wanted young, impressionable consumers that believed a sponsor's promise of a happy life as close as their products on supermarket shelves.

That new emphasis on demographics twisted the fate of many shows and stars. It brought the demise of Johnny's relationship with Jackie Gleason. *Variety* entertainment reporter Les Brown revealed, "Two of the hardest programs for CBS to sell during the 1969-1970 television season were Red Skelton and Jackie Gleason. A few seasons earlier, when only the mass viewers counted, both were among the first to sell out completely for the year. Conscious now of quality of audience — on age, income, and education levels — the media buyers of advertising agencies considered the two CBS comedians overpriced for the kinds of people they delivered."[31-5] Advertising rates were recalculated to reflect the demographic makeup, and Brown reported that Gleason show's final season represented a loss of $300,000 to the network.

The new schema also rang the death knell for Goodson-Todman's touchstone programs, *To Tell the Truth, I've Got A Secret, Password, The Match Game,* and even the revered *What's My Line?* All were unceremoniously wiped from network prime-time schedules by the end of the 1960s. Suddenly, the game show business was soft. Goodson-Todman's shrinking empire precipitated layoffs and consolidation.

Goodson-Todman once occupied the entire thirtieth floor and additional suites in the architecturally celebrated, bronze and dark glass Seagram's Building in New York. In 1959, when the Four Seasons Restaurant opened in a vast ground floor space originally intended to be a Cadillac showroom, the address became even more prestigious. With the sudden cancellations, Goodson and Todman scaled down their operation to less than half of a single floor. They were forced to explore a new business model in which syndicated programming was sold by a distributor to individual television stations on a market-by-market basis.

Starting with a revitalized, more youthful *What's My Line?*, new versions of other classic game shows kept the company afloat at a time when their network airtime was quickly eroding. For the first time in its history, the production company was out of the business of providing programming to networks. Johnny announced what proved to be Goodson's final two network shows of the era, Gene Rayburn's subdued *The Match Game* and another struggling word game that barely survived two seasons despite celebrity appearances by Bob Hope and Johnny Carson.

Like most Americans, I had come to recognize his voice on television, but I first saw Johnny in 1968 at a taping of *Snap Judgment,* one of the two remaining Goodson-Todman network programs. The word association game was staged at one edge of NBC's massive Studio 8H, which was christened "The Peacock Studio" to commemorate its technical upgrade to accommodate color television.

That taping was preceded by Johnny's warm-up antics. Host Ed McMahon joked, "If there are seven people waiting in line at a telephone booth, Johnny will warm them up." [31-6] His performance was enthusiastic, engaging, and endearing. The laughter and applause was so loud and exuberant that the unbridled energy in the studio was palpable. To anyone who had experienced Johnny's opening act in person, it came as no surprise that he made an impression on everyone from Jackie Gleason to Bob Barker's mother.

Miss Lillian Miller, a perennial television audience member, was among those in attendance that day at *Snap Judgment.* For reasons unknown, Miss Miller adopted an unusual hobby first practiced by a Mrs. Sterling, who reportedly attended every episode during Steve Allen's reign on *The Tonight Show.* Starting in 1949, Miss Miller devoted the second half of her life to attending television tapings, and she was a regular fixture in the studio audience during both Steve Allen's and Jack Paar's tenure in late-night, before becoming Merv Griffin's most loyal audience member. In his book, *Hi-Ho Steverino,* Allen commented on Lillian Miller. "Incredibly, she came to our show every night by train from Philadelphia where she worked as a clerk-typist for the US Army Quartermaster Corps." [31-7]

Lillian wore thick glasses, spoke with equally thick speech, and wore an omnipresent hat. Allen, Paar, and Griffin engaged her in on-air conversations so frequently that Miss Miller was required to join AFTRA, the performers' union. With the migration of entertainment programs from New York to Hollywood, Miss Miller ultimately made the move herself, settling into a small apartment on Vine Street north of Hollywood Boulevard, just a few blocks north of the theater where Merv taped his talk show.

Well into her 80s, Miss Miller frequently took the bus to Television City, where she was treated to priority seating by the CBS pages at countless episodes of game shows announced by Johnny. In a little daytime drama that played out at each of the tapings she attended, Miss Miller always called Johnny's attention to the fact that she was present, which always resulted in Johnny discretely passing her a few of the $1 bills he distributed as audience prizes.

Johnny kept busy working throughout the turbulent 1960s on the Gleason show, the declining *Snap Judgment,* and *The Match Game.* He also worked on three syndicated offerings, newcomer *He Said, She Said* and revivals of *What's My Line?* and *To Tell the Truth.*

In 1969, Goodson-Todman lost its final network berths. In 1970, *The Jackie Gleason Show* was cancelled. Johnny took stock of the business, his career, his finances, and his marriage. He was sixty years old, and he decided that it was time to retire.

CHAPTER 32
THE BIG IDEA

Dr. Joyce Brothers, a psychologist, television personality, and former game show champion, tackled the topic of the popularity of audience participation programs in a 1963 interview. She spoke of the genre providing an escape mechanism for viewers' tension: "As long as the shows are honest, they fulfill a healthy need. They are a socially acceptable outlet for the aggressions of the public, and are certainly better than yelling at children or hitting siblings." [32-1]

On the occasion of the sixtieth anniversary of the formation of AFTRA, the good doctor revisited the question of the category's longevity. She pointed out how game shows resonate with the childlike fantasy and fascination we all share about getting something for nothing. Dr. Brothers also discussed the appeal of viewers vicariously participating in the competition. "The game show provides for many people the kind of excitement and stimulation that watching a sports contest does. You are emotionally involved, but it's not the end of the world if the person you're involved with loses; so you're not gambling a lot of emotional involvement when you're watching. You're getting the excitement, but not the worry. You're also identifying with the person who's playing…for a moment you're not you, you're the person spending all that money or jumping up and down with joy." [32-2]

Goodson and Todman were America's biggest producers of game shows. They inspired more people to jump up and down with joy than any other entity on Earth, with the possible exception of the inventors of the pogo stick. Their most prized and profitable program was *The Price is Right*.

It was the show that most fully exploited the genre's strengths as described by Dr. Brothers. The show enjoyed the longest run of all broadcast games, and has awarded more winnings than any other — in 2006, the program's owners boasted a grand total of over half a billion dollars in cash and prizes. Bob Stewart sparked the notion for a contest based on the pricing of items when he was a staff producer at the local NBC station in New York. It was a perfect game for the 1950s consumption-oriented society.

While the invention of television's most successful game might seem like the result of copious hours of struggled creativity, Stewart forged the basic concept while on the streets of New York. His introduction to Mark Goodson was also an al fresco affair. Stewart recounted, "I got to Goodson-Todman in a roundabout way. In August '56, I was out of work, and I bumped into Monty Hall on the street. He said, 'I know the attorney who represents Goodson and Todman. You got any ideas?" [32-3]

Monty was a native of Ontario, Canada, where he had been a host and producer before moving to New York as a sportscaster. He hoped that a salable proposal from Stewart would make him the logical choice for the show's host. The Goodson-Todman attorney made an appointment, and Stewart pitched *Three of a Kind*, his original idea that later begat *To Tell The Truth*.

On a subsequent visit to the production company's offices, Goodson invited Stewart to join him for lunch. He explained that he was interested in the game of identities, but he needed something entirely fresh, "new, novel; something different." Stewart gave a cursory description of the general concept behind a show he called *The Auctioneer*. "You bid for things and if you don't go over the retail price, you win it." [32-4] Stewart remembered that Goodson was immediately interested.

Stewart recalled, "I got the idea from an auction I used to watch on Fiftieth Street during my lunch hour." [32-3] While many of the midtown gift shops had similar merchandise, the store at the corner of Seventh Avenue that caught Stewart's attention used an auction as a unique way of selling its silverware, glassware, and household goods. The store manager invited shoppers to bid on his inventory, and with the excitement of the auction, items often sold above what would have been the asking price. As an observer, Stewart thought that those bidding even a nickel over the actual retail price were, in a way, "losers," while the bidder, who was closest to the retail value without going over, was the best judge of prices and a "winner" in the transaction.

Stewart remembered that he and Goodson returned after lunch to the production company's offices. The pair soon had secretaries bidding on the lamps and furniture. The process of molding the basic idea into a television show brought various twists and turns. Once it was decided that four bidding players would be the optimum number of participants, it seemed appropriate to start each with a bank of money from which they could bid. The mechanics of displaying both the increasing bids and the decreasing bank totals might prove to be too visually awkward, so it was decided that each bidder would simply come to the auction with seemingly unlimited funds.

Once the format for *The Price is Right* was refined, the show was presented in run-throughs to both CBS and NBC. Surprisingly, both networks offered to immediately buy the show. CBS was Goodson-Todman's first and top client, and it was the higher rated network; it was more likely to deliver a strong lead-in audience for the program and increase chances for success. With a highly-rated line-up already on the air, CBS did not anticipate an opening in the daytime schedule for another six months.

NBC was prepared to take the show immediately, and they offered a thirteen week guarantee, but they seemed set on placing it in a suicide slot at 10:30 a.m., directly opposite Arthur Godfrey, the top-rated, dean of daytime performers. Stewart lobbied for getting the show on the air quickly; he said he was simply anxious for a job. A bit of Todman's shrewd business acumen next came into play. The game plan for the new game show was to sell it to NBC and watch it wither opposite Godfrey. Once it was cancelled, they hoped to take it to CBS with the understanding that the failure was only due to the troubled time period NBC had provided. It would have been a chance to say "yes" to both networks' offers for the show.

Todman engineered a deal with NBC for thirteen weeks of shows. As was customary at the time, a pilot was then shot onto kinescope to see how the production would stand on its feet prior to a live, debut broadcast. Stewart remembered that sample show as being laden with technical flaws and unanticipated staging problems from its first moments. Host Bill Cullen was almost choked by his microphone cable during his entrance, when the turntable on which he was perched began its rotation. Among other gaffes, the electronic readouts that displayed the bids failed to operate. All in all, the pilot was a disaster.

High expectations for *The Price is Right* were dashed to such an extent that NBC was willing to buy its way out of the contract. The network offered the full thirteen weeks of payment in return for only seven weeks of production — a programming bookmark to give NBC adequate time to prepare a replacement for the time period, but the buyout deal was never consummated.

The Price is Right debuted on November 26, 1956, from the Ziegfeld Theater, a venue financed by William Randolph Hearst for impresario Florenz Ziegfeld's *Follies*, and the former home of the hit Broadway musical *Show Boat*. To the surprise of Goodson, Todman, Stewart, NBC, and certainly Arthur Godfrey, the lowbrow show that auctioned refrigerators and furniture became one of the era's biggest success stories. Within thirteen weeks, the program where "bargain hunters match their shopping skills," "the exciting game of bidding, buying, and bargaining" was outperforming Godfrey. It ultimately unseated the old redhead, continuing as NBC's daytime anchor for seven years and scoring well with an additional, weekly prime-time berth during six of those seasons.

When the Ziegfeld Theater was tapped for another theatrical production, *The Price is Right* moved to the Colonial Theater at Broadway and West 62nd Street, a facility that originated one of the first transcontinental color television demonstrations. In 1963, NBC felt the show had run its course. *The Price is Right* was picked-up by ABC for two more years from that network's Ritz Theater on West 48th Street (presently the Walter Kerr Theater - the name was changed to commemorate the work of the former drama critic for the *New York Times* and the *New York Herald Tribune*.)

The Price is Right evolved from the flawed pilot and through the early months of its run. Stewart's original idea to present unique, esoteric items — even occasional museum pieces — was scrapped in favor of the appliances, dining room sets, and household merchandise that played more directly to the home viewers' materialism. To keep it fresh and unpredictable, once bidding was concluded and a winner named, host Bill Cullen often announced that there was a surprise bonus associated with the item.

With that mechanism, gifts with humorous connections to the initial prize added to the entertainment and variety. A barbeque grill was paired with a mile of hot dogs; a live (NBC) peacock accompanied a color television; and the winner of a grand piano received a live elephant, which presumably could be used to supply replacement ivory. Television historian and educator Matt Ottinger reported that the winning bidder, a Texas farmer, refused $4,000 in cash in lieu of the pachyderm, resulting in Stewart having to fly one in from Kenya.

Although the universe of exciting and glamorous prizes seemed unlimited, the list was actually quite short, consisting of little more than cars, boats, trips, and furs. That led to the addition of truly unusual prizes that included a 16-foot Ferris wheel, a chauffeur-driven 1928 Rolls-Royce, a Pacific island, yachts, and even an airplane. Some required creative solutions to the logistical problems of transporting them through the streets of New York and loading them into the shows' originating theaters. When the program invited home viewers to mail postcards with their bids on weekly home showcases, avalanches of mail arrived. Entries needed to be farmed out to an independent company to sort through for the closest bids.

Goodson-Todman again avoided being embroiled in scandal after it was learned that *The Price is Right* contestants were occasionally provided with ceiling prices over which they were not to bid. As all players shared that same information, and no one participant was given an advantage or disadvantage, the outcome of the game play was not manipulated to favor any individual contestant.

Bill Cullen, America's most prolific game show personality, rode a wave of popularity on the original version of *The Price is Right*. The show awarded thousands of sports cars during fifty years on NBC, ABC, and CBS.

Johnny was not associated with the original incarnation of *The Price is Right*. For most of its run, that honor went to NBC's Don Pardo, who performed the role masterfully. When the program moved to ABC in 1963, Pardo turned down a lucrative offer to change channels. He remembered that he was earning approximately $50,000 while working NBC's daytime and prime-time versions of *The Price is Right*. One day at the studio, Mark Goodson offered Pardo $100,000 to move with the show to ABC. Pardo said he hesitated to shake hands on the deal, but asked for time to consider the proposition.

Pardo's wife encouraged him to accept the offer, but he recalled they took a vacation in San Marten without her knowing his intent to disregard her advice. He chose to remain true to his rare, lifetime contract with David Sarnoff's network. As a soldier under "The General" that year, Pardo read the first NBC bulletin reporting shots fired at President Kennedy's motorcade in Dallas. He was still well-entrenched at NBC a decade later, working on other Bob Stewart productions, as well as on the original version of *Jeopardy!*

Considering the guaranteed years of steady work, the ability to hear about addi-

Left: Don Pardo, one of American broadcasting's greatest voices, was the announcer during the NBC years of *The Price is Right*. Right: Eternally young Johnny Gilbert described the prizes when America's biggest giveaway show enjoyed a berth on ABC.

tional programs that yielded added talent fees, and the freedom from the insecurity of freelancing, Pardo concluded that turning down Mark Goodson's offer was the right decision. Pardo recalled that his wife was furious. For months, she called him a "coward," but he remained certain his decision was correct, especially after being cast for *Saturday Night Live*, citing the prestige of being associated with that hip, successful comedy.

Pardo enjoyed one of the longest and most prestigious careers of any announcer. He began in 1938 as a radio actor at WJAR in Providence, his hometown station. He eventually won a lifetime contract at NBC, New York. After retiring from the network, the honored broadcaster continued to work past the age of ninety, commuting from his retirement home in Tucson, Arizona, for *Saturday Night Live* broadcasts.

With Pardo remaining at NBC, Johnny Gilbert was hired to announce the ABC incarnation of *The Price is Right*. Like Johnny Olson, Gilbert had been a vocalist and host before transitioning to the announce podium. Gilbert became a specialist in the art of game show announcing, as had Johnny Olson, Bill Wendell, Charlie O'Donnell, John Harlan, Jack Clark, Johnny Jacobs, Jay Stewart, Kenny Williams, and Gene Wood. Gilbert became best known for his over twenty-five years with *Jeopardy!*

The Price is Right eventually ran out of steam; the prime-time version ended on September 11th, 1964, and one year later, the daytime series signed-off. It was a decade of transition for television, as programmers reflected the country's evolving social values. Madison Avenue time buyers were also chasing the changes, beginning the revolution that placed an ever-increasing importance on demographics. By the late 1960s, it was universally accepted at the networks — especially CBS — that older, rural audience needed to be youth-enized — or euthanized.

In the 1970s, Robert Wood, Paley's new President, told CBS affiliates, "The winds of change are at a gale force. Everything is being tested and challenged...We have to attract new viewers, viewers who are part of every generation, viewers who reflect the growing degree of education and sophistication that characterizes American society, viewers who live in every part of the country...We are taking a young, fresh, new approach to programming." [32-5]

CBS not only retired Goodson-Todman's *What's My Line?*, *I've Got A Secret*, *Password*, and *To Tell the Truth* from prime-time schedule, but by 1970, they had also cleared most game shows from their daytime lineups. Only NBC remained significantly invested in the traditional category with mid-day shows. ABC picked-up NBC's discarded *Let's Make a Deal* by offering Monty Hall a sweeter deal than he enjoyed at General Sarnoff's web. ABC also locked into Chuck Barris' *The Dating Game* and *The Newlywed Game*, two variations on old themes that reflected the new zeitgeist of the times.

Much of the dubious credit for CBS' complete obliteration of audience participation, quiz shows, and game programs went to programming wunderkind Fred Silverman, who came to the corporate ranks directly from local television in Chicago and New York. His success with CBS children's and daytime fare led to a coveted vice presidency in which he lorded over all network programming decisions. As CBS programming chief Michael Dann told *Variety's* Les Brown about the man who soon succeeded him. "Freddie's my expert, and if he wants to drop a game show or go with soaps all day long, that's okay with me." [32-5]

During Goodson-Todman's twenty-year relationship with CBS they provided numerous long-running, successful shows. It was assumed that the network programmers would want to meet with the producers to discuss any new programming plans, perhaps over a friendly lunch. In any other business that would likely be the norm, but show business was never known for its indulgence in well-mannered protocol. According to Bennett Cerf, Goodson had not been given the simple courtesy of a telephone call from CBS.

Cerf said that he was paged at a New York airport while waiting to board a plane for a vacation in Barbados. It was a reporter calling from the *New York Times* asking for a comment about the cancellation of *What's My Line?* When Cerf told the reporter that he knew nothing about the show being pink-slipped, the reporter responded that he was certain it was true. Cerf said, "I immediately called Mark Goodson in his office in New York...Goodson said, 'I haven't heard a word about it...I'll check immediately.' He called back in about ten minutes and said, 'You're right! They've decided that all the game shows are going out...they're going to throw out all of the games.'" [32-6]

CBS had enough of the parlor game played by the elite of the aging society set attired in their tuxedos and evening gowns. They did not fit for a company focused on attracting viewers who were far more likely to be wearing jeans. Also judged irrelevant for the times were Goodson's other quaint, guessing games. Gone forever was the peculiar practice of Garry Moore handing cartons of cigarettes to departing *I've Got A Secret* contestants. In fact, untold millions of dollars in tobacco advertising soon disappeared from the airwaves by government decree. The bounty from one of broadcasting's most beneficent benefactors went up in smoke, and anticipation of the lost revenue was the top topic of discussion in network boardrooms.

Game show producers also needed to reinvent their business strategy. Syndication served as the most viable distribution model for the genre, and Goodson-Todman returned to prominence after a lean period with the help of an unlikely ally — the FCC.

In 1971, television continued to transition. David Sarnoff and Philo Farnsworth, two long-time rivals from the birth of the medium, both passed away. The last cigarette commercials aired on New Years Day, and the Prime-Time Access Ruling changed the playing field.

The regulation was birthed in a contentious era during which President Nixon was unhappy with what he perceived as a network news bias against White House policies. Vice President Spiro Agnew repeatedly attacked the broadcast media in scathing public rants, some written by Nixon's speechwriter, Pat Buchanan. William Safire, another Nixon wordsmith, armed Agnew with this memorable salvo: "In the United States today, we have more than our share of nattering nabobs of negativism. They have formed their own 4-H club — the hopeless, hysterical hypochondriacs of history." Although he later resigned his elected office in disgrace, the Vice President impugned the network news broadcasters as "a tiny, enclosed fraternity of privileged men elected by no one."

In the hopes of creating an environment in which new and diversified sources of programming could gain access to television screens during peak viewership hours, the FCC passed a long-pending decree in which network programming was limited to a maximum of three hours per weeknight.

The Prime-Time Access Rule was championed by Westinghouse, KDKA's owner and one of the first companies to experiment with wireless a half-century earlier. Founded by George Westinghouse, the inventor of an innovative air braking system for trains, Westinghouse expanded its realm from transportation to electric power generation, to household and industrial products, and then into media ownership. Its broadcasting division, known as Group W, already produced several syndicated offerings, including *The Mike Douglas Show* and *The David Frost Show*.

Don McGannon, Group W's CEO, had a plan in place to offer more syndicated fare to local stations if the networks could be forced to relinquish their lock as their affiliates' evening program supplier, as well as be stripped of their ownership of much of their programming. It worked. As a result of the Prime-Time Access ruling, a daily half-hour of prime-time television reverted from the networks to local stations, with an explicit dictate that reruns of network fare could not be used to fill the time.

While the FCC's intent was, in part, to encourage local and creative programming alternatives, most stations simply bought pre-packaged, nationally syndicated series for the time period. In addition to Group W's business, the ruling also bolstered Goodson-Todman's. Where *What's My Line?* and *To Tell The Truth* had tested the syndication waters with revivals in 1968 and 1969 respectively, there was then a fertile field in which the company could nurture other evergreen titles, including new adaptations of *I've Got A Secret*, *Concentration*, *The Price is Right*, and *Match Game*. Although not in his plans at the time, all six series featured Johnny, America's favorite game show announcer.

By the spring of 1972, the three networks had totally abandoned prime-time audience participation shows. Johnny's employer produced only one daytime program, *Password*, for ABC, a show Johnny did not work. His experiment as a Broadway performer had failed to pan out, and the Olsons were preparing to spend their golden years together in West Virginia, far from any television studios. Simultaneously, Goodson-Todman was preparing *I've Got A Secret* and *The Price is Right* for fresh forays in syndication.

In a videotaped pitch for *The Price is Right*, Goodson and anticipated host, Dennis James, were seated at a desk explaining the planned updates to the program's original format. They crudely demonstrated the basic idea behind one of the many new games, and they presented a sampling of footage of James filling-in for Monty Hall on an episode of *Let's Make A Deal* that showed his skills as an adept wheeler dealer. James recounted that he received a last minute call at his country club to substitue for Monty, who had suddenly taken ill. Bill Todman just happened to have seen the show and asked for a videotaped copy. [32-7] Nobody knew it at the time, but that sequence of seemingly random events was part of the genesis of Goodson-Todman's all-time most successful undertaking. The Olsons had no idea that a project was brewing that would cancel Johnny's planned retirement from broadcasting.

CHAPTER 33

COME ON DOWN!

There are several defining moments in twentieth century American history. Most came in an instant, such as the 1929 stock market crash that began the Great Depression, the 1941 bombing on Pearl Harbor that marked the nation's entry into World War II, and the September 11, 2001 attack on the World Trade towers that ushered in a new era of global terrorism. Another shift was more gradual, almost glacial by comparison.

In the wake of the assassinations of President John Kennedy, Senator Robert Kennedy, and civil rights leader Reverend Martin Luther King Jr., a political and sociological chiasm was fashioned in great part by the differing views concerning the highly polarizing Vietnam War. The tectonic movement that created the so-called "generation gap" stirred the nation's status quo with aftershocks that included the investigation of criminal activity by, and the subsequent resignation of, a US President.

As always, television programmers attempted to reflect America's changing tastes and remain relevant, but the turbulent times made that challenge greater than ever. While *All in the Family* was a prime-time breakthrough for CBS, the network's daytime schedule was still hopelessly floundering with reruns of anachronistic situation comedies. Although entertaining, the mid-morning line-up that included *The Beverly Hillbillies*, *The Andy Griffith Show*, *The Lucy Show*, *My Three Sons*, and *Family Affair* was not engaging the viewers that advertisers coveted. The so-called Tiffany Network sought to regain some of its luster.

Fred Silverman, former CBS daytime programmer, had turned his attention to structuring the network's prime-time grid. CBS hired Bud Grant from NBC as its new Vice President of Daytime Programming. Grant's strength at NBC had been game shows; he understood and had confidence in the genre. With *Let's Make A Deal* a runaway success for NBC, and a 1971 revival of *Password* drawing a sizeable audience for ABC, Grant looked to re-introduce game shows into the CBS daytime line-up for the 1972-1973 season.

He purchased *Gambit* starring Wink Martindale from Merrill Heatter and Bob Quigley, the producers behind the success of *Hollywood Squares*. He also bought *The Joker's Wild* based upon Jack Barry's three-year-old pilot hosted by Allen Ludden. With the network's blessing, Barry re-cast himself in the role of emcee. Barry once again appeared on American television screens a dozen years after his disgrace in the quiz show scandals as the host and producer of *Twenty One*. Soon, Dan Enright returned from relative obscurity in Canada to reunite with his former partner.

Grant also made a call to a trusted supplier that would change Goodson-Todman's fate and change Johnny's life. Grant learned that Mark Goodson had a revival of *The Price is Right* in the works for syndication, and he envisioned the show as the perfect answer to the Monty Hall-Stephan Hatos, prize-laden hit, *Let's Make A Deal*. He requested a network version of the series for his new daytime block.

Although the show had previously been successful for both NBC and ABC, that was years before. It took only a few run-throughs for the Goodson-Todman creative team to realize that the original format of *The Price is Right* was hopelessly slow and tedious in the context of the times. Grant encouraged Goodson to scrap the original format if necessary to build a fresh, flashy, and exciting version of the classic. With that, the game show guru mobilized his minions for a major overhauling of Bob Stewart's original hit. In an unusual demonstration of faith and confidence, Grant and Goodson ultimately signed for a network program without a pilot episode. Roger Dobkowitz, a newcomer on Goodson's staff who later became the new show's guiding force, observed after thirty-six years of working with CBS, "The most creative program people just trust their gut."[33-1]

As always, development at Goodson-Todman was a group effort; two of the brightest brains in games were marshaled for the new mission. Frank Wayne, the company's senior statesman, earned the title of Executive Producer, and Jay Wolpert was awarded the role of Producer for *The New Price is Right*. Director Marc Breslow, Goodson's trusted friend, was also assigned to the project early on to devise the presentation and staging, as well as participate in the overall creative process. Wolpert recalled, "We worked close to 14 hours a day to develop the show — me and about a half dozen other creative executives who were part of the Goodson coterie. We'd sit around his pool. That sounds grand, but believe me, we were not swimming. We worked very, very hard while Goodson swam in the pool."[33-2]

The game that had been at the core of the Bill Cullen-hosted version was pared down to a quick pricing round, in the vernacular of the show's producers, the "one-bid" round. It harkened back to an unexpected moment during a broadcast of *The Price is Right* in the 1950s when the live program was running long. Producer Bob Stewart described that impromptu incident to illustrate the intuitive nature of his relationship with Cullen, the emcee that Mark Goodson referred to as an "on-stage producer."

Stewart recalled the morning when the studio clock was showing less time than was needed for the usual bidding on a prize. Always on the stage during production, he held up a single finger to Cullen, and the host created the first "one bid" round on the spot by informing the contestants that they would only get one chance to bid on the next item. The mechanism was perfect for the streamlined revival. On the basis of a single bid in the newly-formatted auction, one of the four contestants selected from the audience instantly won his way up on stage to play one of a variety of rotating games.

The diversity of those different, quick-playing pricing games was the innovation that reflected the new generation's shorter attention span, kept each episode unique and fresh, and provided a structure that allowed the show to evolve as new games could be introduced and others retired. Another important element in modernizing the format was the decision to pre-interview and choose contestants from the pool of audience members in attendance on any given day. Their surprise, on-camera selection had the potential to generate exceptional energy and could reinforce the viewers' identification with the players. It paralleled a successful innovation in contestant selection that Hall and Hatos were using on *Let's Make a Deal.*

Each episode of *The New Price is Right* climaxed with a retooling of the original show's "home showcase" that had generated millions of postcard entries from viewers during the 1950s. Instead of a collection of six or seven prizes presented for the home audience's bids, it was imagined that the three players who appeared during the course of the half hour would return to each bid on one of three showcases, each consisting of half as many gifts.

When that fourth act of the show proved to be too lengthy and too unwieldy, it was decided that only the program's two top winners would each bid on one of two exciting showcases, each usually containing three or four prizes. The contestants' challenge was the same — to bid closer to the actual retail price of their own showcase without exceeding that value. Unlike the home showcases of old, the audience did not need to wait days for resolution; the values of the showcases were revealed and the winner announced instantly. The original home showcase feature was revived occasionally, usually as a holiday promotion, and viewer response was, as always, overwhelming.

With the auction that was at the heart of the concept reduced to a single bid from each participant, the pace of the show was dramatically accelerated. With each auction winner then playing another pricing game that was generally limited to a maximum of three or four minutes, the lightening fast presentation meant a visually stunning show with a steady stream of eye-appealing prizes.

Despite all the progress in revitalizing *The Price is Right*, Mark Goodson expressed concern early in the development process. Understanding that the brisk tempo meant drastic reductions in the time between the reveals of prizes, one product description would follow another and another, sometimes with only seconds between sponsor plugs. Goodson felt the audience might lose its patience with endless, sponsored prize and product plugs; he felt that the entire show might sound like a half-hour commercial. It became apparent that the casting of the right announcer would be a crucial consideration.

As planned, Dennis James emceed the syndicated version, but CBS had Bob Barker in mind to host its daytime show. The forty-eight-year-old veteran broadcaster gained a national following fronting *Truth or Consequences,* and he had been on Bud Grant's radar for a future opportunity. Barker said, "I know that Bud and I had a close relationship. He appreciated me." [33-3] *The New Price is Right* was the right vehicle for the gifted ad-libber, and Grant told Goodson that the network strongly supported Barker as host.

Barker remembered the call from Goodson in which he explained the completely revamped format. He said, "We're going to call it *The New Price is Right.* I want you to host it. Would you be interested?" Barker joked, "And Mark, incidentally, was always very generous, but two or three years later, I found out that he had talked with Bud Grant, who had said, 'I'll buy that show for CBS if you get Bob Barker to host it.' I didn't know that when we negotiated. If I had, Mark would have been even more generous than he was." [33-4]

After Barker agreed to front the program, he had second thoughts. Grant recalled, "We were in rehearsals, and I got a call from Bob, asking if he could buy me lunch.

In 1972, after thirty-three years of living and working together, Johnny and Penny Olson were preparing for retirement when their plans suddenly changed.

We went to the Brown Derby in Hollywood. After exchanging the usual pleasantries over coffee, Bob said he didn't want to do the show. I almost fell off the chair."

Barker told Grant that from what he had seen, he was concerned that the show could be better produced, and he offered to do *Joker's Wild* or *Gambit* instead of *Price*. Grant remembered telling his lunch partner, "Barker, you will do *Price* because those other two shows are good, solid game shows that require a traffic cop to run them, and you're not a cop. You have far more talent!" [33-2] Barker reconsidered, and he later declared it to be the most fortuitous decision in his fifty-year television career.

Barker was locked, and attention then turned to the role of announcer. Had plans for *The New Price is Right* called for production to be in New York, it would have been a simple job to determine whether Johnny's availability could mesh with the taping schedule. If not, another announcer could have been tapped to free up Johnny for the new assignment. From all reports, Johnny was Goodson-Todman's first and only choice to handle the extensive amount of scripted copy containing dozens of prize and product descriptions woven throughout the program.

By the age of sixty, Johnny had long come to peace with the fact that his days as a host were over, and he and Penny were contemplating retirement. As game shows were being dropped from network schedules, the couple had begun searching for the perfect locale for their senior years. They decided on a community not far from the heavenly little St. Charles Church at White Sulphur Springs, West Virginia, that had so impressed Penny and inspired her album of hymns. The Olsons purchased several acres in nearby Lewisburg, and they were planning their dream home when the dream was interrupted by a call offering Johnny new opportunities in California.

The prospect of accepting work on the other side of the country was the source of much discussion and contemplation for the Olsons. They had never been that far apart for more than a few weeks at a time, and it proved to be a difficult decision. Johnny was interested, but at his age, he did not want to seriously delay their retirement plans. Twenty-eight years after her previous move to the show business mecca, Penny was reticent to again relocate to Los Angeles, but she also knew how much satisfaction Johnny derived from his work. Years later, Johnny shared with his colleagues that Penny had encouraged him to make the move. He explained that after seeing so many television programs come and go after a year or two, she believed that the stop in California would only be a brief detour along the road to their retirement.

Initially, Johnny hoped that Penny would accompany him on the return to Hollywood, and he looked to create a parallel arrangement to the one they had enjoyed in New York. Johnny would maintain an apartment near the studios, and the couple would spend their leisure time in an affluent suburb. Instead of Greenwich, the couple's getaway would be in Palm Springs where other Goodson staffers had second homes. Penny demurred, and decided to make the move to West Virginia to start building their retirement home.

Once Mark Goodson confirmed Johnny's relocation to Los Angeles for *The New Price is Right*, he told Bob Barker about having cast him as the show's announcer. Barker was only familiar with Johnny's work on network programs from New York.

However, by a strange coincidence, Matilda "Tille" Barker Valandra, Barker's mother, had seen Johnny years earlier at one of his countless personal appearance, and he had made a memorable impression. Tillie surprised her son with a rave review that contributed to the host and announcer forming a strong bond based on mutual respect. The on-air pairing of Barker and Johnny proved wonderfully successful, and it endured for the remainder of Johnny's career.

In 1972, new publicity photos came with a new assignment.

With Johnny headed for Hollywood and Penny for West Virginia, the Olsons placed their Greenwich home up for sale. It was the second of two houses that the couple had owned in that up-scale Connecticut community. Years earlier, they were convinced by a local real estate agent that they could realize a significant profit, so the Olsons sold their first Greenwich home, but they did not stray far. Penny had grown to enjoy the small town ambiance. They had become established in their church, and they were regular patrons of their favorite local haunts, especially Manero's Steakhouse. Greenwich was a convenient forty-five-minute train ride from Grand Central Terminal for Johnny, so the couple soon bought a larger home nearby. It was for that second Connecticut home that Johnny made an unusual purchase to commemorate his earliest career ambitions.

He always cherished memories of performing as a vocalist. As a youngster, Johnny sang in a glee club, warbled on the roof of his high school, and vocalized at his hometown theater. He had crooned as "The Buttermilk Kid" for his first job in radio, he had recorded popular and novelty songs, and he had travelled to Chicago and Hollywood as a vocalist during the era of big bands. Although he ultimately made the decision to return to broadcasting, Johnny shared every singer's dream to play The Palace. The Palace Theater in New York was the holiest shrine of live entertainment from its 1913 opening and through the 1920s, 1930s, and 1940s.

The theater's builder declared it "The Valhalla of Vaudeville." Among the superstars to trod the boards of The Palace stage were Harry Houdini, Will Rogers, Fanny Brice, Sophie Tucker, Ethel Barrymore, Ethel Merman, Bob Hope Al Jolson, Jimmy Durante, Judy Garland, and Jack Benny. When the Palace Theater closed in the 1960s, Johnny purchased one of the magnificent, tall mirrors that had adorned the theater's ornate lobby. He had it shipped to Greenwich and mounted on the wall of the stairway spanning the first and second floors, the only place tall enough to accommodate it. He never owned bragging rights to having played the world-famous Palace, but he owned a piece of the theater.

Before closing the quarter-century, New York chapter of his career, Johnny had a chance to reminisce about his earlier escapades in Milwaukee. His Midwest alma mater, WTMJ, was celebrating its forty-fifth broadcasting anniversary in May 1972, and the station included Johnny in their retrospective. Via videotape, Johnny joined Jack Bundy, his old bandmate, Don McNeill, a Chicago radio legend, and other station alumni in a series of vignettes and promos reflecting on Milwaukee radio and television's glorious history. Johnny then flew over WTMJ's coverage area on his return to Hollywood.

Most of the Goodson-Todman team and the television business were relocating to Los Angeles. Goodson maintained homes and offices on both coasts, and he lived in a custom-decorated bungalow at the Beverly Hills Hotel when in California. Johnny rented a modern, up-scale fourth-floor apartment on La Cienega Boulevard near Santa Monica Boulevard in Los Angeles. While the apartment was bright and airy, convenient to restaurants and shopping, adjacent to nightlife on the Sunset Strip, and offered a pleasant city view, he considered home to be with Penny. At first, he made the cross-country commute every weekend, as she became entrenched in Lewisburg.

In 1975, Penny briefly returned to the spotlight as the subject of an advertising campaign for West Virginia's Greenbrier Valley Bank that focused on local residents of interest. She projected the same exuberant positive energy that had been her style through the years. "I can't stand to see people who are bored with life!" she said. "There's just so much to learn, to see and accomplish! Do you know that it takes energy to be miserable and saves energy to be happy? So why be miserable?"

Penny reminisced about the celebrities she had met and with whom she had worked: Bing Crosby, Lucille Ball, Nelson Rockefeller, and Frank Sinatra. "And I've gotten 390 kisses from Jackie Gleason! One every week we did his show! He's one of the most generous, liberal and unprejudiced men in the world! Jack Benny was very serious about his violin. He would practice all day before a performance." Penny mentioned her love of cooking, reading, art, and music. She took the opportunity to mention with pride that her album, *Heavenly Hymns*, was selected for the Nashville Hall of Fame.

At first, Johnny was uncertain about delaying retirement and relocating to California, but later, he never regretted his decision. The voluminous work during the first forty-four years of his career was all but eclipsed by the fame he enjoyed during what turned out to be one of his final assignments. Johnny was best remembered as the second banana on *The Price is Right* starring Bob Barker, the longest running game show in network television history.

CHAPTER 34
CBS: THE STARS' ADDRESS

In 1972, eighteen-year-olds were registering to vote in their first presidential election, The Supreme Court was preparing its ruling on Roe vs Wade that made abortion legal, cigarette ads were nowhere to be found on television or radio, and a break-in was discovered at the Democratic National Headquarters at the Watergate hotel, office, and apartment complex.

That summer, Johnny relinquished his roles on his New York-based series; his announcing job on *To Tell The Truth* went to Bill Wendell, and his work on *What's My Line?* went to Chet Gould. Johnny moved to California and quickly settled into an apartment in West Hollywood to begin new challenges on both the daytime and syndicated versions of *The New Price is Right*, as well as a new weekly syndicated run of *I've Got A Secret*.

Both shows needed to stockpile episodes for their debuts in early September. Work began first with Steve Allen on the old panel show that Johnny knew well. Johnny and Ira Skutch, his partner on *He Said, She Said, Play Your Hunch, Snap Judgment,* and *The Match Game* were reunited, 3,000 miles away from their previous ventures. Also present on the first day of taping was Gene Rayburn, another old friend and on-air partner, who appeared as a debut-week panelist. Adding to his sense of déjà-vu, Johnny was working on a soundstage at Metromedia Square on Sunset Boulevard. Just across narrow Van Ness Avenue, Johnny was less than 200-yards from where he had worked thirty years earlier during World War II at KFWB radio.

In a suite of offices located under the stage where *I've Got A Secret* taped, *The New Price is Right* took form. Frank Wayne, Jay Wolpert, Marc Breslow, and a full staff of production personnel were creating games, reviewing music, writing scripts, overseeing the design of the set and the game props, as well as establishing the systems that would enable Goodson-Todman's most complex series to be efficiently produced at the ambitious rate of four episodes a day.

Roger Dobkowitz was on the staff of *The Price is Right* from those early days of pre-production, and he rose through the ranks to become one of the show's producers, as well as its heart, soul, and guiding force through many of his incredible thirty-six seasons with the program. In 1972, he was fresh from college, and he landed his job that May after his college thesis about audience participation television programming had found its way to Mark Goodson.

Roger remembers gearing-up for the show's debut. "We only had five games at the beginning: Any Number, Bonus Game, Double Prices, Grocery Game, and Bullseye."[34-1] Ultimately, the original five games expanded to more than one hundred inventive games of combined luck and skill, of which as many as seventy were rotated at any given time to keep each day's episode fresh and unpredictable.

Roger recalled the very first time he met Johnny. "I'd heard his name and I'd heard his work. We were down in the basement and upstairs they were taping *I've Got A Secret*. Johnny came by the offices and said 'hi' to everybody. He was just a happy-go-lucky guy — he came in all smiles, shook everybody's hand, and left."[34-2] Over the next thirteen years, their professional relationship and friendship grew, and Roger came to know and respect Johnny as one of broadcasting's most dedicated and reliable pros.

The New Price Is Right staff continued to toil at Metromedia Square for another six months. After *I've Got A Secret* wrapped its run, production offices for *The New Price is Right* were merged into Goodson-Todman's expanding west coast headquarters further west on Sunset Boulevard. Once taping started, Wayne, Wolpert, Breslow, Dobkowitz, and the team that Roger remembered included Barbara Hunter, Nancy Meyers, Pamela Freeman, Heather Harwood, Robert Lane, and Karen Kelly caravanned to CBS on tape days.

In mid August 1972, Johnny arrived for two quick rehearsal days of *The New Price is Right* at CBS Television City. He was undoubtedly impressed as the state-of-the-art complex was one of the premiere broadcast facilities in America (it remains so, as the home to competing networks' *American Idol* and *Dancing With the Stars)*. In 1938, CBS had built Columbia Square in Hollywood for radio, only to later reconstruct much of the property to accommodate television. New ground was broken, and in the fall of 1952, barely one month after NBC first utilized its new Burbank television studios, CBS began production at Television City. Located just a few miles from the network's Columbia Square, CBS boasted that it operated the world's most sophisticated video production facility.

The new complex was built on land that was once the location of a race track and the Gilmore Field sports stadium. Gilmore Field was constructed in 1938 to accommodate the Hollywood Stars, a minor league professional baseball team of the Pacific Coast League that was owned in part by Bing Crosby, Barbara Stanwyck, and Cecil B. DeMille. The adjacent Gilmore stadium was home to the Bulldogs, the first professional football team in Los Angeles, and it was where presidential candidate Harry Truman delivered a 1948 campaign speech to war-weary voters.

CBS Television City originally contained four primary studios, each approximately 10,000-square-feet. Two were designed for audience programs and two were designed for dramatic presentations. There were additional smaller insert stages, a news studio, voice-over studios, a photography studio, and a darkroom. There was a huge set construction shop, as well as drapery, wardrobe, and make-up departments, several rehearsal halls, numerous dressing suites, elegant conference rooms, extensive office facilities, and even a barber shop. The state-of-the-art engineering and distribution facilities regularly fed the hundreds of stations that comprised the CBS network. The three-story building was sleek, clean, and minimalist, with a modern décor in black, white, and grey — the shades of early television — all contrasted with dramatic red accents.

CBS Television City was designed by the Pereira and Luckman architectural firm, which was responsible for the NASA Space facility at Cape Canaveral and

CBS Television City under construction in 1952. It became a state-of-the-art enclave for production, engineering, sales, and management.

the Los Angeles International Airport master plan. Later on his own, Pereira designed numerous California landmarks, including the Los Angeles Art Museum, the Malibu campus of Pepperdine University, Marineland of the Pacific in Palos Verdes, The University of Southern California master plan, and the Transamerica Pyramid building in San Francisco. Pereira and Luckman received a Merit Award from the American Institute of Architects for Television City's style and functionality. The firm designed the facility for future expansion to the east and west of the original building to accommodate as many as twelve studios, but those plans were never utilized.

In 1956, when Elvis Presley first appeared on *The Ed Sullivan Show*, he performed at CBS Television City. Over the years, the complex was home to dozens of illustrious, dramatic programs, including the *Playhouse 90* anthology series and the few episodes of *The Twilight Zone* that were not shot on film at MGM.

Among the lighter fare produced at CBS Television City were *Art Linkletter's House Party*, *The Judy Garland Show*, and Dinah Shore's program, *Dinah!*, plus *The Smothers Brothers Comedy Hour*, *The Glen Campbell Goodtime Hour*, *The Sonny & Cher*

Comedy Hour, Tony Orlando & Dawn, The Captain and Tenille, The Jacksons, Maude, the first six seasons of *All in the Family,* the later years of *The Mike Douglas Show,* as well as the first season of *Welcome Back, Kotter.*

Bob Hope, Bing Crosby, Frank Sinatra, Doris Day, Steve Martin, Groucho Marx, Elton John, Billy Crystal, Robin Williams, and Whoopie Goldberg made appearances at CBS Television City. Johnny's new assignment on *The New Price is Right* took him to Studio 33, hallowed ground shared with *The Carol Burnett Show,* and previously occupied by *The Burns and Allen Show, The Jack Benny Show,* and *The Red Skelton Show.*

The Columbia Broadcasting System was the creation of Arthur Judson, a talent agent, and a great deal of the network's subsequent success was the result of its skillful exploitation of the public's hunger for big name stars. From humble beginnings in 1927, CBS rose to prominence in the late 1940s in what many in the industry termed "talent raids." NBC had fired the first shot in the battle by wooing Bing Crosby and Kate Smith from William Paley's CBS stable. In 1948, Paley returned fire when he lured Jack Benny from NBC with a $2 million tax-sheltered arrangement designed in such a way as to greatly enhance the star's wealth.

Benny's creative deal with CBS was structured by MCA, the powerful talent agency started by Dr. Jules Stein, who had signed Johnny's musical group, The Hips Commanders. The agency represented the top talent of the day, including Jack Benny, and negotiated for many of their top earners to be paid as corporate entities that would own their product. CBS had exclusivity, but as owners of their programs, artists' income was not categorized as wages; they were defined as profits to be taxed at the lower IRS capital gains rates.

To elicit Madison Avenue's cooperation, Paley made an unprecedented guarantee. The American Tobacco Company agreed to continue to sponsor Benny through the move from Sarnoff's airwaves, with CBS agreeing to rebate their advertising agency $3,000 for every rating point that Benny lost in the shuffle, as measured by the C. E. Hooper Company. At CBS, Benny scored a Hooper rating of 27, three points higher than at NBC. In June 1950, the next shots in the talent war were fired from Rockefeller Center. General Sarnoff signed Groucho Marx to an eight-year, $3-million capital-gains contract, and drafted both Bob Hope and Kate Smith with five year deals.

Freeman Gosden and Charles Correll were the stars of *Amos 'n' Andy,* which was Johnny's favorite radio show and the anchor of the NBC schedule, when the duo defected to CBS. Edger Bergen, Red Skelton, and Jack Benny's pals, George Burns and Gracie Allen ultimately followed the golden goose to Paley's playground. In the 1950s, listeners were regularly reminded, "The stars' address is…CBS."

In 1972, Johnny found CBS in Hollywood very different from CBS of the 1950s and 1960s in New York. Most of the games, soap operas, and variety shows were being produced under one roof instead of at theaters and production facilities spread across the city. In addition, the building contained suites of offices that housed the programming and finance executives, and senior management bigwigs who occasionally dropped in to the studios.

By that time, New York corporate chiefs were all sequestered away from the studios in a stark, minimalist tower on Sixth Avenue at West 52nd Street. There, programming, sales, and management personnel toiled in a nondescript, dark corporate office building of Canadian granite and smoked glass nicknamed Black Rock that contained no video production facilities and gave little hint that it had any connection with the world of entertainment, broadcasting, or show business.

Television City's Studio 33 in 1952. Despite an estate in West Virginia and an apartment in West Hollywood, Johnny spent most of his time during the final thirteen years of his life in this 10,000-square-foot dream factory.

The New Price is Right began taping on August 19 with a single episode, followed by two episodes the following day. Soon the team was staging as many as five half-hour episodes a day, providing sufficient output to feed both the network and the syndicated pipelines. Johnny settled into a narrow dressing room with no amenities other than a simple bathroom and closet, and with scarcely enough room for a sofa and television. It was the location, just steps from the stage and across a narrow hallway from Bob Barker that imbued the humble room with power. Barker occupied the star dressing suite that was home to Carol Burnett, Red Skelton, and Jack Benny.

The biggest change for Johnny was that, with the exception of a few senior Goodson-Todman staffers, he knew almost none of the people with whom he worked. After decades in New York, Johnny was friendly with seemingly every crew member and technician at all of the city's studios, and those whom he did not know certainly knew him. While Johnny instantly developed a friendly, professional rapport and an upbeat spirit of camaraderie with crew members, anecdotes and remembrances suggest that he seemed lonely at first, when he was not in front of an audience.

Before long, Johnny seemed to be universally admired by all, from the program's star and producers down the ranks to those performing the least glamorous tasks in the entertainment factory, including janitorial workers, commissary workers, and security

Johnny at his stage-left podium, between prize descriptions on *The Price is Right*. He was masterful in simultaneously watching the on-stage action and his television monitor, listening to both Bob Barker and the director's cues, and waving for audience applause while flawlessly reading page after page of copy.

guards. Bob Boden became a respected television executive at Fox broadcasting after having held positions at CBS, ABC, and Sony. In 1981, Boden was paying his dues as an unpaid intern on *The Price is Right*, a show he would later oversee as a member of the network programming staff. He recalled the day he learned that the voice of America's most popular game shows belonged to a kind and compassionate man.

Bob said, "I remember one of my first days on the set, waving the audience to applaud. But I was mistakenly standing in a place where I was in Johnny Olson's eye line and was distracting him while he was announcing. In explaining the problem, Johnny could not have been more kind, more gentle or more supportive. That was the beginning of some nice conversations we had over the following months…He wasn't about Hollywood, and he wasn't about stardom or fame."[34-3]

The staging for *The New Price is Right* was unique. With contestants selected from the audience and so much of the action taking place in front of the first row of seats, the

300 spectators were brightly lit and clearly visible throughout much of the show. Marc Breslow created a unique template for direction that stood for decades, with reverse angle shots from the stage shooting the contestants standing in the audience section. With this arrangement, the appearance and demeanor of the audience members were far more important than they had been on any previous Goodson-Todman show.

That made Johnny's skill at making merry especially important for *The New Price is Right*, and he rose to the occasion with an especially exuberant warm-up. Author Maxene Fabe described the frenzy from the audience's point of view. "Suddenly, there is Olson, a short, balding, bespectacled man, wearing a suit and tie, doing the frug, the funky chicken, the bumps and a few grinds. Before the audience can recover, he has leaped down from the stage and into the lap of the nearest middle-aged woman. As he proceeds from person to person, his banter is carefully interlaced with important instructions: 'Don't chew gum on camera; don't whistle; kiss Bob Barker if you want to, but don't kill him.'" [34-4]

On shows from the first week of *The New Price is Right* tapings, Johnny identified contestants in the audience with the words "stand up!" The quartet was then invited en masse to "come on down!" The presentation was quickly changed, and each contestant was called to contestants' row individually and immediately, and the three-word phrase "come on down" took on prominence and urgency.

Production Assistant Bobby Lane was among the staffers who participated in Johnny's warm-up specifically to demonstrate the kind of manic energy that the show hoped to capture from its contestants when Johnny called their names. Roger Dobkowitz inherited the job, and over time, he greatly expanded the interplay until it escalated into something like a vaudeville act. He remembered, "If I did something that got a laugh, we kept it in, and if Johnny did something that got a laugh, he kept it in." [34-2] Eventually, the burlesque included running, jumping, assorted one-liners, a pair of oversized boxer shorts, and an unexpected, staged kiss.

With the new high-octane introduction of contestants, Johnny put his own spin on a three word phrase. Old kinescopes reveal that the line had been used on occasion to call a game show contestant from the balcony to the stage back in the New York theaters. Also, "come on down!" had more recently been heard repeatedly in an annual local advertising campaign that saturated the New York area airwaves. As spokesman for National Airlines, veteran sports broadcaster Jim Dooley continually advocated for winter weather weary New Yorkers to visit Florida with an inviting, enticing and enthusiastic "so come on down!" Sports legends, including Yogi Berra, joined Dooley in reciting the popular line that was always accompanied by a welcoming wave of the hand.

Johnny knew the commercials, the airline, and even the flight path well from his weekly commutes between the two cities for Gleason's show. He made "come on down!" a national catch phrase that endured into the twenty-first century. Of those magic three words, Bob Barker said, "Olson started what it has become with his delivery. As an announcer, he was quite incredible. He not only had a great voice, but if you watch *The Price is Right* for an hour, you realize the announcer covers a lot of copy. Johnny would go through hour after hour without a flub." [34-5]

On September 4, 1972, *The New Price is Right* debuted along with *Joker's Wild* and *Gambit*, replacing aging reruns of the network's vintage prime-time sit-coms. All the pieces came together and *The New Price is Right* was an instant hit, scoring a 40 share and multiplying CBS' coveted young adult audience five-fold over the sitcoms that had filled the mid-morning hours. Its success helped to return audience participation programming to the CBS daytime lineup for years to come after

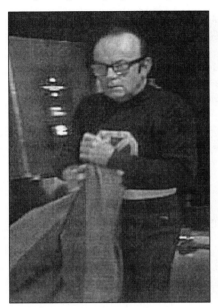 

Left: Johnny transformed into "Captain Klutz" for a *Price is Right* showcase skit. Right: Johnny "Santa" Olson and the North Pole's friendliest elves in a Christmas showcase on *The Price is Right*. (Left to right) Dian Parkinson, Janice Pennington, Johnny, and Holly Hallstrom.

a long dry spell for game shows on network television.

Johnny and Barker bonded quickly from the earliest rehearsals. Before long, the host generously conferred on Johnny a level of inclusion that few announcers ever enjoyed. Elevated from an unseen voice to an on-camera sidekick, Johnny enjoyed a commensurate increase in pay. The pair's complementary on-air chemistry and ongoing interplay added an element that enhanced the new incarnation of the Goodson classic.

Starting in 1974 with a spoof of "Little Red Riding Hood," Johnny took great delight in his regular appearances in the program's creatively-themed prize showcases. They were conceived in the imaginative mind of producer and future screenwriter, Jay Wolpert, who supervised the select few staffers that helped him concoct the zany scripts. Barbara Hunter warmly remembered the cartoon-like escapades. "Johnny was always a great sport about dressing up. He loved doing the showcases…it gave Johnny a chance to shine, and I think he did." [34-6]

Johnny's enjoyment of those skits was evident in the fact that he saved dozens of his original scripts from those sometimes elaborate, humorous sketches in which he appeared as a wide variety of characters including The Big Bad Wolf, the educator in "Johnny's School House," and Captain Klutz, which was adapted from a *MAD Magazine* feature authored by Goodson-Todman writer Dick DeBartolo. Scores of future "Flaky Flick" parodies cast Johnny as Captain Quirk in a *Star Trek* spoof, Quasi-Murphey in "The Halfback of Notre Dame," Sam Spaced in "The Maltese Mustang" and swashbuckler Errol Olson in "The Sea Gawk." *The Price is Right* brought Johnny popularity among a whole new generation of television viewers and gave him moments in the spotlight that he missed from his days as a host.

While the hours were long taping multiple episodes each day, the cast, crew, and staff enjoyed a close camaraderie during the early years. Most remember Studio 33 as a fun and magical place to report for work. Former model Holly Hallstom recalled some of the high jinx that Jay Wolpert encouraged during rehearsals, including one time when an old junk station wagon was secretly substituted for the show's favorite prize, a new car. Johnny began reading the scripted plug, but saw the old klunker on his monitor. "It's a new — uh, old — uh, what the heck is that?!"

Frank Wayne was Executive Producer. Phil Wayne Rossi, his son, Barbara Hunter, and Roger Dobkowitz followed Jay Wolpert as producers. Directors Marc Breslow, Paul Alter, and Associate Producer Kathy Greco were also key personnel. *The Price is Right*, its cast, and staff broke numerous records and received a long string of awards for longevity, popularity, and production excellence. There was no secret that, over the decades, there were private personality clashes and public scandals. Some, such as Breslow's removal from the show following disagreements with Bob Barker, were handled discretely and equitably. Others, including cases of alleged harassment, discrimination, and wrongful termination, wound through the judicial system. Despite the backstage drama, which was intense at times, the on-air product never suffered.

Mark Goodson earned a well-deserved reputation among the networks for delivering first-class productions, and his commitment to quality was evident on the show that boasted "A fortune in fabulous prizes may go to these people...." Later, the show was introduced as "Television's most exciting hour of fantastic prizes." From its 1972 debut, the set pieces, electronic displays, music, and sound effects reflected Goodson's attention to detail. The set was designed by Don Roberts, who was well-known for his work on Hollywood-based sitcoms, and was simultaneously Art Director and Set Decorator for CBS' new *Joker's Wild*. Monty Hall was said to have later commented on the similarity between the three-door set of *The Price is Right* and his earlier *Let's Make A Deal*.

Design and fabrication of many of the larger and more elaborate games and props posed challenges that were tamed in the CBS set shop. In the era before compact microprocessors were commonplace in game show electronics and displays, the advanced circuitry required for many of those new games was custom-designed and hand-built at the electronics shop at CBS Television City. Likewise, artwork and graphics were created in-house. Mark Goodson was always a stickler for the bells and buzzers that communicated the status of game play to the home audience. He birthed *The New Price is Right* with an especially rich cacophony of sounds.

The show also featured the deepest library of original music created for any game show. Under the supervision of Bob Israel's Score Productions, a young composer who had a background in rock, experience in scoring films, and was early to master the Moog synthesizer, Edd Kalenhoff, created countless hours of thematically linked music cues. Roger Dobkowitz remembered, "Shows like *Let's Make a Deal* had a small band, usually not much more than an organ and drums." He recalled that Goodson's senior producers were proud that their new music was "completely orchestrated" and used "a lot of brass that gave our show a different sound."[34-2]

Original tunes, their variations, and multiple remixes were recorded by a full orchestra in London in order to avoid the jurisdiction of the American Federation of Musicians. The music offered a more creative, richly orchestrated palette than had ever been available to score a game show. After almost forty years, the original main theme continued to sound contemporary, only being re-recorded once, note-for-note, for an upgrade to stereo. Mike Malone, and later, Stan Blits, the program's music mavens, were responsible for the underscoring that enhanced Johnny's vocal presentations.

Blits was another long-time staffer at Goodson-Todman. In 2008, he advanced through the ranks of *The Price is Right* to Co-producer in the wake of Roger Dobkowitz's departure. Stan wrote of Johnny, "A more professional talent could not have existed...I honestly cannot remember one single time when he made a mistake on the air."[34-7]

Johnny never missed an episode of *The Price is Right*. In fact, Johnny proudly told one producer that he had not missed a performance or tape date since 1948. Stan Blits was among many in show business to know the secret behind Johnny's perfect attendance record. It was not any miracle of eternal good health, because Johnny worked despite illnesses. "No matter how sick he was, he would hang in there until the end. One time, he was so sick to his stomach that he had to throw up, so he just kept a trash can next to his lectern and barfed into it between 'Come on downs.' Now that's a trouper."[34-7] Holly Hallstrom also remembers the incident. "The director was telling Johnny to 'push it' because we were running behind. Johnny, sick as he was with the flu, throwing up into the wastebasket, was spitting out copy like a machine gun, and it was flawless!"[34-8]

Johnny played a role in one of the most memorable and the most discussed moments from over 6,000 episodes of the show. Bob Barker recalled, "A young lady wearing a tube top was called to be a contestant. She began jumping up and down and came out of the top. She came on down, and they came on out. When I came through the doors and they were screaming, I thought, 'Well, this audience loves me — there's no doubt about that!' And then I realized no audience had ever liked me this much. I turned to Johnny and said, 'What's going on out here?' Johnny said, 'Bob, this girl has just given her all for you.'"[34-5]

Producer Barbara Hunter recalled the moment vividly. "I just remember the smile on Johnny's face, and he was laughing...Barker thought they were all clapping and yelling for him…and then Johnny said, 'Bob, they have given their all for you.' I think that was probably his funniest line." As for the contestant, a Yolanda Bowsley, "I almost ran out of the studio, I was so embarrassed for this woman." [34-6]

There was another incident of unintentional, behind-the-scenes nudity in the early years of *The Price is Right*. Janice Pennington was an up and coming personality in the early 1970s, having appeared in the party scenes on *Rowan and Martin's Laugh-In*, and in a Playboy pictorial spread before she was chosen to be one of the original models for the show. She introduced her friend, actress Anitra Ford, to Mark Goodson, who promptly hired Ford to join the television family.

Anitra remembered, "I had a bikini that I really liked to wear for the showcases that had gold loops on both sides. One time I was trotting along backstage and Johnny Olson was right behind me when all of a sudden I heard this plop. I looked down and there was my bikini bottom on the floor. I was bottomless. I turned around and Johnny had just disappeared. We never spoke about it." [34-1] In another moment of spontaneous mayhem, one that was shared with the audience, Janice Pennington drove one of the new cars she was steering into camera view, right past its mark, crashing into the set. Her simple explanation, "I hit the clutch instead of the brake."

Over the thousands of episodes recorded live-to-tape, there were dozens of other unanticipated disruptions that were captured and aired as they happened. They included a contestant fainting, and refrigerators tipping and spilling their contents onto the show's models. Another occurrence involving one of "Barker's Beauties" presented what was one of the most challenging moments in Johnny's extensive career. With his countless thousands of hours in front of audiences over the course of more than forty years in every aspect of show business, there was no situation that could throw Johnny.

Events were never more awkward than at a taping of *The Price is Right* when beloved model Janice Pennington was seriously injured in an on-stage accident. One of the program's regular camera operators was unexpectedly absent, so another was dispatched from an adjacent studio. He was insufficiently rehearsed in the fast-paced choreography of cameras, cables, props, and people that were integral to each show. Janice always started each episode positioned extreme downstage right, where she was prepared to hand off the host's microphone as Bob Barker made his entrance. Seconds into the show, the heavy lens assembly mounted on the front of the camera nearest Janice struck her. She was knocked headfirst some three or four feet from the raised stage to the concrete floor below.

"Right after Bob is introduced on each show, that one camera swings around and catches a shot of the audience," Stan Blits said of the usual action. "It's a fast move." [34-7]

Janice was knocked unconscious, suffered a concussion, and tore ligaments in her shoulder. While the audience looked on, and witnesses were only able to stand by cringing helplessly, the beloved model lay unconscious at the feet of the front row of guests for more than fifteen minutes until paramedics arrived.

Johnny was concerned for his dear co-worker's condition and frustrated by his inability to offer any aid, but he rose to the challenge to defuse as much of the fear and awkwardness as possible and keep the audience calm. He reassured and kept their interest during the approximately half-hour delay. Then, Johnny had to again pump-up the crowd to the customary frenzy in order to begin re-taping the episode. Johnny had again proven himself masterful in adapting to any circumstances.

Janice's ligiment injuries never fully healed properly, but after a period of recovery,

The best-remembered members of the *Price* family, (left to right) Johnny Olson, Dian Parkinson, Bob Barker, Janice Pennington, and Holly Hallstrom.

she was welcomed back to the show. She and the other Barker's Beauties also joined Johnny in his return to prime-time on the syndicated, evening incarnations of *The Price is Right* that ran concurrent with the daytime hit. His old fans in Wisconsin heard his familiar voice once again on the *Milwaukee Journal's* station, WTMJ-TV, Monday evenings at 6:30. Mark Goodson's originally intended host, Dennis James, fronted that nighttime half-hour starting in 1972 and filled in for Bob Barker during a week of daytime episodes in December 1974.

Twenty years later, Barker answered questions from studio audiences and reflected on what were obviously warm memories of his time with Johnny. "Johnny Olson was legendary. When I started doing *The Price is Right*, Goodson-Todman had several game shows on. And every show wanted Johnny Olson. He not only did a great warm-up, and *Price is Right* is probably the toughest show in television for the announcer...I would be startled when he fluffed. He read beautifully, and not only that, he had a great voice for *Price is Right*. A great voice, period. He was wonderful." [34-9]

Barker's show business sensibilities were always keen. He intuitively knew how to charm an audience, and how to draw out a contestant's personality to make the most of their moments in the spotlight. Barker also never lost sight of the basic appeal of *The Price is Right*, saying, "Everything we do is based on prices — that is such a strong premise." [34-5] He told the *New York Times*, "How much stuff costs is what people think about every day, anyway. The premise is so overpowering…everyone identifies with prices." [34-10]

After thirty-five years of pricing games and a fifty-year career in television, Barker retired at the age of eighty-three following the taping his last program on June 6, 2007. With a record nineteen Emmy awards and an expanding list of lifetime

Johnny was proud as a papa at his colleague Janice Pennington's wedding. (Left to right) Carlos de Abreu, Johnny, and Pennington.

achievement and hall of fame honors, Barker was American television's most celebrated personality. Although his father passed away when he was only six years old, Barker was able to share most of his success with Tillie, his mother. After her second husband died during the 1970s, Tillie lived with Barker at his Hollywood home in an attached guest house above the garage until her passing in 1993 at the age of ninety-four.

Barker, his friends, and his co-workers all agree that having been able to enjoy a wildly successful career at the work he enjoyed most was the source of his greatest happiness. In 1981, his greatest sadness was the loss of his high school sweetheart, wife and partner Dorothy Jo, to lung cancer. Johnny and others observed that her passing precipitated a period of depression in Barker's life that friends reported was profound and deep.

As a producer and writer on his first radio programs, Dorothy Jo was a constant source of support and encouragement, and she helped establish Barker's friendly, relatable on-air persona. Barker remembered with reverence, "She worked with me and supported me all the days of her life. That's the kind of girl she was." Bob laughed recounting one of their evenings at home, "At the end of the day, we would sit down with a glass of wine and have chat time. One night she poured the wine and said, 'Now, let's chat about anything but you.'" [34-11]

CHAPTER 35
THE SOUND OF SUCCESS

Johnny's unique vocal delivery was loose and fluid in style, with an ever-present, subtle hint of infectious laughter. Johnny could achieve great impact with his reach into the tenor range. His voice perfectly suited the technology of early television; its pitch, strength, and tonality cut through music and applause and projected from the small speakers with energy and clear diction that filled living rooms. As the technology advanced, improved audio quality revealed more of his vocal nuances and presentation.

Tom Kennedy admired what he called Johnny's "Clear, crisp, clarion tones...that crystalline voice." The host observed, "A lot of people thought that in radio you had to have a deep, resonant voice, and all that...but personality is what it's all about, and Johnny had that personality in his voice."[35-1]

Johnny's gifts went beyond the character of his voice and his flair for interpretation. Bob Barker was another of the emcees that publicly marveled at his impeccable reading skills and his ability to cover what few errors he made. In 2009, *The Price is Right* Producer Roger Dobkowitz reflected, "In all the years Johnny announced for our show it's hard to remember him making a mistake."[35-2] It motivated one memorable moment of rehearsal high-jinx. In an attempt to break his concentration, staffers undressed Johnny — opened his shirt, unbuckled and lowered his pants — while he continued to read flawlessly.

None of that precision in delivery was accidental or left to chance, nor was it simply the result of his hearing-impaired mother's repeated requests for him to "speak up." Johnny meticulously pre-read and extensively marked each piece of his written copy for phrasing, intonation, pronunciation, pace, and style.

The hand-written slashes he used to designate breaks between phrases went beyond standard breath marks; he developed his own personal syntax of markings, a collection of notations to guide every aspect of his delivery. He underlined words or brief phrases to indicate emphasis. Double and triple underlines were his cues to convey extra emphasis.

Vertical lines separated similar sounding syllables that might otherwise seem slurred. His flowing strokes through words marked where he could most effectively use the musical modulations in tone and timbre that made his personal presentation so identifiable. Open-bracketed words or phrases marked the beginning of copy to be presented as new thoughts for the ear, much as a new paragraph is used in writing

SHOW #185N

SECOND SHOWCASE:

YOUR SHOWCASE CONTAINS ALL THE PROPS USED BY "THE "PERFECTION" OF
PRESTIDIGITATION" THE MASTER MAGICIAN...FUMBLE FINGERS"!! AND HERE
HE IS WITH HIS LOVELY ASSISTANTS ABOUT TO PERFORM THAT GREAT
ILLUSION, "THE DISAPPEARING BODY". INTO THE FIRST COMPARTMENT GOES
THE LOVELY ASSISTANT...THE CURTAINS CLOSE, A FEW MAGIC PASSES WITH
HIS HANDS, HE UTTERS THE MAGIC WORDS "THE PRISO IS RIGHTO" AND
BEHOLD, SHE APPEARS IN ------NOW, THAT'S NOT HER, THAT'S A
NEW REFRIGERATOR (*** A 19 CUBIC FOOT FROST-FREE REFRIGERATOR
WITH MEAT KEEPER, CANTILEVERED ADJUSTABLE SHELVES AND CONVENIENT
GLIDE-OUT ROLLERS...FURNISHED BY WHITE-WESTINGHOUSE. (P)

SHE'S STILL BACK IN THIS FIRST COMPARTMENT...
WELL, FUMBLE FINGERS WILL JUST HAVE TO TRY HARDER...A FEW FANCY
GESTURES, A MUTTERED ABRA-CADABRA AND FLASH, SHE HAS BEEN SPIRITED
THROUGH THE AIR, AND HERE SHE IS------------NOW, THAT'S NOT
HER, THAT'S A COLOR TV CONSOLE (***) THE ZENITH "PANORAMA"..
A SOPHISITICATED 25 INCH DIAGONAL CHROMACOLOR II TV CONSOLE, WITH
COLOR SENTRY...THE AUTOMATIC PICTURE CONTROL SYSTEM...FURNISHED
BY ZENITH RADIO CORPORATION. (P)

SHE'S STILL HERE IN THIS COMPARTMENT.!!!
CALLING UPON ALL HIS POWERS, AND MUTTERING HOCUS POCUS AND
ALAKAZAM...AND FLASH, SHE HAS BEEN TRANSFERRED THROUGH THE AIR AND
LANDS IN---------------THAT'S SOME OTHER GIRL AND SHES WEARING
A MINK COAT (***)

(MORE)

SHOW #185N

<u>SECOND SHOWCASE</u>:

FROM THE DUFINO CUSTOM COLLECTION FURNISHED BY ZINMAN FURS, OF
CAMDEN, NEW JERSEY...AN EXQUISITE COAT OF SNOWTOP MINK OVALS...
IT'S A STUNNING DOUBLE BREASTED FASHION WITH SHOULDER EPAULETTES,
SLEEVE TABS, ANGLED FLAP POCKETS AND MATCHING LEATHER TIE BELT.

STILL HERE, HUH...TELL YOU WHAT, LET'S CHANGE PLACES...YOU DO
THE MAGIC AND I'LL DISAPPEAR...THE MOMENT IS TENSE AS THE CURTAINS
CLOSE AND THE LOVELY ASSISTANT GOES INTO HER MAGIC DANCE AND
UTTERS THE MAGIC WORDS. "GET OUT OF HERE AND GET OVER THERE"...
AND FLASH, FUMBLE FINGERS HAS BEEN TRANSPORTED THROUGH THE AIR
AND IS FOUND-----------------HE'S NOT THERE, HE MUST STILL BE IN
THE OTHER COMPARTMENT...THE CURTAINS OPEN, AND HE'S NOT THERE...
OH FUMBLE FINGERS, WHERE ARE YOU...AND FUMBLE FINGERS REPLIES...
I'M HERE IN MY NEW CAR (***)
THE PONTIAC GRAND PRIX SJ COUPE... OPTIONS INCLUDE PADDED LANDAU
TOP, STEEL-BELTED RADIAL WHITEWALL TIRES, BUMPER GUARDS, DOOR
EDGE GUARDS...FURNISHED BY PONTIAC.

AND TO KEEP YOUR NEW CAR RUNNING SMOOTHLY, THERE'S 33 QUARTS
OF CASTROL GTX...FOR PERFORMANCE YOU CAN FEEL...CASTROL GTX, THE
ALL-SEASON MOTOR OIL.

AND TO KEEP IT LOOKING NEW...A CAR CARE ASSORTMENT FEATURING
TURTLE WAX...THE WORLD'S LARGEST SELLING LIQUID CAR WAX...
CLEANS, POLISHES, PROTECTS IN ONE EASY OPERATION...TURTLE WAX,
WITH THE HARD-SHELL FINISH.
AND YOUR SHOWCASE WON'T DISAPPEAR, IF THE PRICE IS RIGHT.

for the eye. Quotation marks were adapted as a guide to utilize a technique known among voice-over talent as "billboarding."

Johnny's addition of "(P)" cued a pause, and handwritten exclamation marks indicated his choice to use added energy in conveying a key phrase. He added word prompts as superscripts or in the margins for style, including "dry, eerie, sweet, cry, mysteriously, weird, soft, big, and low."

Johnny was also fluent in the use of foreign diacritical markings such as the German umlaut, the Spanish tilde, the French grave accent, acute accent, and cedilla. He put that knowledge to use to assure correct foreign pronunciations when pre-reading scripts that included foreign phrases, such as items of French or German cuisine, or sightseeing attractions to be found on European trips that were frequently offered in *The Price is Right* showcases. By the end of his preparation, a page of complex copy often had more of Johnny's added ink than had been used to print the original script. Once fluent in his personal language of notations and symbols, one can almost hear Johnny's interpretation while silently reading his marked scripts.

Performers preferred working with Johnny not only for his flawless readings, engaging delivery, and legendary warm-up, but also for his intuitive support of their efforts. From his years as a host, he understood when he could best add a comment to help an emcee in his pacing or in a transition. He intuitively knew when to deliver a straight line, to add a chuckle, or simply to lay back to help the star shine. If adding a humorous line risked upstaging the star, he knew how to sublimate his own creativity.

Johnny's simple tools remained unchanged through the decades. In the 1950s and early 1960s, he regularly used a RCA 77DX ribbon microphone. In the late 1960s and early 1970s, he was often behind an Electrovoice 635A or RE11. There was a music stand for his copy, one paper cup for water, and another to hold a throat lozenge he used while off mike. He preferred a single, hand-held Brush Clevite-style earphone that he would hold to his ear for the director's cues, and then rest on the music stand when he began to read. In 1952, Cleveland Graphite Bronze, an automotive parts manufacturer, merged with the Brush Development Corporation and produced the low-fidelity earphones and other radio equipment that were so familiar to broadcasters of the era.

Johnny loved the business, and he was known to occasionally drop in at radio stations while traveling, usually simply to meet the air personalities and tour the facilities. His voice was so distinctive and recognizable that he was often asked to lend his tones to commercials, promotional announcements, and local station identifiers. He generously contributed audio bits for fellow broadcasters, often a simple, "This is Johnny Olson in New York (or later, Hollywood) and whenever I'm in town I listen to…"

In 1971, a creative radio programmer approached Johnny to record a few lines for his station's weekend special programming. Johnny accepted no money to record station IDs and promos at Mark Century Studios in New York City for Tom McMurray of WBT, Charlotte, North Carolina. Those voice tracks ran for many years, adding sparkle and magic to the 50,000 watt station's "Sunday Night Hall of Fame" that was heard by millions up and down the east coast.

CHAPTER 36
MAKING MIRTH

Beyond his skills as an announcer, Johnny was highly respected for his ability to work any studio audience into a frenzy of anticipation in the moments just before airtime. Buddy Piper, the creator of television's classic *Concentration* and host of NBC's *The Bible Story Game*, remembered that Johnny's warm-up skills were well-crafted as early as the late 1940s, when Piper watched him run through a television audience with an umbrella that he used to shield guests from the periodic leaks that emanated from the early water-cooled studio lights.

Audience warm-ups have been a part of broadcasting from radio's infancy, beginning when the public was first invited into a studio to view a program. Early on, warm-ups consisted simply of a word of welcome from the producer, an introduction of the cast, an occasional question and answer session hosted by a staff member, and/or a rousing musical number if the program featured a live band.

Ed Sullivan stepped on stage each week to briefly welcome the studio audience just before his Sunday night show took to the air. "How are you all? How many are here from out of town?" He then admonished, "Everybody in the audience is honor-bound to be happy. So look happy! In thirty seconds, Art Hannes is going to introduce me and he will be absolutely astonished that I showed up. They didn't think old Smiley would do it!" [36-1]

In the world of game shows, all of Johnny's contemporaries had their own presentation. Kenny Williams of *Video Village* and *The Hollywood Squares* fame started his warm-up by bounding on-stage bellowing, "Hello! I'm Kenny Williams from Baltimore, Maryland. Where are you from?" Jay Stewart had a seemingly unlimited memory for one-liners that he enthusiastically shared while interviewing audience members at *Let's Make A Deal* and the dozens of other shows he worked during his four decades in broadcasting. Gene Wood, best remembered from *Family Feud,* selected audience members to join him on-stage to participate in his impromptu skewed recreations of scenes from such well known stories as "Romeo and Juliet" and "Tarzan."

On *Truth or Consequences,* host Bob Barker performed his own warm-up, interacting with audience members in order to identify the outgoing, emotionally demonstrative members of the crowd that he would later choose to participate in the various stunts planned for that specific episode. He shared, "I did my own warm-up and selected my own contestants. I would talk with them enough that I would be confident that I had found the best possible contestant for each consequence." [36-2]

Then the staff usually provided a series of sight gags and quick quips that reached a crescendo as the clock ticked towards the top the show.

Moments before airtime, the *Truth or Consequences* audience was brought to hysterics by two men awkwardly struggling to don brassieres and girdles over their clothes. At the moment of maximum hilarity, the show started with close-ups of laughing audience members while the announcer roared, "Hello there! We've been waiting for you! It's time to play *Truth...or Consequences!*"

Johnny helped to elevate the traditional pre-show mood-setting session to an art form. The importance of that unique skill to the success of a program, and Johnny's pride in his proficiency, were reflected in the design of his business card from the late 1960s - he listed three talents: "TV Announcer, Warm-up Specialist, and Audience Host." His dedication to his craft was evidenced by the fact that he maintained files in which he kept humorous quiz questions and answers, fill-in-the-blank quotations, comic and contest material, as well as anecdotes and jokes collected through the years. It was the equivalent of a magician's bag of crowd-pleasing tricks, and Johnny seemed to have an endless supply of that material committed to memory and always ready for any unexpected, lengthy delay.

Johnny had learned from experience the importance of working to an attentive, receptive, and reactive audience, one that could even be cajoled into laughing and applauding on cue. He developed an adrenalin-enriched warm-up act capable of simultaneously energizing an audience, relaxing the inhibitions of even its most staid members, and creating a wild, party-like atmosphere.

He was the subject of a great many newspaper and magazine write-ups as well as broadcast interviews for his excellence in a job that was a strange hybrid of entertainer, party host, psychotherapist, cheerleader, borscht-belt tummler, court jester, and cub scout den mother. Johnny told *Time* magazine that he was a specialist in "the mass breakdown of tensions. I'm a psychological second banana, who acts as a liaison between audience and performer. I don't pretend to be a comedian, just someone in whom the audience can develop confidence." [36-3]

In a 1962 Sunday *New York Times* feature story by reporter John P. Shanley, Johnny shared his observations on everything from sociology to meteorology as it affected his work with audiences. Of the weather, he explained, "It's a psychological factor. On a rainy night you have to work harder to get them in a good mood." [36-4] Johnny also observed that audiences were less reserved and would laugh more enthusiastically when the house lights were dimmed. He often asked for the cooperation of the lighting director during his warm-ups.

Being the youngest of ten children apparently contributed to his skills as a people person. Johnny said, "In a family that size, you've got to learn how to give and take, how to appreciate the tastes and peculiarities of others, and that's really the basis of understanding people." Johnny explained "I am not a jokester, I leave that to the star. I don't want to step on his toes. I just try to get the audience in a receptive mood... if the studio audience reacts well, it can help a star in his timing." [36-4]

The ability to lead an audience in laughter was based on first developing rapport and a sense of trust with them. On many of the shows he worked in New York,

Johnny used to go out on the street while the audience was waiting in a queue. He explained, "I would go up and down the line out in front of the theater, say 'hello,' and get them acquainted with me, so when they came in the theater they felt they knew me."

In another serious reflection on the science of making merry, Johnny said, "You have to present the idea of the show and how the audience can have a good time and

What's his line? Making merry! Johnny took a moment to pose for a photo while charming a Sunday night *What's My Line?* audience moments before the live broadcast.

participate...On a variety show like Jackie Gleason's, I'm sort of the liaison between the performer and the audience." He explained how he stood off to the side of the performer while still in the audience's view and led their reactions. In differentiating his approach to that of a comic, Johnny said, "A lot of comedians go out and do a warm-up and tell a lot of funny material...it gets fantastic laughs. Now you come on the air and the star comes out with a joke, and there's nothing."

Johnny spoke of his observations of people from having interacted with well over two million audience members through the years. He noted that people from New York and Los Angeles were more receptive. "They're the solidest; they're hep to show business...folks in California are real friendly. I think L.A. audiences see it all and may even get it all, but the L.A. audience is more reserved, where New Yorkers react with gusto." Johnny continued, "Midwesterners are slow starters...and they like broad humor. Southerners get the gags a little sooner, and yet, somehow their reactions come a little more slowly...but they're great for interviews."[36-4]

Despite these observations of regional peculiarities, Johnny's in-studio warm-up spoke the universal language of fun. His familiar NBC peacock dance, complete with bumps, grinds, and faux striptease, was a fun and effective icebreaker. During warm-ups, he explained the game and the audience's role in the show while giggling and dancing wildly up and down the aisles. Johnny told mildly suggestive jokes that dated back to his days as a club singer, while he landed on people's laps, planted

Johnny center-stage on the *Match Game* set, rehearsing the audience's applause on the count of "1, 2, 3 . . . pow!"

kisses on the cheeks of older ladies, and peeled off dollar bills in an engaging and frenetic frenzy of energizing, pre-show excitement. It was all calculated and crafted to ease shyness, overcome reservations, minimize self-consciousness, relax inhibitions, unhook hang-ups, and create an environment in which audience members bonded with the strangers around them and felt more comfortable reacting audibly to the program.

After his explosive, dancing entrance, Johnny introduced himself and lightheartedly took audiences through warm-up exercises, having them repeat "Ho, ho, ho! Ha, ha, ha! Hee, hee, hee!" and assorted giggles and Woody Woodpecker-style guffaws. While he bopped and boogied around the studio seemingly at random, he was actually checking to assure that each of his guests was unencumbered by coats and packages, with their hands free to be coached and rehearsed in creating double-time, super-charged applause.

Dancing up and down the aisles, Johnny made a personal connection with as many individual audience members as possible while creating merriment. A kiss on an aging matron's cheek might include, "Well, how are you, sweetheart?" As he pulled down the hem of her skirt, he added, "Are your knees bothering you? They sure are bothering me! Ooh-ooh, I'll meet you after the show, honey!"

Dick DeBartolo said of his favorite Olson-ism, "He would go through the audience asking women 'Are you married?' Somewhat flirtatiously, he would ask the slightly older women until he found one slightly older woman who was not married. He'd ask 'Are you married?' and she would say, 'No, I'm not.' And Johnny would say, 'You'd better not wait too long for your ship to come in, because your pier might collapse!'" [36-5]

The engaging silliness was always interspersed with instructions in how to react, as well as a rundown of cues for laughter and applause. "At the top of the show, we'll have all the lights up bright and we'll all be applauding. The cameras will be panning your pusses — ah, faces, and believe me, some of your pusses need panning! Wo-ho! So sit up straight, or sit up like you're straight, yooo-hooo! And gosh-darn-ya, smile like you're having a good time. Don't you remember the last time you had fun, dear? I sure do! Ha-ha-ho! C'mon now, look happy; I don't want any sourpusses on this show. You wanna look good for your friends and family, your in-laws and your out-laws. Oooh, you're good! You're going to be great today. So let's try your applause; when we applaud we give it all we got. On the count of three, everybody. When I introduce our host let's make it big, big, BIG. Are you ready, gang? Let's do it! One… two…three…POW! Go! Go! Go! Go! Go! Go!"

Johnny's performance reached a comedic crescendo with "Okay, the time has come! Let me hear that laughter now. Ha ha, ho ho, whee hee! Let's see that big smile. Bee-yoo-tee-ful!! Take a deep breath of New York's freshest air. (cough). Ha, ha, whee! Folks, you're the best! There's just a moment to go, so there's no time if you have to go now! Huh-hoo, hee-hee, ha-ha-ho!" Johnny danced exuberantly, with a few suggestive burlesque bumps and grinds, over to his microphone with barely a second to spare before delivering a show's scripted opening announce copy, all while the audience was at its peak, reacting to John's choreographed mayhem and willingly contributing to the audible enthusiasm he had encouraged.

Unlike other warm-up acts, Johnny's continued throughout the show. During commercials, he came back and pumped the audience's energy level with one-line non-sequiturs, including, "Anybody out there celebrating a birthday? Anniversary? Parole?" Even while the cameras were hot and the microphones open on shows with a light announce load, he roamed up and down the aisles during the program. He whispered comments about the game to random audience members, as well as cued applause and laughter from among them. Sometimes, he ran to the microphone from the rear of the studio, seemingly just in time to pick up his cue to speak. It was all part of keeping audience members alert, entertained, engaged, and reacting to the action.

Television production crew members were rarely shy when talking among themselves about audience warm-up acts. They had heard them all, and they had heard them repeated day after day. While all warm-up personalities had a collection of well-crafted routines that got repeated in the course of their work, Johnny developed a number of tricks that kept each day in the studio fresh.

Ray Angona, six-time Emmy winning Technical Director for *The Price is Right* and *Match Game,* said, "Johnny would involve the production personnel and the crew members who were on stage just before tape rolled. He would interact with them during the warm-up, often setting them up to deliver the punch lines from the jokes that we had all come to know."[36-6]

Ray also reflected on one measure of Johnny's generosity that helped to endear him to his co-workers. "During the course of his warm-up, in addition to welcoming the audience on behalf of the executive producers, Johnny would also work into his act the names and titles of three or four crew members. It was a small touch, but gratifying when he mentioned your name. You knew that he cared about you and your contribution to the show." [36-6]

Bob Stewart, the creator of *The Price is Right, To Tell The Truth,* and *Password,* reflected more than a decade after Johnny's death that the announcer was "A terrific guy. One of the best in the business."[36-7] Gene Rayburn enjoyed working with Johnny on a number of shows, including an astounding sixteen seasons of *The Match Game.* On a 1974 broadcast, he simply said, "I did a show without Johnny once, and I never realized how good he was until I tried to do a show without him."

John Daly, the host of *What's My Line?* worked with Johnny during that series' long run. In 1965, he complemented him on the air with a straightforward analysis. "He talks to our audience in the theater before the program begins, and I don't think anybody in television has a better running start than we do. He's such a friendly, engaging, sincere, nice guy that audiences respond to him, and it makes it much easier for us when our time comes."

Holly Hallstrom summarized the joy that Johnny found in his work, "He was a ham to the nth degree. He loved his warm-up. He loved having that audience laughing…and he'd do his little bump and grind…and all those little old blue-haired ladies would go insane, and oh, he loved it." [36-8]

"He is the star of the show in warm-ups." Tom Kennedy remembered Johnny's act from their time together on Goodson-Todman shows. "When he walked out in front of that audience…I, for the first time, had a full appreciation for what he does. This guy is fantastic, and I had a whole new reverence for him." [36-9]

Johnny said that successful warm-ups created the illusion among the audience members that "everyone's a part of the family." His advice to me as a newcomer best explained his overall attitude and philosophy. "The audience members are your guests, and you're their ambassador to show business. You are the liaison between the audience and the performers. Be gracious and generous. Never leave the studio until you've spoken with everyone who has a question or simply wants to say 'hello.'"

CHAPTER 37
STRIKING A NEW MATCH

In 1972, *The Price is Right* was successfully repackaged for CBS. Next, *The Match Game* was revived for the network as *Match Game '73* with an all-star panel inspired by the success of NBC's celebrity-laden *Hollywood Squares*. On July 2, Johnny opened the debut episode of *Match Game '73* saying, "Get ready to match the stars!" He introduced the celebrities, and then Gene Rayburn welcomed the audience by saying, "This is your old favorite, updated with more action, more money, and as you can see, more celebrities."

The revival utilized the humorous and often double-entendre style of questions created by Dick DeBartolo that saved the original run of *The Match Game*. They were the catalyst for the comedy and set the bawdy and sometimes outrageous tone for the show. The pilot episode featured some familiar faces from the Goodson-Todman stable, and was carefully cast for the seemingly contradictory qualities of variety and compatibility — "contrast and complement," as producer Ira Skutch described it.

Skutch recalled that the first to be suggested was Richard Dawson, who had just become a darling of the production company while serving as a panelist on the recently revived but short-lived *I've Got A Secret*. Arlene Francis was flown in from New York to lend her talents, elegance, and network appeal. She was joined by Betty White, the queen of television games, the first Emmy-winning female game show host, and the lucky charm who had helped to sell more game show pilots than any other celebrity player.

Rounding out the panel were Jack Klugman, Bert Convy, and JoAnn Pflug, who each brought a unique ingredient to the mix. With Gene Rayburn and Johnny piloting the sample show, the *Match Game* revival was so well-received by CBS that only minor, mostly cosmetic changes were made before the program went to series.

For the first week of shows, Jack Klugman, Richard Dawson, and JoAnn Pflug remained. They were joined by Michael Landon, Vicki Lawrence, and Anita Gillette. Klugman soon bowed out with the request that the producers give his wife a shot as a panelist. He joked to Ira Skutch that it would make his marriage much more pleasant. Brett Somers Klugman and Charles Nelson Reilly first appeared on the panel in the show's third week and helped to drive the program's success for the remainder of the run.

The importance that Goodson placed on casting panels posed a special challenge on *Match Game '73*. The ability to play the game and blend with the personalities of the other celebrities was compounded by the need for guests to possess an appreciation, if not a gift, for comedy. Although vital, the desire to tickle the audience's funny bone was never to take precedence to the game. Dawson understood the delicate balance, explaining, "Some of the worst celebrities on game shows are stand-up

Match Game host Gene Rayburn with a carefully cast panel that included (left to right) Joan Collins, Richard Dawson, and Patti Deutsch (with her back to the camera).

comics. They're getting big laughs with an ad-lib, and the contestant's ten thousand bucks is going down the drain. All someone has to do on 'Match Game' is try that once, and they're never invited back." [37-1]

Host Gene Rayburn had proven himself to be a witty and capable facilitator on the straightforward *Match Game* a decade earlier on NBC, but viewers got to see so much more of his quick mind and Peck's bad boy, puckish persona on the CBS retooling. An educated eye appreciated his exquisite balancing act between playing straight man for the celebrities' humor, enhancing the party with generous doses of his own comedic gift, and always moving the game along.

Johnny privately shared that Rayburn was one of the hosts with whom he most enjoyed working. Rayburn was quick with a quip, clever when breaking the theatrical fourth wall, and adept with physical comedy when wrestling with the cameras, ripping apart the set, and climbing over the audience. With Director Marc Breslow and his camera crew proactively anticipating the celebrity ad-libs and madcap unpredictable action, *Match Game '73* made for quick-cut, compelling viewing, as it played upon the strength of live television's illusion that anything could happen at any time.

Match Game '73 was not your father's *Match Game*. DeBartolo led an Emmy-nominated team of writers that included Bobby Sherman, Joe Neustein, Patrick Neary, and Elliot Feldman. DeBartolo broke new ground in suggestive material that first challenged CBS' censors. A representative of the Standards and Practices department reviewed each episode's questions in advance, and DeBartolo owned up to the old writers' trick of including material that was clearly out of bounds, knowing it would be excluded. Those were calculated sacrifices to help with getting some of the questionable material to squeak through. Dick recalled, "When the questions started going into bedlam, you always had to show that there were three legitimate answers so that you weren't just coming up with questions knowing people would laugh, but would leave the contestants stumped for clean answers."[37-2]

The network's arbiters of morality were also on-set to police the linguistic mayhem. Producer Ira Skutch and writer Dick DeBartolo remembered that the show stopped tape the first time a celebrity player used the word "boob" to denote a woman's breast. DeBartolo recalled, "The guy from Standards and Practices checked with his wife, who said 'why not?' and after it was used once, it became acceptable on the show." [37-2]

George Carlin took notice. The recipient of the Mark Twain Prize for American Humor was famous for exploring America's language mores, and his "Seven dirty words" routine was used by the United States Supreme Court to set standards for broadcasting indecency and obscenity. Carlin included in his comedy act an observation that, while the word "tit" was considered inflammatory, the equally benign "boob" was thoroughly tolerated. As evidence of the word's widespread acceptance as non-offensive, he remarked, "Hey, 'boob' is an answer on *Match Game!*"

DeBartolo also remembered that after panelist Marcia Wallace used the word "genitals," backstage briefings became the norm before tapings. Celebrity casting executive Diane Janover was assigned the distinctive duty of reviewing the show's acceptable language. All were schooled in *Match Game*-ese, a particular lingo — "urinate" was replaced with "tinkle." Contestants and celebrities were told not to use any of the many unacceptable euphemisms for fornication; the preferred phrase was "make whoopee." Johnny was pre-emptive in his warm-up as he included advice for audiences to "go along with the fun," suggesting they simply giggle their way through "questions about booze, broads, and boobs."

It all came together to blend into what *New York Times* television writer Virginia Heffernan called a "wacky leerfest that modeled the promiscuous, drunken, risqué, gender-bending behavior of '70s celebrities for an unlikely daytime audience — under the guise of being a quiz show." [37-3]

Johnny made occasional on-camera appearances on both incarnations of *The Match Game*. On the original NBC version, he briefly assumed hosting duties after Gene Rayburn left the podium for comedic effect. The walk-off was in response to a practical joke instigated by Bill Cullen in which all of the players answered a question with an arbitrary word unrelated to the question, "pickle."

In 1975, Johnny served double duty as announcer and panelist, substituting for Charles Nelson Reilly when the actor overslept for one Sunday morning taping after forgetting to reset his alarm clock for the beginning of daylight savings time. Rayburn also brought Johnny onstage on a few unrehearsed occasions during the nine-year run. In 1975, Johnny delivered his signature "Come on down!" as the definitive answer to the question, "Johnny Olson's beautiful wife, Penny, said, 'Last night it was very hard to sleep. All night long Johnny kept shouting *(blank)*.'" In 1978, Johnny was on-camera again to deliver his famous call of "Come on down!" which was the top answer in a bonus round audience match.

Fred Allen was credited with saying, "Imitation is the sincerest form of television." That thinking was in evidence when Mark Goodson's creative team looked to capitalize on the tremendous success of their re-tooled *Match Game*.

Johnny, part of the party atmosphere on *Match Game*.

The concept of a spinoff was not unique to modern media. William Shakespeare spun Falstaff out of *Henry IV* for inclusion in *Henry V* and *The Merry Wives of Windsor*. Mark Twain's *Huckleberry Finn* was a spinoff from *Tom Sawyer*. Author Alex McNeil conjectured that the practice in television dated back at least to 1955. "The first one I can think of is *The Adventures of Champion*... Gene Autry was so successful with his own show on CBS that he spun off his horse." [37-4]

In the *Match Game* audience match bonus round, players were asked to match the most popular answers given in a poll of previous audience members. That feature was adapted as the basis for *Family Feud*. Although Jack Narz was the anticipated host, Richard Dawson expressed interest in fronting the new show. Roger Dob-kowitz remembered that the run-throughs with Dawson went exceedingly well, and with his huge popularity from *Match Game* and *Hogan's Heroes,* he was chosen to helm the new game.

Johnny voiced the pilot episode that featured members of the Speir household feuding with the Madvig clan, but Gene Wood was cast to announce the series because Johnny's schedule was full. The veteran announcer was lucky that other work precluded his participation, as by all accounts, *Family Feud* became one of the more contentious sets during some difficult years of friction between Dawson and Producer Howard Felsher.

Despite behind-the-scenes high drama, *Family Feud* quickly became one of America's most loved television shows, counting Sammy Davis Jr. among its many fans. Sammy and Altovise, his wife, were such loyal viewers that Altovise came to tapings on several occasions. Finally, Sammy could not resist the temptation to visit Richard Dawson, his old friend, and watch the show in person. Producer Cathy Dawson recalled the show made the most of the occasion by having Sammy enter at the top of the program, totally surprising the audience. Sammy pretended to be the host of that episode of *Family Feud* before Dawson made his entrance and continued the merriment.

Family Feud was an immediate hit following its July 12, 1976 daytime debut on ABC, and the show became a top-rated program within a year. By the fall of 1977, it had sparked a syndicated version that expanded from one night to two nights, and then to five nights a week. With the addition of prime-time all-star specials, *Family Feud* kept its staff and the crew assigned to Studio 54 at ABC's Prospect lot cranking in high gear during its nine-year run.

After reaching an all-time low at the end of the 1960s, Goodson-Todman was again a vibrant, thriving concern by the mid 1970s. Johnny was then in his sixties, but he was along for the ride and doing what he enjoyed most — working on multiple hit television shows and playing to enthusiastic studio audiences.

CHAPTER 38

HOLLYWOOD, THE RETURN

Johnny's move to California proved to be a good career choice. While the weekly *I've Got A Secret* fizzled, *The New Price is Right* sizzled. It was an immediate hit and remained strong despite the network's juggling of the show's time period. The revival of *Match Game* the following year also delivered noteworthy Nielsen numbers out of the box, was fun to work, and was creating positive word of mouth at the network, suggesting that it would enjoy a long run. Overall, it was a new renaissance period for game shows. By 1975, there were a total of twenty-six regularly scheduled games on the airwaves, making it the most prolific year for the category in television history.

Johnny occasionally lamented the industry's migration to Los Angeles, admitting that he missed the energy of New York and the proximity to his wife. The Olsons made the best of the awkward, bi-coastal arrangement. Johnny was in his mid-sixties, and the regular, cross-country travel was a hardship, but it was a trip he enthusiastically made most weekends.

Starting in 1973, tapings of *Match Game* on alternate weekends limited his ability to visit Penny as often as he would have liked. He also logged more days in the studio when *The New Price is Right* reduced its daily production load from four to a less exhausting three episodes. After years sharing a large Connecticut home with his wife, living a bachelor's lifestyle in his Hollywood apartment was lonely. Co-workers reported over the years that they occasionally saw Johnny with female companions at restaurant dinners. His friends were all far too respectful to ever question the nature of the relationships.

Johnny's love for Penny was indisputable. Being away from his dear soulmate was a choice he made for the benefit of his career, and because he simply enjoyed the work and his friendships in the television community. He spoke of Penny often, and always mentioned her during interviews. On one chat with Tom Snyder, he delayed a commercial break long enough to hold up a picture of his beloved and give Penny credit for her contributions as a co-host on his early programs.

His production partners remembered him as eternally up-beat, passionate, and positive. With his endearing demeanor, he was sought out for opportunities that allowed him to expand beyond his bread-and-butter audience participation shows.

The work load that he enjoyed in New York quickly became equaled, if not surpassed, in California.

Johnny briefly returned to the world of vaudeville working with hosts Sammy Davis, Jr. and Mickey Rooney on thirteen hours of huge, glitzy, kitschy, variety television called *NBC Follies*. Joey Heatherton, Jerry Lewis, Wayne Newton, Andy Griffith, Petula Clark, Peter Lawford, Diahann Carroll, The Weavers, and John Davidson were among the guests appearing in big musical production numbers and original comedy sketches. No expense seemed to be spared to re-launch the once reliable vaudeville format on television.

After a successful pilot aired in the summer of 1973, NBC locked Sammy Davis, Jr. for the new extravaganza with an exclusive, five-year, $3 million overall deal. Johnny was signed to provide his enthusiastic voice and masterful warm-up skills. The original Hollywood Playhouse on Vine Street, later renamed the El Capitan Theater, had been home to the last big weekly television vaudeville hit, ABC's *The Hollywood Palace*. It was refurbished for the new venture, and the Thursday night slot in which Dean Martin brought the network some of its biggest ratings was opened to assure success for *NBC Follies*.

New York Times critic John J. O'Connor wrote that the new show was "pleasantly and attractively entertaining," [38-1] but with only mediocre ratings, the big-budget variety offering never commanded the advertising revenues needed to generate a profit. Thirteen weeks after its debut on September 13, 1973, *NBC Follies* was history. Johnny simply drove to his next gig, untainted by his association with cancelled shows, while fortunes were made and lost, careers created and deflated, and executives re-hung their artwork in ever-changing offices.

The return of another abiding classic was next. NBC purchased *Twenty One, Tic Tac Dough,* and *Concentration* from Jack Barry and Dan Enright in the era of the game show scandals. They produced *Concentration* before granting a license in 1973 for Goodson-Todman to create and distribute a revival of the evergreen hit. *Concentration* had always violated the traditional thinking about daytime game shows needing to be "radio on television" in order to be accessible to homemakers visually involved in household chores. NBC's longest running daytime game show had been on the air since 1958, and America loved watching contestants try to solve a picture and word puzzle, revealing parts of the puzzle by matching pairs of prizes.

After nearly 4,000 episodes, *Concentration* rested for only six months before returning in syndication. Howard Felsher produced, Ira Skutch directed, and an electronic game board replaced the thirty archaically noisy, solenoid-driven, mechanical, three-sided rotating trilons that for years had revealed prizes, segments of the rebus puzzle, and an occasional crew member's hand. From 1973 to 1979, friendly and familiar host Jack Narz was joined by Johnny at a rented studio at Metromedia Square to officiate over this updated version of *Concentration*.

Concurrently, *Now You See It* also teamed Johnny with Narz in 1974 and 1975. On that visually intensive program created by Frank Wayne, contestants concentrated to find words disguised in a sea of sixty-four letters that were the correct answers to questions posed by the host. The production shared Studio 33 with *The Price is Right* at CBS, and Johnny was in familiar territory, ensconced in the utilitarian dressing room that was a second home for the final thirteen years of his life.

In 1974, Johnny substituted for Gene Wood as announcer on *Tattletales* with the program's host Bert Convy and long-time friend, executive producer Ira Skutch. *Tattletales* was the show that evolved out of the earlier *He Said, She Said* that Johnny had worked, in which couples competed to see who knew the most about their mates.

Host Jark Narz reviewing a winning contestant's solution of a bonus round rebus (Piccadilly Circus) before Johnny described her prizes on the 1970s revival of *Concentration.*

Celebrities appearing on game and quiz shows traditionally played for charity, but in a new twist, *Tattletales* audience members shared the celebrity couples' winnings. The audience was divided into thirds with each of the three celebrity pairs playing for one segment of the audience.

To keep it simple, the show paid off on the spot. As the audience left Television City's Studio 31, each of the over 200 participants was handed a check, usually amounting to less than $10, from an automatic check-writing machine. According to Mark Evanier, homeless people regularly attended *Tattletales* tapings for the funds that might feed them for a few days. There were merchants located around Beverly and Fairfax Boulevards that put up signs reading, "We cash *Tattletales* checks."

During a 1974 return to New York, Johnny appeared as a mystery guest on *What's My Line?* and gave host Larry Blyden one of the longest responses to the standard question, "What are you doing now?" Johnny detailed his incredible twenty-one half-hours of television each week in California, consisting then of the weekday and weekly syndicated versions of *The Price is Right*, plus *Match Game*, *Concentration*, and the new *Now You See It*.

In 1975, Microsoft appeared, Jimmy Hoffa disappeared, and Johnny's airtime and income increased significantly, when CBS and Goodson expanded *The Price is Right* to become the first daily, hour-long game show. A one-week test proved the idea viable, and Johnny's salary was permanently boosted approximately 30 percent, as prescribed by the AFTRA code. The new taping schedule was ambitious, with three one-hour episodes produced in a day. Producer Barbara Hunter recalled, "We would get there at eight in the morning and get through at ten at night. Johnny was rehearsing three shows, warming-up three audiences, and then taping three shows... the schedule was so rigorous." [38-2]

It was a period of renewed prosperity for television games, and Johnny remained fully employed during that last decade of his life. In fact, 1975 was the most prolific year in his long career. Monday, Tuesday, and Wednesday of most weeks were dedicated to producing a total of nine, one-hour episodes of *The Price is Right*. There was also a weighty workload with other tape days for his other programs. *Now You See It*, *Concentration*, and *Match Game* all conformed to the traditional half-hour format. By the 1970s, all such series were taping five or more episodes a day. *Match Game*, which enjoyed a weekly syndicated run concurrent with its daytime version, often recorded a sixth show on its twice-monthly Saturdays and Sundays in the studio.

Barbara Hunter worked her way from receptionist to producer at *The Price is Right* before advancing to become a CBS network programming executive. She recalled, "Johnny would hop a plane...I think he would even leave on the red-eye, maybe Wednesday after taping, and then come back on Sunday for Monday's taping. I remember him saying they knew him so well by that point that they would just bump him up to first class." [38-2] Barbara recalled that Penny flew to join her mate for a few days in Hollywood on no more than a couple of occasions.

At the age of sixty-five, Johnny's calendar was even more crammed than it had been in the late 1940s as one of broadcasting's most prolific performers, when he walked from studio to studio through midtown Manhattan, between NBC, CBS, ABC, DuMont, and Mutual, sharing greetings with the familiar doormen and street vendors along his usual route. The only hint of Johnny's age can be heard on recordings of his warm-ups during his final work years, when he was occasionally winded after his enthusiastic dancing entrance onto the stage. His on-air performances remained as vibrant, energetic, crisp, and clear as they had always been.

Alex Trebek was first discovered by Lin Bolen, NBC's controversial, tougher-than-nails Vice President of daytime programming, as the embodiment of the next generation of hosts. He joined the stable of Goodson-Todman emcees with *Double Dare*, which Johnny announced between December 1976 and February 1977. Despite Johnny's and Trebek's best efforts, that program was one of several well-honed games that became short-lived shows created or produced by Jay Wolpert.

Wolpert was the 1969 Tournament of Champions winner on the original *Jeopardy!* before becoming one of the brightest and most creative minds in the game show industry. Although he enjoyed great success and left a legacy as one of the premier architects and producers of the 1972 revival of *The Price is Right*, and contributed to the development of *Match Game, Card Sharks,* and *Family Feud,* other programs Wolpert originated as an independent producer didn't fare as well. Although always expertly crafted, a number of Wolpert concepts were considered by some to be "too smart" for the genre. Like so many game show formats, program development executives periodically reconsider the *Double Dare* concept for new adaptations or revivals.

The staging for Wolpert's *Double Dare* was awkward. Two contestants in sound-proofed and view-proofed booths were challenged one at a time to identify people, places, or things from an increasing list of clues. The winner's attempt in the bonus round was impeded by a hallmark of Jay Wolpert's shows, "spoilers" or "blocks," as featured on his *Hit Man* for NBC and *Whew!* for CBS, as well as *Faker's Fortune* and other un-aired program concepts he developed.

The Bronx-born Wolpert went on to appear as an actor in a couple of motion pictures — *I Love Trouble* starring Nick Nolte and Julia Roberts, and *Father of the Bride Part II* with Steve Martin and Dianne Keaton. Wolpert ultimately found movies to be an apt outlet for his creativity. His greatest success and financial rewards came as screenwriter for Walt Disney Pictures' *The Count of Monte Cristo* and the trilogy of *Pirates of the Caribbean* motion pictures.

Chester Feldman created and Mark's son, Jonathan Goodson, produced *Card Sharks.* Johnny announced both 1978 pilots and a number of the NBC episodes for that adaptation of the ancient card game variably known as "Acey-Deucy" or "Pisha-Paysha." Contestants answered survey questions reminiscent of *Family Feud* for the opportunity to predict whether unrevealed playing cards would be higher or lower than the preceding card. It was an engaging format that enjoyed two different three-year runs in both network daytime and syndicated versions.

As the most reliable voice and warm-up performer in game shows, Johnny was the obvious choice to substitute for fellow announcer Gene Wood on another revival of a classic, *Password Plus,* which hit the air in January, 1979. Taped at NBC's studios in Burbank, as the name implied, *Password Plus* was an update of the original 1960s Bob Stewart creation. After twenty years with a show with which he was closely associated, that was the final incarnation of *Password* that Allen Ludden hosted before he succumbed to stomach cancer in June 1981.

In that popular word game, contestants were paired with celebrity players with the challenge of using one-word clues to communicate a password to their partners. As always, game play alternated between the two teams until one team was successful in guessing the word. In that updated version, a game-within-a-game was added wherein each password in a series of five was, in itself, a clue to the answer of a puzzle about a person, place, or thing. Contestants who solved the puzzles advanced with their celebrity partner to a timed bonus round with the goal of discerning ten words in sixty seconds.

Indicative of the nature of the small community of game show specialists, Howard Felsher, a former Barry & Enright staffer, Goodson-Todman team member, and controversial figure from the quiz show scandals, was Executive Producer of *Password Plus*, and *I've Got A Secret* creator Allan Sherman's son Bobby was Producer. The show's set designer, Bente Christensen, continues to this day in her domain with *The Price is Right*.

Starting in August of 1979, in an era of renewed interest in astrology and the birth of the so-called "new age movement," Johnny again joined forces with producer Ira Skutch to announce *Mindreaders*. Dick Martin of *Rowan and Martin's Laugh-In* fame was the capable and affable host for the program that ran for only five months on NBC. *Mindreaders* was based on experiments with ESP, and featured two teams, each composed of four players of the same sex, headed by a celebrity who tried to guess responses to questions given by the members of his team. The team members would then guess the responses of studio audience members before having the chance to discern answers given by their celebrity teammate.

Another new game from Goodson-Todman debuted in 1980. America's most prolific host, Bill Cullen, entered his fifth decade on television with *Blockbusters*, co-created by puzzle-meister Steve Ryan. The game was played using a five by four grid of hexagons, each designated by a letter that was the first letter of the answer to a question. With each correct answer, a player or team of two players captured one of the hexagons as they tried to string together sufficient hexagons to traverse the grid horizontally or vertically. Thirty-six years after being hired at NBC in New York, Johnny made the trip over the hills that separated Hollywood from the San Fernando valley to the network's Burbank facility to serve as substitute announcer with Cullen, one of his oldest friends in the business.

Johnny continued his association with Bob Barker on 1981's *That's My Line*, a non-game, prime-time show that highlighted unusual occupations. Johnny's work on that early experiment with what later came to be known as "reality TV" was followed two years later by three specials entitled *Life's Most Embarrassing Moments*. Johnny was back with old friends, when he announced those one-hour compilations of outtakes and goofs. Steve Allen served as host, and Johnny's old pal Bert Parks was among the celebrity guests.

Goodson-Todman then raided its vaults for *Television's Funniest Game Show Moments*, which Johnny voiced in 1984. Although the program failed to foster an ongoing series at the time, it was a forerunner of a slew of "clip shows" over the subsequent decades that inexpensively and effectively boosted ratings, especially for the FOX and NBC networks.

In Los Angeles, as he had in New York, Johnny packed as much work as he could into his weeks, and he maintained a level of physical energy that belied his age. When asked about maintaining that boundless enthusiasm, he often offered an explanation along the lines of this response from a videotaped interview. "When I leave that dressing room, I turn it on. When I cross that threshold, to me it's opening night on Broadway." It appeared to all that his energetic presence was derived from his sincere love of performing. His claim that he hadn't missed a performance since

1948 was never challenged, despite the fact that he was regularly working as many as six series simultaneously. His workload far surpassed any announcer not serving on staff for a station or network.

With what spare time he might have enjoyed, Johnny was happy to add his voice to other shows when asked. He was featured on episodes of three CBS sitcoms, *Archie Bunker's Place, Maude,* and *WKRP in Cincinnati.* On the November 8, 1976 episode of a spin-off from *All in The Family,* Johnny provided the voice of the announcer on a fictional game show when Maude and friend Vivian appear on *Beat The Devil.*

On a November, 1980 episode of the sitcom about life at an Ohio radio station, WKRP's salesman Herb Tarlek was exposed as the head of a dysfunctional household when his clan appeared on the fictional reality show, *Real Familes,* hosted by *Hollywood Squares'* Peter Marshall and announced by Johnny. Johnny's signature style was instantly recognizable when he intoned, "From Hollywood, California, look out, because it's time for the new show all of America's talking about...." Unfortunately, because of the cost and the logistics involved in re-licensing the music originally used in the series, Johnny's voice was removed from that episode when reruns of *WKRP in Cincinnati* were syndicated in the 1990s.

In 1983 and 1984, Johnny was again tapped to fill-in for colleague Gene Wood and temporarily team once more with Gene Rayburn as the voice of *The Match Game-Hollywood Squares Hour.* This short-lived conglomeration of two hits failed to gel as a single offering, despite featuring notable guest stars. Co-host Rayburn recalled that program was the assignment he liked least during his long career, in part because of his having to share the emcee duties with a performer with whom he failed to develop any on-air rapport. John "Bowzer" Bauman, a former member of the singing group Sha Na Na, hosted the *Hollywood Squares* portion of the show during which Rayburn participated among the other celebrity players.

For two of his last series, Johnny was paired with a relative of two of his old colleagues. Affable broadcaster Tom Kennedy was the brother of host Jack Narz and brother-in-law of Bill Cullen. While Kennedy first met Johnny when he was a celebrity guest on *Match Game* in 1964, he had heard his work many times before, even as a youngster. Like Bob Barker's mother, Kennedy's mom had been a fan. He remembered, "My mother used to listen to *Ladies Be Seated*... and it just didn't register with me that this was the guy who was entertaining my mother decades before I met him." [38-3]

Kennedy's *Body Language* debuted on June 4, 1984, and was in production sharing CBS Television City's Studio 33 with *The Price is Right,* at the time of Johnny's death. A variety of charades, the classic party pastime, had been among the very first games on television, and in 1948 as *Pantomime Quiz,* was the first television show to win an Emmy award. Tom Kennedy hosted the 1984 version in which each word communicated by pantomime filled in a blank in a sentence that identified a person, place, or thing. Johnny opened *Body Language* episodes with the explanation, "It's a game for the uninhibited" on which celebrities let their "bodies do the talking." Television's first lady of physical comedy, Lucille Ball was an occasional guest.

On *Body Language* Johnny was working with old friends Chester Feldman from *I've Got A Secret* and director Paul Alter from *To Tell The Truth,* colleagues whom he had known since the 1950s, and members of the game show community that he considered family.

In the summer of 1985, Johnny was teamed with Tom Kennedy for another syndicated season of *The Price is Right* to consist of 170 episodes scheduled to air between September 9, 1985 and May 30, 1986, with repeats continuing until September 5. Kennedy remembered his concern about stepping into Bob Barker's big shoes. He told David Hammett, a mathematics and probability consultant to the game show industry, "I was privileged to be asked to do it; the show is a classic, beautiful...it made me appreciate Bob Barker's job. I had to learn 45-50 games; it doesn't sound like much until you try to remember your marks, cues, etc." [38-4] Johnny was comfortable and confident with the assignment that, sadly, he never completed. Tom Kennedy remembers being shocked when he received a call notifying him that Johnny, a man he said he "loved to pieces," had passed away. [38-3]

Even at the age of seventy-five, Johnny had not slowed down. He had shied away from retirement thirteen years earlier, choosing to continue the work he loved, and had he lived past 1985, the opportunity would have been his to remain fully employed. *Body Language* continued on CBS' schedule until the following January, and *The Price is Right* was an unstoppable hit in both daytime and primetime syndication. In 1985, Goodson was reportedly in the process of planning new syndicated versions of shows to which Johnny was inextricably linked, including a return of *Match Game* with Gene Rayburn for the following year.

America's premier television game show announcer was silenced on October 12, 1985. Philosopher George Santayana mused, "There is no cure for birth and death, save to enjoy the interval." By all accounts, Johnny did.

CHAPTER 39
SIGN OFF

In 1968, while jotting notes for a planned autobiography that he never completed, Johnny recalled that his sole source of encouragement in the earliest years of his radio work came from the only other performer in his family, his sister Pearl. She was a pianist, who toured in vaudeville, and Johnny noted that her premature passing was most likely the result of her work schedule. While entertaining in traveling Chautauqua tent shows that trekked through rural America, Pearl had contracted tuberculosis, known at that time as "the white plague." For the last years of her life, Pearl moved to the warmer climate of San Antonio, Texas, before losing her battle against the disease at the young age of thirty-five. Johnny noted, "She toured on the Chautauqua circuit where I think she more or less worked herself to death."

That was an ironic comment considering that many friends and colleagues hypothesize that Johnny's own hectic schedule of working during the bulk of the week in Los Angeles, flying cross-country to Miami for the Gleason show on Fridays, and/or to West Virginia for precious hours with Penny, and then returning to Los Angeles Sunday nights, contributed to his demise. Such was his schedule during his final week of work at the age of seventy-five.

Following his last taping of *The Price is Right* on Wednesday, October 2nd, 1985, Johnny drove directly to the Los Angeles International airport. From there, he flew to West Virginia for the weekend. It was a tedious journey because there were no direct flights, and he would not arrive until the following morning. Upon returning to the Los Angeles airport on Sunday evening, October 6, Johnny apparently felt ill. The director of *The Price is Right*, Marc Breslow conjectured for the press, "He must have figured something was wrong after he got in his car."

From the variation in his usual route, it was surmised that Johnny attempted to drive himself from the airport to St. John's Hospital in Santa Monica, but he never completed the ten-mile trip. Johnny was reportedly found hours later at the side of the road. He was unconscious and slumped over the steering wheel of his car. From there, he was transported to St. John's emergency room.

The following morning, Monday, October 7, fifteen minutes into readying Studio 33 for another week of taping, a shocked crew was given the news of Johnny's condition. *The Price is Right* did not tape that week. St. John's nursing supervisor Maureen Freudider confirmed for the Associated Press that Johnny died six days after his hospitalization, on Saturday, October 12, of a cerebral hemorrhage. Penny had flown to

Los Angeles and was at his bedside when he passed away. Breslow said, "He never regained consciousness," and he confirmed that Penny was in Los Angeles arranging for a cremation on the day after the death of her husband of forty-six years. There was no memorial service in Los Angeles.

Model Holly Hallstrom's voice cracked with sadness twenty-four years later: "We never got to say 'goodbye.' We never got to talk about how wonderful he was and how much we loved him, and what he had meant to each of us individually, and the special little Johnny stories. Johnny always, always, always made me understand that we...had been given a gift. When I was looking into that camera, I was looking at people in possibly the worst of places or the worst of situations or the worst of times. And I was looking right at them and I was thanking them for giving me this opportunity. And I was wanting them to feel how happy they made me." [39-1]

Marc Breslow told UPI, "There isn't a single person at CBS who didn't love Johnny Olson. He never missed a show in fourteen years...doing *The Price is Right* was the most fun he had, and he did his job better than anybody."

Newspapers from coast to coast carried the news of the silencing of a favorite television voice. Old fans from Johnny's days at WTMJ read of his passing the following morning in the Sunday *Milwaukee Journal,* in which Mark Goodson was quoted as saying that his faithful announcer "can never be replaced."

Bob Barker recorded a touching tribute to his friend that aired with a subsequent episode on October 29. Johnny's last recorded show aired on November 8, 1985. The timing was ironic because only two months earlier, The Academy of Television Arts and Sciences saluted Johnny at the Daytime Emmy awards banquet for his extensive career that included forty years in television. Johnny was spry and energetic that evening, as he sprinted to the stage to accept the award from Barker. Johnny then joked about working on *The Price is Right* for another forty years.

Frank Wayne, Goodson-Todman's senior seignior, said the company was shocked by his colleague's death. He recalled having to review previous episodes of *The Price is Right* to transcribe transitional phrases Johnny had been ad-libbing for the past thirteen years. Until a permanent replacement could be found, *The Price is Right,* as well as Johnny's other programs, continued with substitute announcers, including Gene Wood, Bob Hilton, and stand-in-turned-announcer, Rich Jeffries, all from the Goodson-Todman stable.

The company faced the prospect of trying to fill Johnny's huge shoes on America's most popular daytime game show. After on-air tryouts, the consensus among those involved in the process was that Gene Wood's voice was not right for the program, and Rich Jeffries' performance was sub-par. It was agreed that Bob Hilton brought an excitement and youthful energy to the show. Bob Boden recounted that Hilton, a former actor and game show host, was the leading contender until Bob Barker expressed displeasure in having someone that young and telegenic, who could be considered a potential replacement, in the role of second banana.

When none of the announcers who filled-in proved to be a suitable fit, and other names that were raised were shot down, CBS executive Barbara Hunter had an inspiration. Hunter had been a producer on *The Price is Right,* working with Jay Wolpert,

Roger Dobkowitz, and Phil Wayne on the Studio 33 stage before ascending to a network programming post to work with daytime chief Mike Brockman. She knew firsthand the rigors of the job that needed to be filled. Barbara Hunter played a VHS reference tape of another CBS game show featuring an announcer not previously considered as Johnny's replacement. Hunter recalled, "I was the CBS executive on *Press Your Luck* and thought that Rod would be great as the new announcer." [39-2]

Rod Roddy proved to be a great choice to carry on *The Price is Right* tradition following Johnny's death in 1985. Rod had the announcing and warm-up skills necessary for the demanding program.

It was a moment that proved to be fortuitous for a former radio personality, Robert "Rod" Roddy, who was given a successful on-air audition. Barbara Hunter continued, "I would have him up to the office to watch and listen to Johnny's tapes." [39-2] The prevailing opinion was that his style was compatible with the sound Johnny had created for the show, and that his appearance was that of a character performer, rather than a leading man, who might draw attention from the program's host.

Roddy was offered the opportunity of his career. Instead of immediately accepting the job to announce television's number one network game show, he hired an attorney to negotiate a contract that included a starting salary more than double the AFTRA minimum scale and provided for regular pay increases for as long as he remained with the program.

Bob Boden was a member of the CBS programming team and participated in the search for Johnny's replacement. He recalled, "The Goodson organization wanted somebody who would get in there, be great and work for scale, because that's what

Johnny did. But by the time we got to the end of the casting process, Rod had risen to the top and Barker was in his court. And that's when the discussion took place that if we want this guy we've got to pay him the market rate and not scale." [39-3]

Game show announcing was a second career for Rod Roddy, a Texan who had built an impressive resume as a major market radio personality at Dallas' legendary KLIF, and Buffalo's WKBW, among other stations. Rod was inspired by a friend's success in New York's commercial voice community. In the mid-1970s, he departed for Los Angeles to try his hand with voice-overs. He barely made ends meet, and only worked occasionally on spots for Pennzoil, Pillsbury, Kal Kan, and Kitty Litter. He was also on-camera, dressed as a jockey, in a humorous pitch for a Texas-based chain of muffler repair shops. Then, an unexpected break involving Casey Kasem, a legendary voice talent, brought Rod a network commitment.

As a youngster in the Midwest, Kasem performed on *The Lone Ranger*, the popular Mutual Radio Network show. His versatility behind the microphone led to a long, prolific career. As a radio disc-jockey he was best-known for hosting *American Top-40*, and as an animation voice actor he gave life to numerous characters, including Shaggy from *Scooby-Doo*. Kasem auditioned and won the narrator role on *Soap*, the controversial ABC-TV situation-comedy. *Soap* dealt with adult themes including sexual promiscuity, adultery, interracial marriage, and sexual impotence. The program also featured Billy Crystal portraying American television's first openly gay lead character in a sitcom, Jodie Dallas.

Following a *Newsweek* review panning the show and criticizing its subject matter, a number of prominent church groups registered their objections. As its September 13, 1977 debut neared, *Soap* became increasingly controversial. Kasem had long been a politically conscious performer known to turn down work that he found contrary to his beliefs, and he bowed out. It left Kasem's agent, Don Pitts, in a lurch, until he was able to sell Rod Roddy as a last minute replacement.

Roddy's ability to emulate Kasem's style brought him his first big break with a network program, along with the credibility and professional profile that led to additional opportunities. Subsequent work with Producer Jay Wolpert on game shows *Whew!* and *Hit Man*, plus *Battlestars*, *Press Your Luck*, *Dream House*, and *Love Connection* gave Rod experience with audience warm-ups and helped him develop the unique skills required for delivering the fast-paced product descriptions on *The Price is Right*.

With Barbara Hunter's guidance, Roddy refined a style compatible with Johnny's legacy, and a persona well-suited for the celebrated show. Rod made the job his own and enjoyed a long run on *Price* until after the digestive tract discomfort and weakness he was experiencing was diagnosed as colon cancer. The discovery was made following a hospital emergency room visit for a fall suffered at L.A. Studios, one of Hollywood's premiere commercial recording facilities. Rod was told his condition was extremely serious and that immediate surgery was imperative to remove tumor tissue. With the first of several surgeries performed on September 11, 2001, Rod fought long and hard until his death two years later, on October 27th.

There was bittersweet joy when I was hired by Bob Barker, Syd Vinnedge, and Roger Dobkowitz to fill-in for my ailing friend on *The Price is Right*. Burton

Richardson, a long-time member of the Fremantle family and fellow announcer, alternated with me at Johnny and Rod's old podium. After Rod discouraged me from visiting him at his Century City hospital room I was concerned that he had interpreted my role as an act of disloyalty. I was uncertain about continuing as his temporary replacement.

I sought the advice of two of Rod's oldest friends, one in New York, the other in Florida. Both adamantly reassured me that there was nothing disrespectful or parasitic in substituting for our mutual friend. They reminded me that Rod had gotten the job himself after his predecessor's illness. They conjectured that he might ultimately find solace in the fact that fill-in duty was assumed by a friend, who would gladly relinquish the position if and when his health returned. Sadly, that never happened. Roddy died at 3:45 p.m. on October 27, 2003.

Rod was interned at Greenwood Memorial Park in Fort Worth on November 1, 2003, following a memorial service officiated by Susan Stafford. The original letter-turner on *Wheel of Fortune* and Roddy had been dear friends going back to his days at Texas' KLIF radio. Susan had been married to the station's owner, radio legend Gordon McLendon, had subsequently earned a doctorate in clinical psychology, and became an ordained minister.

Burton Richardson and I sat together, directly behind Bob Barker and Roger Dobkowitz and near the coveted announcer's podium, at a well-attended, touching private memorial held on the CBS Studio 33 stage. As he had with the staff and crew at Television City, Rod had developed a loyal following among viewers. He relished his camera time when appearing, as Johnny had, in the program's showcases. Rod was a dedicated pro throughout his years on Price, and had performed valiantly through the pain and weakness of his illness, checking out of the hospital as often as possible to return to the stage for tapings during his final months. The loss of the show's second announcer was a blow, and it naturally generated reflections and comparisons. Those who had worked over the years with Johnny sorely missed him. After his familiar and familial relationship with the crew, Rod or any other performer could only be perceived by some crew members as a bit aloof.

CHAPTER 40
THE END GAME

Johnny's fifty-eight-year presence on radio and television was not only the measure of a successful career, it allowed the man behind the talents to achieve a certain level of immortality through the memories of those who enjoyed his work. A generation of Americans heard his voice regularly for the better part of their lives. While few knew the man, and most likely never even knew his name, John's occasional, brief, and familiar presence in their homes was always associated with moments of entertainment and joy.

Johnny was never as interested in fame or wealth as much as he was motivated by the warm feelings of acceptance, appreciation, fellowship, and gratitude that was behind the smiles of those who found humor or simply derived a sense of human connection from their in-person interaction with him. The inner joy that Johnny derived from the cumulative impact of those moments of laughter from the millions of strangers he briefly befriended was undoubtedly the source of his endless energy. No other explanation can illuminate the source of the enthusiasm Johnny brought to the four, five, six, or even seven performances per day, for the four, five, six, or even seven days per week of work, for such an extended period of years.

So many of the programs on which Johnny worked endured through the decades, a number of them over multiple runs and revivals. They are testaments to the Mark Goodson-Bill Todman producing team's ability to fabricate flawless formats and its sharp eye for execution and presentation. Goodson's intuitive sense of what made a successful show work in terms of the refinement of the game, its functional staging, as well as its pacing were pivotal to the longevity of the company and the programs it produced.

By the time of Johnny's death in 1985, the basic games had been on television for so many years that many had become thoroughly familiar parts of the culture — the television equivalent of comfort food. Goodson's team was often on the mark in knowing just how far to tweak to accommodate for the changing times. Certainly the *Price is Right* and *Match Game* adaptations of the 1970s were prime examples of striking the right balance between exploiting the familiarity of a classic and presenting a fresh product in step with contemporary tastes. Johnny's style seemed to reflect that same balance between comfortable tradition and modern stylishness. Perhaps the sound of genuine enthusiasm was, and is, simply timeless.

Goodson's personal attention to detail was evidenced by his collection of various bells, chimes, and gongs, and the hours spent experimenting with microphone placements to create the sounds that have since become standard for indicating correct and incorrect answers. The producer looked to innovate with electronic scoring displays, neon, and rotating set pieces. Led by Ted Cooper, Goodson's in-house art department created detailed miniature models of the sets for each show so that every aspect of appearance and staging was refined before blueprints and specifications for the actual set, scenery, and electronics were drafted. Dick DeBartolo remembered Goodson lavishing attention on every minute detail of the set when a show was first being staged. DeBartolo recalled that on NBC's *The Match Game,* the producer was almost obsessed with the way the folded question cards popped into view as they emerged from being pushed, clipped to a stick, through a small tunnel.

For one of that show's sound effects, an electric cash register was dismembered to allow for a microphone to be placed near its motor. DeBartolo said, "Goodson was all over a show the first couple of months…he was into everything." [40-1] At the time of his death, the queen of television panelists, Kitty Carlisle Hart, said that the producer's strength was the cleverness he used to devise a game and the meticulous care he took with every element of its production; "He had infinite attention to detail." [40-2]

A few years after Bill Todman's death in 1979, Goodson purchased his former partner's share of the company. In 1982, the enterprise was renamed Mark Goodson Productions. The announcers' signature sign-off that had been heard on broadcasts almost daily for some thirty-five years, "This has been a Mark Goodson – Bill Todman Production" was changed. The new wording was purposely designed to maintain much of the same spoken rhythm and to include a brief silence to mark the passing of its co-founder. The scripts read, "This has been a Mark Goodson (pause) Television Production."

The company continued to set new records for ratings and revenues. The Los Angeles offices were moved from 6430 Sunset Boulevard in a declining Hollywood neighborhood to a new up-scale office complex built at the former site of a large church on Wilshire Boulevard, in the heart of Los Angeles' Miracle Mile District. However, Goodson's long reign was destined to end. On December 18, 1992, at age seventy-seven, the undisputed king of American game shows fell to pancreatic cancer.

Jonathan Goodson had joined his father's company in 1973 as legal counsel, and he had proven himself an able producer and executive. He succeeded his father as President and CEO, while Bill Todman's brother, Howard, longtime Business Manager for the company, served as Treasurer. However, the dynasty was in its last days as a family business. By 1995, it took on new life as part of what became known as a content provider in the new millennium's global media marketplace, but not before a pen stroke by Jonathan Goodson closed a landmark deal with Sony.

In 1994, tape machines in the basement of CBS Television City were running around the clock for months, as tens of thousands of recorded episodes of Goodson-Todman shows were restored, archived, and dubbed. Shows dating back to 1950 and earlier were unspooled for the first time in decades. Jonathan licensed the Mark Goodson Productions library of past programs to Sony for its new Game Show

Network. It was a multi-million-dollar deal that netted Johnny and dozens of other performers their largest posthumous paychecks.

The USA cable network had exploited the appeal of game shows, programming a daytime block of favorites in the mid 1980s. The idea for a 24-hour game show station was explored by televangelist Pat Robertson for his Family Channel the following decade. Starting in June 1993, *Trivial Pursuit*, and later, *Boggle, Jumble,* and *Shuffle,* four original game shows from Wink Martindale and partner Bill Hillier, attracted an audience and generated income as the first interactive television games. The real-time, play-along component of those game shows utilized a "900" telephone number for home players, an innovation co-created by Martindale, the respected television host, and Hillier, the imaginative producer, who was a direct descendant of one of the fathers of television, inventor Vladimir Zworkin.

Well-known producer Woody Fraser, a veteran responsible for *The Mike Douglas Show,* added two more original shows to the Family Channel weekday schedule. *Wild Animal Games* was one of Ryan Seacrest's first hosting roles, and *Family Challenge* was Ray Combs' final emcee job before his death. Michael Burger ably carried that show's torch as the Family Channel's experiment with games continued.

Reruns of classics were added to the daytime lineup, proving there was a new audience for perennials such as Monty Hall's *Let's Make A Deal* and the ever-popular *Name That Tune.* Robertson was unable to support too many more originals or to contract for sufficient rerun programming to expand beyond the hours of game shows being offered as a Family Channel daytime block.

Sony had already purchased the assets of Merv Griffin Enterprises, including the hits *Wheel of Fortune* and *Jeopardy!* for $250 million. Sony also owned Chuck Barris' properties, including *The Dating Game* and *The Newlywed Game,* as well as the assets of the old Jack Barry-Dan Enright partnership that included *The Joker's Wild.* More pieces of the Game Show Network puzzle came together when former Paramount executive Mel Harris became head of the television division of Sony Pictures Television in 1992. The idea for Sony to capitalize on those holdings by launching its own 24-hour game show channel was the result of collaboration between Harris and Dick Block, a former colleague and consultant for United Video. The Tulsa-based company provided electronic program guides for cable television and handled the satellite distribution for several superstations, including WGN of Chicago, WPIX of New York, and KTLA of Los Angeles.

Bob Boden was hired as an outside consultant to formulate the master plan before joining the network's president Russ Myerson at Game Show Network's new offices in the summer of 1994. There, in a modest brick building across the street from Sony's production facilities in Culver City, the former home of the legendary MGM Studios, GSN launched on December 1, 1994.

Sony's intent was to form a three-way equity partnership with Mark Goodson Productions and United Video. Jonathan Goodson told *Broadcasting and Cable* magazine that his family's interests would be better served by licensing exhibition of the vast library, and only a few months before Game Show Network's launch the deal was restructured. The new agreement still gave Sony's access to the mother lode of product — close to 35,000 episodes of the classics that Goodson-Todman had stock-piled over the decades. Sony further fortified its game show holdings by purchasing the fruits of Bob Stewart's post Goodson-Todman labors.

As a result, iconic programs such as *Tic Tac Dough,* and *The $10,000 Pyramid* with its subsequent incarnations shared a home on the Game Show Network with *What's My Line? To Tell The Truth, I've Got A Secret,* and other Goodson classics. Suddenly, by satellite, Johnny's voice was re-launched multiple times a day, much as it had been during the years when he shuttled between CBS, NBC, ABC, and DuMont.

In 1996, Dan Sullivan, Manager of Videotape Technical Operations at CBS Television City, remembered the preparation necessary to launch Sony's new network. "CBS entered into a contract with Mark Goodson Productions to transfer their entire library of approximately 34,000 programs from their current formats, which consisted of 16-mm kinescopes, two-inch and one-inch videotape, to serial digital betacam format. We worked around the clock, seven days a week, for fifteen months...34,637 shows were transferred. Approximately 2,700 of these programs originated on kinescope." [40-3]

The Goodson family did not retain ownership of those videotapes for long. Three years after Mark Goodson's death, his family sold the rights to the collection of game show formats and the vast library of taped and filmed shows. It was the beginning of a litany of deals that crossed the Goodson-Todman legacy with such unlikely names as Weird Al Yankovic, Pamela Anderson, and former competing producer Reg Grundy.

In a way, Johnny's legacy had come full circle, back to the world of music and radio, as the Goodson-Todman assets passed to the hands of recording company executives well-known in the synergistic radio and record industries. The Scotti Brothers was an entity to be reckoned with in those businesses. Ben and Tony Scotti's record label controlled the output of artists as diverse as Electric Light Orchestra, Sarah Vaughn, James Brown, and Weird Al Yankovic. Radio station programmers knew the Scotti Brothers well from their aggressive promotion of the careers of entertainers as varied as Dolly Parton and teen idols Sean Cassidy and Leif Garrett.

The Scotti Brothers ventured into television in 1979, initially with the weekly *America's Top Ten* starring radio countdown guru Casey Kasem. Combining forces with entertainment executive Joseph E. Kovacs, television distributor George Back, and advertising veteran and production CEO Syd Vinnedge, the new enterprise grew under the banner All American Television. A comedy special starring newcomer Roseanne Barr, and the NBC game show *Wordplay* were other early endeavors for the new entity. Thanks to a discerning eye and shrewd instincts, the tiny company soon ranked as the 15th largest firm in the US motion picture and video production industry, not too far behind behemoths Sony, Disney, Time Warner, and Universal.

Unhappy with the ratings of a new prime-time soap opera set on the beaches of Southern California, in 1990 NBC cancelled *Baywatch* after a single season. With a finger on the pulse of pop culture, All American Television sensed the potential international appeal of the show and purchased the rights as well as the twenty-three episodes already produced for NBC. As Syd Vinnedge recounted for the press years later, "The [*Baywatch*] property was recognizable and distinctive, whether you liked it or not... There was a buzz about it and we built on that." [40-4]

The company raised $10 million by pre-selling international broadcasting rights and used that capital to produce additional episodes that fueled a worldwide frenzy for the fantasy lifestyle embodied by the image of Pamela Anderson running in slow motion on the sandy beach at Santa Monica. It was a steroid-and-silicone-enhanced version of the cultural phenomenon popularized by Annette Funicello, Frankie Avalon, and Gidget that had sparked the imagination of a previous generation just a few miles up the Pacific Coast Highway at Surfrider, Leo Carillo, and Point Dume Beaches in Malibu.

Awash in a tsunami of profits, All American Television expanded its holdings with a $25 million purchase of 50 percent of Mark Goodson Productions in 1995. In 1996, All American Television paid Interpublic Group, a consortium with extensive holdings in the world of advertising, the remaining $25 million for the other half of the Goodson assets that the Group acquired the previous year. The deal included additional substantial payments for a percentage of the profits from the ongoing deal with CBS for the jewel in the Goodson-Todman crown, *The Price is Right*.

An October, 1996 filing with the Securities and Exchange Commission confirmed that All American Television had total control of the over forty Goodson-Todman game show formats that are listed as an appendix in this book, as well as the library of more than 30,000 recorded episodes. [40-5] Ben Scotti told the press, "The Goodson acquisition is an important element in our strategic plan to produce and distribute programming for every country in the world." [40-4] Veteran producer Bob Noah, who had worked with producers Barry and Enright, as well as the team of Merrill Heatter and Bob Quigley before his long tenure at Goodson-Todman, was retained to help All American Television exploit its new assets.

The game continued on the international playing field. In 1997, All American Television, the company named for Tony Scotti's success as a football hero during his high school days, was acquired by Pearson P.L.C., the British media conglomerate that owned The Financial Times, Penguin Books, Reg Grundy Productions, and Madame Tussaud's Wax Museum. At $373 million in cash and the assumption of $136 million in debt, for the Scottis, Syd Vinnedge, George Back, Joseph Kovacs, and the others who joined in the venture in the few short years, the price was right.

The Goodson-Todman legacy transferred one last time in 2001, when Pearson was acquired by RTL Group's British subsidiary FremantleMedia RTL. An outgrowth of Radio Television Luxemburg, it was Europe's largest television, radio and production company. Majority-owned by German media conglomerate Bertelsmann, RTL's FremantleMedia was one of the most successful entities in global broadcasting, owning television, and radio stations throughout Europe, as well as formats including *Pop Idol*, the hit British talent contest that spurred *American Idol* in the USA and Fremantle's equivalent in a dozen other countries. That star-making competition became a planet-wide franchise that was beyond the comprehension of the creator of *The Original Amateur Hour*, Major Bowes.

As Executive Producer, Syd Vinnedge continued to guide the American version of *The Price is Right* on CBS. Through FremantleMedia's international licensing agreements, Bob Stewart's original creation and the other Goodson-Todman formats that brought Johnny his greatest fame, survive on the airwaves.

CHAPTER 41
EPILOGUE

When totaled, Johnny lent his voice to more than two dozen series as a Goodson-Todman employee for a quarter century. More than one senior executive with the company recalled that in all that time, Johnny never negotiated for money. Apparently his richest reward was being in and around the business that he loved. He told one author, "I'm never more alive than when the lights are up, the audience is hot, the music starts and I say 'here's the star of our show...'"

Paper trails bear out the informal nature of his long relationship with Goodson-Todman Productions. On July 21, 1975, Jonathan Goodson wrote a letter that included the following excerpts:

"Dear Johnny: Although you have long been the announcer on *Match Game* and *The Price is Right*, we do not yet have a written agreement with you."

Then seeking to set the record straight, the company put forth this simple confirmation, "...it will then be understood that you have been rendering services for us under the terms of this form contract...and that future services will be under this contract until either of us informs the other to the contrary."

A similar agreement dated October 30, 1975, specified the same terms for the daytime and nighttime runs of *The Price is Right*, the daytime and nighttime runs of *Match Game*, and *Concentration*.

The simple, one-page agreements that Johnny signed did little more than merely reflect the AFTRA union terms under which all television and radio performers work. It also provided for a simple, ten-day notice by either party to alter compensation or to end the relationship that ultimately spanned four decades. That unusual arrangement between a major production company and talent spoke volumes about the parties' character, priorities, and trust.

The letter also served to confirm what many inside and outside of the business have found incongruous — that the man universally respected as the best announcer and best warm-up performer in television, after decades of building a reputation for excellence and working on the most-celebrated programs in the genre, was not represented by a talent agent. In addition, he worked at the peak of his career for the union-mandated minimum scale salary.

That fact can best be interpreted as a testament to Johnny's love of the work, and may also offer insight into his lack of ego. As Bob Boden observed, "I think the fact that Johnny worked for scale was a combination of factors. Among them, he never asked for more and was never offered more."[41-1] Roger Dobkowitz reported, "Johnny was proud that he was never out of work. He said that not a week ever went by during which he wasn't on the air. I think this ties in to the fact that he worked for scale. It was a way to guarantee that he would always work."[41-2]

His enjoyment of people and the talent that he called "making good talk" was obvious in the time Johnny took to chat with tourists and audience members. The late Jay Stewart, long-time network voice and the announcer on *Let's Make A Deal*, first met Johnny on a bitterly cold winter day when they were both working at NBC-TV in New York's Rockefeller Center. Jay recounted with amazement that, as he was darting from a cab into a side entrance of the RCA building, he paused long enough to see Johnny wrapped in scarf and gloves and doing something he often did: he was walking and talking along the line of people on West 50th Street, people who were waiting to come in from the cold to see a taping. Jay said he was astounded, "It's freezing cold, and Johnny's outside doing warm-up before they're even in the studio!"[41-3]

Years later, Jay saw Johnny again. That time, they passed in the lobby of the building at 1155 North La Cienega Boulevard in West Hollywood, where each coincidentally maintained an apartment for a time. Jay remembered, "Johnny was almost jogging. He had one of his polyester pairs of pants and a jacket over his arm, and said he was running to CBS."[41-3]

In addition to his more visible work, Johnny was always active in community service and was a dedicated supporter of charitable causes. The legacy of his involvement in over 2,000 blood drives, polio fund raisers, war bond rallies, and appearances at goodwill functions of every stripe brought aid and comfort to countless Americans in need.

In late 1943, there was an all-school bond drive and rally to buy Corsair aircraft for the US Navy. The Wauwatosa High School in the Milwaukee suburb of Wauwatosa, Wisconsin, needed $137,000 in bond sales to rate the privilege of an aircraft being christened off the assembly line with the name "Spirit of Tosa" painted on its cowl. Two seniors, Fred Seegert and Jim Sweitzer, produced the day-long rally that featured music, skits and variety acts. The Wauwatosa High School auditorium was packed, with front row seats for the fundraiser reserved for purchasers of $1,000 war bonds. Johnny was there, broadcasting his local WTMJ "Johnny Olson's Rumpus Room," and was considered a major draw that added to the event's success. Also, on the home front during World War II, Johnny and Penny adopted a French war orphan through the Foster Parents Plan for War Children.

On January 19, 1953, Johnny fronted another of the many non-broadcast fundraisers he graciously hosted during his career. Staged at the RKO Dyker Theater in Brooklyn, this one likely had special meaning for the second-generation American of Norse ancestry. It benefited the Norwegian Hospital Building Fund. Among the many facilities to reap the rewards was the Hillsboro Medical Center, which opened its new hospital in Hillsboro, North Dakota, later that year.

Johnny worked with Jerry Lewis during the earliest days of his fundraisers for the Muscular Dystrophy Association when the telethons were local News York affairs broadcast on DuMont's WABD. Johnny continued as the announcer for the five years starting in 1966 when the program first became a Labor Day weekend institution, and while Lewis' "Love Network" of over 100 stations first spread the goodwill coast-to-coast.

After his move to Los Angeles, each year Johnny was found introducing celebrities and reading pledges at The United Cerebral Palsy annual fundraiser that broadcast from those ABC-TV studios on Prospect Avenue, where years earlier, he had renewed his acquaintance with Lawrence Welk.

In the vein of giving back to his industry, with old cronies Hugh Downs and Arlene Francis, Johnny founded and served on the Board of Governors of the Institute of Broadcast Arts. A school chartered in 1968 to train developing broadcasters, the Institute operated at local broadcast stations in Chicago, Milwaukee and other cities in seven states, offering courses taught by working professionals.

Johnny's occasional on-air partner, Steve Allen, made mention of the announcer's many extra-curricular charitable activities. During a 1980 appearance on David Letterman's NBC show, Allen joked that Johnny "is now working in Los Angeles with the ASPCA. Whenever there's a cat stuck up in a tree, he yells, 'Come on down!'"

Johnny was survived by only one of his ten siblings, Richard, his older brother in South Dakota. Of course, most distressed by Johnny's passing was Penny. The love of Johnny's life continued to live for the next fourteen years in the childless couple's spacious retirement home in the lavish Buckingham Acres development in Greenbrier County, West Virginia. Although Johnny was cremated in Los Angeles, his ashes rest in Lewisburg, a sleepy, picturesque community of 3,000, located approximately fifty miles Northwest of Roanoke along the Seneca Trail. Lewisburg comes alive each August to host the West Virginia State Fair, an event Johnny attended annually.

Roger Dobkowitz was a guest at the retirement home that Johnny and Penny rarely got to enjoy together. He recalled it was a large, single-story, ranch-style estate with an exterior that reflected the colonial style so popular in the region. Their home was set on sufficient acreage to assure that no neighbors were visible. The interior was lavish yet tastefully appointed with white carpeting and antique furniture that included numerous display cases and armoires with elegant, collectibles and art objects.

The Olson home was located just ten miles from The Greenbrier, one of the most regal and most historic resorts in America, and a landmark destination for the rich and famous since opening in 1778. The Greenbrier was Johnny and Penny's favorite for dinners to commemorate special occasions, but the resort also held a secret: it was the location of the United States government's classified Emergency Relocation Center. Between 1959 and 1962, a covert 112,000 square foot underground bunker and bomb shelter was built, and for thirty years was in a constant state of readiness, prepared to house and feed hundreds of dignitaries and their families, and to serve as the emergency location for the legislative branch of Congress in the event of an international crisis. In 1995, the underground bunker was finally closed and its secrets revealed.

While Penny was a well-known and popular member of the community with numerous friends, Johnny's absence left a huge void. Managing the couple's business affairs created one well-documented challenge for Penny that ended up in the West Virginia Supreme Court of Appeals. In 1979, Johnny had invested in a parcel of undeveloped land on US Route 219 near their home. Sixteen years later, looking to liquidate the investment, Penny unwittingly listed the property with two real estate agencies. She accidentally sold the land to two different buyers, a residential real estate developer and a gas station-convenience mart company. Two purchase agreements were dated only nine days apart.

Penny spent months in legal actions. A jury found, and all parties agreed that, from a legal standpoint, at age 83, Penny lacked the understanding and capacity to enter into the conflicting agreements. The case was resolved with both deals being nullified, and Penny losing the significant closing costs incurred at the time she deeded the property to the developer.

Four years later, in 1999, Penny suffered failing health. She called upon Bob Carpenter, her closest family member, to help permanently close her home. The bulk of Johnny's large collection of tapes, kinescopes, photos, and writings were donated for historical preservation, and the remainder of the Olson estate was sold at auction by the DuMouchelles fine arts gallery in Detroit during the second weekend of June, 1999. The large collection of Meissen and Dresden porcelain, Chinese ivory and jade carvings, antique furniture, crystal, furs, and artwork fetched over $100,000 in three days of brisk bidding.

Penelope Kathleen Olson died a year later on August 17, 2000, at the Brier Nursing Home in nearby Ronceverte. Her remains were entrusted to Okey McCraw, Jr. at the McCraw Funeral Home in Lewisburg. Penny's will designated fourteen heirs, including Mrs. Marc Breslow and a stepmother, who each received small sums of money. The balance of her estate was left to Mr. Carpenter.

A Greenbrier County native interviewed in 2008 spoke excitedly of her memories of the Olsons, detailing how she had regularly seen the couple at church, how Johnny treated Penny to dates at the Greenbrier resort, as well as how they were so obviously enamored with one another and Lewisburg. Another acquaintance, a female chauffer who occasionally drove John and Penny Olson to and from special evenings at the Greenbrier, echoed the sentiments of so many who were impressed by Johnny's easy-going, friendly manner: "He was very well spoken, sophisticated, sweet and personable."

CHAPTER 42
IN MEMORIAM

Johnny was eulogized as "America's most heard voice" and "American television's number one announcer." The liner notes from Penny's *Hymns of Hope and Inspiration* indicate that her dear hubby was a spiritual man, having written as many as seventy religious hymns.

Although praise from Mark Goodson did not flow freely during their time together, he marked Johnny's passing with a full-page remembrance in the *Hollywood Reporter:* "All of us who worked at your side for more than 30 rewarding years will never forget your professionalism, your unfailing enthusiasm, your loyal friendship. Thank you, Johnny, for letting us know you."

Two years after Johnny's death, on the occasion of the fifteenth anniversary of *The Price is Right* on CBS, Goodson read a poem he authored honoring the milestone. He posthumously acknowledged Johnny's contributions with the lines, "And I can't let this anniversary end without mention of our dear good friend, Johnny Olson. Who loved the show, the audience, and each and every game. Johnny has a permanent place in our hearts and our *Price is Right* hall of fame."

As Johnny's career was the inspiration for my life's work, I am proud to have given a new home to an attaché case filled with his personal effects, and a collection of his most prized personal mementoes. The attaché was a gift from Goodson and was a dusty home to some of Johnny's treasured trinkets, from jewelry and old photographs to his union cards and his CBS ID badge.

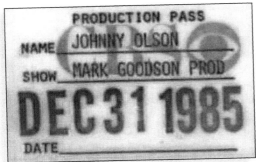

Among Johnny's personal effects saved by Penny was the CBS identification badge he wore while working during the final year of his life.

The most interesting items Johnny saved in that attaché include newspaper and magazine clippings dating back to 1931, a collection of scripts from favorite shows on which he performed, and personal notes. There is the award from the Academy of Television Arts and Sciences honoring his forty years in television and his contribution to *The Price is Right* during what was his final season on the show. There is the microphone that he used during his many years announcing *What's My Line?* in

Above: Fourth Avenue, as it appeared when Johnny was a child. The street was renamed Johnny Olson Boulevard for the Cottonwood County Centennial in 1970. Facing page: Minnesota Congressman and Senator William Windom for whom Johnny's home town of Windom was named.

New York. That RCA 77DX had been mounted with a gold plaque indicating that it was awarded to him by the CBS studio staff at the end of the show's seventeen-year run.

Johnny's random jottings include bits of history of the broadcasting industry from the birth of wireless to the social and political impact of television through the 1960s. In conversation, he reflected on the milestones in the development of wireless broadcasting, from Marconi through historic short wave broadcasts, and to Admiral Richard Byrd and his men at the South Pole to the transmission of voice and picture from the moon.

While he was always respectful of the people who populated the industry he loved, Johnny spoke from his unique vantage point. He had been a constant presence as executives, producers, directors, stars, and even entire networks came and went over the course of his fifty-eight-year tenure during the most vital era in American broadcasting.

Of his own history, Johnny reflected back to his earliest memories of cruelly cold weather and patched clothing. Temperatures fall well below zero in Windom every winter, and he quipped, "When I took Penny there for her first visit after we were married, the mercury fell to 42 degrees below zero in her honor." He was quick to add that, in summer, Windom is a very pleasant place. "I have warm memories of the courthouse in the square, a bandstand adjoining the jail a block away. And no matter how far away from there I've been, I've always subscribed to the local weekly newspaper, the *Cottonwood County Citizen*."

Johnny made heralded returns to his hometown. Even without any names included in the caption, he was easily identifiable in the *Cottonwood County Citizen's* photo of the twenty-fifth reunion of Windom High School's class of 1928. The city rolled out the red carpet on June 6, 1970, for the Cottonwood County Centennial, which honored both Johnny and television star William Windom.

Although the Emmy award-winning actor was born in New York, he was inextricably tied to Johnny's hometown of Windom because the city was named for the actor's great-grandfather, also William Windom, who was a Congressman and later a Senator representing Minnesota, as well as a member of President Lincoln's so-called Kitchen Cabinet. The senior Windom also served as Secretary of the Treasury under both Presidents James Garfield and Benjamin Harrison. For $1 the actor purchased a small island that serves as a wildlife refuge in the city that bears his and his great-grandfather's name.

Following a parade, the city council presented Johnny with a commemorative award and renamed 4th Avenue "Johnny Olson Boulevard" in his honor. It was a celebrated homecoming that meant a great deal to Windom's favorite broadcaster. On that visit for the Cottonwood County Centennial, Johnny renewed his relationships with childhood friends including Glen Peterson, his high school rooftop performing partner. Johnny added, "I was interested through high school in an attractive girl named Evelyn McCullough, recorded by the yearbook as 'fond of fun and merriment, and ever ready with a laugh.' She is married and still lives in Windom."

Reminiscing about his family life as the youngest of ten children, Johnny recalled that all members of his clan were good at working with their hands. He said the Olsons were, "a family of tinkerers, builders and fixers." He proudly claimed that the Olson women could use hammers and saws as well as needles and sewing machines. "The only time I heard my gentle mother use strong language," and Johnny claimed it was only the word "darn," "was when something went wrong with a kitchen cabinet

A selection of Johnny Olson's memorable appearances on *The Price Is Right*.

she was remodeling." He remembered, "With their skills, my older brothers actually built from odd parts our first electric washing machine."

Johnny also wrote of his most colorful career recollections. They include broadcasts from ships, prisons, hospitals, and zoos, as well as appearances at over 2,000 country fairs. His anecdotes run the gamut from babies being born and the terminally ill in audiences dying during his broadcasts, to the FBI's arrest of a criminal wanted for interstate auto theft who appeared on *What's My Line?*

Appearing on the program one Sunday night as an elephant trainer, the fugitive was recognized by a viewer during the live broadcast. He was taken into custody by authorities minutes later in the wings, just after he bid host John Daly adieu. Then, there was the lady who approached John after one show and thanked him for the infusion of psychic energy that gave her the will to continue. She told Johnny that she had rushed to his warm-up directly from her husband's funeral.

Johnny wrote that he faced microphones in all fifty states, and had vivid memories of many poignant moments, one during a show at a Veterans Administration hospital in Springfield, Missouri. He recalled that most of the patients were ambulatory, but that many of the more seriously wounded wanted to see the program, too. "They were wheeled into the room in chairs and beds. I was singing 'Wagon Wheels.' Just as I got to the last part, one boy, God rest his soul, gasped his last. The orderlies came in and covered him up right in front of me. While the show concluded, they slowly wheeled him away."

Johnny was perpetually upbeat, friendly, and professional in demeanor. Most people never sensed that he was not immune from career frustrations. Based on observations of at least one host's occasional callousness, a couple of Johnny's co-workers have conjectured that their friend may have silently harbored his fair share of concerns about respect, money, and camera time, even at the height of his success. He did go out of his way to be certain that one young producer Johnny worked with in his later life was fully aware that, before his years as an announcer, he'd had a successful career as a television host in his younger days.

Despite any speculation about his innermost thoughts and feelings, all who knew Johnny agree that he outwardly approached his work each day with great grace, dignity, humility, and enthusiasm. His oft-voiced adage: "Let not trifles ruffle your temper."

His co-worker for a decade, model Holly Hallstrom, echoed the sentiments of so many of John's collegues, "Everybody loved Johnny, everybody respected Johnny, and everybody felt safe with Johnny...we really admired Johnny, he was a twinkle-in-the-eye kind of person, special, a generous and gracious humanitarian who epitomized professionalism...He was precious, and everybody accorded him so." [42-1]

On a personal note, she said, "I just adored him. And he was so positive, his energy, just to be around him...His eyes were always smiling, always turned up in the corners...Everything that came out of his mouth was so positive, I just gravitated to him just because he felt so good to be around...I feel so blessed to have worked with him." [42-1]

If Johnny was ever angry, frustrated or negative, nobody remembers hearing a single curse word, foul remark, or confrontational comment from him. Holly remembered one moment when, uncharacteristically, he was not a source of light and good humor. During a delay in the final rehearsal near the end of a particularly long tape day, when things were not going well and the producers were outspoken in disagreement over some creative issue, Johnny was not happy. He shook his head and whispered, "Oh Geez, let's just get this over with and get out of here." [42-1]

Johnny took tremendous pride in his performance and his reputation, and he retained a passion for the business that remained seemingly untainted by cynicism and sarcasm. I carry much of what Johnny taught me to every taping. Yet, as I attempt to emulate his professionalism, I am continually challenged by the high standards he set. Johnny presided over twelve half-hour episodes of *The Price is Right*, plus twelve installments of *Match Game*, during weeks that included a seven-episode tape day or two for *Concentration*, as well as stockpiling episodes of *Now You See It*. That workload was a herculean challenge, clearly well beyond my own capabilities at a much younger age.

While I regularly announced as many as fifteen episodes of *Supermarket Sweep* in a single recording session, modern post-production techniques did not require me to perform in real time, with the requirement to simultaneously keep a parade of audiences energized. Although I have warmed-up audiences during long days when multiple, one-hour episodes of *Weakest Link* and *Deal or No Deal* were taped, I was freed from the responsibility of doing double-duty because I was not simultaneously performing as announcer on those shows. Through those experiences, I gained a heightened appreciation for Johnny's physical stamina, professional dedication, and emotional discipline.

Johnny left the world without children, and he likely spent more hours on the job than he did with Penny. Tributes for which he might be proudest come from those with whom he toiled through his six decade career. Director and producer Ira Skutch, who worked with him on several series, often daily during a period of twenty-five years, and who was a guest at his home in Greenwich, Connecticut, remembered him as "a unique individual." Skutch recalled his co-worker as even tempered, never depressed nor elated, adding, "During the four years of *Play Your Hunch*, he was always cheerful…totally reliable."[42-2]

Dick DeBartolo's told of his memories, saying, "He was a sweetheart. I assume he was very well-off, but you always felt like he was just a working guy. There was certainly no pretense."[42-3]

Host Tom Kennedy was working with Johnny on both *Body Language* and the nighttime *Price is Right* when he was shocked by a telephone call at home informing him that his on-air partner had passed away. Kennedy recalled, "I don't remember eulogizing him on the show…but…I was privledged to know him, and privledged to work with him. He was one of the most outstanding, unforgettable figures I ever met." Of Johnny's 50-plus year contribution to radio and television, Kennedy said, "He was a real, vital, living, breathing museum piece…a thread that went through the entire fabric of broadcasting history." [42-4]

Barbara Hunter was side-by-side with Johnny daily, through most of his tenure on America's most loved game show. Like everyone, she remembered him with warmth and fondness. "Johnny was lovely…I have a great picture of Johnny from what I think was my last day on the set. I look at it often, and I never saw a different side of Johnny…He was always courteous, always kind. In all the work he did, I never heard a harsh word from Johnny."[42-5]

In discussing the importance of having a trusted on-air partner, Bob Barker said, "When you're in ad-lib situations with people, you want to know that they have the good taste and good judgment not to embarrass you." He called Johnny, "One of my favorite people, and one of the favorite people of all television viewers in the United States." Barker recalled, "When Johnny died we were really in a panic because he was such a part of the show."[42-6]

Johnny valued his relationships with the many stage managers, stylists, stagehands, lighting, camera and sound people that he considered teammates. He would be happy

Veteran television announcers Charlie O'Donnell (left) and Don Pardo (center) with the author discussing Johnny's legacy in 2007.

to know of the legacy of goodwill he left. Between 1998 and 2003, I worked on several shows, including *The Price is Right*, standing at Johnny's podium in Studio 33, "The Bob Barker Studio" at CBS Television City. His many friends and co-workers from the thousands of episodes he taped there still remember him fondly, some with great affection. They are unanimous in their admiration for him and in their high regard for him as an always warm, pleasant, up-beat colleague and friend. The most frequently repeated comment about him leaves a legacy he would undoubtedly be proud of: "He was always the consummate professional."

By his attitude, actions, demeanor, and deeds, and in his shared respect for and from his fellow man, in his 75 years John certainly made his mother proud. He recalled her last words to him: "Goodbye, then Johnny. Be a good boy — be sure to pray."

LADIES BE SEATED

The script from the debut radio and television simulcast of *Ladies Be Seated* on the ABC radio and television networks from New York City, 2:30 PM, February 25, 1945.

VIDEO		AUDIO	
#1 LS of audience standing and singing.	FADE IN #1	MUSICAL SIGNATURE SUNG BY AUDIENCE – "You Are My Sunshine"	

TITLE 1	LAP DISS
	Over #1

The Blue Network of the American Broadcasting Company

TITLE 2	LAP DISS
	Over #1

Presents Johnny Olsen in

TITLE 3	LAP DISS

"LADIES BE SEATED"

#2 TIGHT SHOT	TAKE #2
of audience	

PAN audience as they sing.

#3 MCU announcer	TAKE #3	ANNOUNCER
		(as they finish chorus) Ladies, be seated!

#1 LS of audience	TAKE#1	AUDIENCE (sitting)
as they sit.		

#3 MCU announcer TAKE #3	**ANNOUNCER** Welcome to the first television presentation of the popular radio show, heard every weekday over the Blue Network at two-thirty – Ladies Be Seated. The show where anything can happen, and usually does. The show where you get money for being funny. And now, here's your master of mirth, that minstrel of merriment – Johnny Olsen!
Announcer turns and gestures upstage.	APPLAUSE UP FULL AND SUSTAINED. FANFARE BRINGS HIM ON.
#1 MS of upstage TAKE #1 Entrance, taking in some audience. Catch Olsen as he enters and hugs one of the contestants.	**OLSEN** (He ad libs) **ANNOUNCER** (off) Hey, Johnny!
Olsen gives another hug… then goes to announcer and her.	**OLSEN** (making a take) Huh?… Oo ooooh!
#3 MED two-shot TAKE #3 Olsen & announcer.	**ANNOUNCER** Wait a minute, Johnny… Wait a minute! **OLSEN** Hah?… When I see those eyes, those lips, Those nose?… **ANNOUNCER** But those audience! **OLSEN** (indicating studio audience) You mean all these people here? **ANNOUNCER** (indicating camera) I mean all those people there.

<table>
<tr><td></td><td>

OLSEN
(peering into camera) I can't see 'em, Helen.

ANNOUNCER
No, but they can see you, and I think it might be a good idea to say hello to them and start the show... Well, it's all yours, Johnny. (going off) See you later.
</td></tr>
</table>

Olsen comes in tighter.	OLSEN (Olsen ad libs opening. Gets in plug and introduces Penny.)
#1 MS of Penny TAKE #1 and first contestants.	APPLAUSE AS PENNY TAKES BOW.
PAN with Penny and contestants.	OLSEN & PENNY (asks Penny if she has two service men for the first stunt. She brings them up.)
#3 tight three-shot. TAKE #3	OLSEN & CONTESTANTS (Olsen interviews them.)
READY #1 for MS of stunt.	1. DOUGHNUT ROUTINE (Two men – six doughnuts hanging on strings. Contest to eat around holes without biting through.)
#1 MS of stunt. TAKE #1	MUSIC – Cancan from "Gaite Parisienne." START MUSIC ON OLSEN'S CUE – "Go."
#3 catch BCU's.	MUSIC OUT ON OLSEN'S CUE – "The Winnah."
READY #2 for pay-off.	
#2 PAN with contestants. TAKE #2	OLSEN (Pays off contestants. Calls for applause.) CHASER MUSIC AS THEY RETURN TO SEATS.

....TIME (   )

#1 MCU of Johnny TAKE #1 Penny brings two women in.		**OLSEN & PENNY** (Olsen interviews two housewives brought up by Penny.)

#3 three-shot   TAKE #3   **OLSEN & CONTESTANTS**
(He describes what they are to do. Calls for raincoats. The women put them on.)

READY #1 for stunt

READY #2 for audience reaction.   NO MUSIC DURING THIS STUNT.

#1 MS of stunt.   TAKE #1   **2. BOAT ROUTINE:**
(Housewives get in canvas boat. Pans are tied to their heads and a little water poured in. They are given brooms and told to paddle as they sing "Row, Row, Row Your Boat." They are not supposed to spill the water as Johnny makes them go faster and faster. Olsen yells while an assistant is swinging a big bucket … he lets them have it. It turns out to be puffed rice. Pays off contestants. Calls for applause.)

#2 PAN with contestants TAKE #2   CHASER MUSIC AS THEY
RETURN TO SEATS.

.................................TIME (   )

#1 MS of Penny as   TAKE #1   **PENNY & LADY**
she brings up lady.   Johnny, I want you to meet a very lovely lady, etc.

NO MUSIC DURING HEART-THROB.

#3 tight two-shot   TAKE #3   **OLSON & LADY**
3. HEART-THROB: Olsen interviews mother with four sons in service. At the end she is given a bouquet of flowers.

Olsen comes in tighter.	**OLSEN** (Gets in short plug for next week and invites studio audience.)
...............................TIME (	)
#1 tight three-shot. TAKE #1	**OLSEN, PENNY & A WIFE** Gag interview with wife.
	The wife is asked if she will unveil a statue. MUSIC – "Pomp and Circumstance." START ON OLSEN'S CUE, "Bring on the statue."
	4. <u>STATUE ROUTINE</u>: (Penny blindfolds wife and leads her upstage. The husband has been previously taken to dressing room and fixed up. Johnny comes to camera and tips off audience that the statue will be her husband. "Statue" is brought in swathed in sheets and pillowcase. Wife unveils "Statue" revealing husband in Red flannels. Pay-off comes when blindfold is removed and she finds it is her husband.)
#3 med. Three-shot TAKE #3	**OLSEN, PENNY & WIFE** (Pays off contestants. Calls for applause.)
#2 PAN with wife TAKE #2 as she sits.	**CHASER MUSIC AS SHE RETURNS TO SEAT**
...............................TIME (	)
#3 tight four-shot TAKE #3	**OLSEN** (Interviews three servicemen. Tells them they are to have privilege of dancing with the famous danseuse, Madam Lazonga.)
	MUSIC – 1. WALTZ; 2. CONGA; 3. JITTERBUG.

DOLLY BACK #1
to catch dance.

5. MADAME LAZONGA:
(They are taken offstage and the
"madame" is brought on. She is a life-
size rubber dummy. The first serviceman
dances a waltz with her; the second a
conga; the third a jitterbug number,
during which the air escapes and
Madame Lazonga collapses.)

OLSEN
(Pays off contestants. Calls for applause
and says it is time for the finale by "the
entire company.")

AUDIENCE STANDS AND SINGS
"You Are My Sunshine."

#3 MCU announcer   TAKE #3

ANNOUNCER
(after one chorus) SINGING IN BG.

READY #1 for CU of Olsen

Well, time's up for tonight. Don't forget
to sit down with us again next week at
this same time for another program of
LADIES BE SEATED. But before
signing off, a final word from Johnny
Olsen.

#1 CU of Olsen   TAKE #1

OLSEN (over singing)
(He gives closing commercial and con-
cludes with)...

And remember, you get money for being
funny on LADIES BE SEATED.

DOLLY BACK #1
to take in audience.

MUSIC SIGNATURE UP FULL –
(Third chorus)

TITLE 4   LAP DISS
This has been a presentation of the
American Broadcasting Company.

FADE OUT   FADE OUT MUSIC ON APPLAUSE

THE LASTING LEGACY OF GOODSON-TODMAN PRODUCTIONS

The television formats purchased by All American Communications from Mark Goodson Productions, subsequently acquired by FremantleMedia. (Starred entries indicate that Johnny Olson was featured as the program's announcer.)

Beat the Clock	*Password Plus* *
Blockbusters *	*Play Your Hunch* *
Body Language *	*Rate Your Mate*
By Popular Demand	*Say When!*
Call My Bluff! *	*Showoffs*
Card Sharks *	*Snap Judgment* *
Child's Play	*Spin To Win*
Choose Up Sides	*Split Personality* *
Double Dare *	*Super Password*
Family Feud	*Tattletales* *
New Family Feud	*That's My Line* *
Get the Message *	*The Match Game* *
He Said, She Said *	*Match Game* *
Hit the Jackpot	*The Name's The Same*
It's News To Me	*The Price Is Right* *
Judge For Yourself	*To Tell The Truth* *
Make The Connection	*Trivia Trap*
Mindreaders *	*Two For The Money*
Missing Links *	*Winner Take All*
Now You See It *	*What's My Line?* *
Number Please	*What's Going On*
Password	

JOHNNY OLSON'S CREDITS

Radio Host

WIBU – *Various programs*
WIBA – *Various programs*
KGDA – *Various programs*

WTMJ – *Various programs including:*
"Chamber Music Society of Lower
  Basin Street"
"Comic Caravan"
"The Falstaff Show"
"Johnny Olson's Rhythm Rascals"
"Johnnie Olson and His Eight Broth-
  ers Rhythm Rascals"
"Johnny Olson's Rumpus Room"
"Masters of Rhythm"
"Platter Puzzlers"
"Quiz Battle of the Century"
"Romantic Balladier"
"The Rhythm Rascals"
"Winsom"

Regional Midwest – *Various programs
  including:*
"The 1940 Laugh Parade"
"Can You Beat It?"
"Oshkosh B' Gosh Radio Program"

KMPC – *Various programs including:*
"The Foreman of the Flyin' Y"
"The Johnny Olson Show"
"Johnny Olson's Rumpus Room"

KFWB – *Various programs including:*
"Chef Milani"
"Man on the Street"
"Missing Persons"

New York:
"Break the Bank" (Mutual, ABC,
  NBC)
"Everything Goes" (NBC Blue)
"Get Rich Quick" (WJZ)
"Johnny Olsen on Broadway"
"Johnny Olsen's Luncheon Club" (ABC)
"Johnny Olsen's Rumpus Room" (WJZ)
"The Johnny Olsen Show" (Mutual)
"Johnny Olson Pantry Party"
  (NBC Blue)
"Johnny Olson's Get Together" (ABC)
"Johnny Olson's Prince Charming"
  (WOR)
"Ladies Be Seated" (NBC Blue/ABC)
"Ladies'Man, Johnny Olsen" (WOR)
"Let Yourself Go" (NBC Blue)
"The Mary Small Show" (NBC Blue)
"Meet The Girls" (NBC Blue)
"Movie Quiz" (Mutual)
"The Mutual Movie Matinee" (Mutual)
"National Wives Week" Specials
  (Mutual)
"On Stage Everybody" (ABC)
"Second Chance" (NBC)
"Swing Shift Follies" (NBC Blue)
"What's My Name?" (Mutual, NBC)
"Whiz Kids" (CBS)

"Whiz Quiz" (NBC Blue)
"Weekly War Journal" (NBC Blue)
"Yankee Doodle Quiz" (NBC Blue)

Television Host

"Break The Bank" (NBC, CBS, ABC)
"Doorway to Fame" (DuMont)
"Fun For The Money" (ABC)
"Homemakers' Jamboree" (WJZ-TV)
"Johnny Olsen's Rumpus Room"
    (DuMont)
"Kids and Company" (DuMont)
"Ladies Be Seated" (ABC)
"Monday Night Fights" (DuMont)
"Mrs. America Pageant" 1963
"On Broadway Tonight" (CBS)
"Play Your Hunch" (NBC)
"Tic Tac Dough" (NBC)
"TV Auction Club" (WOR-TV)

Television Announcer

"A Penny to a Million"
"Archie Bunker's Place"
"Blockbusters"
"Body Language"
"Break the Bank"
"Call My Bluff!"
"Card Sharks"
"Concentration"
"Double Dare"
"Get the Message"
"Glenn Miller Time"
"He Said, She Said"
"Hold That Note"
"I Made The News"
"I've Got A Secret"
"Jackie Gleason and His American
    Scene Magazine"
"Keep It in the Family"
"Keep Talking"
"Life's Most Embarrassing Moments"
"Manhattan Honeymoon"

"Masquerade Party"
"Match Game"
"Match Game-Hollywood Squares
    Hour"
"Maude"
"Mindreaders"
"Missing Links"
"Name That Tune"
"NBC Follies"
"Now You See It"
"Password Plus"
"Play Your Hunch"
"Second Honeymoon"
"Snap Judgment"
"Split Personality"
"Stop the Music"
"Tattletales"
"That's My Line"
"The Dom DeLuise Show"
"The Jackie Gleason Show"
"The Kate Smith Show"
"The Match Game"
"The Peggy Fleming Show"
"The Price Is Right"
"The Steve Lawrence Show"
"The Strawhatters"
"The USIA Worldwide Show"
"The Young and the Restless"
"Tic Tac Dough"
"To Tell The Truth"
"What's My Line?"
"WKRP in Cincinnati"
"You're in the Picture"

Film

"The Sin of Mona Kent"

Theater

"The Selling of the President"

APPENDIX D

JOHNNY OLSON'S FAMILY

Johnny's brother, Richard Olson, made these incomplete notes in an attempt to identify all of the members of the extended family. The portrait (which also appears on page 19) was taken at a 1914 reunion at the home of Elling and Ellen Elness, Johnny's maternal grandmother and grandfather. The family moved onto this land in Jackson County, Christina Township, Minnesota, in 1873. Homestead was granted on May 28, 1881.

Back row (left to right):
1. Hans Telefson *(a neighbor, not a relative)*
2. Sivert Olson *(Hannah's husband, Johnny's father)*
3. Ellen Elness *(Hannah's mother, Johnny's grandfather)*
4. Delbert Elness *(son of Andrew Elness)*

5. Andrew Elness *(brother of Hannah)*
6. Theodore Elness *(brother of Hannah)*
7. *(unidentified)*
8. Ole Elness *(brother of Hannah, holding Orland Elness)*
9. Bessie Elness *(wife of Ole)*
10. Hannah Elness Olson *(Johnny's mother)*

11. Leonard Wick *(Ella Olson's Husband)*
12. Elling Elness *(Hannah's father, Johnny's grandfather)*
13. Sam Olson *(son of Hannah)*
14. Alex Elness *(Hannah's brother)*
15. Gea *(wife of Alex)*
16. Elsus Elness *(Hannah's brother)*
17. Minnie Elness *(wife of Edward)*
18. Annie Elness *(wife of Theodore)*
19. Hannah Mickelson *(cousin of Hannah)*
20. Carey Elness *(wife of Andrew)*
21. *(unidentified)*
22. Calmer Elness *(Hannah's brother)*
23. Clara Elness *(wife of Calmer)*

Middle Row (left to right):
1. Alex's Son
2. Tilford Elness *(son of Theodore)*
3. Ralph Elness *(son of Calmer)*
4. Orvin Elness *(son of Alex)*
5. Emmett Elness *(son of Alex)*
6. Harold Olson *(son of Hannah)*
7,8. Ralph Wick held by his mother, Ella Olson *(daughter of Hanna)*
9. Irene Elness *(daughter of Ole)*
10. *(unidentified)*

Bottom Row (left to right):
1. *(unidentified)*
2. Curtis Olson *(son of Hannah)*
3. Johnny Olson *(son of Hannah)*
4. *(unidentified)*
5. Lehland Elness *(son of Edward)*
6. Clifford Elness *(son of Edward)*
7. Richard Olson *(small child in front of Richard unidentified)*
8. Petra Elness *(daughter of Theodore)*
9. *(unidentified)*
10. *(unidentified)*
11. *(unidentified)*
12. *(unidentified)*
13. Corrine Elness *(daughter of Andrew)*
14. *(daughter of Andrew)*
15. *(unidentified)*
16. *(unidentified)*
17. *(unidentified)*
18. Emma Elness *(daughter of Theodore)*
19. Hilda Olson *(wife of Sam)*
20. *(daughter of Calmer Elness)*
21. Alberta Elness *(daughter of Calmer Elness)*

RESEARCH ASSISTANCE

Linda Fansen, Mark Nind, Barry Wick, also Steve Beverly, Bob Boden, Roger Dobkowitz, A.J. Elias, Mark Evanier, Jim Hilliker, Bob O'Brien, Jack O'Brien, Matt Ottinger, David Ruprecht, David Schwartz, and Stuart Shokus.

ADDITIONAL ACKNOWLEDGEMENTS

Bernie Alan, Maiquel Alejo, Art Alisi, Paul Alter, Ray Angona, Don Azars, Bob Barker, Don Barrett, Kevin Belinkoff, Peter Berlin, David Besbris, Leah Biel, Stan Blits, Bob Boden, Marla Boden, Michael Brockman, Michael Burger, Bill Carruthers, Byl Carruthers, Bob Chic, Joe Cipriano, Wally Clark, Chris Clementson, Charlie Colarusso, Jerry Collins, Brian Conn, Corey Cooper, Doug Davidson, Michael Davies, Cathy Dawson, Dick DeBartolo, Mark DeCarlo, Roger Dobkowitz, Chris Donnen, Johnny Donovan, Geoff Edwards, Bill Egan, Mark Evanier, James Farah, Andy Felsher, Howard Felsher, Rob Fiedler, Rich Fields, Pat Finn, Marc Fisher, Ed Flesh, Arthur Forrest, Dan Fox, Woody Fraser, Steve Friedman, Scott Fybush, Art Gilmore, Jonathan Goodson, Mark Goodson, George Gray, Kathy Greco, Marc Green, Ron Greenberg, Sharon Lord Greenspan, Phil Gurin, Holly Hallstrom, Bob Hamilton, George Hamilton, David Hammett, Jim Hampton, John Harlan, Tony Harrison, Kristin Hegel, Shelly Herman, Mike Hill, Bill Hillier, Bob Hilton, Howard Hoffman, Ray Horl, Al Howard, Barbara Hunter, Mandel Ilagen, Mark Itkin, Art James, Gary Johnson, Claudia Jordan, Maryanne Jorgenson, Steve Kamer, Marvin Kaplan, Cynthia Kazarian, "Shotgun" Tom Kelly, Mick Kennedy, Tom Kennedy, Sallie Kleiman, Leonard Koss, Stuart Krasnow, Jerry Kupcinet, Steve LeBlang, Eric Leiber, Ken Levine, Bob Levy, Roger Lodge, Sue MacIntyre, Ron Maestri, Sandy Martindale, Wink Martindale, Mark Maxwell-Smith, Joel McGee, Jade Mills, Jeff Mirkin, Beverly Morrison, Don Morrow, Jack Narz, Barrie Nedler, Caleb Nelson, Todd Newton, Charlie O'Donnell, Gary Owens, Jeff Palmer, Don Pardo, Chuck Pharis, Buddy Piper, Don Pitts, Beverly Pomerantz, Dave Price, Doug Quick, Steve Radosh, Mark Ragonese, Bill Ratner, Gene Rayburn, Marco Antonio Regil, Richard Reid, Scott Reside, Joey Reynolds, Rachel Reynolds, John Ricci, Burton Richardson, JD Roberto, Rod Roddy, Jim Rossi, Phillip Wayne Rossi, Michele Roth, Bob Sadoff, Pete Salant, Adam Sandler, Debra Schaub, David Schwartz, Ryan Seacrest, Brandi Sherwood, Tom Shovan, Owen Simon, Susan Simons, Rudi Simpson, Alan Skinner, John Sly, Herb Small, Mike Soliday, Aaron Solomon, Alan Solomon, Maggie Speak, Pammela Spencer, Bob Stewart, Jay Stewart, Sande Stewart, Marc Summers, Jake Tauber, Jeff Thisted, Randy Thomas, Jan Tobin, Peter Tomarken, Gia Trasatti, Pamela Usdan, Linda Vanoff, Syd Vinnedge, Rita Venarri, Art Vuolo, Mark Walberg, Marc Wanamaker, Frank Wayne, Marc Weilage, Barry Wick, Terry Wilkie, Jay Wolpert, Gene Wood, Rod Woodcock, Chuck Woolery, Fred Wostbrock, and Dr. Murray Zucker.

Photographs are from the author's personal collection, supplemented by photos from Fred Wostbrock, David Schwartz, and Barry Wick.

REFERENCES

The primary reference sources for this work were interviews and conversations with Johnny Olson.

Chapter 1
[1-1] Author's personal interview with Gene Rayburn, Encino, California, December 22, 1998
[1-2] Author's personal interview with Barry G. Wick, Rapid City, South Dakota, February 5, 2009

Chapter 2
[2-1] Cottonwood County Citizen, May 9, 1951

Chapter 3
[3-1] The David Sarnoff Library Collection, The David Sarnoff Research Center, Princeton. New Jersey
[3-2] Archer, Gleason L., "Big Business And Radio," The American Historical Company, Inc., New York, 1939

Chapter 4
[4-1] Barnouw, Erik; "A Tower of Babel: A History of Broadcasting in the United States to 1933," Oxford Press, 1966
[4-2] Enman, Charles, "One Against the World," The Ottawa Citizen, September 13, 1999

Chapter 5
[5-1] Windom High School "Cricket," 1928, Windom, Minnesota, courtesy of The Cottonwood County Historical Society, 2007

Chapter 6
[6-1] Fisher, Marc, "Something in the Air: Radio, Rock, and the Revolution That Shaped a Generation," Random House, 2007
[6-2] NBC Library of Congress Collection, Motion Picture, Broadcasting and Recorded Sound Division, Folders 836 and 837
[6-3] Maslin, Janet, "Color Adjustment (1992)," The New York Times, January 29, 1992
[6-4] Ely, Melvin Patrick, 'The Adventures of Amos 'n' Andy: A Social History of an American Phenomenon," The Free Press, 1991

Chapter 7
[7-1] "Doctor Says Voice on TV Caused Seizures," Associated Press, The New York Times, July 11, 1991

Chapter 9

9-1 Cottonwood County Citizen, May 16, 1951
9-2 Trout, Robert. Interviewed in "CBS Radio at 50: An Autobiography in Sound," September 18, 1977
9-3 "America's Story," Library of Congress, Washington, D.C.
9-4 Floherty, John J, "Behind the Microphone," J.B. Lippincott, 1944

Chapter 10

10-1 Harry Bartell, "Struts and Frets – On KFWB," unpublished manuscript
10-2 Lasky, Betty, "RKO: The Biggest Little Major of Them All," Prentice-Hall, 1984
10-3 Archives, Pacific Pioneer Broadcasters, Hollywood, CA, 2007
10-4 Schaden, Chuck, interview with Frank Nelson, "Nostalgia Digest," Book twelve, Chapter six, October-November, 1986
10-5 McMahon, Ed, and David Fisher, "When Television Was Young," Thomas Nelson, 2007
10-6 Lebo, Harlan, "Casablanca: Behind The Scenes," A Fireside Book, Simon & Shuster, 1992

Chapter 11

11-1 Mogel, Leonard, "This Business of Broadcasting: A Practical Guide to Jobs & Job Opportunities in the Broadcasting Industry," Billboard Books, 2004
11-2 Hutchens, John K., "Radio Notebook; New Blood On Blue," New York Times, January 9, 1944
11-3 Buxton, Frank, and Bill Owen, "The Big Broadcast: 1920-1950," Flare Books/Avon Books, 1972

Chapter 12

12-1 U. S. Census Bureau report released May 20, 1946 reporting 90.4% of U. S. homes had radios in 1945, up 17.9% from 1940.
12-2 Collins, Jerry, Newsletter Number 265, The Old Time Radio Club, December, 1998
12-3 "Johnny Roventini; Bellboy Called for Philip Morris in Ads," New York Times, December 3, 1998
12-4 "Johnny Roventini," Variety, Dec. 10, 1998
12-5 "Television Review – Balaban and Katz," The Billboard, March 9, 1946

Chapter 13

13-1 Myerson, Bess, and Susan Dworkin; Miss America, 1945: Bess Myerson and the Year That Changed Our Lives," Newmarket Press, 2000
13-2 "Bess Myerson reflects on fame, Miss America and Judaism," Chicago Jewish News, October 6, 1995
13-3 "Impeachment?" Redbook, April 1974
13-4 The David Sarnoff Library Collection, The David Sarnoff Research Center, Princeton. New Jersey

Chapter 14

14-1 Schaden, Chuck, interview with Frank Nelson, "Nostalgia Digest," Book Twelve, Chapter Six, October-November, 1986
14-2 "Fox 5 History," WTTG-TV, July 14, 2008
14-3 "Happy Birthday MBS," Time, September 15, 1941
14-4 "Radio and Television Program Reviews – What's My Name?" The Billboard, February 19, 1949
14-5 McMahon, Ed, and David Fisher, "When Television Was Young," Thomas Nelson, 2007

Chapter 15

[15-1] "Inventions," Time, February 22, 1926

[15-2] "Television," Time, April 18, 1927

[15-3] Bob Hope Collection, Motion Picture, Broadcasting and Recorded Sound Division, Library of Congress

[15-4] Fisher, Marc, "Something in the Air: Radio, Rock, and the Revolution That Shaped a Generation," Random House, 2007

Chapter 16

[16-1] Ritchie, Michael, "Please Stand By: A Prehistory of Television," The Overland Press, 1994

[16-2] National Congress of Parents and Teachers, "The PTA Magazine," National Parent-Teachers, 1953

[16-3] Bob Barker interview, Archive of American Television, Academy of Television Arts and Sciences Foundation, July, 2007

[16-4] McMahon, Ed, and David Fisher, "When Television Was Young," Thomas Nelson, 2007

[16-5] Author's personal interview with Jim Young, Wildwood, Missouri, February 23, 2009

[16-6] Author's personal interview with Arthur Forrest, Las Vegas, Nevada, May 1, 2008

Chapter 17

[17-1] "Just a Homebody," Television Forecast, July 9, 1949

[17-2] Rovin, Jeff, "TV Babylon," Signet, 1984

[17-3] "Top TV Town," Collier's, March 17, 1951

[17-4] Look, March 27, 1951

[17-5] Lamparski, Richard, "Manhattan Diary," BearManor Media, 2006

Chapter 19

[19-1] Cottonwood County Citizen, May 16, 1951

[19-2] Murphey, Mary, "The Prizes... The Applause... The Pain," TV Guide, January 21, 1984

[19-3] Newcomb, Dr. Horace, "The Encyclopedia of TV," The Museum of Broadcast Communications, Chicago, 1997

[19-4] "Big As All Outdoors," Time, October 17, 1955

[19-5] "Oceans of Empathy," Time, Feb. 27, 1950

[19-6] Singer, Arthur J., "Arthur Godfrey: The Adventures of an American Broadcaster," McFarland, 1999

[19-7] Interview with Tom Kennedy, WABC radio, Mark Simone, December 6, 2008

[19-8] Holms, John P., and Ernest Wood, "The TV Game Show Almanac," Chilton Book Company, 1995

[19-9] O'Connor, John J., "How a Taste for the Offbeat Led to an Institution," The New York Times, May 7, 1997

[19-10] Dmytryk, Edward, "Hollywood's Golden Age As Told By One Who Lived It All," BearManor Media, 2003

[19-11] Kisseloff, Jeff, "The Box," Viking, 1995

[19-12] Lebo, Harlan, "Casablanca: Behind The Scenes," A Fireside Book, Simon & Shuster, 1992

Chapter 20

[20-1] "The Search for the Gimmick," Time, December 17, 1951

[20-2] "The Search for the Gimmick," Time, December 17, 1951

20-3 Bob Stewart interview, Archive of American Television, Academy of Television Arts and Sciences Foundation, 1998

20-4 "Lords Of Fun And Games," Sports Illustrated, June 24, 1963

20-5 Fabe, Maxene, "TV Game Shows," Doubleday Dolphin, 1979

20-6 NBC Library of Congress Collection, Motion Picture, Broadcasting and Recorded Sound Division

20-7 Newcomb, Dr. Horace, "The Encyclopedia of TV," The Museum of Broadcast Communications, Chicago, 1997

20-8 Carter, Bill, "Mark Goodson, Game-Show Inventor, Dies at 77," New York Times, December 19, 1992

20-9 Author's personal interview with Mark Goodson, Hollywood, California, June 1, 1985

20-10 Author's personal interview with Roger Dobkowitz, Glendale, California, January 19, 2009

20-11 Author's personal interview with Bob Boden, Los Angeles, California, September 20, 2008

Chapter 21

21-1 Fabe, Maxene, "TV Game Shows," Doubleday Dolphin, 1979

21-2 Bennett Cerf interview, Columbia University Libraries Oral History–Notable New Yorkers, 1967

21-3 Talbot, David, "Brothers: The Hidden History of the Kennedy Years," Simon and Schuster, 2007

21-4 Author's personal interview with Bill Egan, Los Angeles, California, September 1994

21-5 Jordan, Sara, "Who Killed Dorothy Kilgallen," Midwest Today, May 16, 2009

21-6 Fates, Gil. "What's My Line? Inside the History of TV's Most Famous Panel Show," Prentice-Hall, 1978

21-7 Ira Skutch, "I Remember Television: A Memoir," Rowman & Littlefield, 1989

Chapter 22

22-1 Sherman, Allan. "A Gift of Laughter. The Autobiography of Allan Sherman," Fawcett, 1966

22-2 Fates, Gil. What's My Line? Inside the History of TV's Most Famous Panel Show," Prentice-Hall, 1978

22-3 Ira Skutch, "I Remember Television: A Memoir," Rowman & Littlefield, 1989

22-4 Newcomb, Dr. Horace, "The Encyclopedia of TV," The Museum of Broadcast Communications, Chicago, 1997

Chapter 23

23-1 "Fox 5 History," WTTG-TV, July 14, 2008

23-2 Dannen, Fredric, "Hit Men: Power Brokers and Fast Money Inside the Music Business," Vintage Books, 1990

23-3 Press, Dr. Stephen J., "Passion, Profession & Politics," Buy Books on the Web, 2004

23-4 "Lords Of Fun And Games," Sports Illustrated, June 24, 1963

23-5 Author's personal interview with Mark Evanier, Las Vegas, Nevada, June 12, 2008

Chapter 24

24-1 Bob Stewart interview, Archive of American Television, Academy of Television Arts and Sciences Foundation, 1998

24-2 Kisseloff, Jeff, "The Box," Viking, 1995

24-3 "Lords Of Fun And Games," Sports Illustrated, June 24, 1963

24-4 Author's personal interview with Dick DeBartolo, New York, October 9 and October 20, 2008

24-5 "Broadcasters Disagree With Electrical Wizard," New York Times, October 3, 1926
24-6 Floherty, John J, "Behind the Microphone," J.B. Lippincott, 1944

Chapter 25
25-1 NBC Library of Congress Collection, Motion Picture, Broadcasting and Recorded Sound Division, Folder 200
25-2 Torricelli, Robert & Andrew Carroll, "In Our Own Words: Extraordinary Speeches of the American Century," Simon and Schuster, 2000
25-3 Bennett Cerf interview, Columbia University Libraries Oral History–Notable New Yorkers, 1967
25-4 Tony Randall Interview, Archive of American Television, Academy of Television Arts and Sciences Foundation, 2008
25-5 Frank Stanton interview, Archive of American Television, Academy of Television Arts and Sciences Foundation, 2000, 2001
25-6 Moffitt Library, The Media Resources Center of the University of California, Berkeley
25-7 Streitmatter, Rodger, "Mightier Than the Sword: How the News Media Have Shaped American History," Westview Press, 1998
25-8 Barnouw, Erik, "A History of Broadcasting in the United States," Oxford University Press, 1966

Chapter 26
26-1 "The $64,000 Question–Life with the Creators of Breathless Tuesday," Newsweek, September 5, 1955
26-2 Dobkowitz, Roger, "A Historical Study of Prime-Time Network Television Audience Participation Programs 1948-1968"
26-3 "The American Experience: Quiz Show Scandal," PBS/Krainin Productions, Inc./Educational Foundation, 2000
26-4 Kisseloff, Jeff, "The Box," Viking, 1995
26-5 Author's personal interview with Jack Narz, Hollywood, California, 1994
26-6 Nelson, Valerie J., "Jack Narz dies at 85," Los Angeles Times, October 16, 2008
26-7 "Big Fuss Over TV Quiz Shows," Life Magazine, September 15, 1958
26-8 "Charges 'Shocked' Van Doren," New York Times, November 3, 1959
26-9 Newcomb, Dr. Horace, "The Encyclopedia of TV," The Museum of Broadcast Communications, Chicago, 1997
26-10 "How to Rig Contestants," Life Magazine, November 16, 1959
26-11 Congress, House Subcommittee on Interstate and Foreign Commerce, "Investigation of Television Quiz Shows," 86th Congress, 1st Session, November, 1959, Washington, D.C., U.S. Government Printing Office, 1960
26-12 "The American Experience: Quiz Show Scandal." PBS/Krainin Productions, Inc./WGBH Educational Foundation, 2000
26-13 "The Wizard of Quiz," Time, February. 11, 1957
26-14 "The Big Fix," Time, October 19, 1959
26-15 Umberger, Daryl, "Quiz Show Scandals," St. James Encyclopedia of Pop Culture, CBS Interactive Incorporated, 2009
26-16 Congress, House, Committee on Interstate and Foreign Commerce, "Investigation of Television Quiz Shows," 86th Cong., 1st Sess., October 1959, Washington, D.C., U.S. Government Printing Office, 1960

26-17 Mclellan , Dennis, "Steve Carlin, 84; Produced TV's '$64,000 Question' Quiz Show," Los Angeles Times, March 7, 2003

26-18 "Van Doren & Beyond," Time, November 16, 1959

26-19 Van Doren, Charles, "All The Answers," The New Yorker, July 30, 2008

26-20 Murphey, Mary, "The Prizes… The Applause… The Pain," TV Guide, January 21, 1984

26-21 "Quiz Show Scandals Changed U.S. TV," NPR Radio, "All Things Considered," August 19, 2008

Chapter 27

27-1 Congress, House Subcommittee on Interstate and Foreign Commerce, "Investigation of Television Quiz Shows," 86th Congress, 1st Session, November, 1959, Washington, D.C., U.S. Government Printing Office, 1960

27-2 "How to Rig Contestants," Life Magazine, November 16, 1959

27-3 McMahon, Ed, and David Fisher, "When Television Was Young," Thomas Nelson, 2007

27-4 "Quiz Show Scandals Changed U.S. TV," NPR Radio, "All Things Considered," August 19, 2008

27-5 Kisseloff, Jeff, "The Box," Viking, 1995

27-6 Transcribed interview with Dennis James, "The New Price is Right" press kit, 1972

27-7 "The Specialist," Time, November 1, 1968

Chapter 28

28-1 Bacon, James, "How Sweet It Is – The Jackie Gleason Story," St. Martin's Press, 1985

28-2 Stelter, Brian, "Bad Today, Gone Tomorrow," New York Times, September 20, 2008

28-3 "John Guedel, 88, Producer Who Shaped Early Television," New York Times, December 24, 2001

28-4 Ingram, Billy, "TV Party - Television's Untold Tales," TV Party, 2002

28-5 "The Specialist," Time, November 1, 1968

28-6 Author's personal interview with Dick DeBartolo, New York, October 9 and October 20, 2008

28-7 Author's personal interview with Mark Evanier, Las Vegas, Nevada, June 12, 2008

Chapter 29

29-1 Kisseloff, Jeff, "The Box," Viking, 1995

29-2 Cottonwood County Citizen, May 16, 1951

29-3 "The Specialist," Time, November 1, 1968

Chapter 30

30-1 Kisseloff, Jeff, "The Box," Viking, 1995

30-2 "Lords Of Fun And Games," Sports Illustrated, June 24, 1963

30-3 Fabe, Maxene, "TV Game Shows," Doubleday Dolphin, 1979

30-4 Kitty Carlisle speaking at "Television and Video Preservation 3," Library of Congress hearings, New York, March 19, 1996

30-5 Morgan, Henry, "Here's Morgan! The Original Bad Boy of Broadcasting," Barricade Books, 1994

30-6 Hyatt, Wesley, "The Encyclopedia of Daytime Television," Watson-Guptill Publications, 1997

30-7 Cohen, Adam, "Welcome to the Campaign That Makes 'Selling' a President Look Good," New York Times, September 26, 2004

30-8 Interview with Jack O'Brien conducted for the author by David Ruprecht, Los Angeles, California, January 11, 2009

Chapter 31

31-1 Shribman, David, "Look for Questions to Go Unanswered at Debates," Pittsburgh Post Gazette, September 21, 2008

31-2 Kelley, Beverly Merrill, "Reelpolitik II: Political Ideologies in '50s and '60s Films," Rowman & Littlefield, 2004

31-3 Schroeder, Alan, "Presidential Debates: Forty Years of High-risk TV," Columbia University Press, 2000

31-4 Minow, Newton N., "Equal Time: The Private Broadcaster and the Public Interest," Atheneum, 1964

31-5 Brown, Les; "Television–The Business Behind The Box," Harcourt Brace Jovanovich, Inc., 1971

31-6 "The Specialist," Time, November 1, 1968

31-7 Allen, Steve, "Hi-Ho, Steverino!: My Adventures in the Wonderful Wacky World of TV," Barricade Books, 1992

Chapter 32

32-1 "Out of Isolation," Newsweek, August 5, 1963

32-2 AFTRA Magazine, "AFTRA Sixty–a Celebration," American Federation of Television and Radio Artists, 1997

32-3 Kisseloff, Jeff, "The Box," Viking, 1995

32-4 Bob Stewart interview, Archive of American Television, Academy of Television Arts and Sciences Foundation, 1998

32-5 Brown, Les; "Television–The Business Behind The Box," Harcourt Brace Jovanovich, Inc., 1971

32-6 Bennett Cerf interview, Columbia University Libraries Oral History–Notable New Yorkers, 1967

32-7 Transcribed interview with Dennis James, "The New Price is Right" press kit, 1972

Chapter 33

33-1 Author's personal interview with Roger Dobkowitz, Glendale, California, January 19, 2009

33-2 "The Right Stuff," "Entertainment Weekly," June 15, 2007

33-3 Bob Barker interview, Television Critics Association, Winter Press Tour, Hollywood, California, January 19, 2007

33-4 Bob Barker interview, Archive of American Television, Academy of Television Arts and Sciences Foundation, July, 2007

33-5 Author's personal interview with Barbara Hunter, North Hollywood, California, October 22 and November 11, 2008

Chapter 34

34-1 "The Right Stuff," "Entertainment Weekly," June 15, 2007

34-2 Author's personal interview with Roger Dobkowitz, Glendale, California, January 19, 2009

34-3 Author's personal interview with Bob Boden, Los Angeles, California, September 20, 2008

34-4 Fabe, Maxene, "TV Game Shows," Doubleday Dolphin, 1979

34-5 Bob Barker interview, Archive of American Television, Academy of Television Arts and Sciences Foundation, July, 2007

34-6 Author's personal interview with Barbara Hunter, North Hollywood, California, October 22 and November 11, 2008

34-7 Blits, Stan, "Come On Down! Behind the Big Doors at The Price Is Right," Harper Entertainment, 2007

34-8 Author's personal interview with Holly Hallstrom, San Diego, California, May 3, 2009

34-9 Bob Barker interview, Television Critics Association, Winter Press Tour, Hollywood, California, January 19, 2007

34-10 New York Times, June 13, 2006

34-11 Bob Barker interview, USA Today, Gannett, May 13, 2007

Chapter 35

35-1 Author's personal interview with Tom Kennedy, Oxnard, California, September 3, 2009

35-2 Author's personal interview with Roger Dobkowitz, Glendale, California, January 19, 2009

Chapter 36

36-1 "Big As All Outdoors," Time, October 17, 1955

36-2 Bob Barker interview, Archive of American Television, Academy of Television Arts and Sciences Foundation, July, 2007

36-3 "The Specialist," Time, November 1, 1968

36-4 Shanley, John P., "Audience Warmer-Up," New York Times, April 8, 1962

36-5 Author's personal interview with Dick DeBartolo, New York, October 9 and October 20, 2008

36-6 Author's personal interview with Ray Angona, Hollywood, California, May 10, 1994

36-7 Bob Stewart interview, Archive of American Television, Academy of Television Arts and Sciences Foundation, 1998

36-8 Author's personal interview with Holly Hallstrom, San Diego, California, May 1, 2009

36-9 Author's personal interview with Tom Kennedy, Oxnard, California, September 3, 2009

Chapter 37

37-1 Fabe, Maxene, "TV Game Shows," Doubleday Dolphin, 1979

37-2 Author's personal interview with Dick DeBartolo, New York, October 9 and October 20, 2008

37-3 "Filling in the Blanks on a Staple of Daytime," The New York Times, November 25, 2006

37-4 McNeil, Alex; "Total Television: A Comprehensive Guide to Programming From 1948 to the Present"Penguin Books, 1980

38-1 Fishgall, Gary, "Gonna Do Great Things: The Life of Sammy Davis, Jr.," Simon and Schuster, 2003

38-2 Author's personal interview with Barbara Hunter, North Hollywood, California, October 22 and November 11, 2008

38-3 Author's personal interview with Tom Kennedy, Oxnard, California, September 3, 2009

38-4 Tom Kennedy interview with David Hammett, Los Angeles, California, transcribed February 6, 1996

Chapter 39

39-1 Author's personal interview with Holly Hallstrom, San Diego, California, May 1, 2009

39-2 Author's personal interview with Barbara Hunter, North Hollywood, California, October 22 and November 11, 2008

39-3 Author's personal interview with Bob Boden, Los Angeles, California, September 20, 2008

Chapter 40

[40-1] Author's personal interview with Dick DeBartolo, New York, October 9 and October 20, 2008

[40-2] Carter, Bill, "Mark Goodson, Game-Show Inventor, Dies at 77," New York Times, December 19, 1992

[40-3] Dan Sullivan speaking at "Television and Video Preservation 2," Library of Congress hearings, Los Angeles, March 6, 1996

[40-4] Pederson, Jay, "International Directory of Company Histories – Volume 20," St. James Press, 1998

[40-5] All American Communications, Inc., Securities and Exchange Commission Form S-4 Filing, October 28, 1996

Chapter 41

[41-1] Author's personal interview with Bob Boden, Los Angeles, California, September 20, 2008

[41-2] Author's personal interview with Roger Dobkowitz, Glendale, California, January 19, 2009

[41-3] Author's personal interview with Jay Stewart, Hollywood, California, November 21, 1987

Chapter 42

[42-1] Author's personal interview with Holly Hallstrom, San Diego, California, May 1, 2009

[42-2] Ira Skutch interview, Archive of American Television, Academy of Television Arts and Sciences Foundation

[42-3] Author's personal interview with Dick DeBartolo, New York, October 9 and October 20, 2008

[42-4] Author's personal interview with Tom Kennedy, Oxnard, California, September 3, 2009

[42-5] Author's personal interview with Barbara Hunter, North Hollywood, California, October 22 and November 11, 2008

[42-6] Bob Barker interview, Archive of American Television, Academy of Television Arts and Sciences Foundation, July, 2007

ADDITIONAL BIBLIOGRAPHY

Abramson, Albert; *The History of Television, 1942 to 2000*; McFarland, 2003

Bacon, James; *How Sweet It Is – The Jackie Gleason Story*; St. Martin's Press, 1985

Barnouw, Erik; *Tube of Plenty: The Evolution of American Television*; Oxford Press, 1975

Barnouw, Erik; *A Tower of Babel: A History of Broadcasting in the United States to 1933*; Oxford Press, 1966

Blum, Daniel; *Pictorial History of Television;* Chilton Company, 1959

Brown, Les; *Television; The Business Behind The Box*; Hartcourt Brace Jovanovich, 1971

Buxton, Frank, and Bill Owen; *The Big Broadcast: 1920-1950*; Flare Books/Avon Books, 1972

Campbell, Robert; *The Golden Years of Broadcasting*; RutledgeBooks/Scribners, 1976

Castleman, Harry, and Walter J. Podrazik; *Watching TV: Four Decades of American Television*; McGraw Hill, 1982

Castleman, Harry, and Walter J. Podrazik; *The TV Schedule Boo: Four Decades of Network Programming from Sign-on to Sign-off*; Mc Graw Hill, 1984

Dobkowitz, Roger; *A Historical Study of Prime-Time Network Television Audience Participation Programs 1948-1968,* Masters Thesis, 1971

Dunning, John; *On The Air: The Encyclopedia of Old Time Radio*; Oxford University Press; 1998

Eddy, William C.; Television: The Eyes of Tomorrow; Prentice Hall, 1945

Erickson, Hal; *Syndicated Television: The First Forty Years, 1947-1987*; McFarland & Company, 1989

Fabe, Maxene; *TV Game Shows*; Doubleday, 1979

Fates, Gil; *What's My Line? The Inside History of TV's Most Famous Panel Show*; Prentice-Hall, 1978

Floherty, John J.; *Behind the Microphone*; J.B. Lippincott, 1944

Gilmore, Art and Glenn Middleton; *Radio Announcing*; Hollywood Radio Publishers, 1946

Greenfield, Jeff; *Television: The First Fifty Years;* Harry Abrams, 1977

Griffin, Merv, with Peter Barsocchini; *Merv: An Autobiography*; Simon & Schuster, 1980.

Hagedorn, Ann; *Savage Peace: Hope and Fear in America, 1919*; Simon & Schuster, 2007

Head, Sydney W., and Christopher H. Sterling; *Broadcasting in America*; Houghton Mifflin Co., 1987

Hilmes, Michele and Michael Lowell Henry; *NBC: America's Network*; University of California Press, 2007

Hoerschelmann, Olaf; *Rules of the Game: Quiz Shows and American Culture*; State University of Nerw York Press, 2006

Holmes, John P. and Ernest Wood; *The TV Game Show Almanac*; Chilton Book Company, 1995

Jaker, Bill, Frank Sulek and Peter Kanze; *The Airwaves of New York: Illustrated Histories of 156 AM Stations in the Metropolitan Area, 1921-1996*; McFarland, 1998

Kisseloff, Jeff; *The Box: An Oral History of Television, 1920-1961*; Viking, 1995

Kubey, Robert: *Creating Television: Conversations with the People Behind 50 Years of American TV*; Lawrence Erlbaum and Associates, Inc., 2003

Lackmann, Ron; *The Encyclopedia of American Radio*; Checkmark Books, 1996

MacDonald, J. Fred; *One Nation Under Television*; Pantheon Books, 1990

McMahon, Ed, and David Fisher; *When Television Was Young*; Thomas Nelson, 2007

McNeil, Alex; *Total Television*; Penguin Books, 1980

Newcomb, Horace; *The Encyclopedia of Television*; The Museum of Broadcast Communications, 1997

Newcomb, Horace; *The Encyclopedia of Television*; CRC Press, 2004

Norbom, Mary Ann; *Richard Dawson and Family Feud*; Signet, 1981

Paar, Jack; *P.S. Jack Paar: An Entertainment;* Doubleday, 1983.

Paley, William S. *As It Happened: A Memoir;* Doubleday, 1979.

Ritchis, Michael; *Please Stand By: A Prehistory of Television;* The Overland Press, 1994

Sanford, Herb; *Ladies and Gentlemen, The Garry Moore Show: Behind the Scenes When TV Was New;* Stein & Day, 1976.

Schatz, Thomas; *Hollywood: Critical Concepts in Media and Cultural Studies;* Taylor & Francis, 2004

Schwartz, David, Steve Ryan and Fred Wostbrock; *The Encyclopedia of TV Game Shows;* Facts On File, 1995

Shulman, Arthur, and Roger Youman; *How Sweet It Was. Television:* A Pictorial Commentary; Bonanza, 1966

Ira Skutch; *I Remember Television: A Memoir;* Rowman & Littlefield, 1989

Slater, Robert; *This... Is CBS, A Chronicle of Sixty Years;* Prentice Hall, 1988

Sterling, Christopher H. and John M. Kittross; *Stay Tuned: A History of American Broadcasting;* Lawrence Erlbaum Associates, 2002

Stone, Joseph, and Tim Yohn; *Prime Time and Misdemeanors: Investigating the 1950s TV Quiz Scandal – a D.A.'s Account;* Rutgers University Press, 1992

Weinstein, David; *The Forgotten Network: DuMont and the Birth of American Television;* Temple University Press, 2006

Windom High School Yearbooks; *Cricket;* Windom, Minnesota, 1927, 1928

Newspapers
The Chicago Tribune, The Cottonwood County Citizen, The Los Angeles Times, The Milwaukee Journal, The New York Times, The Wall Street Journal, The Washington Post, The Windom Reporter

Magazines
AFTRA Magazine, The Atlantic, The American Heritage, Billboard, Broadcasting, Daily Variety, Ebony, Electronic Media/TV Week, The Hollywood Reporter, Jet, Life, Look, Newsweek, Old Time Radio Club Newsletter, Popular Science, Popular Mechanix, Radio Guide, Radio Mirror, Radio and Television Mirror, Saturday Evening Post, Science Illustrated, Sports Illustrated, Telecast, Television Forecast, Time, TV Guide, Variety

Personal Interviews
Ray Angona, Paul Alter, Bob Barker, Bob Boden, Cathy Dawson, Dick DeBartolo, Roger Dobkowitz, Bill Egan, Mark Evanier, Arthur Forrest, Mark Goodson, Holly Hallstrom, Bill Hillier, Al Howard, Barbara Hunter, Tom Kennedy, Don Morrow, Jack Narz, Charlie O'Donnell, Don Pardo, Buddy Piper, Gene Rayburn, Rod Roddy, Phil Wayne Rossi, Bob Stewart, Jay Stewart, Frank Wayne, Gene Wood

The Academy of Television Arts & Sciences Foundation Archive of American Television Interviews
Bob Barker, Charles Cappleman, Albert Freedman , Roger King, Don Pardo, Ira Skutch, Frank Stanton, Bob Stewart

CBS Photo Archives

The Cottonwood County Historical Society

FremantleMedia USA

Office of the Greenbrier County Clerk; Lewisburg, West Virginia

The United States Library of Congress

The North Dakota State University Libraries

Pacific Pioneer Broadcasters Archives

The Paley Center for Media

The University of Southern California Television Collection of the Cinematic Arts Library

The Wisconsin Historical Society

Where required, every effort has been made to secure permission from all copyright holders. We apologize for any omission, and will make any necessary correction and insert the appropriate acknowledgement in subsequent printings.

INDEX

INDEX

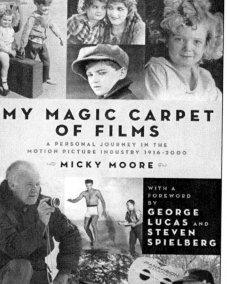

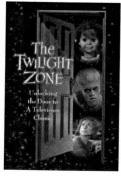

Breinigsville, PA USA
15 December 2010
251491BV00005B/93/P

9 781593 93471